New York City

Selection of

527 Restaurants

& 60 Hotels

2007
2nd edition

Dear reader

We are thrilled to present the second edition of the Michelin Guide New York City. Our teams have made every effort to update our selection to fully reflect the rich diversity of the restaurant and hotel scene in the Big Apple.

The Michelin Guide provides a comprehensive selection and rating, in all categories of comfort and prices. As part of our meticulous and highly confidential evaluation process, Michelin American inspectors conducted anonymous visits to restaurants and hotels in New York City. Michelin's inspectors are the eyes and ears of the customers, and thus their anonymity is key to ensure that they receive the same treatment as any other guest. The decision to award a star is a collective one, based on the consensus of all inspectors who have visited a particular establishment.

Our company's two founders, Édouard and André Michelin, published the first Michelin Guide in 1900, to provide motorists with practical information about where they could service and repair their cars, and find quality accommodations and a good meal. The star-rating system for outstanding restaurants was introduced in 1926. The same system is used for our present American selections.

We sincerely hope that the Michelin Guide New York City 2007 will become your favorite guide to the restaurants and hotels of the Big Apple. On behalf of all our Michelin employees, let us wish you the very best enjoyment in your New York City dining and hotel experiences.

Jim Micali
Chairman and President, Michelin North America
Jean-Luc Naret
Director, Michelin Guides

Table of Contents

Table of Contents

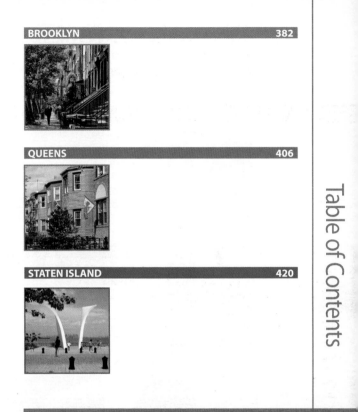

WHERE TO STAY

Table of Contents

How to use this Guide

Hotels classified according to comfort
(more pleasant if in red)

🏠 Comfortable enough
🏠 Comfortable
🏘️ Very comfortable
🏘️ Top class comfort
🏰 Luxury in the traditional style

The Hotel

Map References
(Hotels)

Mini/Maxi Prices
prices do not include applicable taxes

359 Colombus Ave.

Phone:	555-867-5309
Fax:	555-867-5400
Web:	www.thehotel.com
Prices:	rooms: $395 - $645 • suites: $850 - $1,300 • restaurants: $$

Hotel symbols

149 rooms No. of rooms and suites
  ♿ Wheelchair accessible
  Exercise room
  Spa
  Swimming pool
  Equipped conference room

149 Rooms
2 Suites

Star for good food

❀ to ❀❀❀

Perch ❀❀

Seafood

43 E. 38th St.

Phone:	333-900-8877
Fax:	333-980-1212
Web:	www.perch.us
Prices:	$$$$

Open daily 9am - midn
Closed Christmas

Restaurant symbols

Cash only
♿ Wheelchair accessible
Garden or terrace dining
Brunch
A particularly interesting wine list
Jacket required

The city's special-occasion spot for more than 40 years, t
restaurant now operates under the auspices of chef and own
Bill Smith. It's no wonder that his restaurant, with its roman
main dining room lighted with 900 custom candles, and set w
Limoges china and Louis XVI-style furnishings, is prized for
enchanting evening out.

In this sanctuary of classic French cuisine, you can choose yo
own dishes within the framework of a three-, four-, or five-cou
prix-fixe menu. Although it constantly changes, the selecti
includes a long list of French favorites (peppered filet mign
with braised endive, boneless quail stuffed with ris de veau, Gra
Marnier soufflé), many interpreted with California products. F
non-meat eaters, a vegetarian tasting menu is always an optio

On the wine list, you'll discover an excellent selection of Fren
varietals, including Riesling and Gewürztraminer from t
chef's native Alsace region, as well as white Burgundy and r
Bordeaux.

NYC areas or neighborhoods

Each area is color coded...

■ Manhattan
■ The Bronx
■ Brooklyn
■ Queens
■ Staten Island

Wine Country Napa Valley

Castro Cole Valley

52 - Restaurants

How to use this Guide

Restaurants classified according to comfort (more pleasant if in red)	X̂ Comfortable enough	X̂X̂X̂ Very comfortable	X̂X̂X̂X̂X̂ Luxury in the traditional style
	X̂X̂ Comfortable	X̂X̂X̂X̂ Top class comfort	

Name, address and information about the establishment

Map References (Restaurants)

Inspectors' favorites for good value

Price classification (Restaurants)

- ෂ under $25
- $$ $25 to $50
- $$$ $50 to $75
- $$$$ over $75

Antica Osteria ☺

Italian X̂X̂

m2 2 Market St.

Phone:	555-855-2222
Fax:	555-855-4700
Web:	www.anticarestaurant.com
Prices:	$$$

Tue - Thu 11am - 10pm
Fri - Sun 11am - midnight
Closed Mon

Meat lovers, rejoice! The Brazilian concept at this restaurant means that for one set price, you can eat all you want. A variety of meats (pork loin, ribs, top sirloin of beef, sausage, chicken) is cooked on skewers over an open fire and brought straight to your table by a waiter clad in gaucho garb. They'll keep bringing food until you tell them to stop. A small sign placed on your table will inform the staff of the state of your appetite: turn up the green side, *sim por favor* ("yes, please, I want more") or the red side, *nao obrigado* ("no thanks, I'm full").

To go with all that tasty meat, there's a salad bar, a buffet of side dishes, and your choice of dessert. Wine racks and Brazilian landscape paintings embellish the colorful dining space.

San Francisco

Boros

American X̂

:roft Way (bet. College & Piedmont Aves.)

Thu - Tue 11am - 10:30pm
Closed Wed & January 3 - 15

s star at this Mediterranean meze house, where low
a casual, convivial atmosphere add to the appeal. The
ng room with its bright walls and inlaid-tile tables
ne for sharing meze (the menu lists over 20 different
h homemade yogurt with cucumber and garlic to
pe leaves to pan-fried cubes of calf's liver. Most of
come from Turkey, but there are Greek and Lebanese
tems like char-grilled octopus and hummus.

of small plates doesn't float your boat, there's also
of daily specials, including meat kebabs and grilled
aiter will fill you in on the delightful desserts, such as
d kadayif filled with almonds, pistachios and honey.

ancisco

Appetizers

*Tartare of Ahi Tuna,
Moroccan Spices, Lemon
Confit, Fresh Herbs*

*Trio of Cold Artisan Foie
Gras: Orange Terrine, Epici
Poached, Truffled Torchon*

*Sesame-crusted Hamachi, Ye
Plum, Shiitake Mushroom
Salad*

Entrées

*White Sturgeon en papillote,
Cabbage, Jacked Beans,
Smoked Duck and Razor Clam*

*Brioche-crusted Halibut,
English Peas, Bacon and
Lettuce, Poultry Jus*

*"Surf & Turf" Roasted Veal
Sirloin, Poached Langoustine,
Salsify Gratin, Truffle
Hollandaise*

Desserts

*Chocolate Composition:
Gianduja Bonbons,
Marshmallow and Fudge,
White-chocolate Ice Cream*

*Coffee Mousse Bar, Dark
Chocolate Sauce, Havana
Cream*

*Coconut Soufflé, Exotic Fruit
and Chocolate Pearls*

Sample menu for starred restaurants

How to use this Guide

A brief history of New York City

From sushi to steak frites—and everything in between—New York jams a staggering world of food into about 320 square miles. With more than 17,300 eating establishments to feed its eight million residents (at last count), there's a restaurant on nearly every corner. Besides being a food-lover's paradise, the most populous city in the U.S. is a global melting pot, a cultural magnet, an economic powerhouse. It's not for nothing that New Yorkers have a reputation for being swaggering and brash. Theirs is one great city.

It's also a relatively young one. European settlement began in earnest here in 1625, when the Dutch East India Company established the Nieuw Amsterdam trading post at the southern tip of Manhattan Island. That name, which comes from an Algonquian term meaning "island of hills," suggests that the natives ventured farther than the colonists, who for the better part of 200 years remained on flat land near the shore, behind a defensive wall (today's Wall Street).

The transfer of authority from Dutch to British hands in 1664—and the new name, after the Duke of York—was hardly earth-shattering for early New Yorkers, most of whom had little allegiance to either crown. They were here to make money.

Manhattan, as it turns out, was perfectly suited to global trade, thanks to the snug arrangement of other landmasses (today's Staten Island, New Jersey and Brooklyn) around its harbor. As port activity grew, so did friction with the British system of "taxation without representation," the bulk of which fell on importers and exporters. When war broke out, the British took over the city almost immediately, and occupied it until independence.

After briefly serving as the U.S. capital, New York established the commercial links and financial

Brigitta L. House/MICHELIN

20 years, fed by waves of European immigrants, who would help build the city not just with their hands but with their ideas.

These immigrants, who clustered in little enclaves around the city, contributed something else to New York's culture. From foreign lands they brought their own foodways and family recipes, which melted into the multicultural stew that is New York City. With an ever-growing influx of people from around the globe, New York maintains the ethnic diversity that still defines its restaurant scene today.

institutions that led the new nation into the Industrial Age. In 1792 brokers met under a buttonwood tree at Wall and Williams streets and founded the forerunner to the New York Stock Exchange, then based largely on handshakes. Around the turn of the century, Manhattan's gridiron plan was laid out, and the exploding population spread northward into what was then mostly pastureland.

Then came the 363-mile-long Erie Canal, which in 1825 linked the city with the Great Lakes. Shipping costs to and from Buffalo dropped 90 percent virtually overnight, and New York became the nation's preeminent port and shipbuilding capital. The city's leading businessmen leveraged this advantage skillfully, investing their profits in new building projects, which were carried out by a steady supply of cheap labor. New York's population doubled every

In the second half of the 20C, the city solidified its international position in industry, commerce and finance, and its skyline, newly bristling with skyscrapers, reflected that prosperity. To this day, the dynamic metropolis attracts plucky types who are looking to succeed in New York's proving ground (as the words to Frank Sinatra's famous song attest: "If I can make it here, I can make it anywhere . . .").

Of course, restaurateurs and chefs number among those risk-takers who have worked up an appetite for the Big Apple. Whether their ventures are hole-in-the-wall red-sauce joints in Little Italy, Lower East Side Kosher delis, or Uptown culinary palaces ruled by renowned chefs, they all revel equally in one thing: they're all part of the dizzying dining world in New York City, the reigning U.S. capital of great cuisine.

Where to **eat**

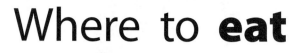

Alphabetical list of Restaurants

Where to eat

Alphabetical list of Restaurants

Restaurants by cuisine type

Greek

Anna's Corner	411
Avra Estiatorio	200
Eliá	396
Estiatorio Milos	260
Ithaka	335
Molyvos	267
Periyali	110
S'Agapo	415
Snack	295
Taverna Kyclades	418
Trata Estiatorio	349

Indian

Banjara	64
Bay Leaf	252
Bombay Talkie	42
Copper Chimney	104
Däwat	209
Dévi	90
Diwan	209
Jackson Diner	413
Sapphire	368
Saravanaas	111
Surya	159
Tamarind	112
Vatan	114

Italian

Abboccato	250
Acappella	304
Acqua Pazza	250
Al Di Lá	392
Ama	284
Antica Venezia	132
Ápizz	178
Areo	393
Aroma Kitchen and Wine Bar	133
A Voce	84
Babbo	120
Barbetta	251
Becco	253
Beccofino	379
Beppe	99
Bianca	135
Bice	201
Bottega del Vino	203
Bread Tribeca	305
Bricco	256
Bruno	204
Cacio e Pepe	64
Canaletto	205
Cellini	207
Centolire	331
'Cesca	360
Crispo	138
Da Antonio	208
Da Silvano	138
da Umberto	45
Del Posto	40
De Marco's	139
Downtown Cipriani	287
Esca	260
Etcetera Etcetera	261
Falai	179
Felidia	211
Fiamma Osteria	282
Frankies 457 Spuntino	397
Fresco by Scotto	212
Gabriel's	361
Giambelli 50th	213
Gigino at Wagner Park	79
Gigino Trattoria	307
Giorgione	288
Gnocco	66
Gusto	144
Il Buco	146
Il Cantinori	146
Il Cortile	170
Il Mulino	147
Il Nido	214
Il Palazzo	170
Il Riccio	334
'inoteca	180
Isle of Capri	334
I Trulli	106
La Masseria	266
Lavagna	71
Le Zie 2000	46
Locanda Vini & Olii	399
Lupa	149
Lusardi's	339
Macelleria	149
Max SoHa	166

Restaurants by cuisine type

Where to eat

Latin American

Calle Ocho	359

Malaysian

Fatty Crab	141
Nyonya	171

Mediterranean

Ammos Estiatorio	198
AOC Bedford	133
Barbès	201
Barbounia	98
Beyoglu	328
Brick Cafe	412
Dona	210
Extra Virgin	141
Fig & Olive	332
Frederick's Madison	333
Isabella's	362
Nice Matin	365
Olives	109

Mexican

Alamo (The)	197
Crema	44
El Parador	211
Fiesta Mexicana	412
Itzocan	68
La Esquina	171
Maya	340
Maz Mezcal	341
Mexicana Mama	151
Noche Mexicana	365
Rocking Horse	48
Rosa Mexicano	227
Zarela	236

Middle Eastern

Mamlouk	72
Taboon	276

Moroccan

Café Mogador	65
Park Terrace Bistro	372

Persian

Persepolis	344

Puerto-Rican

Brisas Del Caribe	379

Russian

Firebird	261
Russian Samovar	272

Scandinavian

Aquavit	199

Seafood

Aquagrill	285
Atlantic Grill	328
BLT Fish	100
Blue Fin	254
Brooklyn Fish Camp	394
Fresh	307
Grand Central Oyster Bar	213
Jack's Luxury Oyster Bar	68
Le Bernardin	240
Lure Fishbar	290
Mary's Fish Camp	150
Mermaid Inn (The)	72
Oceana	192
Ocean Grill	366
Pearl Oyster Bar	155
Pearl Room (The)	400
Sea Grill (The)	274
Tides	183
Water Club (The)	235

Southern

Londel's	165
Miss Mamie's Spoonbread Too	364

Southwestern

Mesa Grill	108

Spanish

Alcala	197
Barça 18	98
Bolo	102
Casa Mono	103
Degustation	65
El Cid	139
El Faro	140
La Paella	70
Picasso	225
Sevilla	157

Steakhouse

Ben Benson's	253
Blair Perrone	202
BLT Prime	100
BLT Steak	202
Bobby Van's Steakhouse	203
Bull and Bear	205
Capital Grille (The)	206
Cité	258
Del Frisco's	259
Frankie & Johnnie's	262
Gallagher's	263
Keens Steakhouse	264
Maloney & Porcelli	219
MarkJoseph Steakhouse	80
Michael Jordan's	220
Monkey Bar	221
Morton's	221
Nebraska Beef	81
Nick & Stef's	268
Old Homestead	151
Peter Luger	388
Rothmann's	227
Smith & Wollensky	231
Sparks Steak House	231
Strip House	158
Wolfgang's Steakhouse	235

Thai

Bann Thai	411
Jaiya	106
Kittichai	289
Land Thai Kitchen	363
Pongsri Thai	56
Prem-on Thai	157
Sea	403
Sripraphai	417

Turkish

Antique Garage	284
Sip Sak	230
Turkish Kitchen	113

Vegetarian

Gobo	144
Pure Food and Wine	110

Venezuelan

Flor's Kitchen	143

Vietnamese

Le Colonial	217
Nam	310
Omai	47
Sapa	111
Thai So'n	57

East Side Street Sign

Starred Restaurants

Within the selection we offer you, some restaurants deserve to be highlighted for their particularly good cuisine. When giving one, two or three Michelin stars, there are a number of things that we judge, including the quality of the ingredients, the technical skill and flair that goes into their preparation, the blend and clarity of flavors, and the balance of the menu. Just as important is the ability to produce excellent cooking time and again. We make as many visits as we need, so that our readers can be sure of quality and consistency.

A two- or three-star restaurant has to offer something very special in its cuisine; a real element of creativity, originality or "personality" that sets it apart from the rest. Three stars – our highest award – are given to the very best restaurants, where the whole dining experience is superb.

Cuisine in any style, modern or traditional, may be eligible for a star. Because we apply the same independent standards everywhere, the awards have become benchmarks of reliability and excellence in more than 20 European countries, particularly in France, where we have awarded stars for almost 80 years, and where the expression "Now that's real three-star quality!" has entered into the language.

The awarding of a star is based solely on the quality of the cuisine.

Exceptional cuisine, worth a special journey

One always eats here extremely well, often superbly. Distinctive dishes are precisely executed, using superlative ingredients.

		page
Jean Georges	XXXX	354
Le Bernardin	XXXXX	240
Per Se	XXXXX	242

Excellent cuisine, worth a detour

Skillfully and carefully crafted dishes of outstanding quality.

		page			page
Bouley	XXXX	300	Del Posto	XXXX	40
Daniel	XXXXX	316	Masa	XX	244

A very good restaurant in its category

A place offering cuisine prepared to a consistently high standard.

		page			page
Annisa	XX	118	Jewel Bako	X	62
Aureole	XXXX	318	Kurumazushi	X	188
A Voce	XX	84	La Goulue	XX	324
Babbo	XXX	120	Lever House	XXX	190
Café Boulud	XXX	320	Modern (The)	XXX	248
Café Gray	XXX	246	Oceana	XXX	192
Country Restaurant	XXX	86	Perry Street	XXX	126
Craft	XXX	88	Peter Luger	X	388
Cru	XXXX	122	Picholine	XXX	356
Danube	XXX	302	Saul	XX	390
Dévi	XX	90	Spotted Pig	X	128
Etats-Unis	X	322	Sushi of Gari	X	326
Fiamma Osteria	XXX	282	Veritas	XX	96
Fleur de Sel	XX	92	Vong	XX	194
Gotham Bar and Grill	XXX	124	Wallsé	XX	130
Gramercy Tavern	XXX	94	wd~50	XX	176

Starred Restaurants

Bib gourmand

This symbol indicates our inspectors' favorites for good value. For $40 or less, you can enjoy two courses and a glass of wine or a dessert (not including tax or gratuity).

Bon appétit!

Where to eat

Where to eat for less than $25

Where to have brunch

Where to have brunch

© Jeff Greenberg/NYC & Company, Inc.

SoHo dining

Where to have a late dinner

Where to eat

Where to eat

Chrysler Building

Manhattan

Manhattan - Times Square

Chelsea

Center of New York's art world and gay community, Chelsea is situated west of Avenue of the Americas (Sixth Avenue) between 14th and 30th streets. It's a place of stark contrasts—busy commercial avenues intersect quiet residential side streets, and tiny neighborhood cafes abut gargantuan dance clubs. You'll find restaurants in this eclectic neighborhood cater to a wide range of tastes, from French bistros and old-fashioned Spanish places to sushi bars and authentic Mexican eateries. Be sure to check out **Chelsea Market** *(75 Ninth Ave., between 15th & 16th Sts.; 212-243-6005; www.chelseamarket.com)*. This 1898 Nabisco factory (where the Oreo cookie was first made, in 1912) was reopened in 1997 as an urban food market. Interspersed with stores selling flowers, meats, cheeses and other gourmet essentials are cafes, bakeries, and several soup-and-sandwich shops.

A Bit of History – Chelsea got its name in 1750, when British army captain Thomas Clarke bought a farm here (bounded by 21st and 24th streets, Eighth Avenue and the Hudson River) and named it after his London neighborhood. In 1813 the property passed to Clarke's grandson **Clement Clarke Moore**, a scholar and literary figure best known for writing *A Visit from St. Nicholas (aka The Night before Christmas)*. In the 1820s Moore helped shape the development of the district by setting aside land for park-like squares, giving the neighborhood a distinctly English feel, even as its population increasingly hailed from Germany, Italy, Scotland and Ireland. He also specified that residences had to be set back from the street behind spacious front yards. The Hudson River Railroad opened along 11th Avenue in 1851, spawning slaughterhouses, breweries and tenements. From about 1905 to 1915, several motion-picture studios operated here. Dock activity

Along Eighth Avenue

© Martha Cooper

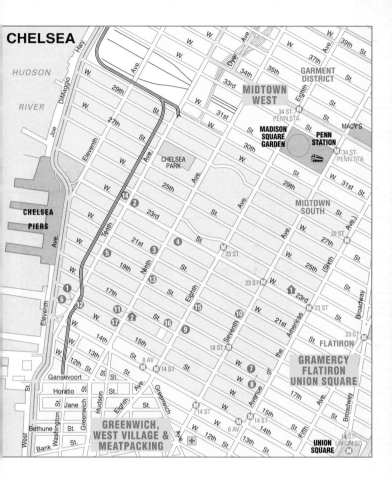

CHELSEA

along the Hudson River began to decline in the 1960s, opening up warehouses and industrial spaces for new uses. Slowly artists moved in, and town houses began to be refurbished.

Chelsea's Gallery Scene – More than 100 world-class **galleries** now occupy garages and lofts on the district's western flank (concentrated between 20th and 30th streets, west of Tenth Avenue), offering museum-quality exhibitions alongside up-and-coming group shows. Be sure to pick up a **Gallery Guide**, which contains a fold-out map locating all the galleries in the area. The guide also lists opening receptions, a fun way to drink in the scene. On 20th, 21st, and 22nd streets, a lovely **historic district** preserves Clement Clarke Moore's vision of elegant city living in some of Chelsea's loveliest brownstones. While you're in the neighborhood, check out the ever-evolving waterfront area, home to the mammoth Chelsea Piers recreation complex and the Hudson River Greenway.

Del Posto ❀ ❀

001

85 Tenth Ave. (bet. 15th & 16th Sts.)

Subway:	14 St - 8 Av	Mon – Thu 5:30pm - 11pm
Phone:	212-497-8090	Fri – Sat noon - 1pm & 5:30pm - 11pm
Fax:	212-807-6320	Sun noon - 10pm
Web:	N/A	
Prices:	$$$$	

Lydia Gould Bessier

Grand design often acts as a distraction for less-impressive food, but in the case of Del Posto, it's simply a complement. Spacious balconies reign from three levels overlooking the stunning first-floor dining room, while dark paneled walls, graceful columns and glittering chandeliers complete the opulent décor.

A project by the blockbuster partnership between Mario Batali and the Bastianich family, Del Posto was getting major press long before it opened, simply because of its provenance. The praise is well deserved. Elegantly prepared Italian classics fill the menu. Perfect al dente pastas pop here, while delicate fish and succulent roasts are often sized for two or more. The impressive wine list showcases a tremendous spectrum of Italian producers and varietals, and the excellent desserts deserve a try for their harmony of sweet ingredients.

Sophisticated, professional and polite service adds to the experience; you might even spot Lidia Bastianich herself making rounds in the dining room to greet a chosen few.

Manhattan Chelsea

Appetizers

Spaghetti with Spicy
Crab, Saffron and
Caramelized Shallots

Garganelli Verdi al
Ragù Bolo

Risotto with Morels

Entrées

Veal Chop for two with
Black Trumpets and
Watercress

Cacciucco with Red
Mullet and Green-
Onion Crostino

Pork Loin with Cipolla
Ripiena and Preserved
Figs

Desserts

Kremeschnitte: Semolina
Mousse, Blackberries,
Green-Apple Sorbetto

Apricot Cassata di
Gelato: Almond Cake,
Baked Meringue,
Apricot Moscato
Brodo

Panna Cotta: Almond
Milk, Moscato Sorbetti
and Orange-Flower
Marmellata

ITALIAN

Bette

002

461 West 23rd St. (bet. Ninth & Tenth Aves.)

Subway:	23 St (Eighth Ave.)	Open daily noon - 3:30pm
Phone:	212-366-0404	& 5:30pm - 11:30pm
Fax:	N/A	
Web:	N/A	
Prices:	$$$	

This stylish low-key setting, hidden away on 23rd Street (look for the apple doorknob), comes alive in the evening. That's no surprise, since owner Amy Sacco is well known as the queen of the New York City nightlife scene. Sacco has decked out her restaurant with pop-style portraits of glamorous women, dark wood wainscoting and sultry lighting. A panel of glass separates the elegant bar from the dining room, and the drinkers from those trying to enjoy a peaceful meal.

At lunch the fashion and publishing crowds come to pick at salads. At night, the beautiful people pour in to see and be seen as well as to sample the likes of lobster spaghetti, grilled meats and fish.

Will this restaurant have the longevity to survive after the initial buzz has worn off? Bette on it.

Bombay Talkie

003

189 Ninth Ave. (bet. 21st & 22nd Sts.)

Subway:	23 St (Eighth Ave.)	Sun – Thu 5pm - 10:30pm
Phone:	212-242-1900	Fri – Sat 5pm - 11:30pm
Fax:	212-242-6366	Closed July 4
Web:	www.bombaytalkie.com	
Prices:	$$	

Street food from India steals the spotlight at this Chelsea restaurant, opened in early 2005. Owner Sunitha Ramaiah named Bombay Talkie after the 1970 film that inspired her, and Thomas Juul-Hansen designed the dining space accordingly with painted murals of Indian movie stars and an LCD flat screen running Bollywood films in the downstairs bar.

Styled as an Indian teahouse, Bombay Talkie divides its menu into sections dubbed "Street Bites," "Dinner by the Roadside" and "Curbside." Regional dishes range from Kathi rolls and dosas to pork vindaloo. East meets West in a mesmerizing mix on the house cocktails list.

Don't skip dessert here; the delicate flavors of Mariebelle cardamom ganache or carrot Halwa will leave you with sweet dreams.

Chelsea Bistro

004

358 W. 23rd St. (bet. Eighth & Ninth Aves.)

Subway:	23 St (Eighth Ave.)	Tue – Sat 5pm - 11pm
Phone:	212-727-2026	Closed Sun & Mon
Fax:	212-727-2180	
Web:	N/A	
Prices:	$$	

The bright red façade of Chelsea Bistro stands out amid the other storefronts on this block, beckoning diners inside. An intimate atmosphere created by velvet curtains, tapestry-patterned banquettes, a brick fireplace and candlelight set the mood for a romantic evening.

Cuisine sticks to French favorites like roasted free-range chicken, grilled pork chops with silky mashed potatoes, steak frites and duck with orange confit sauce. Desserts are equally classic, with signatures including tarte Tatin, crème brûlée, and profiteroles blanketed with warm chocolate sauce. To accompany your meal, you can choose among some 250 wines; the list concentrates on French and American vintages.

The glass-roofed Garden Terrace Room brings the outdoors in (without the cold) year-round.

Cookshop

005

156 Tenth Ave. (at 20th St.)

Subway:	23 St (Eighth Ave.)	Mon – Sat 11:30am - 3pm
Phone:	212-924-4440	& 5:30pm - midnight
Fax:	212-242-1803	Sun 11:30am - 3pm & 5:30pm - 10pm
Web:	www.cookshopny.com	Closed July 4 & Christmas Day
Prices:	$$	

This Chelsea newcomer, owned by the husband-and-wife team behind Five Points in the Village, wins rave reviews from a sophisticated crowd. Soft lighting, a warm design and closely spaced tables lend an intimate air, while thoughtful service makes regulars out of many first-timers.

Large blackboards lining the walls highlight the chef's passion for market-fresh products on the daily changing menu. The roster reads like a geography lesson, with enticing choices such as Catskill duck, Montauk squid and Vermont quail grouped by cooking method rather than category. The concise wine list offers a fine selection at sensible prices.

Since Cookshop's popularity has soared, reservations are a must—unless you prefer to dine at one of the bar tables, in which case it's first come, first fed.

Manhattan Chelsea

Craftsteak

006

85 Tenth Ave. (at 15th St.)

Subway:	14 St - 8 Av
Phone:	212-400-6699
Fax:	212-352-1690
Web:	www.craftsteaknyc.com
Prices:	$$$$

Sun – Thu 5:30pm - 10pm
Fri – Sat 5:30pm - 11pm

Opened in May 2006, Craftsteak is the latest addition to Tom Colicchio's New York restaurant empire. A cavernous space in a remote location on edge of the Meatpacking District, this urban-chic steakhouse fills a dramatic and dazzling space, complete with views of the Hudson River. Craftsteak draws diners from all neighborhoods, and its boho-banker crowd is as appealing as its dark, contemporary décor.

The kitchen turns out flawless fare, high in quality and imagination. Ingredient-focused, yet simple, the dishes wow foodies, celebrities and fashionistas alike. An extensive raw-bar menu rounds out the first-course selections, while Hawaiian grass-fed Angus beef, corn-fed Hereford and Australian Wagyu beef are main-course standouts. Prices are high, though, so come on an expense account.

Crema

007

111 W. 17th St. (bet. Sixth & Seventh Aves.)

Subway:	18 St
Phone:	212-691-4477
Fax:	212-691-6084
Web:	www.cremarestaurante.com
Prices:	$$$

Tue – Sun noon - midnight
Closed Mon & July 4

Monterrey-born chef Julieta Ballesteros showcases the regional cuisine of her homeland at her newest venture, Crema. Already carrying a loyal following from sibling Mexicana Mama in the West Village, Crema is as artsy as the crowd it draws. Inside, it's pure Mexico City stylish from the colorful décor to the upbeat Mexican music. An open kitchen brings the space to life.

The food here is equal parts upscale and casual. Vibrant presentations of flavorful dishes show the chef's flair for the creative. Choose the tostadas topped with grilled scallops, avocado, chipotle aïoli and mango salsa, or opt for the grilled ribeye steak with homemade mole sauce. The prix-fixe lunch menu, which includes an appetizer, entrée, and a side dish or drink, is a particularly good value.

da Umberto

008

107 W. 17th St. (bet. Sixth & Seventh Aves.)

Subway:	18 St	Mon – Fri noon - 3pm & 5:30pm - 11pm
Phone:	212-989-0303	Sat 5:30pm - 11pm
Fax:	212-989-6703	Closed Sun
Web:	N/A	
Prices:	$$	

You're likely to hear as much Italian as English spoken at da Umberto—a good clue to the authenticity of the cuisine. The chic dining room fills nightly with a crowd of regulars, many of whom are celebrities and power brokers. Getting a table here is half the battle, but whether you're a frequent diner here or not, you'll be greeted warmly.

Northern Italian specialties—house-made pasta, hearty risotto, grilled fish and a veal chop with a fresh rosemary and cognac sauce—are complemented by a long list of daily specials to further tantalize your palate. The *bistecca alla Fiorentina*, a steak for two, is a signature dish. Knowledgeable servers cater to the smartly dressed clientele, efficiently checking back on a regular basis to make sure everyone is happy.

Gascogne

009

158 Eighth Ave. (bet. 17th & 18th Sts.)

Subway:	14 St - 8 Av	Open daily noon - 3pm & 5:30pm - 11pm
Phone:	212-675-6564	
Fax:	212-627-3018	
Web:	www.gascognenyc.com	
Prices:	$$	

A jewel in the heart of Chelsea, Gascogne sparkles with its cuisine, which celebrates rustic fare from southwestern France. Fine cassoulet, foie gras and veal kidneys flamed with Armagnac are examples of the carefully prepared dishes. In true French fashion, the bar stocks a good selection of aged Armagnac for after-dinner sipping.

If you're on a budget, go for the prix-fixe pre-theater menu (cash only), which is offered all evening on Monday. Weekend brunch is also a good bet, with a fixed-price menu offering the likes of rabbit terrine with black truffles, and roast pork loin with white bean ragout. In cold weather, ask for a table by the window overlooking the charming, flower-filled garden—complete with a Christmas tree in season; in summer you can dine outside in this shady space.

Le Zie 2000

Italian 🍴🍴

010

172 Seventh Ave. (bet. 20th & 21st Sts.)

Subway:	23 St (Seventh Ave.)	Open daily noon - 11:30pm
Phone:	212-206-8686	
Fax:	212-924-9984	
Web:	www.lezie.com	
Prices:	$$	

The cooking of Italy's Veneto region takes center stage in this pastel dining room. Start your meal by sharing the cicchetti for two, an antipasto that includes sardines in *saor* (a traditional sweet and sour preparation), fried artichokes with olive sauce, fava beans with Pecorino, stewed eggplant, cod mousse and more—served with grilled polenta, the Venetians' signature starch. Then move on to the hearty homemade pastas and a fish or meat course. Heading the dessert menu is creamy tiramisu, a confection that originated in Venice. All of Italy's viticultural regions are spotlighted on the wine list, which boasts more than 200 labels.

Open for brunch, lunch and dinner, Le Zie's small outdoor patio makes it a perfect place to while away a sunny day.

Matsuri

Japanese 🍴🍴

011

369 W. 16th St. (bet. Eighth & Ninth Aves.)

Subway:	14 St - 8 Av	Sun — Wed 6pm - midnight
Phone:	212-243-6400	Thu — Sat 6pm - 1am
Fax:	212-835-5533	
Web:	www.themaritimehotel.com	
Prices:	$$	

Matsuri is a place to soak up the scene, and what a scene it is! True to its name ("festival" in Japanese), Matsuri exudes a party vibe, especially in the evening. Housed in a cavernous space underneath the Maritime Hotel *(see hotel listings)*, the restaurant is the domain of chef Tadashi Ono, whose commitment to using the freshest ingredients requires him to have fish and organic grains flown in daily from Japan. Sake black cod is a staple of the seasonal menu.

In the multilevel dining room, large Japanese lanterns hang like bright moons from the dark vaulted ceiling. And the stars are here, too, in a galaxy of celebs and supermodels who frequent the place. Be sure to try a few of the 200 different types of sake, which includes Matsuri's own house brew.

Morimoto

012

88 Tenth Ave. (at 16th St.)

Subway:	14 St - 8 Av	Sun – Wed 5:30pm - 10:45pm
Phone:	212-989-8883	Thu – Sat 5:30pm - 11:45pm
Fax:	212-989-8822	
Web:	www.morimotonyc.com	
Prices:	$$$	

From the A-list crowd that frequents this hot spot to the kitchen's artful presentations, it's all about looks at Morimoto, which was one of New York's most anticipated openings (by Philadelphia restaurateur Stephen Starr) in January 2006. The knockout interior design is defined by a large-scale artwork composed of glass bottles that divides the dining room. Tables and banquettes are scattered among different levels, creating a dramatic effect.

Adding to the big-city buzz, the open kitchen turns out innovative, colorful courses peppered by a mix of Japanese, Asian and European influences. Dishes double as eye candy, with a modern panache applied to the cooking method and even more so to the presentations. Every dish that arrives at the table seems to manifest a more dazzling display.

Omai

013

158 Ninth Ave. (bet. 19th & 20th Sts.)

Subway:	23 St (Eighth Ave.)	Sun – Thu 5:30pm - 10:30pm
Phone:	212-633-0550	Fri – Sat 5:30pm - 11:30pm
Fax:	212-633-0576	
Web:	www.omainyc.com	
Prices:	$$	

Don't look for a sign to identify this little restaurant in the hub of Chelsea—there isn't one. Once you find the place, though (watch for the pots of bamboo outside), you'll step into a space tastefully underdecorated with exposed brick walls and Southeast Asian accents.

Vietnamese dishes here manage to be creative while staying true to their roots. Omai's takes on entreés such as roasted duck, jumbo shrimp and sautéed chicken are perfumed with tamarind, curry and coconut, and lemongrass. Want something lighter? The menu offers options from spring rolls to rice and vegetables to noodle dishes. Finish your meal with a tempting dessert, such as the coconut pyramid with tapioca pandan sauce. Hint: avoid the middle row of tables if you don't want to be jostled while you eat.

Manhattan Chelsea

The Red Cat

Contemporary ✕✕

014

227 Tenth Ave. (bet. 23rd & 24th Sts.)

Subway:	23 St (Eighth Ave.)	Mon – Thu 5pm - 11pm
Phone:	212-242-1122	Friday – Saturday 5pm - midnight
Fax:	212-242-1390	Sunday 4:30pm - 10:30pm
Web:	www.theredcat.com	Closed Christmas Day
Prices:	$$	

With its wood-paneled walls, and red-and-white color scheme enlivened by contemporary art, The Red Cat's dining room has a New England-meets-the-big-city air. A stylish and sophisticated crowd adds to the ambience; this is the kind of place you can tell is cool, but not so cool that you'd rather be elsewhere.

Innovative American fare here often includes varying preparations of a sautéed Chatham cod, or a pan-roasted organic chicken. It's the kind of menu that has wide appeal, as the food is creative enough to be unusual, but not so weird that Mom can't enjoy it. A classic example is the lobster and potato chip salad, a highlight of the chef's irreverent culinary style.

The restaurant's location makes it convenient to browsing Chelsea's tony art galleries.

Rocking Horse

Mexican ✕

015

182 Eighth Ave. (bet. 19th & 20th Sts.)

Subway:	14 St - 8 Av	Sun – Thu 11am - 11pm
Phone:	212-463-9511	Fri – Sat 11am - midnight
Fax:	212-243-3245	
Web:	www.rockinghorsecafe.com	
Prices:	$$	

From its elegant design to its upscale cooking, Rocking Horse Cafe is not your run-of-the-mill Mexican restaurant. The sleek dining room is the perfect match for the contemporary Mexican-accented cuisine.

Niman Ranch pork, free-range chicken and fresh vegetables provide the filling for supple burritos, quesadillas and enchiladas at lunch, while sophisticated dishes like black tiger prawns with caramelized papaya and poblano chiles, and Chiltepe chile-crusted tuna take the stage at dinner. As an appetizer, the house-made guacamole is flavorful and lightly spiced, served with warm corn tortilla chips. Save room for the oh-so-rich tres leches cake, topped with sliced bananas and banana cream.

Snag a seat by the retractable wall and take in the lively street scene while you sip a Margarita.

Sueños

016

311 W. 17th St. (bet. Eighth & Ninth Aves.)

Subway:	14 St - 8 Av	Sun – Wed 5pm -11pm
Phone:	212-243-1333	Thu – Sat 5pm - midnight
Fax:	212-243-3377	
Web:	www.suenosnyc.com	
Prices:	$$	

Sueños ("dreams" in Spanish) is a literal dream come true for chef/owner Sue Torres. Formerly of Rocking Horse Cafe, also in Chelsea, Torres supervises the operation of the kitchen and the dining room at this restaurant, which opened in 2003.

There's nothing timid about the place; from the brightly painted magenta and orange brick walls to the bold, chile tasting menu, Sueños celebrates the best of Mexico. Dining spaces center on a glass-enclosed patio, complete with a fountain and flowers. This place has a festive spirit, with flavor-packed dishes like tequila-flamed shrimp with avocado black bean salad and fun "make your own taco" menus. Like the food? You can even take cooking classes in the restaurant or follow the chef to Mexico to learn her secrets.

202 😋

017

75 Ninth Ave. (bet. 15th & 16th Sts.)

Subway:	14 St - 8 Av	Mon 8:30am - 4pm
Phone:	646-638-1173	Tue – Sun 8:30am - 10pm
Fax:	646-638-2188	
Web:	N/A	
Prices:	$$	

Set in Chelsea Market, 202 gives shoppers in the Nicole Farhi boutique a respite from difficult fashion decisions (Does that dress really make me look fat?). Grab a table—there's no separation between shop and restaurant—and order a guiltless tuna burger, or a seasonal salad. While these dishes are shopping-friendly, there is enough hearty fare on the menu—created by British chef Annie Wayte—to satisfy more ravenous appetites. And if you felt any angst over the crispy fish and chips you inhaled, by the time you finish that last luscious bite of chocolate pot de crème, you'll wonder why you ever fretted over such a silly thing.

Sister to Nicole's in Midtown (10 E. 60th St.), 202 offers a classy vibe and service sans attitude. Don't overlook the daily specials noted on the blackboard.

Manhattan Chelsea

Chinatown

Sprawling Chinatown is a veritable city within a city. Narrow streets at its core feel utterly unlike the rest of New York City. Densely packed markets stock everything from lychee to lipstick, while storefront restaurants serve up 20 distinct Asian cuisines in more than 200 restaurants. Especially crowded on weekends, the area marked by pagoda-roofed buildings and Buddhist temples bursts its seams at **Chinese New Year** (first full moon after January 19), when dragons dance down the streets accompanied by costumed revelers and fireworks.

Just Visiting – The first Chinese came to New York in the 1870s from the California goldfields or from jobs building the transcontinental railroad in the western U.S. Most were men who, unlike other immigrants, had no intention of staying—they simply wanted to make their fortunes and return to a comfortable life in China. By the 1880s, New York's Chinese community numbered about 10,000 people. In 1882, the Chinese Exclusion Act was passed to stop further immigration, and growth came to a standstill. Unable to earn passage back to China, many "temporary" residents stayed. In part because single men continued to make up the majority of the population, the neighborhood took on a rough-and-tumble character in the late 19th and early 20th centuries. Opium dens, brothels and gambling parlors sprang up, as did social clubs called tongs.

Here to Stay – Following the 1943 repeal of the Chinese Exclusion Act, a new influx of immigrants arrived in New York from Taiwan and Hong Kong, as well as from mainland China. Garment factories, Chinese laundries, shops and restaurants appeared in the quarter, which has inexorably spread out from its dense heart into neighboring Little Italy and the Lower East Side.

Today New York's Chinatown holds one of the largest Chinese immigrant communities outside Asia. The hub of the neighborhood lies in the area bounded by Worth, Baxter, and Canal Streets and the Bowery. Pell, Doyers, and Bayard streets—the most atmospheric in the district—are so

Chinatown Food Market

© Martha Cooper

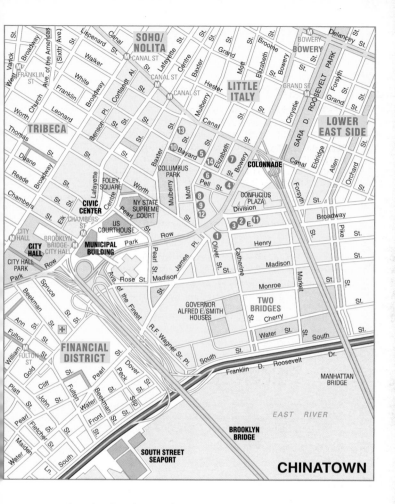

narrow that they're almost always in the shade. Mulberry and Mott streets are lined with shops piled high with displays of bamboo plants, tea sets, silk dresses, Chinese lanterns, fans, and the like. Browse the food markets here for exotic products from duck eggs to Durian fruit, then check out Mott Street when you get hungry; many of the quarter's best restaurants are located here. Be sure to experience **dim sum**, a multicourse meal of small snacks (buns, pastries, dumplings and more) served on rolling carts.

Dim Sum Go Go

001

5 East Broadway (at Chatham Sq.)

Subway:	Canal St (Lafayette St.)	Open daily 10am - 10:30pm
Phone:	212-732-0797	
Fax:	N/A	
Web:	N/A	
Prices:	⊖⊖	

Despite the name, you won't find dancers in white go-go boots here. What you will find is a simple but comfortable place decorated with sleek metal chairs and red voile lining the ceiling. Servers offer good advice about the vast number of dim sum choices, which are served à la carte, rather than from steam carts. That fact makes this a good restaurant to introduce neophytes to the delights of dim sum, before taking them to more authentic Hong Kong-style spots where it helps to know something about the cuisine.

Founded by French-American food writer Colette Rossant, this restaurant serves dim sum all day. There are 24 different types of dumplings alone here; go for the dim sum platter if you want a well-priced sampling.

Fuleen Seafood

002

11 Division St. (bet. Catherine & Market Sts.)

Subway:	Canal St (Lafayette St.)	Open daily 11am - 2:30am
Phone:	212-941-6888	
Fax:	N/A	
Web:	N/A	
Prices:	⊖⊖	

If you fancy Chinese food, you won't dig up a better lunch special in Chinatown—or perhaps all of Manhattan—than the lunch deal at Fuleen Seafood. Less than $5 here buys your choice of an entreé, and they throw in rice and soup on the house. It seems unbelievable, but the locals and those on break from jury duty at the nearby courthouse, who crowd the large, round tables here, know where to go for a good filling meal for an incredibly low price. The long list of main courses offers something for everyone: seafood, shellfish, chicken, beef, pork and vegetable dishes. The lunch special is offered daily from 11am to 3pm.

The simple décor is typically no frills, but the patrons who come here for good food at a good value aren't looking for hip styling and a cool crowd.

Golden Unicorn 😊

003

Chinese 🍴🍴

18 East Broadway (at Catherine St.)

Subway:	Canal St (Lafayette St.)	Open daily 10am - 11pm
Phone:	212-941-0911	
Fax:	212-941-0951	
Web:	N/A	
Prices:	$$	

You'll enter the Golden Unicorn through a commercial building in the underbelly of eastern Chinatown. If it's a weekend, you'll have to elbow your way through the mob to get a number from the woman who runs the show. When she calls your number, she'll direct you to take the elevator to either the second or third floor, where you're in for a dim sum treat at lunch.

Family-size tables in the large rooms leave just enough space for the waitstaff to roll carts of delectable little jewels past each diner. Choose from a mouthwatering array of shrimp and leek dumplings, shu mai, barbecue pork buns, crispy duck and much, much more. Just don't fill up before your favorites have wheeled your way.

Dinner brings Cantonese and Hong Kong fare, but it's the daytime dim sum that really packs 'em in.

Great N.Y. Noodletown 😊

004

Chinese 🍴

28 Bowery (at Bayard St.)

Subway:	Canal St (Lafayette St.)	Open daily 9am - 4am
Phone:	212-349-0923	
Fax:	N/A	
Web:	N/A	
Prices:	💰💰	

If you're looking for fancy décor or friendly service, keep on walking. But if it's tasty, inexpensive Chinese food you seek at almost any hour, stop right here. Great N.Y. Noodletown is a casual place, to say the least: the menu is displayed under the pane of glass that tops the tables, they don't serve beer, they only take cash, and you pay the cashier before you leave.

Although noodles dominate the menu (get them pan-fried, Cantonese-style or in Hong Kong-style lo mein), they aren't the high point of the menu. There's also a choice of salt-baked dishes—the soft-shell crab being one of the better choices—and best of all are the barbecued meats that you can see hanging in the restaurant's window. Roast duck and pork are fantastic here, and the prices are unbelievably low.

Mandarin Court 😋

005

61 Mott St. (bet. Bayard & Canal Sts.)

Subway:	Canal St (Lafayette St.)
Phone:	212-608-3838
Fax:	212-226-6110
Web:	N/A
Prices:	😋😋

Open daily 8am - 11pm

Dim sum is not just for weekend brunch. At Mandarin Court, dim sum is served every day from 8am to 3:30pm. The presentation here is traditional Hong Kong-style; the waiters roll carts full of dumplings, buns, wontons and other savories past your table so you can take your pick. There's even sweet dim sum for dessert (such as egg custard, almond- or coconut-flavored gelatin, and the sesame ball).

If you're really hungry, try one of the regular entreés, which include steaming bowls of broth brimming with noodles, vegetables, meat or seafood. The dining room may not look like much, and it may be a bit noisy with your neighbors a little too close for comfort, but the regulars don't come here for the atmosphere. They're attracted by good Hong Kong-style food at very reasonable prices.

New Yeah Shanghai

006

65 Bayard St. (at Mott St.)

Subway:	Canal St (Lafayette St.)
Phone:	212-566-4884
Fax:	212-566-6111
Web:	N/A
Prices:	😋😋

Open daily 10:30am - midnight

Just off the bustle of Bayard Street in the heart of Chinatown, New Yeah Shanghai offers a taste of Shanghai. Live plants, arched ceilings and Asian decorative accents lend a cave-like, Pacific Rim feel to this otherwise casual restaurant.

Decision-making may be difficult here, where an extensive menu features Shanghai favorites, dumplings galore, all sorts of noodles and many daily specials, as well as seasonal items created specifically for holidays throughout the year. The carefully cooked food is served as promptly as it is prepared by the capable staff, and the large portions are ideal for family-style gatherings (there's plenty to share or to take home leftovers).

New Yeah Shanghai draws a loyal crowd of regulars and locals, and tourists are equally at home here.

Oriental Garden

007

14 Elizabeth St. (bet. Bayard & Canal Sts.)

Subway:	Canal St (Lafayette St.)	Mon – Fri 10am - midnight
Phone:	212-619-0085	Sat – Sun 9am - midnight
Fax:	N/A	
Web:	N/A	
Prices:	🐚	

You'll know what the food focus is here as soon as you walk through the door. On either side of the entrance, two aquarium tanks swim with live fish and lobsters, awaiting your order (actually, they may not be anticipating it quite so fondly, since they're the ones that will soon be on the plate).

Adventurous palates are rewarded here, where barbecued eel on a stick is one of the intriguing selections. If you're not a fish lover, don't worry, there are plenty of other dishes on the menu, including an extensive selection of classic Chinese fare. The walls of the tidy, single dining room are lined with framed Chinese ideograms, the service is attentive and the place is always hopping. Just be sure to bring cash; Oriental Garden doesn't accept credit cards for bills under $60.

Peking Duck House

008

28 Mott St. (bet. Chatham Sq. & Pell St.)

Subway:	Canal St (Lafayette St.)	Open daily noon - 10:30pm
Phone:	212-227-1810	Closed Thanksgiving
Fax:	212-227-1920	
Web:	www.pekingduckhousenyc.com	
Prices:	$$	

Round up a few friends and go for the specialty of the house—you guessed it: Peking duck—at this Chinatown establishment. The slow-roasted duck comes out juicy inside with pleasingly crispy skin, and it's a surefire crowd pleaser (the dish, which consists of a whole duck or the traditional mulitcourse meal, is better enjoyed by two or more). In ceremonial fashion, the chef slices the bird tableside and serves it with house-made pancakes, scallions, cucumbers and hoisin sauce.

Don't care for duck? There's a full menu of other selections, from Szechuan prawns to crispy sea bass to "volcano" steak (strips of filet mignon flamed with Grand Marnier). Those who want a similar dining experience without the Chinatown buzz can visit the restaurant's Midtown sister (236 E. 53rd St.).

Ping's Seafood

009

22 Mott St. (bet. Chatham Sq. & Pell St.)

Subway:	Canal St (Lafayette St.)	Open daily 10am - midnight
Phone:	212-602-9988	
Fax:	212-602-9992	
Web:	N/A	
Prices:	🍴	

Discreet Asian décor highlights this bustling, comfortable place—complete with white tablecloths—in the middle of Chinatown. The menu, as overseen by chef/owner Chuen Ping Hui, concentrates on Hong Kong-style dishes, characterized by their light sauces and simple preparations—especially talented with (but not limited to) seafood. There's little doubt of the freshness of the latter here; a stack of fish tanks near the entrance display the day's catch.

If you're looking for something more on the authentic side, consider the braised sea cucumber, stir-fried pork stomach and dried squid, or cuttlefish and conch in XO sauce (a Hong Kong invention).

Another location in Queens (8302 Queens Blvd., in Flushing) proves that Ping's has a recipe for success.

Pongsri Thai

010

106 Bayard St. (at Baxter St.)

Subway:	Canal St (Lafayette St.)	Open daily 11:30am - 11pm
Phone:	212-349-3132	
Fax:	N/A	
Web:	N/A	
Prices:	🍴	

Tired of Chinese food? Try Pongsri Thai (also known as Thailand Restaurant, per the sign out front), for a taste of the traditional cuisine of Thailand with its hot, sour, sweet and tangy elements. Seafood shines here, and the extensive menu cites choices from spicy fried whole fish to steamed mussels. For vegetarians, there's a wide selection of vegetable curries, as well as noodle dishes like pad Thai. To whet your appetite, try the traditional soups and salads or sample some of the extensive array of appetizers.

While the Chinatown location is the original (it's been here for 35 years), there are two additional outposts in Manhattan: in the Theater District at 244 West 48th Street, and in Gramercy at 311 Second Avenue.

Sunrise 27

011

27 Division St. (bet. Catherine & Market Sts.)

Subway:	Canal St (Lafayette St.)	Open daily 9am - 11:30pm
Phone:	212-219-8498	
Fax:	212-219-8055	
Web:	N/A	
Prices:	☙	

Large windows face the street at Sunrise 27, beckoning diners into the understated restaurant, where golden dragons sprawl across a red-velvet screen at the back of the room.

At lunch, you have a choice of the regular menu or the cart of dim sum that is circulated around the room. For dinner, you'll be hard-pressed to decide among the pages of offerings, which include casseroles filled with the likes of fresh frog with ginger and scallions, or sliced eel. Several chicken dishes (salt-baked or crispy fried) are offered as half or whole portions, catering to a variety of appetites.

The pleasant waitstaff is well-organized, always accessible and thoughtful, providing hot towels between messy courses for guests who can't get enough of the deliciously sweet and sticky sauces.

Thai So'n

Vietnamese ✕

013

89 Baxter St. (bet. Bayard & Canal Sts.)

Subway:	Canal St (Lafayette St.)	Open daily 10:30am - 10:30pm
Phone:	212-732-2822	
Fax:	212-732-2822	
Web:	N/A	
Prices:	☙	

Set on a busy street in Chinatown, Thai So'n is known in the neighborhood for serving high-quality Vietnamese fare at low prices. The place has a simple, dining-hall-like atmosphere, improved by the photographs of the Asian countryside on the walls; comfort is minimal, but that's not why folks come here.

They come for the contrasting flavors and textures that form the basis of the flavorful cuisine, which incorporates fresh vegetables, fiery peppers and herbs like basil, coriander, mint and lemongrass, along with a minimal amount of oil. If it's cold out, try a steaming bowl of Pho (beef or chicken broth full of rice noodles and your choice of other ingredients) to chase away the chill.

The casual atmosphere makes this spot a great choice for groups or families dining with children.

Manhattan Chinatown

Wonton Garden

Chinese ⚕

014

56 Mott St. (bet. Bayard & Canal Sts.)

Subway:	Canal St (Lafayette St.)
Phone:	212-966-4886
Fax:	N/A
Web:	N/A
Prices:	●●

Open daily 9am - 2am

S

Hard chairs and benches here may not lend themselves to lingering, but copious quantities of well-prepared Cantonese cuisine will likely convince you to stay. This style of regional Chinese cooking emphasizes fresh seasonal ingredients, in prepared-to-order dishes.

Typically, Cantonese-style preparations are quick-fried or stewed to preserve their freshness; homemade noodles, for example, are stewed as in lo mein or pan-fried as in chow mein, both overflowing with roast duck, sweet and sour pork, beef, chicken, shrimp or vegetables, depending on your preference. If you've never tried them, the steamed Cantonese roast pork buns are a favorite dim sum dish. Many staff members speak only a few words of English, but the bilingual menu helps guide visitors through the tasty process.

LOUIS ROEDERER

CHAMPAGNE

East Village

The neighborhood bounded by 14th and Houston streets, and Bowery and the East River is the center of alternative culture in New York—rock concerts, poetry readings, and Off-Off Broadway theater productions take place here nightly. Not only does the East Village have a highly developed cafe culture, it's also one of the best places in the city to shop for used books and records and vintage clothes. In general the East Village caters to a very young crowd—almost all the cafes, bars and boutiques attract patrons in their twenties and thirties who, if they 're not living on a limited budget, like to pretend they are.

A Bit of History – In 1651 **Peter Stuyvesant**, the Dutch-born director-general of the New Netherland colony, purchased the land bounded by today's 17th Street, 5th Street, Fourth Avenue, and the East River from the Indians for use as a farm. After surrendering to the English in 1664, Stuyvesant withdrew from public affairs and moved to his manor house on present-day Stuyvesant Street.

Briefly in the early 1800s, the district west of Second Avenue boasted fashionable town houses, home to a social elite that included **John Jacob Astor**, the fur-trade and real-estate magnate who helped develop the surrounding neighborhood starting in 1825, and railroad tycoon **"Commodore" Cornelius Vanderbilt**. The working-class neighborhoods farther east were home to Polish, Ukrainian and German immigrants until the early 20th century. The term "East Village" was coined in the early 1960s to distinguish the neighborhood from the rest of the Lower East Side. The glory days of the East Village were the 1980s, when rock bands like the B-52's, the Talking Heads, and the Ramones made names for themselves at the legendary club CBGB & OMFUG (a.k.a. Country, Bluegrass, Blues and Other Music for Uplifting Gourmandizers).

East Village

© Martha Cooper

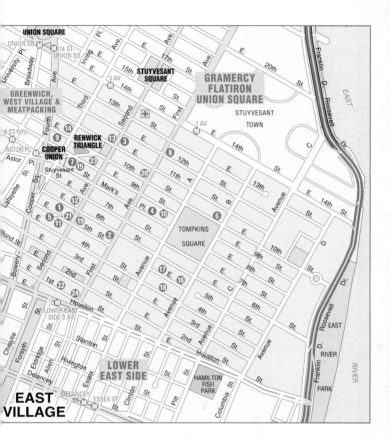

A Taste of East Village – The East Village today contains vestiges of almost all chapters of its history. Laid out in 1834, ten-acre **Tompkins Square Park**, sits roughly at the center of the village. Its 150-year-old elms, flowers and fountains, make the park one of downtown Manhattan's most attractive public spaces. Most of the village's side streets are lined by 19th-century brownstones, spiffed-up tenements, and lush trees. **St. Mark's Place** is the most densely commercial street in the East Village, drawing hordes of students and hippies to its sushi bars, jewelry and sunglass stalls, record stores and head shops. **Second Avenue** is really the district's spine. Here you'll find an astounding variety of ethnic eateries—Italian, Russian, Korean, Thai, Jewish and Mexican among them. Sixth Street between First and Second avenues is known as **Little India** for the many super-cheap Indian and Bangladeshi restaurants that line the block.

Jewel Bako ❀

001

239 E. 5th St. (bet. Second & Third Aves.)

Subway:	Astor Pl	Mon – Sat 6:30pm - 10:30pm
Phone:	212-979-1012	Closed Sun
Fax:	N/A	
Web:	N/A	
Prices:	$$$	

Jewel Bako/Swee Phuah

Jewel Bako—the name means "jewel box"—is the flagship of husband-and-wife restaurateur team Jack and Grace Lamb. And a jewel box it is, with its tables strewn beneath a pair of striking back-lit bamboo arches. Beyond the bamboo tunnels, hidden behind a mirrored wall, lies the little sushi bar. A seat at this bamboo counter, where diners are treated to a taste of the chef's omakase, is highly coveted.

Each piece of sushi is a gem here, including rare varieties like Japanese spotted sardine, needlefish and live octopus flown in from Tsukiji Market in Tokyo. To brighten the taste even further, wasabi is grated fresh at the table, where polished river stones make a pretty rest for chopsticks.

Known for their warm welcome, the Lambs manage to divide their time between their handful of restaurants (including Jack's Luxury Oyster Bar, and the newest, Degustation). Fans of the recently shuttered Jewel Bako Makimono will be glad to know that they can now order their favorite Makimono fare at Jewel Bako.

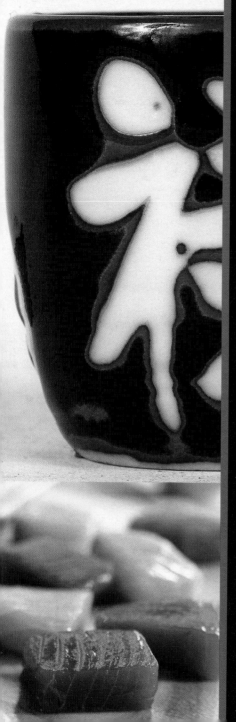

COURSES

Sake-poached Octopus with Sea Salt

Japanese Bonito with Mitsuba Salad and Tosazu Jelly

Poached Sea Eel with Nitsume Sauce and Tempura Bones

Grilled Pen Shell Scallops with Toasted Nori

Yellowtail Nanbanzuke

Toro Tartare

Crispy Giant Tiger Prawns with Green-Tea Salt

Grilled Live Scallop with Japanese Mushrooms and Dashi

DESSERTS

Chocolate and Adzuki-Bean Mousse Cake

JAPANESE

Banjara

002

Indian ✗

97 First Ave. (at 6th St.)

Subway:	Lower East Side - 2 Av
Phone:	212-477-5956
Fax:	212-533-2508
Web:	www.banjarany.com
Prices:	$$

Sun – Thu noon - midnight
Fri – Sat noon - 1am

Named for the Banjara gypsy tribe of Eastern India, this restaurant stands out among the numerous other Indian eateries that mark this Little India section of the East Village. Banjara isn't flashy like most of its Curry Row competition; the dining room is tastefully decorated with fresh flowers on each table and rich-hued Indian tapestries gracing the back wall of the bar area, creating an exotic ambience to match the origin of the cuisine.

Spices add robust flavor, but Banjara eschews the heavy-handed fiery spicing sometimes found in other nearby Indian spots. Authentic regional dishes fill the menu here, from clay-oven-fired tandooris to *dumpakht*, a traditional stew that is sealed in its cooking vessel under a dome of pastry (think of it as the aromatic Indian version of a pot pie).

Cacio e Pepe

003

Italian ✗

182 Second Ave. (bet. 11th & 12th Sts.)

Subway:	3 Av
Phone:	212-505-5931
Fax:	N/A
Web:	www.cacioepepe.com
Prices:	$$

Mon – Fri 5:30pm - 11pm
Sat – Sun 5:30pm - 11:30pm

Lower Second Avenue has its share of Italian restaurants, but this one is worth seeking out. Run by a Roman expatriate, Cacio e Pepe focuses on Roman regional specialties, presenting a generous variety of choices on its seasonally changing menu. For example, the signature Tonnarelli Cacio e Pepe combines house-made tonnarelli tossed in pasta water, olive oil and abundant pecorino cheese and cracked black pepper; the dish is presented in a hollowed-out pecorino wheel and tossed again tableside. The wine list is short but carefully selected to highlight less familiar producers in the most notable Italian regions.

In warm weather, the garden behind the restaurant makes a perfectly lovely setting for dinner. Any time of year, expect service that is warm and attentive.

Café Mogador

004

101 St. Mark's Pl. (bet. First Ave. & Ave. A)

Subway:	1 Av	Sun – Thu 9am - 1am
Phone:	212-677-2226	Fri – Sat 9am - 2am
Fax:	212-533-2159	
Web:	www.cafemogador.com	
Prices:	😊😊	

In the heart of the bohemian East Village, Café Mogador adds a North African note to the neighborhood's ethnic restaurant mix. Moorish lanterns, jars of spices and black-and-white photographs of Morocco lend an exotic air to this little cafe, where prices are approachable and service is cheerful and attentive.

Couscous, a staple of Moroccan cuisine, is interpreted here with an array of veggies (turnips, carrots, cabbage, zucchini and pumpkin) and topped with chickpeas, onions and raisins. Traditional bastilla fills layers of crispy filo with shredded chicken, eggs, almonds and cinnamon, and tagines (meat, poultry or lamb stewed with fruit or vegetables) are always a popular choice. For good measure, the menu throws in hints of the Mediterranean with choices like hummus and charmoula.

Degustation

005

239 E. 5th St. (bet. Second & Third Aves.)

Subway:	Astor Pl	Mon – Sat 6pm - 10:30pm
Phone:	212-979-1012	Closed Sun
Fax:	N/A	
Web:	N/A	
Prices:	$$	

Jack and Grace Lamb have done it again with Degustation. This contemporary tapas bar in the grungy-hip East Village (next door to the Lambs' Jewel Bako) is not your average sangria-soaked tapas bar. Degustation marries unusual flavors and textures with European and Asian influences.

Dimly lit, the tiny space has an industrial-chic feel with slate-lined walls and simple furnishings. The kitchen takes center stage, and the 16 seats all cozy up to a counter around it. Here the chef prepares such tongue-tantalizing dishes as tortillas with shallot confit and quail egg, crispy pork belly with hon shimeji mushrooms, and squid stuffed with braised short ribs. Dessert is equally inventive, boasting the likes of blowtorch-grilled strawberries, ginger granita and basil-mint foam.

Gnocco

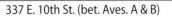
006

337 E. 10th St. (bet. Aves. A & B)

Subway:	1 Av
Phone:	212-677-1913
Fax:	212-477-7610
Web:	www.gnocco.com
Prices:	$$

Mon – Fri 5pm - midnight
Sat – Sun noon - midnight

Gnocco's decidedly comfortable, light-filled front room with its brick walls and paintings of oversize Georgia O'Keefe-style flowers makes this a popular neighborhood hangout. Floor-to-ceiling windows overlook Tompkins Square Park, while the shady back terrace with its vine-covered walls is a great place to sit in nice weather.

Don't leave without sampling the signature gnocco, crispy deep-fried pillows of dough served with thin slices of prosciutto di Parma and coppa. Well-executed homemade pastas, including the more familiar gnocchi, make a fitting first course; then there's a small selection of meat and fish dishes. If you don't have room for dessert, the cantucci accompanied by a glass of *vin santo* makes a light ending to the meal.

Hasaki

Japanese

007

210 E. 9th St. (bet. Second & Third Aves.)

Subway:	Astor Pl
Phone:	212-473-3327
Fax:	212-473-3095
Web:	www.hasakinyc.com
Prices:	$$

Mon – Tue 5:30pm - 11:30pm
Wed – Fri noon - 3pm
& 5:30pm - 11:30pm
Sat – Sun 1pm - 4pm
& 5:30pm - 11:30pm

On weekends, you'll recognize this sushi restaurant by the line that snakes out the door onto the sidewalk. Hasaki doesn't take reservations, but that doesn't seem to deter the devotees of this small, often-crowded place. The lively sushi bar is where the action is; step up and see what all the fuss is about.

Sashimi (buttery yellowtail, eel, King crab, and tuna, not to mention the list of daily specials) is carefully presented and served with soba noodles, a bowl of rice and the requisite wasabi and pickled ginger. Ocean trout carpaccio and fried softshell crab are among the newest additions to the menu. Aside from sashimi and sushi, the menu offers tempura, chicken teriyaki and grilled salmon, among other cooked selections—all at prices that won't break the budget.

Hearth

Contemporary ✕✕

008

403 E. 12th St. (at First Ave.)

Subway:	1 Av
Phone:	646-602-1300
Fax:	646-602-0552
Web:	www.restauranthearth.com
Prices:	$$$

Sun – Thu 6pm - 10pm
Fri – Sat 6pm - 11pm

A joint venture by chef Marco Canora and partner Paul Grieco, Hearth emphasizes Mediterranean-inspired cuisine (the chef's family has roots in Tuscany) on its seasonal menu.

You can watch signature dishes, such as rabbit ballotine, red-wine braised octopus with celery root, cabbage stuffed with veal sweetbreads, and steamed black bass with saffron risotto, being prepared in the open kitchen. Apple-cider doughnuts with apple compote and maple cream will stave away the chill of a crisp fall or winter night.

In addition to the generous menu, the chef offers a five-course tasting. The restaurant's wine dinners provide an enjoyable education in the wine and food of different regions, from the northern Rhone to the Napa Valley.

Hiro

Japanese ✕

009

84 E. 10th St. (bet. Third & Fourth Aves.)

Subway:	Astor Pl
Phone:	212-420-6189
Fax:	212-674-9752
Web:	www.hironyc.com
Prices:	⌘⌘

Mon – Fri 11am - 11pm
Sat 1pm - 11pm
Sun 4pm - 11pm
Closed major holidays

Sushi reigns at Hiro. This relaxed East Village Japanese place has simple, clean interiors with slate floors, redwood furnishings and Asian accents. Nothing fancy, Hiro focuses on the sushi bar, which is manned by several chefs. The polite staff ensures that guests are always satisfied, and reasonable prices and a laid-back attitude entice both professionals and students from nearby NYU (who fuel the restaurant's brisk take-out business).

Hiro offers a wide selection of typical Japanese dishes, such as tempura and teriyaki, along with many specialty sushi rolls displaying creative combinations not often found in similar restaurants. Bento boxes are also available at lunch or dinner, but with the unique maki, colorful presentations and large portions, sushi is the main attraction here.

Itzocan

010

438 E. 9th St. (bet. First Ave. & Ave. A)

Subway:	1 Av	Open daily noon - midnight
Phone:	212-677-5856	
Fax:	N/A	
Web:	N/A	
Prices:	$$	

This little hole in the wall near Tompkins Square Park packs a big punch for its tiny size. Inside there are seats for less than 20 people, but the authentic Mexican food at inexpensive prices (dinner entreés range from $10 to $15) and the lively vibe more than make up for the cramped quarters.

Start your meal with the wonderfully fresh house-made guacamole, which has just the right amount of heat, and a seemingly bottomless pitcher of their terrific sangria. For lunch, you'll find an assortment of burritos and quesadillas. At dinner the choices go upscale (flank steak in chile pasilla; semolina epazote dumplings with roasted poblano peppers) and include several specials. Save room for the moist chocolate mole cake— accented with a whisper of chile pepper.

Jack's Luxury Oyster Bar

012

101 Second Ave. (bet. 5th & 6th Sts.)

Subway:	Lower East Side - 2 Av	Open daily 6pm - 11pm
Phone:	212-673-0338	
Fax:	N/A	
Web:	N/A	
Prices:	$$$	

Peripatetic owners Jack and Grace Lamb shuffled their restaurants around at the end of the summer, moving Jack's Luxury Oyster Bar into the space where Jewel Bako Makimono (now closed) once was. Like its predecessor, this gem of an oyster bar with its narrow rows of tables may be tiny, but its charm is huge.

The chef's tasting menu is the way to go here. Items tend toward fresh seafood—including oysters, of course. You can also order à la carte, or choose from the extensive raw bar list. At the raw bar you can make a delightful meal out of shellfish alone. Ask the gracious staff for advice about which wines go best with which dishes.

The short dessert menu changes regularly, but if it's on the menu, try the baba au rhum cake, served warm with whipped cream.

Jewel Bako Makimono

012

101 Second Ave. (bet. 5th & 6th Sts.)

Subway: Lower East Side - 2 Av   Mon – Sat 6pm - 10pm
Phone: 212-253-7848   Closed Sun
Fax: N/A
Web: N/A
Prices: $$

As of summer 2006, Jack's Oyster Bar moved into the space formerly occupied by Jewel Bako Makimono. Makimono's menu will be added to the offerings at the Lambs' popular Jewel Bako (293 E. 5th St.).

Kanoyama

013

175 Second Ave. (at 11th St.)

Subway: 3 Av   Mon – Sat 5:30pm - midnight
Phone: 212-777-5266   Sun 5pm - 11pm
Fax: N/A
Web: www.kanoyama.com
Prices: $$

The young staff at Kanoyama (formerly known as Koi) caters to a clientele that is fanatical about sushi but prefers the mellow East Village vibe to the power surge of Midtown. Take your place at the seven-seat sushi bar if you want to watch the chefs' amazing knife work and enjoy the warm banter between the sushi men and the regulars. The energy in the tiny dining room is contagious.

Bordering on being overwhelming, the list of daily specials incorporates everything from cooked and sushi appetizers to special sushi rolls and sashimi entrées. It's not inexpensive, but the quality stands up to the price. After all, it's how much of the buttery toro or creamy uni you consume that determines the final tab.

Note that Kanoyama does not accept reservations on Friday and Saturday nights.

Lan

014

56 Third Ave. (bet. 10th & 11th Sts.)

Subway:	3 Av	Sun – Thu 5:30pm - 11pm
Phone:	212-254-1959	Fri – Sat 5:30pm - midnight
Fax:	212-477-5561	
Web:	N/A	
Prices:	$$	

Behind its red awning, Lan reveals a candlelit haven of small white-cloth-covered tables and exposed brick accented by orange-painted walls. In addition to the normal menu of sushi, sashimi and rolls, Lan also features entrées (such as broiled black cod marinated in Saikyo miso sauce), which change according to the season.

Appetizers, like steamed Chilean sea bass with simmered lotus roots, show off the chef's creativity, while meat dishes—a house specialty—combine top-quality products (Kobe beef, Prime ribeye, organic chicken) with Asian techniques. Try the hot pots for two; they come with everything you need to cook your meal at the table. Shabu shabu (thin slices of Prime ribeye with assorted market vegetables and dipping sauces) is a favorite.

La Paella

015

214 E. 9th St. (bet. Second & Third Aves.)

Subway:	Astor Pl	Open daily noon - 11pm
Phone:	212-598-4321	
Fax:	N/A	
Web:	N/A	
Prices:	$$	

Bring some friends to La Paella, so you can sample a wider array of the well-prepared vegetable, meat and seafood tapas. Recalling an Old World Iberian inn with its gold-toned walls, wrought-iron accents and wooden ceiling beams draped with dried flowers, the dark dining space can get crowded in the evening (all the better atmosphere for a party). The romantic setting also makes it a great date place (if you don't mind the noise and the fact that they don't take reservations).

The specialty is—you guessed it—paella, and they serve several types of the traditional Spanish dish, including a vegetarian and an all-seafood preparation, as well as a Basque version, made with chorizo, chicken, shellfish and squid atop a bed of saffron rice. Keep the party going with a pitcher of fruity sangria or a bottle of Rioja from the wine list.

Lavagna

016

545 E. 5th St. (bet. Aves. A & B)

Subway:	Lower East Side - 2 Av	Open daily 6pm - 11pm
Phone:	212-979-1005	
Fax:	212-253-0666	
Web:	www.lavagnanyc.com	
Prices:	$$	

Who says you should quit while you're ahead? Sami Kader didn't, and East Villagers are glad. After successfully launching Le Tableau, just down the street, Kader decided to try his version of an Italian trattoria. It seems he has the Midas touch—at least judging from the crowds that pack the place on weekends.

Any diner at laid-back Lavagna is treated like a friend. And that's what you'll want to be after you sample the refined and innovative cuisine on the short menu, which is supplemented with a host of daily specials. Dishes such as rigatoni with sweet fennel, spicy sausage, peas and tomato cream; or roast pork chop with braised cabbage and butternut squash in *vin santo* sauce. The Sunday night prix-fixe menu, with appetizer, main course and dessert for just $29, is a gourmet bargain.

Le Tableau

017

511 5th St. (bet. Aves. A & B)

Subway:	Lower East Side - 2 Av	Mon – Thu 6pm - 11pm
Phone:	212-260-1333	Fri – Sat 6pm - midnight
Fax:	212-979-1729	Sun 5pm - 10pm
Web:	www.letableaunyc.com	
Prices:	$$	

This modern bistro, with its vivid orange walls, enjoys a good reputation in the neighborhood—and rightly so. The cuisine at Le Tableau boasts excellent quality at a reasonable price, while the soft glow of the gently lit dining room provides a pleasing setting.

Creative brasserie fare includes seasonal offerings such as pomegranate-glazed duck and Berkshire pork loin with yam and walnut gnocchi gratin. Priced at less than $30, the three-course, prix-fixe menu is the best deal (offered before 7pm Tuesday to Saturday, and all night Sunday and Monday); there's also a five-course chef's tasting menu, which includes wines if you so desire. If you order á la carte, save your appetite for the likes of almond cake with apricot coulis and Valrhona chocolate truffle cake.

Mamlouk ☺

018

Middle Eastern ✗

211 E. 4th St. (bet. Aves. A & B)

Subway:	Lower East Side - 2 Av
Phone:	212-529-3477
Fax:	N/A
Web:	N/A
Prices:	$$

Tue – Sun 7pm - midnight
Closed Mon

For an authentic and delightful Middle Eastern meal, head to Mamlouk. Inside, you'll be enveloped in an exotic ambience, furnished with copper-topped tables and wide cushioned seats, and antique jewelry displayed in frames on the walls.

In this cozy atmosphere, hosted by the charming Iraqi owner, you have only to settle back and savor the multicourse, prix-fixe meal (there is no menu). You will be rewarded when you relinquish control at this welcoming restaurant. The repast begins with an assortment of pickles, crudités and fresh-baked pita. Next, a selection of hot and cold meze (lebneh, baba ganoush, hummus) comes to the table. These are followed by several entrées, and finally, dessert.

As a fitting end to the feast, try a hookah, filled with your choice of flavored smokes.

The Mermaid Inn

019

Seafood ✗

96 Second Ave. (bet. 5th & 6th Sts.)

Subway:	Astor Pl
Phone:	212-674-5870
Fax:	212-674-0510
Web:	www.themermaidnyc.com
Prices:	$$

Mon – Thu 5:30pm - 11pm
Fri – Sat 5:30pm - midnight
Sun 5pm - 10pm

With its rough-hewn wood columns, exposed brick walls and dark wainscoting, The Mermaid Inn recalls a New England seaside restaurant. This is no side-of-the-road joint, though. Owned by Jimmy Bradley, the nautical establishment is run like a tight ship.

Seafood stars on the menu, though they often serve a quality pan-roasted chicken to appeal to carnivores. Instead of hot dogs, you might find "cod dogs" on the menu—a terrific version of the fried fishwich. Of course, the lobster sandwich is another sure hit. Oysters or littlenecks from the raw bar, grilled fish and seafood pasta round out the selection.

Those with an incurable sweet tooth will appreciate the demitasse of creamy chocolate or butterscotch pudding that appears compliments of the house to polish off your meal.

Momofuku Noodle Bar

020

163 First Ave. (bet. 10th & 11th Sts.)

Subway:	1 Av	Sun – Thu noon - 11pm
Phone:	212-475-7899	Fri – Sat noon - midnight
Fax:	212-504-7967	Closed major holidays
Web:	www.eatmomofuku.com	
Prices:	⊜⊜	

A consistently popular addition to the East Village dining scene, Momofuku is a peach of a restaurant—which is appropriate since its name means "lucky peach" in Japanese. There are no tables here; diners sit, as they do in noodle bars in Japan, on high stools at long communal counters. It's a great way to make new friends, slurping noodles elbow-to-elbow and watching the chefs' sleight of hand behind the blond-wood bar.

Owner and chef David Chang, a former line cook at Craft, fashioned Momofuku's menu with Asian street food in mind. Ramen noodles share the menu with small dishes; try the steamed pork dumplings filled with Iowa Berkshire black pork, an ingredient that figures prominently. Note that Momofuku doesn't accept reservations.

Mosto

021

87 Second Ave. (at 5th St.)

Subway:	Astor Pl	Mon – Sat 5:30pm - midnight
Phone:	212-228-9912	Sun 4pm - 11pm
Fax:	212-228-6012	
Web:	www.mostoosteria.com	
Prices:	$$	

Named for the juice that results when grapes are first crushed in the wine press, Mosto sticks to what it's good at: offering excellent Italian fare at very approachable prices, with wines to match. The informal dining space, decked out with tropical plants, caters to couples with its intimate candlelit aura, and to groups—or single diners—with its communal table. Loud rock music enlivens the crowded bar scene.

On the menu, you can count on abundant portions of pasta (spinach gnocchi, spaghetti with clam sauce, pappardelle with lamb ragu), and a short list of entrées, from fritto misto di mare to homestyle chicken cutlet. Mosto also offers an affordable roster of Italian wines, available by the bottle, carafe and half-carafe. Expect the service to be pleasant and helpful.

Manhattan East Village

Prune 😂

022

54 E. 1st St. (bet. First & Second Aves.)

Subway:	Lower East Side - 2 Av
Phone:	212-677-6221
Fax:	212-677-6982
Web:	N/A
Prices:	$$

Mon – Thu 6pm - 10:30pm
Fri 6pm - midnight
Sat 10am - 3:30pm & 6pm - midnight
Sun 10am - 3:30pm & 5pm - 10pm

This shoe-box-size bistro began in 1999 as Gabrielle Hamilton's modest vision of a neighborhood restaurant. While it hasn't grown in size since then, it has grown well beyond the East Village in popularity. Despite its cramped quarters, Hamilton's recipe for a home-style eatery has been wildly successful. At Prune she combines vintage bistro décor with a small menu of comfort food—the kind of meals you'd cook for friends in your home.

Loyal fans come here for the chef's unpretentious and slightly irreverent cooking style. Whole grilled fish, fried sweetbreads, and the fluffy Dutch-style pancake served at the acclaimed weekend brunch are a few of the signature dishes. The menu is not broken down by category (appetizers, entrées), so if you just want a plate of veggies, that's no problem.

Soba-Ya 😂

023

229 E. 9th St. (bet. Second & Third Aves.)

Subway:	Astor Pl
Phone:	212-533-6966
Fax:	212-260-0036
Web:	www.sobaya-nyc.com
Prices:	🍜

Open daily noon - 4pm
& 5:30pm - 10:30pm

Students from nearby NYU frequent this place for its Zen-like minimalist ambience and its hearty and inexpensive noodle dishes. Soba (Japanese buckwheat noodles) are made on the premises each morning by the chef, and then presented along with your hot or cold broth and an array of garnishes and ingredients. You can substitute the chewier udon, or wheat noodles (which some say taste more like traditional pasta), if you prefer.

To drink, there's a good selection of Japanese beer and sake to pair with your meal. Homemade ice cream, with unusual flavors like honey wasabi, is made by the owner's wife.

Soba-Ya doesn't accept reservations.

Tasting Room

Contemporary

024

72 E. 1st St. (bet. First & Second Aves.)

Subway:	Lower East Side - 2 Av	Tue – Sat 5:30pm - 11pm
Phone:	212-358-7831	Closed Sun & Mon
Fax:	212-358-8432	
Web:	www.thetastingroomnyc.com	
Prices:	$$	

Diners at the Tasting Room can create their own meal combinations from among the dishes sized as "tastes" (appetizer portions) or "shares" (akin to a reasonably sized entrée). In fact, the tiny dining room invites sharing, since you'll be elbow to elbow with your neighbor.

The chef takes inspiration from fresh market fare; dishes on the changing menu highlight products like Maine diver scallops, heirloom tomatoes, brook trout and local wild matsutake mushrooms. Of special note is the well-chosen selection of American wines, citing more than 350 different labels within a wide price range. The by-the-glass list usually features over a dozen choices and changes nightly.

In summer 2006, the restaurant added a second location in NoLIta *(264 Elizabeth St.)*.

Manhattan East Village

Financial District

Widely considered the financial center of the world, the southern tip of Manhattan isn't as buttoned-up as you might expect. Its ample, U-shaped waterfront, lined with appealing parks, draws hordes of visitors to enjoy views of New York Harbor and catch ferries to Staten Island and the Statue of Liberty. Cradled within are the narrow, twisting streets laid out by New York's first Dutch settlers in the 17th century; developers left the curvy street plan largely intact when they built their gargantuan office towers. Gaze up and you'll feel as though you're at the bottom of a deep well, with only tiny patches of sky visible among the tight clusters of looming skyscrapers.

A Bit of History – The area now known as the Financial District was the birthplace of New York in 1625. Trade flourished here under the Dutch West India Company, and the settlement of Nieuw Amsterdam grew quickly. In 1653 the colonists built a wall of wooden planks between the Hudson and East rivers to protect the settlers from Indian attack. Later dismantled by the British, who took over the colony in 1664, the wall is remembered today on **Wall Street**, which traces the original length (less than one mile) of the fortress.

Legend has it that in 1792 a group of 24 brokers met beneath a buttonwood tree at the corner of Wall and Williams streets, and founded the stock exchange. The New York Stock Exchange wasn't formally organized, however, until 1817. Inside the classical façade of the Exchange today, you'll find one of the most technically sophisticated financial operations on the globe.

Financial District

© Martha Cooper

A Neighborhood Reborn – Two of the Financial District's most famous landmarks, the **World Trade Center** towers, were destroyed in the terrorist attack on September 11, 2001, which left some 2,800 people dead. After that tragic event, the Financial District—indeed, the entire city—understandably saw a downturn in commerce. But in the months that followed, businesses rebounded and restaurateurs put their faith—and their money—back into the area by opening new establishments. Fears that

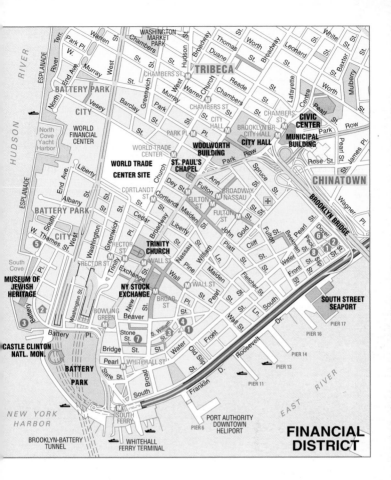

the neighborhood's spirit would always be clouded by that day have, happily, turned out to be unfounded. Today in the Financial District, camera-wielding tourists rub shoulders with briefcase-toting bankers on and around Wall Street, and Battery Park, under the watchful eye of Lady Liberty, teems with cyclists, runners, artists and souvenir peddlers. Restaurants in this area cater to power-lunchers during the day, and to business travelers at dinnertime.

Bayard's

001

American

1 Hanover Sq. (bet. Pearl & Stone Sts.)

Subway:	Wall St (William St.)
Phone:	212-514-9454
Fax:	212-514-9443
Web:	www.bayards.com
Prices:	$$$

Mon – Thu 5:30pm - 10pm
Fri – Sat 5:30pm - 10:30pm
Closed Sun
Closed July 4 & Christmas Day

Facing charming Hanover Square, Bayard's restaurant occupies the beautifully renovated Hanover Bank building, erected in 1853. This landmark Italian Renaissance-style structure has known incarnations as a private residence, as home to the New York Cotton Exchange, and as a private club for overseas merchants. The décor reflects the building's past with maritime artifacts, ships' models and figureheads, and nautical paintings—all discovered during the structure's renovation.

In this elegant atmosphere, you'll dine on fine regional cuisine, from lobster risotto to roasted rack of lamb, equally balanced between meat and seafood and complemented by an extensive wine list. The Blue Bar, done up like a refined yacht, is a clubby place for a drink and a bite from the bar menu.

Bridge Cafe

002

American

279 Water St. (at Dover St.)

Subway:	Fulton St
Phone:	212-227-3344
Fax:	212-619-2368
Web:	www.bridgecafe.citysearch.com
Prices:	$$

Sun – Mon 11:45am - 10pm
Tue – Thu 11:45am - 11pm
Fri 11:45am - midnight
Sat 5pm - midnight

Not many establishments in New York City can claim as colorful a history as this one. Billing itself as "New York's oldest drinking establishment," the business opened in 1794 as a grocery in a two-and-a-half story wooden structure on the bank of the East River. Over the years, the building has housed a restaurant, a saloon, a boardinghouse and a brothel before it became the Bridge Cafe in 1979. The current 1920s structure stands at the foot of the Brooklyn Bridge.

In this simple and cozy atmosphere, embellished by paintings of the bridge, you'll find upscale American food. Gourmet sandwiches dominate the lunch menu, while dinner is a more formal affair with creative selections like the signature buffalo steak with lingonberry sauce. Go Sunday for the popular Bridge Brunch.

Gigino at Wagner Park

003

Italian ✕✕

20 Battery Pl. (in Wagner Park)

Subway:	Bowling Green	Sun – Thu 11:30am - 10:30pm
Phone:	212-528-2228	Fri – Sat 11:30am - 11pm
Fax:	212-528-1756	
Web:	www.gigino-wagnerpark.com	
Prices:	$$	

Sleek sister to the rustic Gigino Trattoria in TriBeCa, this Wagner Park restaurant sits at the tip of Manhattan, between Battery Park's Pier A and the Museum of Jewish Heritage. From its delightful outdoor terrace, you can take in the splendid view of Liberty Island, Ellis Island and New York Harbor (reservations for the terrace are highly recommended in the warmer months). If it's not nice enough to sit outside, the small, contemporary dining room offers plenty of large windows for enjoying harbor views.

Chef's specialties include grilled octopus with black beans, homemade chicken sausage and Gigino's gnocchi with chicken, butter and sage. The wine list is an international affair, showcasing wines, champagne and sparkling wines from Italy, France, South Africa and California.

Harry's Cafe

004

American ✕

1 Hanover Sq. (bet. Pearl & Stone Sts.)

Subway:	Wall St (William St.)	Open 11:15am - midnight
Phone:	212-785-9200	
Fax:	N/A	
Web:	www.harrysnyc.com	
Prices:	$$	

Testosterone rules in this hangout for Wall Street movers and shakers. Located in the historic Hanover Bank building facing Hanover Square, Harry's packs in a crowd of jacket-wearing power brokers who fill the large, masculine room with animated conversation (listen carefully and maybe you'll pick up a stock tip or two).

The menu indulges lighter appetites with starters (truffled steak tartare; crispy oysters), salads, pastas and sandwiches, while bold fare such as deep-fried "original" crackling pork shank and other manly meat dishes give culinary adventurers a lot to chew on (literally, since portions are tremendous).

An impressive list of whiskies, cognacs and cocktails satisfy Wall Street mavens who stop by after work to belt back a few at the bar.

Manhattan Financial District

Liberty View

005

21 South End Ave. (below W. Thames St.)

Subway:	Rector St (Greenwich St.)	Open daily 11am - 11pm
Phone:	212-786-1888	
Fax:	212-786-9988	
Web:	N/A	
Prices:	$$	

True to its name, Liberty View looks out over the Statue of Liberty and the Battery from its perch on the ground floor of an upscale condominium building at the southern end of Battery Park City. In warm weather, area denizens and Financial District movers and shakers both clamor to claim the restaurant's prime outdoor tables.

Unlike in Chinatown, the clientele here is predominantly Western, and the service orients itself towards these guests. Chopsticks, tea and traditional accompaniments to dishes must be requested, but even so, contented regulars appreciate the pleasant interactions and attentive service. The tremendous menu features a good selection of dim sum—notably the juicy buns—and Liberty View's strength lies in this and in the Shanghai-style specialties.

MarkJoseph

006

261 Water St. (bet. Peck Slip & Dover St.)

Subway:	Fulton St	Mon – Thu 11:30am - 10pm
Phone:	212-277-0020	Fri 11:30am - 11pm
Fax:	212-277-0022	Sat 5pm - 11pm
Web:	www.markjosephsteakhouse.com	Closed Sun
Prices:	$$$	

Nestled in the shadow of the Brooklyn Bridge in the South Street Seaport Historic District, MarkJoseph's caters to financiers, Wall Street wunderkinds and tourists with deep pockets. The cozy dining room is a notch above the standard steakhouse design, with art-glass vases and pastoral photographs of the wine country adding sleek notes.

At lunch, regulars devour hefty half-pound burgers (there's even a turkey variety). At dinnertime, Prime dry-aged Porterhouse takes center stage, accompanied by salads and favorite sides like creamed spinach, caramelized onions and hash browns, along with less guilt-inducing steamed vegetables. And what better to wash your steak down with than one of the selections on the generous list of red wines?

Nebraska Beef

007

15 Stone St. (bet. Broad & Whitehall Sts.)

Subway:	Bowling Green	Mon – Fri 11am - 11:30pm
Phone:	212-952-0620	Closed Sat & Sun
Fax:	N/A	
Web:	N/A	
Prices:	$$$	

You could easily walk down Stone Street without noticing the discreet red façade of this little restaurant, three blocks from the clamor of the New York Stock Exchange. But the unpretentious place, with its long bar area opening into a dark, wood-paneled room, is worth seeking out for its comfortable setting and high-quality, grain-fed Nebraska beef, cooked to your liking. In the evening, the bar can get a bit rowdy with its "boys club" crowd, while at midday the dining room has a pleasant atmosphere dominated by Wall Street traders on business lunches.

As far as beef goes, there are no surprises on the menu here (a whopping 32-ounce Prime ribeye that goes by "The Steak!" is the signature dish). The personable and professional waitstaff only adds to the experience.

Quartino 😋

008

21 Peck Slip (at Water St.)

Subway:	Fulton St (William St.)	Mon – Sat noon - 4pm & 5pm - 11pm
Phone:	212-349-4433	Sun noon - 4pm & 5pm - 10pm
Fax:	N/A	
Web:	N/A	
Prices:	$$	

Located on a cobblestone street near the East River in one of the oldest parts of New York, Quartino charms at first sight. This Italian eatery offers a surprising change of pace with its organic cuisine and its simple rustic décor of wooden tables, exposed brick and weathered shutters.

Quartino's Italian menu is all-organic and locally sourced. It's all about the details here, where the Ligurian olive oil is light and grassy, and the yeasty whole-wheat bread is fresh-baked. Meaty Sicilian tuna with string beans and potatoes is perfectly seasoned, while the whole-wheat ravioli filled with spinach, chard and parsley proves that eating healthfully can also be enjoyable.

A sister restaurant, Quartino Bottega Organica, in the Village (11 Bleecker St.) puts more focus on wines.

Gramercy, Flatiron & Union Square

The retail district that stretches from 14th to 30th Streets between the East River and Avenue of the Americas (Sixth Avenue) contains a concentration of fine restaurants with names you'll no doubt recognize. Large 19th-century and early-20th-century buildings line Broadway, and Fifth and Sixth avenues. Originally built as department stores, many of them now house national chains selling clothing or furniture.

Gramercy Park – New York City's only private park anchors this tranquil neighborhood known for its lovely brownstones and good cafes and restaurants. The area was laid out in 1831 by developer Samuel B. Ruggles, who drained an old marsh (Gramercy is a corruption of a Dutch phrase meaning "little crooked swamp") to build an exclusive residential enclave. Enclosed by an eight-foot-high cast-iron fence, to which only local residents have keys, the green rectangle of **Gramercy Park** consists of formal gardens, paths, benches and trees.

A few blocks northwest of Gramercy Park, the lovely six-acre **Madison Square** has been transformed in the past five years into one of downtown's most inviting public spaces. From the 1870s to 1925, a succession of entertainment venues stood on the north end of the square, including the first two (of four) arenas called Madison Square Garden.

Union Square – On the south edge of the district, this pleasant park is crisscrossed with tree-lined paths. The park, so-named because it marked the union of Broadway and the Bowery, was created in 1831; by the mid-19th century it formed the gated focal point of an elegant residential district. In the early 20th century Union Square became a popular place for rallies and demonstra-

Union Square Greenmarket

© Martha Cooper

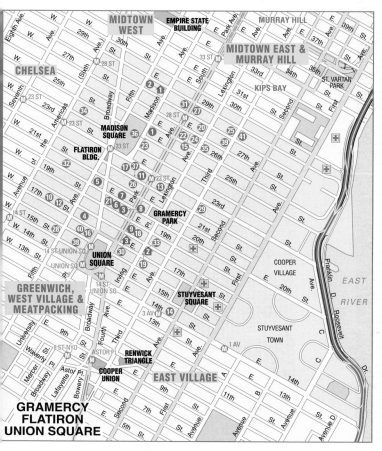

tions; today the tiered plaza on the park's southern end still serves as a stage for protesters, who share space with street performers.

Every Monday, Wednesday, Friday and Saturday year-round, **Union Square Greenmarket** hosts farmers, bakers, flower growers, ranchers and artisanal-food makers from all over New York, Pennsylvania and New Jersey. Neighborhood chefs and residents flock here to forage for the freshest meats, cheeses and vegetables to incorporate into their menus.

Flatiron District – This moniker refers to the area around the **Flatiron Building** (Daniel Burnham, 1902). Even if you've never been to New York City, you've likely seen this building before—it's a popular backdrop in television shows and movies. Viewed from the north side (the side that faces Madison Square Park), the structure looks like an iron—hence the name—the acute angle of its façade formed by Broadway and Fifth Avenue. Though it's only 6 feet wide on this sharp corner, the building rises 22 stories straight up from the sidewalk.

A Voce ✿

001

41 Madison Ave. (enter on 26th St.)

Subway:	28 St (Park Ave. South)	Open daily 11:45am - 2:30pm
Phone:	212-545-8555	& 5:30pm - 11pm
Fax:	212-545-8213	
Web:	www.avocerestaurant.com	
Prices:	$$$	

©Emilie Baltz

Style and substance triumph at A Voce. Located on the first floor of an office building just off leafy Madison Square Park, A Voce is at once hip and comfortable. Brown leather swivel chairs remind diners of a sleek office, while low lighting and dramatic floral displays add sophistication. Floor-to-ceiling windows make for terrific people-watching both inside and out.

This convivial restaurant is jammed day and night with stylish patrons who come not only for the modern interior design, but also for the skillful dishes from chef Andrew Carmellini. While Carmellini honed his skills for years uptown at the much-lauded Café Boulud, he shines on his own here. Showing off his roots, he prepares rustic Italian dishes that pack a flavorful punch without being fussy. Grandma's ravioli is one house specialty, while the homemade pappardelle topped with mint-flavored lamb and a dollop of sheep's-milk ricotta displays an expert technique and talent.

The decibel level in the dining room provides just one hint that this restaurant will remain on many New Yorkers' short list for quite some time.

Appetizers

Carne Cruda with
Walnuts, Celery and
Truffles

Grilled Octopus with
Peperonata, Lemon and
Chorizo

Duck Meatball
Antipasto with Dried
Cherry Mostarda

Entrées

Braised Veal Soffritto
with Soft Polenta and
Orange

Black Bass with
Shrimp Polpettini, New
Potatoes and a Ligurian
Shellfish Broth

Lamb Tortellini with
Escarole, Grapes and
Piave Cheese

Desserts

Bomboloni alla Toscana:
Tuscan Doughnuts with
Chocolate Sauce

Chocolate Panna Cotta
with Amarena Cherries

Lemon-Rhubarb Yogurt
Sorbetti

Country Restaurant ✿

Contemporary XXX

002

90 Madison Ave. (at 29th St.)

Subway: 28 St (Park Ave. South)
Phone: 212-889-7100
Fax: 212-889-7001
Web: www.countryinnewyork.com
Prices: **$$$$**

Sun – Thu 5:30pm - 10pm
Fri – Sat 5:30pm - 11pm

Eric Laignel

Country's name belies its opulent interiors. This sophisticated, jack-of-all-trades restaurant by chef/owner Geoffrey Zakarian (of Town fame) offers something for everyone with two eateries in one.

Located within the recently renovated Carlton Hotel *(see hotel listings)*, Country's downstairs café is a handsome room complete with wood paneled walls and plush banquettes, perfect for those guests who prefer a more informal elegance. The regal upstairs demands more attention with its glamorous Art Deco mosaic floors and Tiffany stained-glass dome. Recalling the glamour of the 1920's, the room's use of rich fabrics, glittering crystal light fixtures and gleaming marble sets it apart from the competition.

Similarly, the food at Country is urban sophistication at its best. Café at Country features all-day dining and its cuisine blends French and American influences, while the Dining Room tempts palates with a four-course tasting menu offering a handful of selections for each course. French-influenced classics are executed with an easy elegance and include many organic and local ingredients. Innovative and appealing, the menu combines both these elements without being too complicated.

Appetizer

Sweet Pea Velouté, Mousseron Mushrooms and Fresh Ricotta

Cèpe Ravioli, Florentine of Spinach and Crisp Prosciutto

Seared Squid, Shaved Celery and Fennel Salad with Dried Olives

Entrées

Poulet Rôti, Morel Mushrooms, Spring Onions and Fines Herbes

Big Eye Tuna, Basque Pipérade and Smoked Garlic Cream

Bison au Poivre, Onion-crusted Potato and Shallot Béarnaise Marmalade

Desserts

Crème Citron, Toasted Brioche, Lemon Sorbet

Almond Pithivier: Choice of Whiskey Vanilla Sauce or Caramel Apple Raisin Sauce along with a Choice of Whipped Crème Fraîche or Vanilla Ice Cream

Chocolate and Coffee Torte, Caramel Crème Anglaise and Praline Ice Cream

CONTEMPORARY

Craft ✿

003

43 E. 19th St. (bet. Broadway & Park Ave. South)

Subway:	14 St - Union Sq	Sun – Thu 5:30pm - 10pm
Phone:	212-780-0880	Fri – Sat 5:30pm - 11pm
Fax:	212-780-0580	
Web:	www.craftrestaurant.com	
Prices:	$$$$	

Craft/Bill Bettencourt

Ever go out to eat with one of those people who wants to change everything about his order ("I'd like the salad, but hold the tomatoes and put the dressing on the side")? Now you can take your pickiest friends to this smart, contemporary restaurant and they can tailor their meals to their own tastes.

At Craft, chef/owner Tom Colicchio (of Gramercy Tavern) offers a choice of basic products—fish and shellfish, charcuterie, roasted meat, salad, vegetables—to be combined however you desire (dessert works the same way). This mix-and-match style has made a star of Colicchio, who also opened the casual Craftbar and 'wichcraft nearby, as well as Craftsteak, on Tenth Avenue. Categorized by "New World" and "Old World" selections, the wine list presents an interesting array of vintages displayed in the huge, glassed-in cellar.

Colicchio believes that cooking is first a craft; he presents ultra-fresh ingredients (wild arugula, Kumumoto oysters, wild boar, local ramps), prepares them simply, and lets the unadulterated taste of each do its own talking. At the end of a meal here, one thing will be clear: Colicchio's daring restaurant is bent on raising the craft of cooking to an art form.

Appetizers

Roasted Quail

Roasted Sweetbreads

Cured Peruvian Octopus

Entrées

Braised Beef Short Ribs

Roasted Chatham Cod

Roasted Heritage Rack of
Pork

Desserts

Brioche Pain Perdu with
Roasted Fruit

Chocolate Soufflé

Doughnuts

CONTEMPORARY

Dévi ❀

004

8 E. 18th St. (bet. Broadway & Fifth Ave.)

Subway:	14 St - Union Sq	Mon — Sat noon - 2:30pm
Phone:	212-691-1300	& 5:30pm - 11pm
Fax:	212-691-1695	Sun 5:30pm - 11pm
Web:	www.devinyc.com	
Prices:	$$	

Dévi/Frink Photography

It's no wonder that the dining-room décor of Dévi seems fit for a goddess, since the Hindu mother goddess inspired the restaurant's name. Once you step inside, you'll be struck by the heavenly interior, which blends elements from both Indian homes and temples. In this sumptuous setting, gauzy jewel-tone fabrics swathe the walls; banquettes covered in a patchwork of brown, yellow and orange provide cozy seating; and clusters of colored lanterns hang from the red ceiling.

Cookbook author Suvir Saran and Tandoori master Hemant Mathur, who opened the 75-seat restaurant in fall 2004, preside over the kitchen and put a new spin on traditional Indian fare. Southern Indian specialties dominate this imaginative menu. Samosas, an Indian favorite, are ramped up here with goat cheese and spinach or lamb and pecorino. Two tasting menus, one which is vegetarian, offer a terrific way to discover the chef's talents for modernized ethnic cuisine. While the dessert selection abounds with confections like the creamy mango cheesecake, the beverage menu cites traditional Indian drinks and beers in addition to wine.

Appetizers

Bombay Bhel Puri, Rice
Puffs, Tamarind, Mint,
Tomatoes and Onions

Shrimp Balchao

Lamb-Stuffed Tandoori
Chicken, Tandoor-grilled
Pickling Spices

Entrées

Tandoor-grilled Lamb
Chops, Pear Chutney,
Curry-Leaf Potatoes

Tandoori Prawns with
Eggplant Pickle

Kararee Bhindi, Crispy
Tangy Okra Salad,
Tomatoes and Red Onions

Desserts

Mango Cheesecake

Kulfi (Indian Ice Cream)

Tasting of Creams:
Seasonal Fruit and Spice
Flavors

INDIAN

Fleur de Sel ✿

Contemporary French 🍴🍴

005

5 E. 20th St. (bet. Broadway & Fifth Ave.)

Subway:	23 St (Broadway)
Phone:	212-460-9100
Fax:	212-460-8319
Web:	www.fleurdeselnyc.com
Prices:	$$$

Mon – Sat noon - 2pm
& 5:30pm - 10:30pm
Sun noon - 2pm & 5pm - 9pm

Fleur de Sel/Xenia B. Buxo

There are many reasons to dine in this charming French restaurant, whose name ("flower of the salt" in French) refers to a prized type of pure salt hand-harvested on France's Brittany Coast. Foremost among them is the delectable, original cuisine prepared by chef/owner Cyril Renaud. His winning concept at Fleur de Sel is to distill the essence of seasonal ingredients and highlight dishes of his native Brittany with daily tasting menus for both lunch and dinner (the three-course lunch menu is a particularly good deal).

In the evening, a three-course prix-fixe menu, with choices that might range from polenta and snail gâteaux to a pork chop marinated in sugar cane and coffee, joins the nightly six-course chef's tasting (only available for the entire table). Renaud lets his talents loose in the latter, which changes according to the market and his whim. For an excellent finish, order the chocolate selection if it's offered; it is there that the pastry chef really excels.

Weighted toward French varietals, the wine list offers more than 1,000 selections. The sophisticated dining room is embellished with the chef's original watercolors of—what else?—food.

Appetizers

Maine Lobster Salad, Black-Truffle Mayonnaise, Baby Celery, Asian Pear

Goat Cheese and Artichoke Ravioli, Micro-Green Salad, Red-Beet Dijon Reduction

Seared Sullivan County Foie Gras, Dried Fruit Purée, Rose Water

Entrées

Crispy Poussin, Wilted Spinach, Wild Mushrooms, Foie Gras Emulsion

Braised Veal Breast, Celery Root and Black-Truffle Purée, Beurre Noisette Sauce

Seared Halibut, Glazed Endive, Balsamic Vinegar, Oklahoma Pecans, Bacon

Desserts

Gaufrette au Chocolat, Black Mint, Chocolate Ice Cream

Banana Mousse, Crème de Café, White-Chocolate Dentelle

Caramelized Granny Smith Crêpe with Devonshire Whipped Cream

Gramercy Tavern ✿

006

42 E. 20th St. (bet. Broadway & Park Ave. South)

Subway:	14 St - Union Sq	Mon – Thu noon - 2pm & 5:30pm – 10pm
Phone:	212-477-0777	Fri noon - 2pm & 5:30pm – 11pm
Fax:	212-477-1160	Sat 5:30pm – 11pm
Web:	www.gramercytavern.com	Sun 5:30pm – 10pm
Prices:	$$$	

Gramercy Tavern/Paul Walsh

The word "tavern" conjures up images of a cozy, wood-paneled room, tankards of ale and convivial conversation. That country-inn ambience is what Tom Colicchio and Danny Meyer were going for when they opened Gramercy Tavern in 1994. They must have done something right, since their restaurant still stands in relief amid New York's culinary landscape.

At Gramercy Tavern, you'll have a choice of several different dining spaces. In the back of the restaurant, the dining rooms kick the tavern concept up a notch with wood-beamed ceilings, velvet draperies and fine artwork. The division of the space into separate rooms gives each a quiet, intimate feel, away from the lively tavern area in front.

Colicchio's seasonal tasting menus spotlight the best products the market can offer. Many of the dishes, such as the braised rabbit, have an old-time appeal, while the presentations and preparations are decidedly modern. Attentive service by pleasant waiters completes the experience at this elegant spot.

In the front of the restaurant, the flower-bedecked tavern room and appealing bar captures the essence of hospitality seven days a week with its less serious all-day menu.

Appetizers

Marinated Hamachi with Roasted Beets and Lemon Vinaigrette

Roasted Sweetbreads with Bacon, Honey-Glazed Onions, Pickled Jerusalem Artichokes and Sherry Vinegar

Sea Scallops with Salsify, Sauternes, Bay Leaf and Vanilla

Entrées

Roasted Monkfish with Pancetta, Red Cabbage, Jerusalem Artichokes and Truffle Vinaigrette

Organic Chicken with Roasted Seasonal Vegetables and Wild Mushrooms

Rabbit with Roasted Shallots, Garlic Sausage, Olives, Rosemary and Potato Purée

Desserts

Warm Apple Tart with Pistachio Financier, Saffron Caramel and Vanilla Ice Cream

Chocolate Tart with Blood Oranges and Ginger Ice Cream

Coconut Tapioca with Passion Fruit and Coconut Sorbets, Passion Fruit, Caramel and Basil Syrup

Veritas ✿

007

43 E. 20th St. (bet. Broadway & Park Ave. South)

Subway:	23 St (Park Ave. South)	Mon – Sat 5:30pm - 10:30pm
Phone:	212-353-3700	Sun 5pm - 9:30pm
Fax:	212-353-1632	
Web:	www.veritas-nyc.com	
Prices:	$$$$	

Veritas/©Emily Cantrell

In vino veritas. There *is* truth in wine, and the truth is that Veritas spells paradise for oenophiles. Some 100,000 bottles of wine cool their heels in the restaurant's temperature-controlled cellar. It may take you a while to read through the voluminous wine list—or, rather, tome—of 3,000 labels from around the globe. No need to feel overwhelmed, though; the sommelier is always on hand in the stylish dining room to help you choose the right accompaniment to your meal.

Wine may vie for the spotlight here, but the list of creative, perfectly prepared American dishes won't leave you disappointed. Chef Scott Bryan, whose training includes stints at Le Bernadin and Lespinasse, crafts a three-course, fixed-price menu selection that provides the ideal balance of red meat, fowl and fish. He designs his dishes to complement the wine, and the combinations mesh wonderfully together, rather than each ingredient competing for top standing. To finish, a peanut butter torte with banana ice cream, or a chocolate soufflé will give you an easy excuse to sample a dessert wine.

Veritas may be expensive, but it's a fair price to pay for such delightful bacchanalian pleasures.

Manhattan Gramercy, Flatiron & Union Square

Appetizers

Chilled Lobster Salad, Fava-Bean Purée, Peppercorns and Old Sherry Vinegar

Wild Mushroom Ravioli, Mascarpone, Tarragon, and Hon-Shimeji Mushrooms

Crispy Pork Belly, Balsamic Glaze, Cipollini Onions and Apple Salad

Entrées

Tender Braised Short Ribs, Parsnip Purée, Porcini Mushrooms, Glazed Carrots and Barolo

Monkfish Medallions, Melted Cabbage, Smoked Bacon, Salsify and Red-Wine Emulsion

Diver Sea Scallops, Celery Root Purée, Braised Endive and Black-Truffle Vinaigrette

Desserts

Chocolate Soufflé, Caramel Ice Cream and Chocolate Sauce

Maple Crème Caramel, Candied Pecans and Sour Cherry Sauce

Warm Apple Tarte Tatin, Vanilla Ice Cream, Macadamia-Nut Brittle and Butter-Rum Sauce

Barbounia

Mediterranean ✗

008

250 Park Ave. South (at 20th St.)

Subway:	23 St (Park Ave. South)
Phone:	212-995-0242
Fax:	212-995-0560
Web:	www.barbounia.com
Prices:	$$

Sun – Mon 11:45am - 11pm
Tue – Thu 11:45am - midnight
Fri – Sat 11:45am - 1am

You'll leave the concrete, gray world of New York behind when you step through the door at Barbounia. This gorgeous space, with its whitewashed walls, breezy white fabrics and dark woods, transports guests from its Park Avenue South location to the serenity of the Greek Islands. Bright and uplifting during the day, Barbounia is sexy and spirited at night. An open kitchen adds to the upbeat vibe, while the small lounge area near the bar is an alluring spot.

The menu is a blend of Greek, Turkish, Mediterranean and American dishes, with the wood oven serving as a central theme. Barbounia's artfully presented cuisine uses top-quality ingredients, and its authentic style, such as strong Turkish coffee served in a copper vessel, adds to the overall experience.

Barça 18

Spanish ✗✗

009

225 Park Ave. South (bet. 18th & 19th Sts.)

Subway:	14 St - Union Sq
Phone:	212-533-2500
Fax:	212-533-2661
Web:	www.brguestrestaurants.com
Prices:	$$

Sun – Mon 11:30am - 4pm
& 5pm - 11:30pm
Tue – Thu 11:30am - 4pm
& 5pm - midnight
Fri – Sat 11:30am - 4pm & 5pm - 1am

Formerly Park Avalon, this large industrial space has been completely redone in a more contemporary, downtown loft-style décor. Enormous square linen light fixtures hover over leather-topped tables. On one side of the entry, an appealing bar flanked by a communal table and lounge seating makes a pleasant spot for nibbling tapas and sipping sangria.

Barça 18 is the result of a cooperation between B.R. Guest group and acclaimed chef Eric Ripert, of Le Bernardin. As such, you can be assured of innovative preparations and top-quality products here. Dishes like braised octopus, paella with shellfish and chorizo, and patatas Barça (herbed fried potatoes served with both a spicy and a mild red-pepper dipping sauce) spotlight traditional Spanish ingredients and presentations.

Basta Pasta

Contemporary ✕✕

010

37 W. 17th St. (bet. Fifth & Sixth Aves.)

Subway:	14 St - Union Sq	Mon – Fri noon - 2:30pm & 6pm – 11pm
Phone:	212-366-0888	Sat 6pm – 11pm
Fax:	212-366-0402	Sun 5pm - 10pm
Web:	www.bastapastanyc.com	
Prices:	$$	

Talk about East meets West—how about an Italian restaurant from Tokyo? Basta Pasta was founded in Tokyo in 1985 and modeled after the TV show *Iron Chef*. The concept here is cooking as theater; indeed, you'll feel like part of the show as you walk through the open kitchen to get to your table.

Settle in and enjoy the performance, as a team of enthusiastic Japanese chefs plate up a mix of Asian and Italian courses. Several of the dishes, such as spaghetti with flying-fish roe and shiso, show off an interesting fusion in their ingredients and techniques. As an additional feast—this one for the eyes—changing artwork hangs on the walls of the modern dining room. This is delicious dinner theater—and you don't have to call ahead for tickets (but reservations are recommended).

Beppe

Italian ✕✕

011

45 E. 22nd St. (bet. Broadway & Park Ave. South)

Subway:	23 St (Park Ave. South)	Mon – Thu noon - 2:30pm & 5:30pm - 10:30pm
Phone:	212-982-8422	Fri noon - 2:30pm & 5:30pm – 11pm
Fax:	212-982-6616	Sat 5:30pm – 11pm
Web:	www.beppenyc.com	Closed Sun
Prices:	$$$	

Located a half-block from the Flatiron Building, Beppe is a modest place, with an intentionally aged-looking décor made warm and cozy by a working fireplace in winter. Enthusiastic staff members provide knowledgeable, yet informal, service, and their hard work is one of the strengths of this welcoming restaurant. From the hospitable servers to the sausage made from pigs raised on the restaurant's own farm, it's the small details that make a big difference here.

A business-lunch clientele doesn't seem to mind paying uptown prices for food, like the consistently crowd-pleasing pastas, that reflects the best of each season. The kitchen is committed to offering house-made prosciutto and salami, and Italian varieties of produce organically grown in upstate New York.

Manhattan Gramercy, Flatiron & Union Square

BLT Fish

Seafood ✕✕

012

21 W. 17th St. (bet. Fifth & Sixth Aves.)

Subway:	14 St - Union Sq
Phone:	212-691-8888
Fax:	212-255-5180
Web:	www.bltfish.com
Prices:	$$$

Mon – Fri 11:45am - 2:30pm
& 5:30pm - 11pm
Sat 5:30pm - 11:30pm
Sun 5:30pm - 10:30pm

After establishing BLT Steak in Midtown, chef Laurent Tourondel turned from turf to surf. His two raucous seafood restaurants occupy the first and third floors of a Flatiron district town house. Upstairs you'll find an informal but elegant dining room, while, downstairs, New England-style BLT Fish Shack (open daily for lunch and dinner) angles in on favorites like lobster rolls and Key lime pie. Both establishments share the same great raw bar.

Available by the pound, exceptionally fresh fish and shellfish are simply brushed with olive oil and grilled; the popular Cantonese red snapper arrives whole in a colorful display. Seasonally inspired side dishes come in little cast-iron pans or other adorable serving pieces. For meat-lovers, Tourondel always includes one or two "Not Fish" dishes.

BLT Prime

Steakhouse ✕✕

013

111 E. 22nd St. (bet. Park & Lexington Aves.)

Subway:	23 St (Park Ave. South)
Phone:	212-995-8500
Fax:	212-460-5881
Web:	www.bltprime.com
Prices:	$$$

Mon – Thu 5:30pm - 11pm
Fri – Sat 5:30pm - 11:30pm
Sun 5pm - 10pm

Chef Laurent Tourondel had a busy year in 2005. BLT Prime opened in June, hot on the heels of BLT Fish (launched in January). Tourondel outfitted the space formerly occupied by Union Pacific in elegant neutral tones that run from beige to sepia, resulting in a cool, classic New York look. Under the vaulted glass ceiling, a large blackboard reiterates the menu, which is divided into sections by product, with an obvious emphasis on meat—beef, veal, lamb and poultry.

Fish lovers are not forgotten, though; a short selection of fish and shellfish rounds out the list. All dishes are realized by a talented cooking team, and diners are free to choose their own sauces and sides, which include blue cheese tater tots, barbecue onions and stuffed mushroom caps, among others.

The Blue Mahoe

014

243 East 14th St. (bet. Second & Third Aves.)

Subway:	14 St - Union Sq	Mon – Thu 11am - 11pm
Phone:	212-358-0012	Fri – Sat 11am - midnight
Fax:	212-220-9224	Sun 11am - 4pm
Web:	www.bluemahoenyc.com	
Prices:	$$	

Need to get away from it all? Take a break at Blue Mahoe, where after a short while of sipping a Dark & Stormy (made with fresh ginger beer) and listening to reggae music, you'll swear you're no longer in the city. With the restaurant's sexy plantation-style décor, whitewashed walls, leafy greenery and whirring ceiling fans, you'll be mentally transported to the islands in no time.

So settle back and let the kitchen wow you with excellent quality ingredients and well-balanced Caribbean flavors. Coconut shrimp, for instance, are cooked in a rich coconut-tomato sauce; the grilled half-chicken is spiced with pungent jerk seasoning and served over grilled pineapple, with rice and peas on the side. Service can be slow, but the waitstaff is so charming that you won't care.

Blue Smoke 😊

015

116 E. 27th St. (bet. Lexington & Park Aves.)

Subway:	28 St (Park Ave. South)	Mon – Thu 11:30am - 11pm
Phone:	212-447-7733	Fri 11:30am - 1am
Fax:	212-576-2561	Sat noon - 1am
Web:	www.bluesmoke.com	Sun noon - 10pm
Prices:	$$	

Jazz and barbecue make a winning combination, and nowhere more so in the city than at Blue Smoke. One of the few barbecue spots in Manhattan that actually uses smoke (from hickory and apple wood) to cook the meat, Blue Smoke replaces traditional canned or powdered ingredients with fresh versions. Sharing is encouraged, since platters like Rhapsody in 'Cue, a sampler of St. Louis spareribs, pulled pork, smoked organic chicken and a hot link are a challenge for one person. With its inclusion of small producers from Europe and North America, the wine list is surprising for a barbecue joint.

If you're a music fan, you can enjoy the same food downstairs at Jazz Standard while you listen to live jazz and blues. Owner Danny Meyer stamps the restaurant with his signature family-friendly service.

Manhattan Gramercy, Flatiron & Union Square

Blue Water Grill

Contemporary ✕✕

016

31 Union Sq. West (at 16th St.)

Subway:	14 St – Union Sq
Phone:	212-675-9500
Fax:	212-675-1899
Web:	www.brguestrestaurants.com
Prices:	$$

Mon – Thu 11:30am - 4pm
& 5pm - 12:30am
Fri – Sat 11:30am - 4pm & 5pm - 1am
Sun 10:30am - 4pm & 5pm - midnight

Overlooking Union Square, the 1903 Bank of the Metropolis building still welcomes moneyed clients, only now they must be hungry too. Today, the building's soaring ceilings, decorative moldings, floor-to-ceiling windows and white-marble walls enclose the main dining room of the Blue Water Grill. The outdoor terrace functions as a "museum" of beautiful people, who are frequently on display here on sunny days.

In addition to seeing the lovely interior of the former bank, you'll catch fresh seafood, from Maryland crab cakes to live Maine lobster. And don't ignore the sushi and maki rolls, or the raw-bar offerings, which include a good selection of oysters. Live jazz entertains diners every night in the downstairs lounge, and there's a jazz brunch on Sunday.

Bolo

Spanish ✕✕

017

23 E. 22nd St. (bet. Broadway & Park Ave. South)

Subway:	23 St (Park Ave. South)
Phone:	212-228-2200
Fax:	212-228-2239
Web:	www.bolorestaurant.com
Prices:	$$$

Sun – Thu noon - 2:30pm & 5:30pm - 10pm
Fri noon - 2:30pm & 5:30pm - 11pm
Sat 5:30pm - 11pm
Sun 5:30pm - 10pm

From the cranberry-red walls to the friendly service, Spain's sunny personality is perfectly captured at Bolo. This restaurant is brought to you by chef Bobby Flay ("Bo") and restaurateur Lawrence Kretchmer ("Lo") of Mesa Grill fame. Although the spirit is Spanish, it's not traditional; the cooking here reflects Flay's modernized version of Spanish cuisine.

At dinner, meat and fish are often oven-roasted or grilled, and a selection of rice dishes might run from paella to risotto. Lunch offers mains like the pressed Bolo burger with Manchego cheese, Serrano ham, and smoked paprika fries.

Whether you choose an entrée or one of the tempting tapas, you'll find that the food is not inexpensive here. Portions are copious, though, so you won't go away lighter, even though your wallet will.

Butai

018

115 E. 18th St. (bet. Irving Pl. & Park Ave.)

Subway:	14 St - Union Sq	Mon – Fri 11am - 3pm & 5pm - 11pm
Phone:	212-228-5716	Sat 5pm - midnight
Fax:	212-228-5751	Sun 5pm - 10pm
Web:	www.butai.us	
Prices:	$$	

♿

Butai is an ideal place to enjoy contemporary Japanese cuisine in a sleek setting. Quietly restrained at lunch, the scene turns hip when the sun sets and young professionals depart the nearby offices. The modern interior is accented with gorgeous marble and dark wood, and lively lounge music adds to the cool ambience.

Attractive presentations of sushi are available throughout the day, but Butai is best known for its robata grill offerings, which are only available in the evening. One of the few Japanese restaurants in the city to offer robata-style cuisine, Butai also impresses with its visually appealing presentations. Japanese classic starters, such as Agedashi tofu or various sunomono are standouts to begin your robata feast.

Casa Mono

019

52 Irving Pl. (at 17th St.)

Subway:	14 St - Union Sq	Open daily noon - midnight
Phone:	212-253-2773	
Fax:	212-253-5318	
Web:	N/A	
Prices:	$$	

♿

Brought to you by the winning restaurant duo of Joseph Bastianich and chef Mario Batali, Casa Mono opened in fall 2003. A lively crowd has been filling up the tiny, rustic dining room ever since.

They come to sample Spanish wines and sherries and to nibble small plates of mussels with chorizo, Serrano ham, tripe with chickpeas, and crema catalona. All these Spanish dishes are created by chef/owner Andy Nusser, an alumnus of Batali ventures Babbo and Pó.

Slightly cramped, the small quarters do make for a festive atmosphere, and the upbeat servers add to the restaurant's lively personality.

If you can't get into Casa Mono, try its baby sister, Bar Jamón (Spanish for "ham bar") next door; there you can nosh on *bocadillos* (Spanish sandwiches) washed down with a glass of Rioja.

Copper Chimney

020

126 E. 28th St. (bet. Lexington & Park Aves.)

Subway:	28 St (Park Ave. South)
Phone:	212-213-5742
Fax:	212-213-8963
Web:	www.copperchimney.com
Prices:	🍴🍴

Mon – Thu noon - 3pm & 5pm - 10:30pm
Fri – Sun 11am - midnight

Opened in summer 2005 by the folks who founded Pongal, Copper Chimney exudes a trendy ambience that appeals to a young crowd with its candlelit room, loud music, close seating and bare wood tables.

A meal here begins with a small plate of mini-pappadums drizzled with mint and tamarind chutney and served with a neat mound of minced tomato, onion and pepper in the center. Main courses incorporate a wide range of traditional ingredients while emphasizing refined preparation and elegant presentation. All the standards are here, along with more sophisticated offerings, and a good mix of vegetarian dishes. Celebrity mixologist Jerry Banks has tailored cocktails specifically to complement the restaurant's cuisine.

Craftbar

021

900 Broadway (bet. 19th & 20th Sts.)

Subway:	14 St - Union Sq
Phone:	212-461-4300
Fax:	212-598-1859
Web:	www.craftrestaurant.com
Prices:	$$

Mon – Thu noon - 10pm
Fri noon - 11pm
Sat 10am - 11pm
Sun 10am - 10pm

In April 2005, Craftbar, the seductive and always crowded annex to Tom Colicchio's Craft restaurant, moved to bigger digs around the corner to accommodate its burgeoning guest list. Here, at Craft's casual cousin, you can sample Craft-like, top-quality ingredients at a lower price point.

The cuisine successfully blends modern American style with Mediterranean flair. Many of the small plates that made Craftbar famous may be gone now, but sharing items on the extensive new menu is still welcomed. Although the dishes change frequently so customers can enjoy the fresh flavors of select seasonal products, the famous veal ricotta meatballs remain—in order to avoid any heartbreak among the regulars.

Here, as at Craft, you'll revel in a large wine list, with a host of selections by the glass.

Dos Caminos

Contemporary Mexican ✗✗

022

373 Park Ave. South (bet. 26th & 27th Sts.)

Subway:	28 St (Park Ave. South)
Phone:	212-294-1000
Fax:	212-294-1090
Web:	www.brguestrestaurants.com
Prices:	$$

Sun – Mon 11:30am - 4pm & 5pm - 11:30pm
Tue – Thu 11:30am - 4pm & 5pm - 12:30am
Fri – Sat 11:30am - 4pm & 5pm - 1am

If you've never tasted good tequila, here's your chance. The bar at Dos Caminos offers 100 different types of the alcohol made by distilling the fermented juice of the agave plant. Don't taste too many, though, or you won't be able to appreciate the 250-seat dining space, vibrant in pink, orange and brown, and lit by hand-carved light fixtures.

Nor do you want to dull your taste buds before sampling the piquant Mexican cuisine, beginning with excellent guacamole, made to order tableside. Seared-tuna tacos, chorizo-sprinkled Cobb salad, and Oaxacan white- and dark-chocolate fondue bring Mexico to mind while displaying a fusion flair.

Check out Dos Caminos' SoHo location *(475 West Broadway at Houston St.)*, and the newest one, in Midtown *(on the corner of E. 50th St. and Third Ave.)*.

Eleven Madison Park

Contemporary ✗✗✗

023

11 Madison Ave. (at 24th St.)

Subway:	23 St (Park Ave. South)
Phone:	212-889-0905
Fax:	212-889-0918
Web:	www.elevenmadisonpark.com
Prices:	$$$

Sun – Thu 11:30am - 2pm & 5:30pm - 10:30pm
Fri – Sat 11:30am - 2pm & 5:30pm - 11pm

An enterprise by Danny Meyer and the Union Square Hospitality Group, this tony establishment is located in the Art Deco MetLife Insurance tower across from Madison Square. The restaurant boasts a splendid 1930s-style dining room, distinguished by its 30-foot-high ceiling, stylish chandeliers, and huge windows with lovely views.

French-inspired contemporary fare (smoked Columbia River sturgeon with peas and mint; Jamison Farm herb-roasted lamb with tomato confit and Niçoise olives) is the specialty here. A seasonal three-course market menu is available during lunch, and three different tasting menus supplement the prix-fixe à la carte offerings at dinner. Don't skip dessert here; creative confections from the talented pastry chef warrant your full attention.

Manhattan Gramercy, Flatiron & Union Square

I Trulli

Italian ✗✗

024

122 E. 27th St. (bet. Lexington Ave. & Park Ave. South)

Subway:	28 St (Park Ave. South)	Mon – Fri noon - 3pm & 5:30pm - 10pm
Phone:	212-481-7372	Sun 5pm - 10pm
Fax:	212-481-5785	
Web:	www.itrulli.com	
Prices:	$$$	

Located near Madison Square, the family of establishments that falls under the I Trulli umbrella includes something for almost everyone. Next door to the restaurant is a wine bar called Enoteca I Trulli, and across the street, you'll find Vino, which sells Italian wines and spirits.

I Trulli features the cuisine of Puglia, the owner's native region; the restaurant even has its own label of olive oil, harvested and bottled in Italy. Pastas, including the light-as-a-feather *malloreddus* (dumplings filled with sausage) make a wonderful first or second course.

The dining room's rustic fireplace, open kitchen and wood-burning oven evoke the Italian countryside. In the warm seasons, the covered terrace, complete with a trickling fountain, will transport you to the European countryside.

Jaiya 😊

Thai ✗

025

396 Third Ave. (at 28th St.)

Subway:	28 St (Park Ave. South)	Mon – Fri 11:30am - midnight
Phone:	212-889-1330	Sat noon - midnight
Fax:	212-447-1098	Sun 5pm - midnight
Web:	www.jaiya.com	
Prices:	😊😊	

Authentic Thai cuisine brings a mixed crowd of couples, families, and groups of friends back to this simple restaurant, located about eight blocks north of Gramercy Park. There's a reason that groups are drawn to casual Jaiya: generous family-style portions are big enough for sharing, and a group can eat well here for a reasonable price.

Skip the popular pad Thai and satay. A foray into the large number of curries and chef's specialties is bound to delight your palate with authentic tastes of Thailand. The waitstaff is efficient and tries to be helpful by talking diners down from their spice requests. Since the kitchen here does not Americanize the traditional Thai spice levels, ordering a dish "medium spicy" may well yield a more fiery taste than you bargained for.

Kitchen 22

026

36 E. 22nd St. (bet. Broadway & Park Ave. South)

Subway:	23 St (Park Ave. South)	Mon – Thu 5pm - 10:30pm
Phone:	212-228-4399	Fri – Sat 5:30pm - 11pm
Fax:	212-228-4612	Closed Sun
Web:	www.charliepalmer.com	
Prices:	$$	

Residents of Gramercy Park count themselves lucky to have Kitchen 22 as their neighborhood restaurant. This is the kind of casual, contemporary place you'll want to come back to often— and with prices this inexpensive, you'll be able to. Be prepared to stand in line, though; this member of Charlie Palmer's restaurant group doesn't take reservations.

While you wait, claim a spot at the bar and brush up on your geography by studying the unique globe light fixtures. Once your table is ready, you can make your dinner selection from the three-course, fixed-price menu, offering updated American fare. Value is key to the concept here. For $29, you can choose from five seasonally inspired dishes at each course, and still have cash left over to enjoy a bottle from the equally affordable wine list.

Les Halles

027

411 Park Ave. South (bet. 28th & 29th Sts.)

Subway:	28 St (Park Ave. South)	Open daily 8am - midnight
Phone:	212-679-4111	
Fax:	212-779-0679	
Web:	www.leshalles.net	
Prices:	$$	

This brasserie serves as home base for Anthony Bourdain, culinary bad boy and author of the restaurant exposé, *Kitchen Confidential*. Bourdain presides over the kitchen here, turning out classic bistro fare in typically bustling Belle Époque surroundings. Named for the famous Paris market, Les Halles is designed with dark wood moldings, a stamped-tin ceiling and antique light fixtures.

The bold personality of this restaurant, which is popular with local business types, turns the typical business lunch on its head with tasty French classics. Meat steals the show here with juicy hamburgers and steak frites (the fries are to die for) among the most-ordered items.

Visit Les Halles' little sister (it has the same menu) in the Financial District at 15 John Street.

Manhattan Gramercy, Flatiron & Union Square

Mesa Grill

028

102 Fifth Ave. (bet. 15th & 16th Sts.)

Subway:	14 St - Union Sq	Mon – Fri noon - 2:30pm
Phone:	212-807-7400	& 5:30pm - 10:30pm
Fax:	212-989-0034	Sat 11:30am - 3pm & 5:30pm - 11pm
Web:	www.mesagrill.com	Sun 11:30am - 3pm & 5:30pm - 10:30pm
Prices:	$$$	

Between filming shows on the Food Network, writing cookbooks and supervising his empire of restaurants (which includes Bolo and Bar Americain in New York, and Mesa Grill in Las Vegas), celebrity chef Bobby Flay is one busy guy. A graduate of the French Culinary Institute, Flay gravitated not to foie gras and truffles, but to products native to the Americas—corn, chiles, black beans.

While you wouldn't pick Mesa Grill, with its boisterous, brazenly colored dining room, for a quiet evening out, you would come for zesty Southwestern cuisine like yellow-corn-crusted chile relleno, goat cheese "queso fundido," and a great margarita list. Salads and sandwiches dominate the toned-down lunch menu, which is popular with business types. Neighborhood denizens have long favored the weekend brunch.

Molly's Pub & Shebeen

Gastropub

029

287 Third Ave. (bet. 22nd & 23rd Sts.)

Subway:	23 St (Park Ave. South)	Open daily 11am - 4am
Phone:	212-889-3361	
Fax:	212-979-1488	
Web:	www.mollyspubandrestaurant.com	
Prices:		

Molly's is as traditional a pub as you're likely to find in New York. Even the exterior screams "Ireland" with its white stucco façade against dark wood beams, and its antique-looking carved wooden sign. Inside, low ceilings, dark walls and sawdust floors are warmed by the wood-burning fireplace—a great place to defrost those winter chills.

The pub draws patrons of all stripes, from twenty-somethings to seasoned regulars, minus the boisterous happy-hour set. An ideal watering hole for a pint and an awesome burger, Molly's also serves pub classics like corned beef and cabbage, fish and chips, and Shepherd's pie.

Limited seating means you may have to wait for a table. No worries; the bar staff will take good care of you, and the friendly regulars usually have a few good stories to share.

Olives

030

201 Park Ave. South (at 17th St.)

Subway: 14 St - Union Sq
Phone: 212-353-8345
Fax: 212-353-9592
Web: www.toddenglish.com
Prices: $$$

Mon – Thu noon - 2:30pm & 6pm - 10:30pm
Fri noon - 2:30pm & 5:30pm - 11pm
Sat 10:30am - 2:30pm & 5:30pm - 11pm
Sun 10:30am - 2:30pm & 6pm - 10pm

Chef Todd English burst onto New York's dining scene in 2000 when he opened this outpost of his popular Boston restaurant on the first floor of the W Hotel. A link in the chain of English's 13 eateries (Olives is now in six cities, including Tokyo), Olives on Union Square packs 'em in seven nights a week.

The draw? A trendy, elegant setting, a chic crowd in the lounge, and English's innovative Mediterranean cuisine. Handmade butternut squash tortelli, oven-roasted branzino with curried lobster vinaigrette, and pistachio-crusted lamb loin are seasonal highlights. You might even find the likes of brick-oven-baked flatbread topped with fig and prosciutto, which leave standard sandwiches in the dust.

You can purchase a copy of English's cookbook, *The Olives Table*, at the reception desk.

Park Bistro

031

414 Park Ave. South (bet. 28th & 29th Sts.)

Subway: 28 St (Park Ave. South)
Phone: 212-689-1360
Fax: 212-689-6437
Web: www.parkbistrorestaurant.com
Prices: $$

Open daily noon - 3pm & 5pm - 11pm

A black-and-white portrait of actress Simone Signoret welcomes you at the entrance of this French bistro, opened in 1989. Step inside and you're immersed in 1920s Paris: photographs of the City of Light by Robert Doisneau decorate the ivory-colored walls, French singers croon in the background, and red banquettes and bistro chairs cozy up to white-linen-and paper-topped tables in this recently refurbished room.

Park Bistro, as its name suggests, serves the real thing, not gussied-up French nouveau cuisine. For lunch and dinner, the prix-fixe menu (served before 7pm) is a real bargain. À la carte selections showcase French classics (escargots, quiche, duck confit, coq au vin), and the short wine list offers a good and inexpensive selection of Gallic wines.

Manhattan Gramercy, Flatiron & Union Square

Periyali

032

35 W. 20th St. (bet. Fifth & Sixth Aves.)

Subway:	23 St (Sixth Ave.)	Mon – Thu noon - 3pm & 5:30pm - 11pm
Phone:	212-463-7890	Fri noon - 3pm & 5:30pm - 11:30pm
Fax:	212-924-9403	Sat 5:30pm - 11:30pm
Web:	www.periyali.com	Closed Sun
Prices:	$$$	

If it's a break from the city's hustle and bustle you're after, you'll find it here. With its white-plaster walls and wood-beamed ceiling—draped, sail-like, with white fabric—Periyali suggests the rustic ambience of islands in the Aegean.

As you'd expect of a restaurant whose name means "seashore" in Greek, the cuisine angles in on the sunny cuisine of the Greek islands. Fantastic bread and olive oil for dipping begin a wonderful meal here. Entreés encompass rustic fare including traditional moussaka, grilled fish, and souvlaki made with filet mignon.

The dining space, divided into four small rooms, makes a great place to have an intimate rendezvous or to discuss business over a good bottle of Greek wine. At midday the crowd comprises stylish and well-spoken Flatiron business lunchers.

Pure Food and Wine

Vegetarian

033

54 Irving Pl. (bet. 17th & 18th Sts.)

Subway:	14 St - Union Sq	Open daily 5:30pm - 11pm
Phone:	212-477-1010	
Fax:	212-477-6916	
Web:	www.purefoodandwine.com	
Prices:	$$$	

Carnivores beware: this restaurant's name means what it says. A disciple of the raw-food movement, Pure Food and Wine serves only raw vegetarian dishes. If you're a first-timer here, the waiters will explain that to preserve vitamins, enzymes, minerals and flavors in the food, nothing is heated above 118ºF.

Spicy Thai lettuce wraps with tamarind chile sauce, and zucchini and golden tomato lasagna with basil-pistachio pesto don't just taste good, they're good for you—especially if you buy into the purported health benefits of raw cuisine. Either way, the kitchen uses only the freshest organic produce available, and the results are surprisingly flavorful.

The quiet terrace makes a perfect place for a leisurely meal, while the juice bar and take-away counter foster healthy eating on the go.

Sapa

034

Vietnamese ✗✗

43 W. 24th St. (bet. Fifth & Sixth Aves.)

Subway:	23 St (Sixth Ave.)
Phone:	212-929-1800
Fax:	212-929-7070
Web:	www.sapanyc.com
Prices:	$$$

Sun – Fri noon - 3pm & 5:30pm - 11:30pm
Sat 6pm - midnight

Since Sapa opened in fall 2004, throngs of beautiful people clad in the latest prêt-à-porter designs have filled this restaurant on the border of Chelsea and Gramercy. Why all the buzz? A festive atmosphere; a seductive contemporary setting designed by AvroKo with Asian wire lanterns, French garden urns and exotic woods; and an amazing culinary alchemy that expertly marries Vietnamese and French cuisine.

If it sounds schizophrenic, it doesn't taste that way. Named for a North Vietnamese village built by the French in the 1920s, Sapa brines chicken in oolong tea, brushes duck breast with red-curry pineapple glaze and steams mussels and clams in lemongrass-coconut broth. Special happy hour and late-night menus are offered in addition to lunch, brunch and dinner fare.

Saravanaas 😊

Indian ✗

035

81 Lexington Ave. (at 26th St.)

Subway:	28 St (Park Ave. South)
Phone:	212-679-0204
Fax:	212-679-5811
Web:	www.saravanaas.com
Prices:	😋

Sun – Thu noon - 3pm & 5pm - 10pm
Fri – Sat 5pm - 10:30pm
Closed Mon

Set smack in the midst of Curry Row, Saravanaas stands out with its simple, clean contemporary décor. Pastel-hued walls, colorful votives and gleaming aluminum serving pieces brighten the dining room.

The menu embraces a contemporary reflection of time-honored Southern Indian dishes. Thalis, a selection of different dishes served with appropriate condiments, come in small or large sizes for a set price. Dosas, made with rice and lentils, are a specialty here. You can order these wonderfully thin pancakes plain or with your choice of myriad vegetarian fillings. The dosas are so enormous, it's easy to make a meal of just one—for less than $10. And the veggie fillings are so tasty and satisfying, you'll never miss the protein.

Tabla

036

11 Madison Ave. (at 25th St.)

Subway:	23 St (Park Ave. South)	Open daily noon – 2pm
Phone:	212-889-0667	& 5:30pm – 10:30pm
Fax:	212-889-0914	
Web:	www.tablany.com	
Prices:	$$$	

A member of Union Square Hospitality Group, Tabla faces Madison Square, next door to Eleven Madison Park (another of Danny Meyer's restaurants). At Tabla you have two dining options. On the first floor, boisterous Bread Bar at Tabla features a short menu of home-style regional Indian fare at reasonable prices. If you're in the mood for a more upscale dining experience with great people-watching, climb the suspended staircase to the second floor and have a seat in Tabla's sensuous, Art Deco dining room.

There, chef Floyd Cardoz, a native of Bombay, skillfully fuses contemporary American cuisine with spicy Indian accents (as in baby lamb with garam masala jus, or crab cakes with avocado salad and tamarind chutney) on his three-course, prix-fixe menu.

Tamarind

037

41-43 E. 22nd St. (bet. Broadway & Park Ave. South)

Subway:	23 St (Park Ave. South)	Open daily 11:30am – 2:45pm
Phone:	212-674-7400	& 5:30pm – 11:30pm
Fax:	212-674-4449	
Web:	www.tamarinde22.com	
Prices:	$$$	

Unlike the sweet-and-sour tropical fruit for which it's named, Tamarind hits no sour notes. Instead, the restaurant achieves a pleasing harmony between its restrained and sophisticated décor (no goddess statues here) and its regional Indian cuisine.

Cowbells hang in alcoves in the sparkling white dining room, and the back wall holds mirrored niches where a collection of stylized Indian wooden puppets are displayed. Inside the glassed-in kitchen, a serious brigade of cooks busies itself preparing piquant dishes from Goa, Punjab, Madras and Calcutta. The large range of regional cuisine includes masala, curries, and tandoori dishes; goat meat here is a tender delight. A good, balanced wine list and a staff of smiling, attentive servers add the final crescendo to this epicurean aria.

Tocqueville

038

1 E. 15th St. (bet. Fifth Ave. & Union Sq. West)

Subway:	14 St - Union Sq	Open daily 11:45am - 2pm
Phone:	212-647-1515	& 5:30pm - 10:30pm
Fax:	212-645-3098	
Web:	www.tocquevillerestaurant.com	
Prices:	$$	

Named for 19th-century French writer Alexis de Tocqueville, this restaurant puts an American spin on its dishes. Although the chef occasionally spikes the contemporary French-accented cuisine with non-sequiturs (as in a tartare of Japanese yellowtail and tuna) the menu consists mainly of classics. The 200-label wine list features selections from little-known wine regions around the world.

Toqueville's new space, just up the street from the original, is still as intimate as before. Tables snuggle close together in the single dining room, but devotees don't mind the lack of privacy. Service is just as quirky, too, but the new space is so much more elegant that it helps distract diners from the waitstaff's flaws. Lockers in the front hallway offer self-serve coat check.

Turkish Kitchen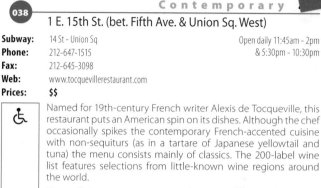

039

386 Third Ave. (bet. 27th & 28th Sts.)

Subway:	28 St (Park Ave. South)	Mon – Thu noon - 3pm & 5:30pm - 11pm
Phone:	212-679-6633	Fri noon - 3pm & 5pm - 11:30pm
Fax:	212-679-1830	Sat 5pm - 11:30pm
Web:	www.turkishkitchenny.com	Sun 11am - 3pm & 5pm - 10:30pm
Prices:		

You'll see red when you step inside the Turkish Kitchen's windowed façade—red walls, that is. The inside of the first-floor dining room is painted bright red, with red fabric-covered chairs. Casual enough for jeans, the place has an exotic feel with copper urns filling wall shelves and alcoves, and colorful martini glasses lining the glowing blue-glass bar. At night, blue-glass votives mounted on the walls cast a romantic light against the claret-colored walls.

Many of the best dishes here are uniquely Turkish, such as the *boregi* (feta-filled phyllo scrolls baked to a crisp), or the lamb, grilled and served in a variety of preparations. Try a glass of Turkish wine or beer to round out your experience. For both lunch and dinner, the set three-course menu is a terrific deal.

Union Square Cafe

American 🍴

040

21 E. 16th St. (bet. Fifth Ave. & Union Sq. West)

Subway:	14 St - Union Sq
Phone:	212-243-4020
Fax:	212-627-2673
Web:	www.unionsquarecafe.com
Prices:	$$$

Sun – Thu noon - 2:30pm
& 5:30pm - 10pm
Fri – Sat noon - 2:30pm
& 5:30pm - 11pm

In New York City, Union Square Cafe is a special place. It was founded by a young entrepreneur named Danny Meyer in 1985, and business has been booming ever since. Given the restaurant's comfortable bistro décor, winning service and excellent modern American cooking, it's easy to see why.

Helpful staff members set the tone for your experience; they're both passionate and knowledgeable about the food and wine. Chef Michael Romano supplements his entrée selection with daily and weekly specials, and the Greenmarket next door figures largely in the planning. Worth a special mention is the tremendous wine list, diverse, well-selected and reasonably priced.

Do as the regulars do, and grab a seat at the bar for a great burger or a three-course meal and a sampling of their wines by the glass.

Vatan 😀

Indian 🍴

041

409 Third Ave. (bet. 28th & 29th Sts.)

Subway:	28 St (Park Ave. South)
Phone:	212-689-5666
Fax:	N/A
Web:	www.vatanny.com
Prices:	$$

Sun & Tue – Thu 5:30pm - 9pm
Fri – Sat 5:30pm - 10:15pm
Closed Mon

When you step inside Vatan, you'll instantly be transported to a Gujarati village on the Arabian Sea in western India. Portraits of Ganesh, the god of wisdom, and of Annapurnadevi, the goddess of prosperity, welcome you at the end of a bamboo-lined corridor. Keep going, and you'll find yourself amid a setting of huts, banyan trees, wisteria vines and a whimsical mural of the Indian countryside.

Take your shoes off and have a seat at one of the low tables. There's no need for decision-making here. The fixed-price, all-you-can-eat menu comprises a 20-course repast of regional Indian specialties—all strictly vegetarian—served by waitresses dressed in bright sarongs. Vatan's flavorful menu proves that avoiding meat isn't a sacrifice.

Live in Italian

At finer restaurants in Los Angeles, Melbourne, Cape Town and of course, Positano.

Greenwich, West Village & Meatpacking

Centering on Washington Square, New York's historic bohemia lies between Houston and 14th streets, and contains within it several distinct areas. From Avenue of the Americas (Sixth Avenue) east to the Bowery, the **West Village** keeps itself young with New York University's student population. **Greenwich Village,** bounded on the east by Avenue of the Americas and on the west by the Hudson River, is the prettiest and most historic of the West Village neighborhoods. The gritty northwest corner of the West Village has been transformed in recent years into an über-hip shopping, dining and clubbing destination known as the **Meatpacking District.** Within these three adjoining areas you'll find a high concentration of eateries, offering cuisines from around the globe.

Greenwich Village – Lined with trees and Federal and Greek Revival row houses, this beguiling tangle of narrow streets is ideal for wandering. The heart of historic **Greenwich Village** is bounded by *(clockwise from north)* Christopher Street, Seventh Avenue South, St. Luke's Place and Hudson Street, inside of which is a skewed layout of crooked streets lined with town houses and old trees. The commercial spine of Greenwich Village, **Bleecker Street** grows increasingly upscale as it nears the Meatpacking District. The stretch of **Hudson Street** between Christopher and Bank streets is lined with restaurants and cafes.

West Village – The area anchored by **Washington Square** is largely defined by the presence of **New York University**, founded in 1831 by Albert Gallatin, secretary of the Treasury under Thomas Jefferson. One of the largest private universities in the country, NYU has an undergraduate population of 40,000 and a steadily rising reputation.

West Village

© Cucina Stagionale/NYC & Company, Inc.

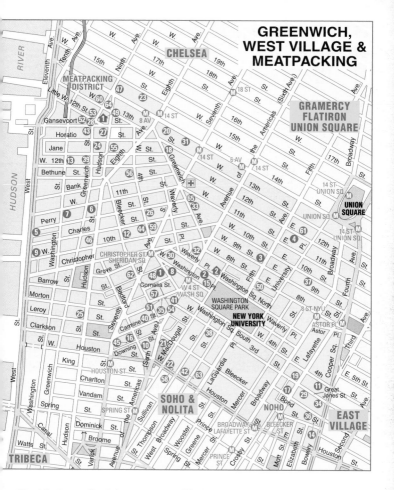

The blocks south of the square are filled with student hangouts.

Meatpacking District – Not so long ago, "trendy" was the last word anyone would ever use to describe the section of the West Village bounded by West 15th, Hudson and Gansevoort streets, and the Hudson River. The Meatpacking District was a rather dangerous place until the 1990s; after meat wholesalers would close for the day, drug dealers and prostitutes prowled its moody, cobblestone streets. The booming economy, along with Mayor Rudy Giuliani's heavy-handed crime policy in the early 90s, cleaned up the neighborhood. Although some meat companies remain, the neighborhood's grit is, for the most part, a fashion accessory. Big-name chefs have made inroads into the district, opening hot and hard-to-get-into restaurants. All these places are packed to the rafters at night, so reserve well in advance.

Annisa ✤

001

13 Barrow St. (bet. Seventh Ave. South & W. 4th St.)

Subway:	Christopher St - Sheridan Sq	Mon – Sat 5:30pm – 10:30pm
Phone:	212-741-6699	Sun 5:30pm - 9:30pm
Fax:	212-741-6696	Closed August 26 - September 4
Web:	www.annisarestaurant.com	
Prices:	$$$	

Annisa

A serene vibe enfolds you inside this West Village restaurant, whose name is Arabic for "women." Indeed, there is much that is feminine about Annisa, starting with the two owners, chef Anita Lo and sommelier Jennifer Scism. Then there's the minimalist décor, softened by a flowing white curtain that lines one wall. Well-spaced, white-cloth-draped tables and curving coral-colored banquettes fill the dining room. Another tribute to the feminine is the wine list; most of its 90 labels are either made by female vintners and/or made at vineyards with female proprietors.

The chef's inventive, seasonally changing menu is American at heart, but Lo's Asian roots reveal themselves regularly in dishes such as miso-marinated sable with crispy silken tofu in a bonito broth. In addition to the à la carte selections, guests are invited to try the chef's five- and seven-course tasting menus (though the entire table is asked to participate, so be sure your fellow diners are up for the feast). The knowledgeable staff will happily answer any questions you have about the menu or the wines.

Appetizers

Seared Foie Gras with Soup Dumplings

White Tuna Tartare with Korean Chile, Black Sesame and Asian Pear

Spicy Grilled Eggplant with Yogurt and Lentils

Entrées

Miso-marinated Sable with Crispy Silken Tofu in a Bonito Broth

Pan-roasted Farm Chicken with Sherry, Chanterelles and Pig's Feet

Smoked Australian Rack of Lamb with Iroquois Hominy, Chile and Lime

Desserts

Poppyseed Bread Pudding with Meyer Lemon Curd

Apple Tart with Caramel Sauce and Vanilla Ice Cream

Chocolate Biscuit Pudding with Banana Mousse

CONTEMPORARY

Babbo ✿

002

110 Waverly Pl. (bet. MacDougal St. & Sixth Ave.)

Subway:	W 4 St - Wash Sq
Phone:	212-777-0303
Fax:	212-777-3365
Web:	www.babbonyc.com
Prices:	$$$

Mon — Sat 5:30pm - 11:30pm
Sun 5pm - 11pm

Babbo/Christopher Hirscheimer

It's not for nothing that Babbo's celebrity chef/owner is known to Food Network groupies as "Molto" Mario. With an empire of New York City restaurants, including Lupa, Esca and Otto, several TV shows and an armful of cookbooks to his credit, Mario Batali is indeed "extremely" Mario. It's amazing that this ponytailed chef, who spent time cooking in a little village in Italy, finds time to man the kitchen at his flagship restaurant, but luckily for diners, he does.

Local seasonal ingredients fresh from the Union Square Greenmarket, made in-house or imported from Italy, make for memorable meals at this boisterous, always-crowded osteria (hint: reserve a table—well in advance—in the quieter second-floor room). Mario is a disciple of the slow-food style of cooking, and the proof is in his rustic, authentic preparations. Homemade pappardelle with wild boar ragu makes an excellent beginning, or, if you're a pasta fanatic, the pasta tasting menu offers a small portion of all the highlights. As *secondi*, the lamb chops, rabbit or sweetbreads all equal a tasty, traditional treat.

The exclusively Italian wine list is one of the most exhaustive selections available in New York.

Appetizers

Asparagus Milanese
with Duck Egg and
Parmigiano

Warm Tripe alla
Parmigiana

Pig Foot Milanese
with Rice, Beans and
Arugula

Entrées

Mint Love Letters with
Spicy Lamb Sausage

Duck with Golden
Beets, Fava-Bean
Barlotto, and Brovada

Spicy Two-minute
Calamari Sicilian-
Lifeguard Style

Desserts

Meyer Lemon
Semifreddo with
Huckleberries

Saffron Panna Cotta
with Rhubarb and
Rhubarb Sorbetto

Date and Walnut
Budino with Vanilla
Gelato and Warm
Caramel

Cru ✿

003

24 Fifth Ave. (at 9th St.)

Subway:	8 St - NYU	Mon – Sat 5:30pm - 11pm
Phone:	212-529-1700	Closed Sun
Fax:	212-529-6300	
Web:	www.cru-nyc.com	
Prices:	$$$$	

As its name suggests, Cru spotlights fine wines in its Greenwich Village dining room. The wine "list" here is more of a book—a 222-page book, to be exact—and ranks as one of the best in New York City. Some 3,500 selections span the globe and include a number of truly exceptional premier cru bottles; nearly a third of the roster is devoted to burgundies.

And since you'll need something to eat while you're enjoying your wine, Cru offers chef Shea Gallante's innovative seasonal tasting menus, which often include his signature homemade pastas among the many courses (Cru is open only for dinner). In addition to the chef's tasting menu, guests may pick and choose from a variety of entrée selections. Fish dishes here, such as sturgeon crusted in sea scallops, Johnson cod or European turbot, particularly sparkle.

All this wonderful food and wine is served by an attentive waitstaff in a smart Art Deco setting of lustrous woods, black-leather banquettes, soft lighting and muted colors. The casual bar area up front serves small plates and doesn't require reservations.

Appetizers

Red Brandywine Tomato Tartare, Whipped Burrata, Genovese Basil and Black-Olive Crisp, Toasted Almond-Milk Vinaigrette

Maine Sweet Shrimp Terrine with Sea Urchin and Shiso Flowers and Pumpkin-Seed Dressing

Grilled Quail with Guanciale, Brussels Sprouts and Hon-Shimeji Mushrooms, and a Curry Emulsion

Entrées

Grain-fed Veal Loin Cooked *Sous Vide*, Smokey Celery-Root Purée, Porcini, Canaletti Beans and Ramps, with a Warm Black-Truffle Anchovy Aioli

House-made Potato Gnocchi with Rabbit Sausage, Fennel Pollen and Sweet Onions, with Baked Ricotta Salata

Turbot "Saltimbocca," Castellucio Lentil Passatina, Roasted Broccoli and Lingonberry Jus

Desserts

Chocolate-Chocolate-Chip Financier with Malted-Chocolate Ice Cream, Caramel Espuma and Espresso Milkshake

Poached Rhubarb with Phyllo Crisp, Saffron and White-Chocolate Mousse, and Buttermilk and Rhubarb Sorbets

Kumquat Poppy-Seed Beignet

Gotham Bar and Grill ✿

004

12 E. 12th St. (bet. Fifth Ave. & University Pl.)

Subway:	14 St - Union Sq
Phone:	212-620-4020
Fax:	212-627-7810
Web:	www.gothambarandgrill.com
Prices:	$$$

Mon — Thu noon - 2:15pm
& 5:30pm - 10pm
Fri noon - 2:15pm & 5:30pm - 11pm
Sat 5pm - 11pm
Sun 5pm - 10pm

Gotham Bar & Grill

French-trained chef Alfred Portale, who has headed Gotham Bar and Grill's kitchen since the restaurant opened in 1984, is as well known for being a defining force in New American cuisine as he is for his towering food designs. In the restaurant's high-ceilinged room with its fabric-swathed light fixtures, the chef offers a monthly changing list of dishes prized for their clean, intense flavors and their top-quality ingredients.

Portale eschews heavier French dishes for fresh vegetables and herbs. The miso-marinated black cod or the yellowfin tuna tartare are just a couple of the longstanding favorite courses that show off Portale's classic flavor combinations. Even the desserts, like a modernized ice-cream sandwich drizzled with warm peanut-caramel sauce, elevate the mundane to the exceptional. Well-trained and professional service strives to anticipate diners' needs.

Don't have time for dinner? Go for the three-course lunch, served weekdays all year long. It's accompanied by a special wine menu that gives you the option of ordering a wine flight (three glasses), a half bottle or a full bottle, all for the same set price.

Appetizers

Yellowfin Tuna Tartare with Japanese Cucumber, Shiso Leaf, Sweet Miso and Asian Ginger Dressing

Muscovy Duck and Foie Gras Terrine with Haricots Verts, Green Lentil Salad, Pickled Onion and Port Glaze

Seafood Salad: Scallops, Squid, Japanese Octopus, Lobster and Avocado, Lemon Vinaigrette

Entrées

Nova Scotia Halibut with Morel Mushrooms, Ramps, English Peas and Fingerling Potatoes

Tandoori-spiced Duck with Basmati Rice, Curried Cauliflower, Sambal and Mango Chutney

King Salmon with Grilled Vegetables, Baby Artichokes and Israeli Couscous, Warm Vegetable Vinaigrette

Desserts

Gotham Chocolate Cake served warm with Espresso Walnut Ice Cream

Hot Cinnamon Rolls with Butter-Pecan Parfait and Spiced Dark Hot Chocolate

Banana Split with Vanilla and Chocolate Ice Cream, Strawberry Compote and Peanut Truffles

Perry Street ✿

005

176 Perry St. (at West St.)

Subway:	Christopher St - Sheridan Sq	Open daily noon - 3pm & 5:30pm - 11:30pm
Phone:	212-352-1900	
Fax:	212-352-1922	
Web:	www.jean-georges.com	
Prices:	**$$$**	

Jean-Georges Management

Jean-Georges Vongerichten's new Gotham venture occupies the ground floor of the southernmost building in a group of glass-tower condominiums designed by Richard Meier. A healthy walk from the subway station, this relatively remote address is located on the corner of the West Side Highway, overlooking the Hudson River. The glamorous dining room is entirely walled in glass covered by sheer white-fabric panels. A mix of round and square banquettes with white-leather seating adds to the contemporary feel. Tables are simply dressed with brown paper placemats and linen napkins.

At Perry Street, the food—a fusion of European, American and Asian cuisines—is as up-to-date as the décor. Inspired à la carte preparations are well executed by a professional staff, who take care to keep the subtle and well-balanced flavors from overwhelming the main ingredient. Juicy rack of lamb encrusted with chile crumbs, and perfectly cooked filet of halibut served atop sweet-pea ravioli represent the global influences of the dishes on the ever-changing menu.

The short but well-selected wine list finds its strength in French vintages.

Manhattan Greenwich, West Village & Meatpacking

Appetizers

Grilled King Oyster Mushroom and Avocado Carpaccio, Charred Jalapeño Oil and Lime

Black-Pepper Crab Dumplings and Snow Peas

Rice-Cracker-crusted Tuna, Sriracha Citrus Emulsion

Entrées

Arctic Char with Steamed Maitake Mushrooms, Smoked Sea Salt and Basil

Lemon Sole with Yukon Gold Potato Ravioli, Paprika Butter

Crunchy Rabbit, Citrus-Chile Seasoning and Soybean Purée

Desserts

Chocolate Pudding, Crystallized Violets and Fresh Cream

Angel Food Cake, Grapefruit Segments, Yogurt and Star Anise

Baked Hazelnut Frangipane, Poached Pear, Amaretto Truffle

CONTEMPORARY

Spotted Pig ✿

006

314 W. 11th St. (at Greenwich St.)

Subway: Christopher St - Sheridan Sq
Phone: 212-620-0393
Fax: 212-366-1666
Web: www.thespottedpig.com
Prices: $$

Mon – Fri noon - 5pm & 5:30pm - 2am
Sat – Sun 11am - 5pm & 5:30pm - 2am

The Spotted Pig

The gastropub craze has hit Greenwich Village in the form of the Spotted Pig. This casual place has become a dining destination, and for good reason. With its brown butcher-paper table coverings, farm-animals design motif, and young, friendly staff sporting Spotted Pig T-shirts, the little pub absolutely oozes character. An upstairs seating area has been added to handle the crowds flocking here, but a wait is a sure thing at this tiny restaurant that doesn't take reservations.

Chef/partner April Bloomfield, an alum of London's River Café and Chez Panisse in Berkeley, California, has obvious talent and interprets top-quality pub food with an Italian flair. The food is not intended to be intricate or fussy, but the seemingly simple dishes exhibit great depth of flavor and stunning contrasts. While standards such as sautéed calf's liver and smoked-haddock chowder are spot-on, sheep's-milk ricotta gnudi, celery and fennel salad with bottarga, and, for dessert, flourless chocolate cake represent a few examples of the upscale "pub grub" that is regularly featured on the daily changing bill of fare.

Appetizers

Roast Jerusalem Artichoke Salad with Marinated Goat Cheese and Hazelnuts

Sheep's-Ricotta Gnudi with Crispy Sage and Brown Butter

Sautéed Squid with Cranberry Beans, Garlic, Parsley and Lemon

Entrées

Char-grilled Calf's Liver with Pancetta, Caramelized Onions and Arugula

Char-grilled Burger with Roquefort Cheese and Shoestring Fries, Rosemary and Garlic

Roasted Halibut with Roast Trevise and Herb Salad

Desserts

Flourless Chocolate Cake with Crème Fraîche

Crème Catalan

Lemon and Lime Tart

Wallsé ✿

007

344 W. 11th St. (at Washington St.)

Subway:	Christopher St - Sheridan Sq	Mon – Fri 5:30pm - 11:30pm
Phone:	212-352-2300	Sat – Sun 11am - 2:30pm
Fax:	212-645-7127	& 5:30pm - 11:30pm
Web:	www.wallse.com	
Prices:	$$$	

Wallsé

You don't see many Austrian restaurants in New York, and this one is a keeper. Residents rejoice that chef Kurt Gutenbrunner, who was born in the 16th-century Austrian town of Wallse, brought his talents to the West Village. His sophisticated Austrian cuisine is served in one of two charming dining rooms, decorated with original 20th-century German and Austrian art from the collection of artist Julian Schnabel (a close friend of the chef).

The ambitious menu showcases traditional dishes (Wiener Schnitzel, Spätzle with braised rabbit, Palatschinken with smoked trout, apples and horseradish) as well as more updated fare (crispy cod strudel with braised leeks and Champagne sauce; thyme roasted rack of lamb with spring vegetables, fingerling-potato purée and Zweigelt), all of which are beautifully presented and rely on market-fresh produce. Of course, Austria's pastries are world-renowned and Wallsé brings a taste of the Old World to New York with its delightful sweets.

The attentive staff can provide good advice about any of the labels on the refined list of Austrian wines, and the specialty cocktails are worth a taste for their delicate balance and blend of flavors.

Appetizers

Maine Lobster with Potato Rösti, Fennel and Lemon Vinaigrette

Palatschinken with Smoked Trout, Apples, Horseradish, and Organic Herbs

Spätzle with Braised Rabbit, Mushrooms, Peas and Tarragon

Entrées

Kavalierspitz with Creamed Spinach, Potato Rösti, and Apple Horseradish

Wiener Schnitzel with Potato-Cucumber Salad and Lingonberries

Wild Striped Bass with Riesling Sauerkraut, Crispy Bacon, and Black-Truffle Sauce

Desserts

Salzburger Nockerl with Huckleberries

Mohr im Hemd with Chocolate Sorbet and Schlag

Apple and Walnut Strudel with Vanilla Ice Cream and Schlag

aki on west 4

008

Contemporary Japanese ✗

181 W. 4th St. (bet. Sixth & Seventh Aves.)

Subway:	W 4 St - Wash Sq	Tue – Thu & Sun 6pm - 10:45pm
Phone:	212-989-5440	Fri – Sat 6pm - 11:45pm
Fax:	212-744-4348	Closed Mon
Web:	www.members.aol.com/akiw4	
Prices:	$$	

At aki, chef/owner Shigeaki "Siggy" Nakanishi goes well beyond the traditional Japanese dishes. Nakanishi did a stint as a private chef to the Japanese ambassador to the West Indies in Kingston, Jamaica, and his cuisine hints at his Caribbean experience. In addition the sushi and sashimi standards, Jamaican jerk chicken is rolled with spicy shrimp paste and veggies in mango teriyaki sauce and served with banana tempura. Even the sushi celebrates the flavors of the islands, with the banana boat roll featuring spicy tuna wrapped with fried banana, and the Caribbean roll mixing mango, avocado and yellowtail. For dessert, green tea tiramisu is topped with passion fruit sauce.

If you want good value, go before 7pm for the four-course prix-fixe menu.

Antica Venezia

009

Italian ✗✗

396 West St. (at 10th St.)

Subway:	Christopher St - Sheridan Sq	Mon – Thu 5pm - 11pm
Phone:	212-229-0606	Fri – Sat 5pm - midnight
Fax:	N/A	Sun 3pm - 11pm
Web:	www.avnyc.com	
Prices:	$$	

The romance of Old Venice comes to Greenwich Village at the bottom of a two-story brick building on this busy avenue bordering the Hudson River. Outside, canopies cover the windows all along the façade, and strings of twinkling white lights festoon the small trees by the entrance. The rustic interior is equally engaging, with its two cozy brick-walled rooms, one with an open fireplace, and the other with a wall of cascading water.

On the menu you'll find a large selection of well-prepared, homestyle Italian pastas, gnocchi, fish, chicken and veal, augmented by a list of daily specials. A meal at Antica Venezia begins with an amuse-bouche offered by the chef, and ends with a complimentary glass of limoncello.

AOC Bedford

Mediterranean ✕✕

010

14 Bedford St. (bet. Downing & Houston Sts.)

Subway:	Houston St	Sun – Thu 5:30pm - 11pm
Phone:	212-414-4764	Fri – Sat 5:30pm - 11:30pm
Fax:	212-414-4765	
Web:	www.aocbedford.com	
Prices:	$$$	

The acronym for the French phrase *appellation d'origine controlée* may seem like a high-falutin' name for a restaurant, but in this case it fits perfectly with the quirky Greenwich Village neighborhood. AOC refers to the French system of designating regional foods and wines, and it symbolizes the restaurant's commitment to using the finest imported and domestic ingredients available.

Cuisine centers on French, Spanish and Italian dishes, using items such as fleur de sel from France, vinegar from Modena, Italy, and Manchego cheese from Spain. The three-course prix-fixe menu (offered from 5:30pm to 7pm) is a treat for early diners. If you want to impress your date, order one of the tableside preparations for two, such as the suckling pig or the crêpes Suzette.

Aroma Kitchen and Wine Bar

Italian ✕

011

36 E. 4th St. (bet. Bowery & Lafayette St.)

Subway:	Bleecker St	Tue – Thu 5pm - midnight
Phone:	212-375-0100	Fri 5pm - 1am
Fax:	212-375-0400	Sat – Sun 6pm - 1am
Web:	www.aromanyc.com	Closed Mon
Prices:	$$	

This sliver of a spot in Greenwich Village has become a festive local hangout, where in warm weather, doors open into the street and the party spills out onto the sidewalk. Aroma's positive energy keeps customers coming back for more fun and food. Luckily, the restaurant's appearance on the Food Network last year didn't result in diners overwhelming the tiny space.

Owners Alexandra Degiorgio and Vito Polosa are passionate about good food and wine, and it shows in the house-made pastas, marinated olives and other fine ingredients, which are a step up from the usual wine-bar fare. All Italian, the unique and fairly priced wine list contains many varietals rarely found outside Italy.

Go Sunday for the prix-fixe family dinner menu and live guitar music.

August

012

359 Bleecker St. (bet. Charles & 10th Sts.)

Subway:	Christopher St - Sheridan Sq	Mon – Thu noon - 3:30pm
Phone:	212-929-4774	& 5:30pm - 11pm
Fax:	646-349-3614	Fri noon - 3:30pm & 5:30pm - midnight
Web:	www.augustny.com	Sat 11am - 3:30pm & 5:30pm - midnight
Prices:	$$	Sun 11am - 3:30pm & 5:30pm - 10pm

The epitome of a cozy, neighborhood place, August radiates warmth from its exposed brick walls to its amiable waitstaff. This charming town house on a bustling street in Greenwich Village offers a small dining room up front, complete with an open kitchen and a wood-burning oven. A bright veranda adds more dining space in the back.

Billed as "regional European," the cuisine ranges across the continent from France to Italy to Portugal to Greece. Grilled lamb and pork gyro, German pancakes, and wood-oven-baked eggs *en cocotte* exemplify the frequently changing offerings featured at brunch; of course, if you want a dish that's closer to home, the August burger (jazzed up with frites and house-made mayonnaise) is available, too.

Barbuto

013

775 Washington St. (at 12th St.)

Subway:	14 St - 8 Av	Sun – Thu noon - 11pm
Phone:	212-924-9700	Fri – Sat noon - midnight
Fax:	212-924-9300	
Web:	www.barbutonyc.com	
Prices:	$$	

When the weather is warm and sunny, and the garage-style doors are open, there's nothing like the ambience at Barbuto. You'll enjoy prime people-watching in this corner of the West Village, not to mention the flavorful, market-based cuisine of chef Jonathan Waxman. Presiding over the kitchen day and night—a rarity in restaurants these days—Waxman plays up the best qualities of his main ingredients. The menu changes daily, except for signatures like oven-roasted chicken, spaghetti carbonara, and skirt steak, which are always available.

The long bar, an appealing spot for a quartino of wine, is normally packed by 5pm, and no wonder. From the celebrity-studded crowd and the lively street scene to the fresh, tasty fare, Barbuto rules as a neighborhood favorite.

Bianca 😊

014

5 Bleecker St. (bet. Bowery & Elizabeth St.)

Subway:	Bleecker St	Sun – Thu 5pm - 11pm
Phone:	212-260-4666	Fri – Sat 5pm - midnight
Fax:	N/A	
Web:	www.biancarestaurantnyc.com	
Prices:	$$	

From its charming owners (the same ones from Teodora on 57th Street) to its intimate seating, Bianca is a darling place that simply radiates warmth. This fetching Italian in the heart of NoLIta is perfect for a date or a get-together with friends. Tables are close together, making diners feel like part of the family, and soft lighting adds to the atmosphere.

Bianca's casual personality extends to its cuisine, genuine Italian food with simple, rustic presentations. Rarely found in the U.S., the *cotechino* (a rustic-style sausage) is a winner. Generous portions of the tasty food and a moderately priced Italian-focused wine list make for a very good value in a city often dominated by overpriced meals.

Open only for dinner, the restaurant does not accept credit cards or reservations.

Blue Hill

015

75 Washington Pl. (bet. Sixth Ave. & Washington Sq. Park)

Subway:	W 4 St - Wash Sq	Mon – Sat 5:30pm - 11pm
Phone:	212-539-1776	Sun 5:30pm - 10pm
Fax:	212-539-0959	
Web:	www.bluehillnyc.com	
Prices:	$$$	

It's not every restaurant that can draw on its own farm for meat and organic vegetables, but luckily for Greenwich Villagers, Blue Hill is one of them. Opened in 2000 by Dan, David and Laureen Barber, Blue Hill occupies a lovely town house near Washington Square Park.

Dan Barber's cuisine incorporates Stone Barns Berkshire pork, New York State guinea hen, Hudson Valley pastured beef, as well as produce grown at the family's farm in Massachusetts. A well-chosen list of international boutique wines complements the food. Note that Blue Hill serves dinner only, though private lunches may be arranged.

If you happen to be up that way, stop by Blue Hill at Stone Barns in Pocantico Hills. This working farm features a restaurant and an educational center, and is a must-see for any serious foodie.

Manhattan Greenwich, West Village & Meatpacking

Blue Ribbon Bakery

Contemporary ✗

016

35 Downing St. (at Bedford St.)

Subway:	Houston St
Phone:	212-337-0404
Fax:	N/A
Web:	www.blueribbonrestaurants.com
Prices:	$$

Mon – Thu noon - midnight
Fri – Sat 11:30am - 2am
Sun 11:30am - midnight

The story of Blue Ribbon Bakery begins with an oven—an abandoned 140-year-old brick oven that brothers Eric and Bruce Bromberg found in the basement of an old bodega in the West Village. Their discovery sparked an idea for a bakery, and they hired a master craftsman from Italy to rebuild the oven. That same appliance now forms the centerpiece of Blue Ribbon Bakery, opened in 1998.

Bread, from challah to country white, baked on-site stars on sandwiches at lunch and appears in a basket at dinner. On the extensive menu you'll find a host of impeccable American dishes, from pigeon to grilled striped bass. But the appetizer list (with some 50 selections) is enough to quell hunger pains alone.

Those in the know frequent the expertly and attractively staffed bar when they want a quick meal.

Bond Street

Japanese ✗✗

017

6 Bond St. (bet. Broadway & Lafayette St.)

Subway:	Bleecker St
Phone:	212-777-2500
Fax:	212-777-6530
Web:	N/A
Prices:	$$$

Sun – Tue 6pm - 11pm
Wed – Sat 6pm - midnight

You'll want to dress to impress at this stylish, always hopping sushi bar—can New Yorkers ever have enough of these?—where the trendy crowd doesn't seem at all concerned about the prices. Sure, they're high—the prices, that is—but the quality of the food stands up to them. Bond Street's ambitious menu lists a wide array of sophisticated sushi, sashimi, rolls and tempura, all well executed and elegantly presented on the plate. The chef, who formerly worked at Nobu, is known for his elaborate creations, like the gold-leaf-topped sushi.

Set in a historic brownstone, the restaurant stretches over three levels: the ground-floor bar/lounge, the main dining room and its lively sushi bar on the second floor, and a third-floor dining space, which includes two tatami rooms.

Café de Bruxelles

018

118 Greenwich Ave. (at 13th St.)

Subway:	14 St (Seventh Ave.)	Open daily noon - 11:30pm
Phone:	212-206-1830	
Fax:	212-229-1436	
Web:	N/A	
Prices:	$$	

Mussels are synonymous with Belgian cuisine, and Café de Bruxelles takes this relationship to heart. You'll know why when you see their menu; it includes an entire section just for mussels—at least ten different preparations. And what would a bowl of mussels be without the café's sublime, crispy frites? Of course, there are plenty of other options, from *waterzooi* to *carbonnade Flamande*; the menu is unabashedly Belgian, for every American to love.

The atmosphere, too, is pure Belgian bistro, complete with photographs of Brussels, exposed brick walls and framed ads for Belgian beer—which the cafe offers plenty of—along with a good list of imported brews. Fair prices make this place popular with a cool, young crowd of Village residents.

Chinatown Brasserie

019

380 Lafayette St. (at Great Jones St.)

Subway:	Bleecker St	Mon – Wed 11:30am - 3:30pm & 5pm - 11:30pm
Phone:	212-533-7000	Thu – Fri 11:30am - 3:30pm & 5pm - midnight
Fax:	212-533-7567	Sat 11am - 3:30pm & 5pm - midnight
Web:	www.chinatownbrasserie.com	Sun 11am - 3:30pm & 5pm - 10pm
Prices:	$$	

Despite a vague feeling of déjà vu, nothing in this restaurant will seem familiar to New Yorkers who remember the space as home to the former Time Café (and Fez downstairs). From the stylish folks behind SoHo's Lure Fishbar and Midtown's Lever House comes a China-chic brasserie with dim sum and then some.

The mammoth place promotes sharing, from the size of the tables to the generous menu. Dim sum is impressive—not quite as authentic as in Chinatown, but approachable for the novice, and served by a friendly staff. In addition to dim sum, the menu includes a mix of Cantonese-American and fusion favorites like General Tso's chicken, and Chinese chicken salad.

Downstairs, the mod lounge—complete with a koi pond—sets the mood for canoodling over creative cocktails.

Crispo

Italian

240 W. 14th St. (bet. Seventh & Eighth Aves.)

Subway:	14 St (Seventh Ave.)	Mon – Thu 5pm - 12:30am
Phone:	212-229-1818	Fri – Sat 5pm - 1am
Fax:	212-229-9979	Sun 4pm - midnight
Web:	www.crisporestaurant.com	
Prices:	$$	

Frank Crispo reigns over the kitchen in his eponymous West Village eatery, recognizable by the black wrought-iron fence that encloses its entrance. Crispo, who cut his teeth in Gotham restaurants like La Côte Basque and Zeppole, presents his culinary artwork against a cozy canvas of rough-hewn brick walls, soft lighting, close-spaced tables and pine flooring.

A do-not-miss starter is the fragrant, air-cured prosciutto di San Daniele, from the Friuli region of northeastern Italy. Its delicate, sweet taste is accented by a variety of Italian cheeses, fruit and vegetables. If you're in the mood for pasta, order the spaghetti carbonara, the restaurant's signature dish and one of the best of its kind in the city.

On weekends, expect a long wait for a table if you don't have a reservation.

Da Silvano

Italian

260 Sixth Ave. (bet. Bleecker & Houston Sts.)

Subway:	W 4 St - Wash Sq	Mon – Thu noon - 11:30pm
Phone:	212-982-2343	Fri – Sat noon - midnight
Fax:	212-982-2254	Sun noon - 11pm
Web:	www.dasilvano.com	Closed major holidays
Prices:	$$	

Think Tuscany. That's the type of simple, rustic food and convivial atmosphere you'll find at Silvano Marchetto's Greenwich Village eatery. Think movie stars. Since he opened in 1975, Marchetto has been pleasing the palates of a good number of film stars, along with a steady supply of media moguls, business leaders and hip Village dwellers.

The menu focuses mainly, but not exclusively (osso buco Milanese, served atop risotto and garnished with gremolata, is a house specialty), on Tuscan dishes and the wine list includes a good selection of Italian labels. Pastas are well-represented here as well, with over a dozen varieties topped with meat, seafood or vegetables.

If you're lucky, you might be able to snag one of the popular sidewalk tables out front for some great people-watching.

De Marco's

022

146 Houston St. (at MacDougal St.)

Subway:	Spring St (Sixth Ave.)	Open daily noon - midnight
Phone:	212-253-2290	
Fax:	N/A	
Web:	N/A	
Prices:	$$	

De Marco's is not your average pizza joint. This cheerful spot on a corner of Houston Street just bordering SoHo is light years away from the typical, ho-hum pizzeria with its neon lights and distracting volume. Exposed brick walls are a focal point in the dining room, which feels significantly nicer than your average pizza joint. Large windows look out over the street, making it a perfect people-watching spot. Cheerful music adds to the atmosphere, and the friendly waiters keep patrons smiling.

Pizza is the standout here, though the menu does provide ample pasta and entrée choices, along with many salads. The De Marco's round pie is the house specialty, with an impossibly thin crust topped with a savory mixture of plentiful mushrooms, sausage, peppers and onions.

El Cid

023

322 W. 15th St. (bet. Eighth & Ninth Aves.)

Subway:	14 St - 8 Av	Tue – Sun 5pm - 11pm
Phone:	212-929-9332	Closed Mon
Fax:	N/A	Closed Sun July - August
Web:	N/A	
Prices:	$$	

This unpretentious little neighborhood eatery may seem out of place in the hip-for-the-moment Meatpacking District, but the truth is, it was here long before the designer boutiques moved in.

Hot and cold tapas provide the food focus in the anything-but-trendy setting, adorned simply with Spanish tiles. Count on the Old World staff to offer careful, kind service to eager crowds. And count on the tapas, from baby eels to chicken, to be flavorful and redolent with garlic. *Gambas al ajillo, chorizo al vino,* and *croquetas* particularly shine. Save room for the signature *torrejas,* a sweet, wine-dipped version of French toast.

A pitcher of sangria makes the perfect quaff here; it comes in red or white versions with enough fruit to liven up the mix, but not so much to clutter your glass.

El Faro

024

823 Greenwich St. (at Horatio St.)

Subway:	14 St - 8 Av	Tue – Thu 11:30am - 11:30pm
Phone:	212-929-8210	Fri – Sat 11:30am - 12:30am
Fax:	212-929-8295	Sun noon - midnight
Web:	www.citysearch.com/nyc/elfaro	Closed Mon
Prices:	$$	

Located in a part of the West Village once known as "Little Spain" for the influx of Spanish immigrants that flocked here in the 1940s after the Spanish Civil War, El Faro began as a bar and grill in 1927. Its current owners, the Lugris and Perez families, purchased the restaurant in 1959 and have run it ever since—and they don't take reservations.

Never mind the aging 1960s-era décor, highlighted by a mural of flamenco dancers that covers the walls of the main dining room; it's the food that stands out here. Paella is a favorite, teeming with seafood and sausages and brought to the table in a traditional double-handled dish. If you crave something light, check out the extensive tapas menu; whatever you order, be sure ask for a pitcher of the house sangria to quench your thirst.

EN Japanese Brasserie

025

435 Hudson St. (at Leroy St.)

Subway:	Houston St	Sun – Thu 5:30pm - 11pm
Phone:	212-647-9196	Fri – Sat 5:30pm - midnight
Fax:	212-647-7550	
Web:	www.enjb.com	
Prices:	$$$	

Brainchild of Japanese restaurateurs and siblings Reika and Bunkei Yo, EN centers on an open kitchen, where the chef and his team craft their own tofu and yuba (the delicate skin that forms when soy milk is heated). A house specialty, yuba appears in dishes such as yuba sashimi and crispy yuba cheese roll stuffed with eel. Tofu, made fresh each night, is available at 90-minute intervals throughout the evening. Signature dishes include black cod in miso, Kakuni-braised Berkshire pork belly in shanso miso and duck-filled croquettes.

True to its name, EN styles itself as a Japanese brasserie. Its industrial-chic, high-ceilinged dining space is decked out in dark woods, glass and stone and embellished with an eye-catching carved-wood screen.

Extra Virgin

026

Mediterranean 🍴

259 W. 4th St. (at Perry St.)

Subway:	Christopher St - Sheridan Sq	Mon – Thu 5:15pm - 11pm
Phone:	212-691-9359	Fri 5pm - midnight
Fax:	212-691-4512	Sat 11am - 4pm & 5pm - midnight
Web:	www.extravirginrestaurant.com	Sun 11am - 4pm & 5:15pm - 11pm
Prices:	**$$**	

Extra Virgin's name, of course, refers to olive oil, which is used liberally in the Mediterranean-inspired dishes served in this West Village brownstone. Mirrors in the bistro-style dining room create a sense of space, and fresh flowers bring the outdoors in. To add to the aesthetics, the young waitresses are as attentive as they are attractive.

Moderate prices mark the menu of simple dishes, where Classics for Two, the restaurant's equivalent of *plats du jour*, change regularly. The specialty cocktails list includes breezy summer specials like blueberry and watermelon margaritas and kiwi caipirinhas. Be sure to save room for dessert, like the warm chocolate cake topped with caramel ice cream. The place is always packed on Sunday for Extra Virgin's popular brunch.

Fatty Crab 😋

Malaysian 🍴

027

643 Hudson St. (bet. Gansevoort & Horatio Sts.)

Subway:	14 St - 8 Av	Sun – Wed noon - midnight
Phone:	212-352-3590	Thu – Sat noon - 4am
Fax:	212-352-3598	
Web:	www.fattycrab.com	
Prices:	**$$**	

Fatty Crab delivers big and bold Malaysian cooking just out of earshot of the bustling Meatpacking district. The diminutive dining room is China-chic, with dark wood tables and antique Chinese chairs, accented with red lacquer and vases of chopsticks on the tables. Rock music complements the entertaining edibles.

Chef Zak Pellacio spent time in Malaysia perfecting his art, and the menu pays tribute to his talents. Go for any of the house specialties, especially the Chili crab, a messy bowl of fun (not ideal for the pre-club crowd) with large pieces of Dungeness crab in a spicy-sweet, tomato chili sauce; or the Fatty Duck, brined, steamed, fried and brushed with a sticky-sweet, soy-chile glaze.

Fatty Crab doesn't take reservations, but it's worth the wait, even during prime time.

5 Ninth

028

Contemporary ✗✗

5 Ninth Ave. (at Little W. 12th St.)

Subway:	14 St - 8 Av	Mon – Fri noon - 5:30pm & 6pm - 11pm
Phone:	212-929-9460	Sat – Sun noon - 5pm & 6pm - 11pm
Fax:	212-929-5103	
Web:	www.5ninth.com	
Prices:	$$$	

One of the Meatpacking's hottest tables, 5 Ninth courts the cognoscenti with an unmarked entrance. Three levels divide the c.1848 brownstone with its shabby-chic décor; an open metal staircase and exposed brick walls suggest the area's erstwhile seediness, while flagstone floors and two fireplaces on each level add sleek touches. A chic crowd prefers the communal table in the enclosed back garden.

Surprising Asian accents and bright flavors bring chef Zak Pellacio's seasonal fare to life. Premium products meld with classic technique to produce unusual and well-balanced dishes. The lunchtime Cuban sandwich may be the best in town. Equally satisfying is the libation list, which runs the gamut from PBR on tap to the White Star Imperial Daisy, made with Moët White Star champagne.

Five Points

029

Contemporary ✗✗

31 Great Jones St. (bet. Bowery & Lafayette St.)

Subway:	Bleecker St	Open daily noon - 3pm & 5pm - midnight
Phone:	212-253-5700	
Fax:	212-529-8643	
Web:	www.fivepointsrestaurant.com	
Prices:	$$	

At Five Points, chef Marc Meyer (who recently launched Cookshop in Chelsea) creates consistently good seasonal American cuisine with Mediterranean flair (such as fava-bean hummus and cornmeal-crusted skate with Sardinian couscous). Many of the dishes—Arctic char, pizzettes, wild salmon—are roasted in the wood oven in the open kitchen.

Lunch is a good time to enjoy updated favorites, like chicken salad dressed with jicama, pineapple and avocado. Locals love the Sunday brunch, which features the likes of lemon-ricotta pancakes, dulce de leche French toast, and a spinach and goat-cheese frittata. Enhancing the atmosphere, a little stream courses through a hollowed-out oak log that runs the length of the dining room.

Drop by during the week from 5pm to 6pm, for $2 oysters and $5 martinis.

Flor's Kitchen

030

170 Waverly Pl. (bet. Sixth & Seventh Aves.)

Subway:	W 4 St - Wash Sq	Sun – Thu 11am - 11pm
Phone:	212-229-9926	Fri – Sat 11am - midnight
Fax:	N/A	
Web:	www.florskitchen.com	
Prices:	🍴🍴	

Flor Villazan whips up Venezuelan comfort food using her family's traditional recipes at this no-frills place. Perhaps "whips up" isn't the right term, since all the dishes are made from scratch. That means no canned corn is used to make the griddle-browned *cachapas* (corn pancakes), and the empanadas are shaped by hand each day. The menu lists a wide variety of ceviches (from shrimp to wild striped bass), and many of the main dishes are served atop yummy plantains. Flor's takes pride in the fact that their food is as good for you as it is tasty. Be sure to try freshly squeezed fruit juices like papaya, mango, tamarind and *papelón* (sugarcane with lemon).

East Siders can get in on the action at Flor's other location *(149 First Ave., between 9th and 10 Sts.)*.

Gavroche

031

212 W. 14th St. (bet. Seventh & Eighth Aves.)

Subway:	14 St (Seventh Ave.)	Tue – Fri & Sun noon - 4pm & 5pm - 11pm
Phone:	212-647-8553	Sat & Mon 5pm - 11pm
Fax:	212-647-1862	Closed major holidays
Web:	www.gavroche-ny.com	
Prices:	$$	

Gavroche is one of the few restaurants on this strip of West 14th Street that is open for lunch, so when you get the urge for some hearty, home-style cuisine *à la Française*, stop by for a plate of coq au vin or steak frites, or settle in for the prix-fixe menu with a choice of appetizer, entrée and dessert. Traditional French bistro dishes are available at dinner, too, along with grilled leg of lamb with raisin couscous, seared tilapia with sautéed potatoes, and wild mushroom ravioli.

Named for the street urchin in *Les Misérables*, Gavroche was opened in 2004 by manager Camelia Cassin. A French-country ambience pervades the small dining room, its bistro tables covered with blue-and-white-checked linen towels. In back, the garden terrace accommodates additional diners in warm weather.

Manhattan Greenwich, West Village & Meatpacking

Gobo

032

401 Sixth Ave. (bet. Waverly Pl. & 8th St.)

Subway:	W 4 St - Wash Sq	Open daily 11:30am - 11pm
Phone:	212-255-3902	
Fax:	212-255-0687	
Web:	www.goborestaurant.com	
Prices:	👓	

Taste, touch, sight, hearing, smell. Gobo (and its Upper East Side sister at 1426 Third Avenue) caters to the five senses with its refined contemporary décor and innovative vegetarian cuisine. Soft neutrals and honey-colored woods highlight the dining area, simply adorned by wooden bowls and glass containers filled with fresh fruit and vegetables.

From quick bites (tea-smoked soy sheets with sautéed mushrooms) to small plates (white bean and cremini-mushroom casserole) to large plates (green-tea noodles with vegan Bolognese sauce), the menu spans the globe for inspiration. An organic juice bar is a perfect alternative to the local coffee shop, and the restaurant even serves organic wines.

The name? It's Japanese for burdock root, long used by herbalists to detoxify the body.

Gusto

033

60 Greenwich Ave. (at Perry St.)

Subway:	14 St (Seventh Ave.)	Mon – Thu noon - 3pm & 5:30pm - 11:30pm
Phone:	212-924-8000	Fri noon - 3pm & 5:30pm - midnight
Fax:	212-924-8055	Sat noon - 4pm & 5:30pm - midnight
Web:	www.gustonyc.com	Sun noon - 4pm & 5:30pm - 10pm
Prices:	$$	Closed major holidays

After significant time spent cooking in Italy, chef Jody Williams worked in the kitchens of some notable New York Italian restaurants before ending up in her own. At Gusto the chef shows off her talents in the rustic, flavorful cuisine that fans follow her for.

From the street-level room with its bright bistro feel to the dark and sultry lower level, the place just oozes style. The appealing and wide-ranging menu hones in on Italy and the Mediterranean with simple but superlative preparations, thoughtfully plated so the presentations don't distract from the food. A full menu is available at the bar, a popular place to dine. Specialty liquors marinate behind the bar and cocktails infused with fresh fruit juices sing with flavor.

It's good to see that Jody has finally found her home.

Hedeh

Contemporary Japanese ✗

57 Great Jones St. (bet. Bowery & Lafayette St.)

Subway:	Bleeker St	Mon – Sat 5pm - midnight
Phone:	212-473-8458	Closed Sun
Fax:	212-473-8509	
Web:	www.hedeh.com	
Prices:	$$	

Opened in late 2003, Hedeh takes the nickname of its chef, Hideyuki Nakajima, formerly of Nobu. Nakajima dreams up an inventive selection of top-quality sushi, maki and sashimi, prepared according to his whim. You'll also find a few crossover dishes inspired by French cuisine (foie gras with balsamic ginger sauce, green-tea crème brûlée), along with the eight-course chef's omakase.

Located at the border of the East Village, Hedeh is a modest place, its contemporary décor limited to neutral colors, soft lighting and a bamboo screen separating the dining room from the sake bar in front. The bar is worth a stop for its impressive list of cold, hot and unfiltered sakes—not to mention Japanese beers. In summer, sake sangria is a popular choice at happy hour.

Home 😊

035

American ✗

20 Cornelia St. (bet. Bleecker & W. 4th Sts.)

Subway:	W 4 St - Wash Sq	Mon – Fri 11:30am - 4pm & 5pm - 11pm
Phone:	212-243-9579	Sat 10:30am - 4:30pm & 5pm - 11pm
Fax:	212-647-9393	Sun 10:30am - 4:30pm & 5:30pm - 10pm
Web:	www.recipesfromhome.com	
Prices:	$$	

Domain of husband-and-wife team Barbara Shinn and chef David Page, Home serves three squares a day, beginning with baked eggs with New York cheddar and homemade salami for breakfast. Bead-board paneling, pine-plank floors and vintage family photographs create a homey atmosphere where you almost expect your own mother to walk out of the kitchen.

Supporters of sustainable agriculture, the owners rely on nearby markets and food shops and local family farms for their kicked-up comfort food; fried chicken, macaroni and cheese with slow-roasted tomatoes, and butterscotch pudding represent a sampling of the home-style American fare served here. Labels from Long Island—including their own vineyard—form the core of the wine list. It seems Dorothy was right all along: There's no place like Home.

Il Buco

036

47 Bond St. (bet. Bowery & Lafayette St.)

Subway:	Bleecker St
Phone:	212-533-1932
Fax:	212-533-3502
Web:	www.ilbuco.com
Prices:	$$

Mon 6pm - midnight
Tue – Sat noon - 4pm & 6pm - midnight
Sun 5pm - 11pm
Closed August 27 - September 7

When independent filmmaker Donna Lennard and her Italian partner Alberto Avalle opened their antique shop in the Village in 1994, little did they guess that they'd be running a restaurant in that same space several years later. Set on cobblestone Bond Street, Il Buco features the aromatic cuisine of Italy and the Iberian Peninsula in a charming dining room that is perfect for a romantic tête-à-tête. Vintage pine pieces and undressed wood tables with painted chairs furnish the room, which is decorated with antique kitchen utensils and plenty of fresh flowers.

The market-based menu changes daily, and constantly looks to the seasons for inspiration. A Mediterranean theme applies to satisfying pasta and risotto dishes, highlights of the tempting selection.

Il Cantinori

037

32 E. 10th St. (bet. Broadway & University Pl.)

Subway:	8 St - NYU
Phone:	212-673-6044
Fax:	212-353-0534
Web:	www.il-cantinori.com
Prices:	$$$

Mon – Thu noon - 3pm & 5pm - 11pm
Fri noon - 3pm & 5pm - midnight
Sat 5pm - midnight
Sun 5pm - 11pm
Closed major holidays

Andy Warhol was a regular at this elegant, off-the-beaten-track restaurant, from the time it opened in 1983. It's not unusual to see other familiar faces here. Nicknamed "the Hollywood Cantina," Il Cantinori has its fair share of celebrity diners (scenes from *Sex and The City* and *The Sopranos* were filmed here). Celebrities, like the not-so-famous patrons, come as much for the food as for the intimate dining room, its tables set with fresh roses. Outdoor seats are shaded by the red-and-green-striped awning.

A meal here starts with a loaf of crusty country bread, complete with fruity olive oil for dipping. The hard part about dining at Il Cantinori is narrowing down your choice from the comprehensive menu of hearty pastas, meat entrées and fish selections. Like the food, the wine list gravitates toward varietals from Tuscany.

Manhattan Greenwich, West Village & Meatpacking

Il Mulino

038

Italian ✗✗

86 W. 3rd St. (bet. Sullivan & Thompson Sts.)

Subway:	W 4 St - Wash Sq
Phone:	212-673-3783
Fax:	212-673-9875
Web:	www.ilmulinonewyork.com
Prices:	$$$$

Mon – Fri noon - 2pm & 5pm - 11pm
Sat 5pm - 11pm
Closed Sun & July

♿

Mouth-watering displays of Italian wines, olive oils, fruits and vegetables tantalize you as you enter the small, flatteringly lit dining room at this Italian institution (opened in 1981) in the heart of Greenwich Village. Reservations are hard to come by; a cadre of regulars packs the place night after night (lunch reservations are easier to get).

Cuisine here centers on the bold, garlicky flavors of the Abruzzi region, where the owners, Fernando and Gino Masci, were born. Everything here is abbondanza-size, from the gorgeous antipasto to the signature veal dishes. Expect larger-than-life black-tie service and hefty prices to match.

Il Mulino also packages its marinara sauce, along with coffee, olive oil and balsamic vinegar, for purchase.

Jarnac

039

Contemporary French ✗✗

328 W. 12th St. (at Greenwich St.)

Subway:	14 St - 8 Av
Phone:	212-924-3413
Fax:	212-414-2505
Web:	www.jarnacny.com
Prices:	$$

Tue – Thu 6pm - 10pm
Fri – Sat 6pm - 11pm
Sun 11am - 2:30pm & 6pm - 10pm
Closed Mon & major holidays

Expect to find a good selection of cognacs on Jarnac's menu, since the restaurant is named for the city in the Poitou-Charentes region of France that is home to the famed cognac producer Courvoisier. Indeed, owner Tony Powe honors the town where he grew up by offering a host of cognacs from a handful of different producers.

Contemporary French fare is interpreted with an American flair here, and the menu changes daily to reflect what's fresh and in season (in spring the menu incorporates products like wild ramps, fava beans and soft shell crabs, while in winter the cassoulet wins raves). All appetizers and salads can be ordered as entrée-size plates.

Fans of Jarnac may want to join the restaurant's club, which offers special dinners, tastings and cooking courses.

Manhattan Greenwich, West Village & Meatpacking

Kirara

040

33 Carmine St. (bet. Bedford & Bleecker Sts.)

Subway:	W 4 St - Wash Sq	Mon – Fri noon - 11pm
Phone:	212-741-2123	Sat – Sun 5pm - 11pm
Fax:	N/A	
Web:	N/A	
Prices:	$$	

If you're feeling adventurous at this family-run restaurant, ask about the omakase, or tasting menu. In Japanese, *omakase* means "to put yourself in the chef's hands," so go ahead and trust his judgment regarding your meal. You'll be treated to an assortment of the chef's choice of appetizers, followed by a generous platter of sushi and sashimi; it's a great idea for sharing. Of course, you can always order off the à la carte menu if you prefer. Gentle pricing ensures that Kirara is a local favorite, and takeout is a popular option for those who live nearby.

Whatever you order, you'll be treated to artfully presented dishes, since chef/owner John Hur is an artist himself. Admire his Japanese-style paintings on the walls of the restaurant.

Le Gigot

French

041

18 Cornelia St. (bet. Bleecker & W. 4th Sts.)

Subway:	W 4 St - Wash Sq	Tue – Sun noon - 2:30pm & 5pm - 11pm
Phone:	212-627-3737	Closed Mon
Fax:	212-627-1188	
Web:	N/A	
Prices:	$$	

"A great place to take a date" is how many regulars characterize this cozy little bistro, located on the same charming West Village block as Pó and Home. Of course, you'd expect to find leg of lamb on the menu (since that's what *le gigot* means in French), and so you will; Senegalese chef Alioune Ndiaye's version is an uncomplicated preparation, served with flageolet beans. Other country French dishes include coquilles St. Jacques and lamb stew. Fresh, healthy bistro food here avoids heavy cream sauces in favor of lighter fare, including several vegetarian selections.

The handful of tables may cluster elbow to elbow, but the service is eager and smiling, and the Gallic ambience, complete with French posters, oversized mirrors and varnished woods, invites romance.

Lupa

Italian 🍴

042

170 Thompson St. (bet. Bleecker & Houston Sts.)

Subway: W 4 St - Wash Sq
Phone: 212-982-5089
Fax: 212-982-5490
Web: www.luparestaurant.com
Prices: $$

Open daily noon - midnight
Closed Thanksgiving & Christmas Day

Brought to you by the team of Mario Batali, Joseph Bastianich, Jason Denton and Mark Ladner (the partnership behind Babbo and Esca), Lupa stands out as a pearl among a string of Italian establishments that line Thompson Street. The restaurant is Roman from its trattoria menu to its name, a reference to the she-wolf in Roman mythology.

Offering the best authentic seasonal ingredients at reasonable prices is the philosophy here. Lupa achieves that goal with its own *salumeria* that features Italian artisanal meats and cheeses, and by making fresh pastas and other products (like canned tuna) in-house. Lunch and dinner both offer a creative and traditional assortment of dishes—including an exemplary spaghetti alla carbonara—along with a generous list of wines from regions throughout Italy.

Macelleria

Italian 🍴

043

48 Gansevoort St. (bet. Greenwich & Washington Sts.)

Subway: 14 St - 8 Av
Phone: 212-741-2555
Fax: N/A
Web: www.macelleriarestaurant.com
Prices: $$

Mon – Fri noon - midnight
Sat – Sun 11am - midnight

In keeping with its past incarnation as a meat warehouse, Macelleria (Italian for "butcher shop") decks out its cavernous space with dangling meat hooks and carving tables to suggest its former use. Its lively, informal ambience is part industrial-chic (high ceiling, brick walls, exposed pipes), part sunny Italian tavola.

And, as you might guess, steakhouse items play a big role on a short menu otherwise filled by Italian fare. Fresh pastas and cheeses influence the daily changing menu. Chestnut ravioli and roasted duck with orange sauce are among the most-ordered dishes. The food isn't inexpensive, but generous portions compensate for the cost. Downstairs, the stone-walled wine cellar—where Italian vintages predominate—doubles as a private dining room.

Mary's Fish Camp

044

64 Charles St. (at W. 4th St.)

Subway:	Christopher St - Sheridan Sq	Mon – Sat noon - 3pm & 6pm - 11pm
Phone:	646-486-2185	Closed Sun & September 1 - 15
Fax:	646-486-6703	
Web:	www.marysfishcamp.com	
Prices:	$$	

Mary Redding opened this tiny Florida-style seafood joint in a West Village brownstone in 2000 and has been enjoying wild success ever since. Her lobster rolls overflow with succulent chunks of meat, slathered in mayonnaise and piled on a buttered hotdog bun—they might be messy, but they sure are good! Other selections such as conch chowder and conch fritters recall Key West cuisine, while lobster pot pie, Chatham cod filet, and raw oysters pay homage to the bounty of New England waters (take a seat at the counter, if you want to watch the chefs deftly shucking your oysters). Sides like French fries, spinach, and grilled corn on the cob accompany the delicious, fresh preparations.

Bear in mind that Mary's only serves seafood, and the restaurant doesn't accept reservations, but the counter couldn't be better for dining on your own.

Mas

045

39 Downing St. (bet. Bedford & Varick Sts.)

Subway:	Houston St	Mon – Sat 6pm - 4am
Phone:	212-255-1790	Closed Sun
Fax:	212-255-0279	
Web:	www.masfarmhouse.com	
Prices:	$$$	

Think French country farmhouse, and you've got Mas, literally (mas refers to the farmhouses of Provence) and figuratively. Amid barn wood and aged beams, a long leather banquette, Prouvé chairs and antique flatware, you'll find yourself ensconced in a rustic-chic ambience. This little slice of old Provence in the heart of the Village draws an equally laid-back, yet hip crowd.

Swiss-born chef Galen Zamarra (who formerly worked at the late Bouley Bakery) revels in putting new spins on classic preparations, as in rainbow trout stuffed with wild ramps. Add to this an intriguing wine list and wonderful service and you have a sure recipe for success. Partyers looking for a place to have a late—as in really late—bite, will appreciate that Mas stays open until 4am.

Manhattan Greenwich, West Village & Meatpacking

Mexicana Mama

046

525 Hudson St. (bet. Charles & 10th Sts.)

Subway:	Christopher St - Sheridan Sq	Tue – Sun noon - 11pm
Phone:	212-924-4119	Closed Mon
Fax:	N/A	
Web:	N/A	
Prices:	⚌	

S

A little restaurant with a big heart, Mexicana Mama raises south-of-the-border cuisine to new heights with food as bright as its décor (purple walls, tables painted in primary colors). Flavors shine in dishes like chicken with mole, and roasted chile relleno served with aromatic green rice that gets its color from the addition of cilantro and poblano chile. Delicious vegetables serve as the inspiration behind quesadillas and burritos, and the pork tacos are always a hit. Save room for the rich *pastel tres leches* (otherwise known as cake with three milks).

This unpretentious and popular place features good food for a good price—and if you're lucky enough to live in the neighborhood, they offer takeout and local delivery.

Old Homestead

047

56 Ninth Ave. (bet. 14th & 15th Sts.)

Subway:	14 St - 8 Av	Mon – Thu noon - 10:45pm
Phone:	212-242-9040	Fri noon - 11:45pm
Fax:	212-727-1637	Sat 1pm - 11:45pm
Web:	www.theoldhomesteadsteakhouse.com	Sun 1pm - 9:45pm
Prices:	$$$$	

This classic steakhouse has stood in the Meatpacking District since 1868, way before it ever became the trendy neighborhood it is today. Old Homestead is a wealthy-guy's-night-out kind of place, with its gentleman's-club-meets-French bistro décor.

Remember that old saying about never eating anything bigger than your head? You'll have to ignore it at this steakhouse, where the "Empire Cut" of prime rib weighs in at two pounds, and the four-and-a-half-pound lobsters are fittingly billed as "whale-size." Signature dishes include the domestically raised Kobe-style beef and the legendary $41 hamburger.

Prices may be high, but the meat is top quality, the service is professional, and the elegant dining rooms are papered with photographs of the district in the early 20th century.

One if by Land, Two if by Sea

048

Contemporary ✕✕

17 Barrow St. (bet. Seventh Ave. South & W. 4th St.)

Subway:	Christopher St - Sheridan Sq	Sun – Thu 5:30pm - 10pm
Phone:	212-255-8649	Fri – Sat 5:15pm - 11:15pm
Fax:	212-206-7855	
Web:	www.oneifbyland.com	
Prices:	$$$	

Despite the name (a reference to the lantern hung in Boston's Old North Church in 1775 to warn the colonists of approaching British troops), Paul Revere did not sleep here. This 18th-century carriage house originally formed part of the Richmond Hill estate. It was restored as a restaurant in the late 1960s and opened in 1972.

Well-executed American fare (spice-marinated Maine lobster; rack of lamb; smoked breast of duck) stars on both the three-course prix-fixe menu and the chef's multicourse tasting. Beef Wellington is the specialty of the house. The lovely two-story brick building, with its four fireplaces, candlelit tables and live piano music, is justly touted as one of the most romantic restaurants in the city. If you have any important proposals to make, this is the place to do it.

Ono

049

Japanese ✕✕

18 Ninth Ave. (at 13th St.)

Subway:	14 St - 8 Av	Mon – Wed noon - 3pm & 5:30pm - 11:30pm
Phone:	212-660-6766	Thu – Fri noon - 3pm & 5:30pm - 12:30am
Fax:	N/A	Sat 11:30am - 3pm & 5:30pm - 12:30am
Web:	www.chinagrillmgt.com	Sun 11:30am - 3pm & 5:30pm - 11:30pm
Prices:	$$$	

Housed in the Gansevoort Hotel *(see hotel listings)*, Ono is all about style. "O-no" is also the reaction Jeffrey Chodorow's wife had when he told her he'd be adding another notch to his restaurant-management belt. The beautiful people flock here to the bamboo-filled outdoor garden, complete with its retractable roof, reflecting pool and cabanas.

The action begins at the bar, where silk-tunic-clad bartenders mix drinks with names like Blushing Geisha and Blue Yuzu. But the real show centers on the open kitchen, where you can watch the chefs prepare robatayaki, meats grilled over an open flame. The large menu focuses on traditional Japanese fare along with creative sushi combinations. And how cool is the edamame "alphabet soup," poured over cubes of tofu carved to form the letters O-N-O?

Otto

050

1 Fifth Ave. (at 8th St.)

Subway:	W 4 St - Wash Sq	Open daily 11:30am - midnight
Phone:	212-995-9559	
Fax:	212-995-9052	
Web:	www.ottopizzeria.com	
Prices:	$$	

Fans of chef Mario Batali flock to Otto, among the more modest of his establishments, which bills itself as an enoteca/pizzeria. The enoteca part refers to the restaurant's remarkable number (700) of unique and good value Italian wines. For the pizzeria part, thin-crust pies are cooked on a flat-iron griddle, and are complemented by a menu of pasta, seafood, cured meats and more. The menu's variety makes it ideal for sharing, and easily accommodates groups and families, who jam the spacious dining room and bar even at off hours.

The lively bar area is a great place to wait for a table and sample some of the excellent wines poured by the glass. For impatient types, Otto also delivers—or you can get your pizza to go, along with a pint or two of the yummy house-made gelato.

Palma

051

28 Cornelia St. (bet. Bleecker & W. 4th Sts.)

Subway:	W 4 St - Wash Sq	Open daily 11am - midnight
Phone:	212-691-2223	
Fax:	212-691-3910	
Web:	www.palmanyc.com	
Prices:	$$	

A new addition to a lively Greenwich Village restaurant row, Palma exudes a Mediterranean vibe with its sunflower-yellow façade, rustic wood beams and candlelit dining area. The menu leans toward Sicilian dishes, with an emphasis on fresh, simply prepared seafood (whole roasted lobster; sautéed swordfish with fresh mint, capers and tomato-olive salad; sea bass grilled with herbs and lemon). The house specialty is the *frutti di mare al cartoccio*. And if you're not up for a big meal, half-portions are available.

Service is casual and efficient, and moderate prices give this place wide appeal. Weekend brunch offers a bargain set-price option that includes baked goods, your choice of entrée (Palermo omelet, Tuscan ham and eggs, Benedict bruschetta) and side item, plus a cocktail.

Manhattan Greenwich, West Village & Meatpacking

Paradou

French French

052

8 Little W. 12th St. (bet. Greenwich & Washington Sts.)

Subway:	14 St - 8 Av	Mon – Wed 6pm - midnight
Phone:	212-463-8345	Thu – Fri 6pm - 1am
Fax:	646-435-0621	Sat 11am - 1am
Web:	www.paradounyc.com	Sun 11am - 10pm
Prices:	$$	

Step into Provence through the weathered French-blue doors of Paradou, which recalls a town in the South of France whose name means "paradise." White-washed walls, high ceilings and tables fashioned out of vintage French wine crates create an airy, country ambience.

Like the atmosphere, the food is Mediterranean in spirit; dishes from that sun-washed region share the menu with the likes of chicken grand-mère and Provençal thick-cut pork chops. After your meal, go straight for the plate of four truffles, handmade by chocolatier Joel Durand in 32 different flavors that capture the essence of Provence. Brunch is an entirely French affair, offering items like crab Napoleon, tarte Tatin and seafood aïoli.

In summer, the verdant garden out back makes a hidden oasis for dining. Ah, paradise.

Pastis

French

053

9 Ninth Ave. (at Little W. 12th St.)

Subway:	14 St - 8 Av	Mon – Thu 8am - 2am
Phone:	212-929-4844	Fri – Sat 9am - 3am
Fax:	212-929-5676	Sun 9am - 2am
Web:	www.pastisny.com	
Prices:	$$	

A classic New York success story, Pastis was one of the first hot spots here, back when the now-booming Meatpacking District was still a bit sleepy. Today this ever-popular restaurant still packs in a fashionable flock from breakfast through dinner, and celebs sightings are a given.

Brought to you by restaurateur Keith McNally, Pastis transports diners back to the south of France circa 1960 with its large decorative mirrors, long zinc bar, bistro tables and walls lined with vintage Pastis ads. The menu includes all the French classics that locals love (skate, onion soup gratinée, steak frites, moules frites—it's really all about the frites here). As you'd expect, the cocktail list leans heavily on the restaurant's namesake anise-flavored aperitif, which originally hails from Marseille.

Pearl Oyster Bar 😊

054

18 Cornelia St. (bet. Bleecker & W. 4th Sts.)

Subway:	W 4 St - Wash Sq	Mon – Fri noon - 2:30pm & 6pm - 11pm
Phone:	212-691-8211	Sat 6pm - 11pm
Fax:	212-691-8210	Closed Sun & February 4 - 10 and
Web:	www.pearloysterbar.com	September 3 - 8
Prices:	$$	

You won't find fresher fish for the price in Manhattan than at Pearl Oyster Bar. This beloved eatery, once just a 12-seat bar, has expanded with a small dining room in order to handle a bustling business of shellfish aficionados, but its no-reservations policy still means that waits can be long.

Chef/owner Rebecca Charles named the restaurant for her grandmother, in memory of childhood summers she spent in Maine. The food is New England through and through: wonderful oysters, creamy clam chowder and the gargantuan lobster roll—chunks of fresh lobster moistened with seasoned mayonnaise, tossed with a hint of celery and parsley and served on a toasted bun with a side of shoestring fries. And don't forget the blueberry crumble pie, another Maine staple, for dessert.

Piccolo Angolo

055

621 Hudson St. (at Jane St.)

Subway:	14 St - 8 Av	Tue – Thu 5pm - 10pm
Phone:	212-229-9177	Fri – Sat 5pm - 11pm
Fax:	N/A	Sun 4pm - 10pm
Web:	N/A	Closed Mon & August 14 - 31
Prices:	$$	

Sited at the "little corner" (piccolo angolo in Italian) of Hudson and Jane streets, this family-run Italian place is constantly packed with a throng of diners willing to wait in line for chef Mario Migliorini's wonderful food. If you're looking for a quiet place, you'd best go elsewhere; Piccolo Angolo is noisy, crowded and the tables are squeezed together like sardines in a can. It may be a tight fit, but the vibe is friendly and welcoming. Mario's brother, Renato Migliorini, runs the front of the house with aplomb.

That said, the house-made pastas are superior, the fresh tomato sauce is redolent with garlic and fragrant with basil, and the toasted garlic bread is even more terrific if you dip it in a bit of fruity olive oil.

The Place

Contemporary ✗✗

056

310 W. 4th St. (bet. Bank & 12th Sts.)

Subway:	14 St - 8 Av
Phone:	212-924-2711
Fax:	212-929-8213
Web:	www.theplaceny.com
Prices:	$$

Mon – Thu 6pm - 10:30pm
Fri 6pm - 11pm
Sat 5:30pm - 11pm
Sun 5:30pm - 10pm

Looking for a restaurant for that intimate tête-à-tête? This is The Place. With its grotto-like dining space carved into a series of cozy, dimly lit rooms with rough stone walls and a beamed ceiling, this is certainly the place for romance. White-linen-clad tables are brightened by candles and fresh flowers, and the service is obliging and efficient.

The food is an ever-evolving roster of carefully prepared American fare, based on fresh market produce. Tender leg of lamb, for example, is roasted to your taste and accompanied by rosemary potatoes and provençal vegetables; homemade fettucini is tossed with roasted tomatoes, toasted garlic, zucchini, baby eggplant, fresh thyme and shaved parmesan.

A second location *(142 W. 10th St.)* plates up equally good food.

Pó

Italian ✗

057

31 Cornelia St. (bet. Bleecker & W. 4th Sts.)

Subway:	W 4 St - Wash Sq
Phone:	212-645-2189
Fax:	212-367-9448
Web:	www.porestaurant.com
Prices:	$$

Mon – Tue 5:30pm - 11pm
Wed – Sun 11:30am - 2:30pm
& 5:30pm - 11pm

Tables aren't easy to come by at this Greenwich Village favorite. Housed in a former coffeehouse/theater (its founder was an out-of-work dancer who staged short plays and served cake and coffee here), Pó was the starting point for clog-wearing chef Mario Batali. He has since moved on from his original kitchen, but the restaurant remains popular for its contemporary Italian fare. The waitstaff buoys up the convivial mood in the tiny dining room with cheerful, attentive service.

High-quality food at reasonable prices rules here; the four- and six-course tasting menus are the best deals. Fresh pastas are delectable, and entrées are rustic works of art, with choices like dark-beer-braised short ribs and grilled guinea hen. The short wine list includes a nice selection by the glass.

Prem-on Thai

058

138 Houston St. (bet. MacDougal & Sullivan Sts.)

Subway:	Spring St (Sixth Ave.)	Mon – Thu noon - 11:30pm
Phone:	212-353-2338	Fri noon - midnight
Fax:	212-353-2320	Sat 3:30pm - midnight
Web:	www.prem-on.com	Sun 3:30pm - 11pm
Prices:	$$	

Perfectly positioned on Houston Street, Prem-on Thai pleases with its modern décor, hip ambience and refined Thai cuisine. The dining space is broken up into several small rooms with a small garden in back. Dark wood tables are left without cloths, and Buddhas, bamboo, and Asian flower decals adorn the rooms (consistently trendy, the men's and women's bathroom stalls are adjacent to each other with a shared sink—not for the overly modest).

On the menu, spring rolls and pad Thai pay homage to the familiar, while crisp and soft noodle curry represents regional dishes rarely found in the city. With every dish, the kitchen pays great attention to presentation. The bargain lunch special, a choice of appetizer and entrée arranged on the same plate, will set you back less than $10.

Sevilla 😊

059

62 Charles St. (at W. 4th St.)

Subway:	Christopher St - Sheridan Sq	Mon – Thu noon - midnight
Phone:	212-929-3189	Fri – Sat noon - 1am
Fax:	212-645-5729	Sun 1pm - midnight
Web:	www.sevillarestaurantandbar.com	
Prices:	$$	

There's something to be said for age. Although Sevilla has been around since 1941, it retains a warm patina in its taberna-style interior. Jose Lloves, who hails from northern Spain, acquired the restaurant in 1962 and has been running it ever since.

Tradition reigns here, starting with the attentive waiters (many of whom have worked here for years), and continuing with the menu, which offers a slice of Spain in its delightful paellas, seafood and meat dishes. Light, refreshing sangria makes the perfect accompaniment to heaping portions of Spanish favorites, all authentically fragrant and garlicky.

Sevilla doesn't take reservations, but if you go during the week when it's a bit quieter, ask for a table by the windows, which look out on one of the most charming blocks in the West Village.

Manhattan Greenwich, West Village & Meatpacking

Spice Market

060

403 W. 13th St. (at Ninth Ave.)

Subway:	14 St - 8 Av	Open daily noon - 3:30pm & 5:30pm - midnight
Phone:	212-675-2322	
Fax:	212-675-4551	
Web:	www.jean-georges.com	
Prices:	$$$	

Another venture by Jean-Georges Vongerichten, Spice Market is a Meatpacking District hot spot. The cuisine concept is inspired by Southeast Asian food—what you might nosh on while roaming marketplace stalls in Thailand or Malaysia. Subtly seasoned dishes (chicken samosas, red curried duck, pork vindaloo) are placed in the middle of the table, for all to enjoy.

Realized by Jacques Garcia, the design transforms the mood inside this 12,000-square-foot former warehouse from industrial to brooding and sexy, in deep shades of red, violet and gold. A large teak pagoda takes center stage, while wooden arches divide the seating areas. The crowd is strictly A-list, especially in the evenings. For those who want to party VIP-style, the private rooms downstairs offer the perfect setting to do so.

Strip House

061

13 E. 12th St. (bet. Fifth Ave. & University Pl.)

Subway:	14 St - Union Sq	Mon – Sat 5pm - 11:30pm
Phone:	212-328-0000	Sun 5pm - 10pm
Fax:	212-337-0233	
Web:	www.theglaziergroup.com	
Prices:	$$$	

A seductive name, yes—but don't go peeling your clothes off just yet. The "strip" here refers to steak, although the suggestive logo and the alluring décor, in deep bordello-red with photos of semi-nude pinup girls on the walls, might lead you to think otherwise.

Broiled New York strip is the signature dish, available in single or double cut. Then there are the standard steakhouse offerings: filet mignon, veal chops and rack of Colorado lamb (besides the requisite lobster; the menu lists a few seafood entrées, too). Sides (all à la carte) such as potatoes crisped in goose fat, and rich black-truffle creamed spinach are not for the faint of arteries, nor are the huge dessert portions.

Additional locations take the Strip House's recipe for success to New Jersey, Florida and Texas.

Surya

Indian ✗✗

062

302 Bleecker St. (bet. Grove St. & Seventh Ave. South)

Subway:	Christopher St - Sheridan Sq	Sun – Thu noon - 3pm & 5pm - 11pm
Phone:	212-807-7770	Fri – Sat noon - 3pm & 5pm - midnight
Fax:	212-337-0695	
Web:	www.suryany.com	
Prices:	$$	

There is much that is sunny about this unassuming little Indian restaurant in the West Village. First, there's the name, which means "sun" in Tamil. Then there's the sleek décor, done in blazing tones of orange and red; and the service, which is delivered with a politeness and a warmth that's rare to find.

Last, but not least, there's a host of meat and vegetable dishes on the menu, which focuses on the aromatic cuisine of Southern India. Lamb, chicken and shrimp are all prepared tandoori-style, cooked over high heat in a traditional Indian clay oven. The sauces that bathe the dishes—aside from the tandoori items—are especially rich, flavorful and well balanced with a desirable elegance.

No time to sit down for lunch? From noon until 3pm, you can pick up a box lunch to go.

Tomoe Sushi

Japanese ✗

063

172 Thompson St. (bet. Bleecker & Houston Sts.)

Subway:	Spring St (Sixth Ave.)	Mon – Sat noon - 3pm & 5pm - 11pm
Phone:	212-777-9346	Closed Sun
Fax:	N/A	
Web:	N/A	
Prices:	ඏ	

Patience is clearly the virtue to have if you're planning dinner at Tomoe Sushi, where the wait in the evening can range up to an hour or more. Why all the buzz? Diners sure don't come for the spartan décor, which consists of a small sushi bar, bare pine tables and specials scrawled on pieces of paper.

They do come, though, for the high-quality fish, which is cut in large pieces for those who don't relish bite-size morsels of sushi and sashimi. Of course, if you're squeamish about sushi, there's cooked seafood, too. You might want to give a second thought to Japanese desserts here. Tomoe's creamy version of cheesecake is scented with green tea and served with a coulis of red fruits.

The only downside? Long waits followed by rushed service can be a drag.

Vento

Italian ✗✗

064

675 Hudson St. (at 14th St.)

Subway:	14 St – 8 Av
Phone:	212-699-2400
Fax:	212-699-2401
Web:	www.brguestrestaurants.com
Prices:	$$

Mon noon - 4pm & 5pm - 11pm
Tue – Thu noon - 4pm & 5pm - midnight
Fri – Sat noon - 4pm & 5pm - 1am
Sun 11am - 4pm & 5pm - 11pm

Vento is a casual incarnation of chef/partner Michael White's SoHo outpost, Fiamma Osteria. When the weather is warm and the breeze is coming off the river, there's no place like Vento's prime corner spot to see and be seen.

The menu is ideal for sharing, and a convivial meal materializes effortlessly from the small plates of cheeses, olives, and other Mediterranean starters. Wood-fired pizzas, house-made pastas, whole-roasted fish, and meats round out your family-style feast. If you run out of room for dessert, house-made gelati and sorbetti are available to go. Brunch brings a chic crowd to the pie-shaped dining space, which is lined on two sides with full-length windows, and a bar in the back.

Stick around to check out the late-night scene in the downstairs bar, called Level V.

Zutto

Japanese ✗

065

62 Greenwich Ave. (bet. Seventh Ave. South & 11th St.)

Subway:	14 St (Seventh Ave.)
Phone:	212-367-7204
Fax:	N/A
Web:	www.sushizutto.com
Prices:	🍤🍤

Mon – Sat noon - 2:15pm
& 5pm - 10:30pm
Sun 5pm - 10pm

Surrounded by vintage clothing stores and coffee shops, Zutto's second outpost holds sway in this little brick town house (the restaurant's original home is at 77 Hudson Street in TriBeCa; there's a third location in Great Neck, on Long Island). Zutto's name may sound Italian, but its tag line, "It's Japanese," dispels any doubt.

Outside, a wrought-iron sign announces the restaurant, while inside, the décor invents an Asian feel with its simple blond wood tables, bamboo shades and Japanese calligraphy. All the usual fare is reasonably priced here. For dinner, the Bento boxes are available in combinations of sushi or sashimi, tempura or shumai, and your choice of teriyaki. Special maki rolls include the buffalo roll, made with spicy tuna, avocado and caviar.

After 100 years of reviewing restaurants, we've still kept our figure.

We've gained something important from a century of evaluating restaurants and hotels: trust. Our professionally trained inspectors anonymously rate quality, service, and atmosphere so you get the real story. To learn more, visit michelintravel.com.

MICHELIN
A better way forward

Harlem

This incredibly diverse neighborhood has a split personality. East of Fifth Avenue and north of East 97th Street lies East Harlem, with its distinctive Puerto Rican flavor. Northwest of Fifth Avenue is central Harlem, the most famous African-American community in America. This area is bounded by West 145th Street to the north, 110th Street to the south, Frederick Douglass Boulevard, West 116th Street and the Hudson River to the west, and Fifth Avenue and the Harlem River to the east.

A Bit of History – Dutch governor Peter Stuyvesant established Nieuw Haarlem in northern Manhattan in 1658. The hamlet remained largely rural until the railroad and the elevated trains linked it to the rest of the city in the first half of the 19th century. By the 1890s, Harlem was an affluent residential area. Overbuilding took its toll early in the 20th century, as the real-estate market slumped and landlords rented to working-class black families moving to better living conditions from the West Side.

Harlem's golden era, the **Harlem Renaissance**, lasted from 1919 to 1929. During this period, writers Langston Hughes and Zora Neale Thurston electrified the world with their originality. Night-clubs—including the original Cotton Club—hosted performances by jazz greats Duke Ellington, Count Basie, and Cab Calloway. Everything changed with the Depression. Jobs became scarce and poverty set in. By the 1960s, a climate of violence and crime overran Harlem, forcing many middle-class families to leave.

21st-Century Renaissance – Today, a renaissance of another sort is taking place. Investors are renovating old brownstones; even Bill Clinton chose Harlem for his post-presidential office. West 125th Street, the main thoroughfare, teems with fast-food joints and chain stores. Tour buses fill with visitors, who come to marvel at the neighborhood's wealth of architectural and cultural treasures, such as the historic **Apollo Theater** *(253 W. 125th St.)*—which still packs in the crowds. And soul food restaurants dish up hearty servings of southern fried chicken, collard greens, black-eyed peas and candied yams.

West 125th Street

© Martha Cooper

With so many outsiders swarming the neighborhood, though, residents wonder if Harlem will be able to retain its unique character as an African-American community. Only time will tell.

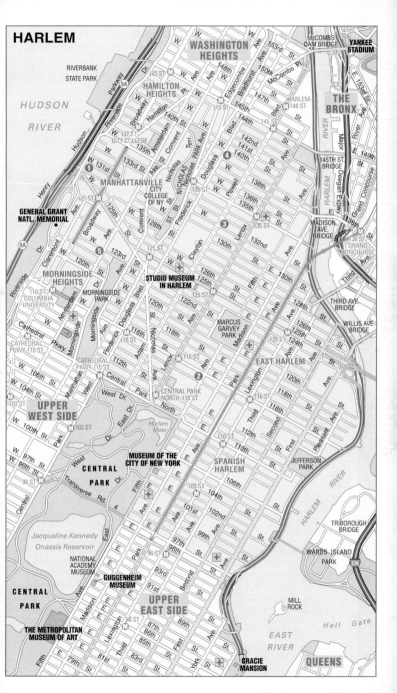

HARLEM

WASHINGTON HEIGHTS

McCOMBS DAM BRIDGE

YANKEE STADIUM

RIVERBANK STATE PARK

HAMILTON HEIGHTS

THE BRONX

HUDSON RIVER

CITY COLLEGE

MANHATTANVILLE

CITY COLLEGE OF NY

HARLEM-148th

MADISON AVE. BRIDGE

GRAND CONCOURSE

GENERAL GRANT NATL. MEMORIAL

STUDIO MUSEUM IN HARLEM

THIRD AVE. BRIDGE

MORNINGSIDE HEIGHTS

COLUMBIA UNIVERSITY

MORNINGSIDE PARK

WILLIS AVE. BRIDGE

EAST HARLEM

CATHEDRAL PKWY. 110 ST

MARCUS GARVEY PARK

UPPER WEST SIDE

CENTRAL PARK NORTH-110TH ST

Harlem Meer

MUSEUM OF THE CITY OF NEW YORK

SPANISH HARLEM

JEFFERSON PARK

CENTRAL PARK

Transverse Rd.

HARLEM RIVER

TRIBOROUGH BRIDGE

Jacqueline Kennedy Onassis Reservoir

WARDS ISLAND PARK

NATIONAL ACADEMY MUSEUM

GUGGENHEIM MUSEUM

MILL ROCK

CENTRAL PARK

UPPER EAST SIDE

Hell Gate

THE METROPOLITAN MUSEUM OF ART

EAST RIVER

QUEENS

GRACIE MANSION

Dinosaur Bar-B-Que 👁️

001

646 W. 131st St. (at Twelfth Ave.)

Subway:	125 St (Broadway)
Phone:	212-694-1777
Fax:	212-694-9072
Web:	www.dinosaurbarbque.com
Prices:	$$

Tue – Thu 11:30am - 11pm
Fri – Sat 11:30am - midnight
Sun noon - 10pm
Closed Mon

Dinosaur Bar-B-Que has become a destination. Though it's off the beaten path in Harlem, Dinosaur lures a spirited crowd from bikers to yuppies who flock here by car (parking is nearby) or subway (a few blocks away) for finger-licking-good barbecue and down-home décor (walls lined with license plates, beer signs, and sports paraphernalia).

Dinosaur is an outpost of the original Syracuse restaurant, and the menu is almost identical. Unlike most New York City barbecue joints, Dinosaur smokes their own meat, and everything from pulled pork, ribs, brisket, sausage and chicken is drenched in the restaurant's succulent sauces—also sold by the bottle to bring home. Sides of honey hush cornbread, mac and cheese, deviled eggs and fried green tomatoes round out the belly-busting meals.

Ginger

002

1400 Fifth Ave. (at 116th St.)

Subway:	116 St (Lenox Ave.)
Phone:	212-423-1111
Fax:	212-423-5955
Web:	www.gingerexpress.com
Prices:	$$

Mon – Thu 5pm - 10:30pm
Fri 5pm - 11:30pm
Sat noon - 4:30pm & 5pm - 11:30pm
Sun noon - 4:30pm & 5pm - 10:30pm

Ginger is an eye-popping sign of the times. Poised between East and West Harlem, which has been experiencing an exciting renaissance after years of neglect, Ginger brings an audacious concept to this bustling neighborhood's culinary scene. This restaurant delivers healthy, fresh and low-fat Chinese food. Avoiding oils, MSG and frying, Ginger's organic-based cuisine is delicious and the portions are large—a good reason to come here with a bit appetite. Marinated spicy tofu is a vegetarian's dream; stir-fry dishes are available with meat, chicken or seafood; and a delightful selection of healthy sides proves a perfect complement to any meal.

The dramatic space is sleek and gorgeous, with warm rosy-toned lighting, sexy dark woods and unique decorative accents showing off an Asian-chic style.

Harlem Grill

003

American 🍴🍴

2247 Adam Clayton Powell Blvd. (bet. 132nd & 133rd Sts.)

Subway: 135 St (Lenox Ave.)
Phone: 212-491-0493
Fax: 212-491-0494
Web: www.harlemgrill.com
Prices: $$

Mon – Sat 6pm - 11:30pm
Closed Sun
Closed Mon in Summer

Opened at the beginning of 2005, Harlem Grill occupies the former Wells Club, which over the years hosted luminaries like Billie Holliday. In its present incarnation, the restaurant re-creates a supper-club feel with its dim lighting, cool bar and regular schedule of musical entertainment. Keep going past the bar into the dining room, permeated by an air of sophistication.

The cuisine here is decidedly contemporary with a nod to the South, offering such selections as fish and grits, and a pork chop with sweet-potato mash. The kitchen demonstrates a light touch that makes the Harlem Grill a worthy dining destination, rather than merely an adjunct to a hip music club. From the Chocolate City to the Harlem Dream, the specialty cocktails are particularly tempting.

Londel's

004

Southern 🍴

2620 Frederick Douglass Blvd. (bet. 139th & 140th Sts.)

Subway: 135 St (St. Nicholas Ave.)
Phone: 212-234-0601
Fax: 212-234-0143
Web: www.londelsrestaurant.com
Prices: $$

Tue – Sat 11:30am - midnight
Sun 11am - 5pm
Closed Mon

Londel's revives the spirit of the Harlem Renaissance with its supper-club ambience and satisfying soul food. Located in the shadows of City University in the middle of Striver's Row—an area known for its distinguished architecture and fascinating history—Londel's celebrates Harlem's artistic spirit with African-American artwork and decorative objects. Diners are treated to live jazz and R&B music every Friday and Saturday night.

Stick-to-your-ribs Southern soul food satisfies with favorites like blackened catfish, smothered pork chops, and macaroni and cheese, all preceded by a basket of warm corn bread. Chicken and waffles, and honey-barbecued baby-back ribs are two of the signature dishes; sweet-potato pie and peach cobbler represent the down-home desserts.

Max SoHa 😊

005

1274 Amsterdam Ave. (at 123rd St.)

Subway:	125 St (Broadway)	Open daily noon – midnight
Phone:	212-531-2221	
Fax:	N/A	
Web:	www.maxsoha.com	
Prices:	**$$**	

Set in the shadow of prestigious Columbia University in the ever-evolving neighborhood of Harlem, Max SoHa is a sweet little place. In the dining room, mirrors double as menu boards, and the staff in the semi-open kitchen turns out a small list of dishes that stays the same through lunch and dinner (in the evening, portions and price tags are a bit bigger). Pastas include a ravioli of the day, while the handful of entrées meanders from *filetto di baccala al forno* to *osso buco di Mamma Bora* (served over risotto Milanese, according to the recipe of the owner's mother-in-law; it's only served on Thursday).

Down the street at 1262 Amsterdam Avenue, little sister, Max Caffé, pampers the locals with breakfast and lunch. The original restaurant, Max, is at 51 Avenue B in the East Village. None of the three locations accepts reservations.

**We've packed your weekend
in this convenient carrying case.**

A long weekend doesn't have to be short on activities. From spas to kid stuff, outdoor fun to nightlife, the Michelin® Must Sees have something for everyone to see and do. To learn more, visit michelintravel.com.

MICHELIN
A better way forward

Little Italy

Little Italy, which once ran from Canal Street north to Houston and from Lafayette Street east to the Bowery, may now be more aptly called Micro Italy. Mulberry Street is the main drag in Little Italy, and the tenacious heart of the neighborhood, which is quickly being swallowed up by neighboring Chinatown. The onetime stronghold of Manhattan's Italian-American population has dwindled to a mere corridor—Mulberry Street between Canal and Broome streets—that caters mainly to hungry tourists, though you can still find some authentic delis, bakeries and gelato shops in the neighborhood. Devotees still frequent Mulberry Street for authentic Italian fare, then go over to Ferrara's bakery *(195 Grand St.)* for Italian pastries (cannoli, tiramisu) and a cup of strong espresso.

A Bit of History – Italians have played a powerful role in shaping New York even before there was a city to shape. Italian explorer Giovanni da Verrazzano, working under the auspices of French king Francois I, was the first European to set foot on the island of Manhattan in 1524. Italians didn't cross the Great Pond en masse until the late 1800s, however. Fleeing rural poverty in southern Italy, many initially settled in the notorious Five Points slum, which stood on what is now a corner of Chinatown, but as families got on their feet they moved north to SoHo, Greenwich Village and Little Italy. In 1880, fewer than 20,000 Italians lived in the city; by 1930 that number had risen to more than a million. Many started their own businesses as tailors, barbers, grocers or restaurateurs, mixing their native dishes, redolent with Mediterranean ingredients like tomatoes, olive oil and basil, into the melting pot of American cuisine.

Outside dining in Little Italy

© Martha Cooper

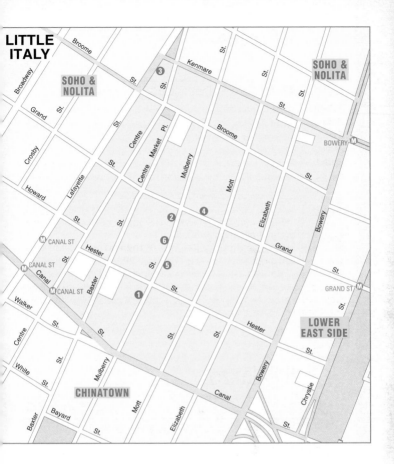

Little Italy Today – A visit to Little Italy basically consists of a Mulberry Street stroll. The stretch between Canal and Grand streets is a veritable restaurant row, with white-aproned waiters sweet-talking diners into choosing their linguine over all others. On weekends from May to mid-October, Mulberry Street is closed to vehicular traffic, making Little Italy one big alfresco party—the **Feast of San Gennaro** in mid-September is particularly raucous. Although these days, you can get better Italian food elsewhere in the city, you still can't beat the ambience on Mulberry Street.

Il Cortile

001

125 Mulberry St. (bet. Canal & Hester Sts.)

Subway:	Canal St (Lafayette St.)
Phone:	212-226-6060
Fax:	212-431-7283
Web:	www.ilcortile.com
Prices:	$$

Mon – Thu noon - midnight
Fri – Sun noon - 1am

Several dining rooms at Il Cortile each have their own ambience, but the most pleasant space is the garden room (*il cortile* is Italian for "courtyard"), more like an atrium with its glass-paneled ceiling, brick walls and abundant greenery. Statues may be plentiful, but this restaurant's décor is among the most restrained in this often over-the-top neighborhood.

Chef Michael DeGeorgio presents a wide array of pastas, meat and seafood dishes, including his ragu del Macellaio, a rich tomato sauce simmered like *nonna* used to make with pork, meatballs, braciola and sausage—offered only on Sundays. Thirty years of sharing family recipes have made Il Cortile a favorite of city politicians, neighbors and tourists.

Il Palazzo

002

151 Mulberry St. (bet. Grand & Hester Sts.)

Subway:	Canal St (Lafayette St.)
Phone:	212-343-7000
Fax:	212-334-6282
Web:	N/A
Prices:	$$

Sun – Thu noon - 10pm
Fri – Sat noon - 11pm

Located on Little Italy's main thoroughfare, Il Palazzo dishes up authentic Italian fare to a host of regulars, especially at dinnertime. The main dining room recalls a winter garden with its flowering plants and well-spaced tables, while the menu lists a generous and varied selection of Old World classics such as veal saltimbocca, chicken Cacciatore, rigatoni alla vodka, linguine with clam sauce, and shrimp scampi. The specials are the reason to come here, though, so be sure to check with your server as to the day's additions.

If you just can't eat another bite at the end of your meal, you can always skip the sweet course and end your meal with a glass of potent grappa or smooth vintage port instead.

La Esquina

003

203 Lafayette St. (bet. Broome & Kenmare Sts.)

Subway:	Spring St (Lafayette St.)	Cafe: open daily noon - midnight
Phone:	646-613-7100	Dining room: open daily 6pm - 2am
Fax:	646-613-1772	
Web:	N/A	
Prices:	$$	

Given all the hype La Esquina has received, it's remarkable that the food is as good as it is. This trendy establishment divides its space and parcels its cool clientele into three distinct dining sections, each sharing the same kitchen. The first is a take-out window and small bar, the second a tiny cafe with about 10 tables, and the third a subterranean dining room (open for dinner only) that requires a "secret" phone number for reservations.

The latter was a tough reservation to get, as it started as the spot to be in SoHo. Now the buzz has calmed a bit and the food can finally take center stage, where it deserves to be. Flavors from the kitchen are carefully balanced, fish tacos are tasty, and desserts are influenced by the fruits of the season.

Nyonya 😳

004

194 Grand St. (bet. Mott & Mulberry Sts.)

Subway:	Canal St (Lafayette St.)	Sun – Thu 11am - 11:30pm
Phone:	212-334-3669	Fri – Sat 11am - midnight
Fax:	N/A	
Web:	N/A	
Prices:	🍪	

Now for something completely different: Malaysian food in Little Italy. Okay, so you don't typically go to Little Italy looking for a Malaysian restaurant, but Nyonya is nonetheless worth seeking out for unique dishes at prices that won't blow your budget. A fusion cuisine that results from the intermarriage of Chinese and Malaysians in order to strengthen early trade ties between the two countries, Nyonya (a word that refers to the woman in such a marriage) pairs traditional Chinese ingredients with Malay herbs and spices.

You're bound to find something you like on the extensive menu, which lists everything from Nyonya seafood rice noodles to curried pork spareribs. Even dessert is interesting; try the *pulut hitam*, a sweet treat made from black rice and coconut milk.

Pellegrino's

005

138 Mulberry St. (bet. Grand & Hester Sts.)

Subway: Canal St (Lafayette St.)
Phone: 212-226-3177
Fax: 212-334-6282
Web: N/A
Prices: $$

Sun – Thu 11:30am - 11pm
Fri – Sat 11:30am - midnight

On a warm summer day, the view from one of Pellegrino's sidewalk tables takes in the heart of Little Italy. You're likely to find a good number of out-of-towners at this restaurant, since the long, narrow dining room is attractive, the umbrella-shaded outdoor tables are inviting and the service is courteous. Children are welcome here; in fact, Pellegrino's even offers half-portions for those smaller appetites.

The food, which stays true to its roots in sunny Italy, includes a balanced selection of pasta, meat and fish. Linguini alla Sinatra, the signature dish named for the beloved crooner, abounds with lobster, shrimp, clams, mushrooms and pine nuts in red sauce. Large portions of tasty food make Pellegrino's a good value in this touristy neighborhood.

Taormina

006

147 Mulberry St. (bet. Grand & Hester Sts.)

Subway: Canal St (Lafayette St.)
Phone: 212-219-1007
Fax: 212-219-0009
Web: N/A
Prices: $$

Open daily noon - midnight

Named for the scenic resort town that towers above the sea on the east coast of Sicily, Taormina remains one of the few culinary strongholds of the slowly disappearing Little Italy neighborhood. The restaurant's contemporary brasserie style showcases light varnished woods and a windowed façade overlooking Mulberry Street. Taormina's elegant setting makes it a good alternative to the assault-on-the-senses style of most of the competition, though the prices here are higher, too.

Pastas, like pappardelle with porcini and linguine della casa (tossed with shellfish, calamari and garlic in a fresh tomato sauce) are homemade and offer a taste of Italy. There's a large and tempting selection of antipasti, and the balanced menu nods to its namesake with a good array of seafood offerings.

ROEDERER ESTATE

Lower East Side

Despite being one of New York's hippest neighborhoods, the Lower East Side has, for the most part, a refreshing lack of attitude and an astounding amount of local pride. "Come one, come all" has been its message to visitors since the 1880s, when it became the quintessential American melting pot. Though today's immigrants tend to be young artists, musicians and designers, artsy types aren't the only ones working on their craft on the Lower East Side. In recent years the neighborhood has become a breeding ground for new culinary talent, while history lives on in the district's many famous ethnic eateries.

The Governor's Farm – The area now known as the Lower East Side—clockwise from north, is bounded by Houston Street, the East River, Pike Street, and the Bowery—was rural long after the southern tip of Manhattan was developed. Peter Stuyvesant, the last Dutch governor of Nieuw Amsterdam, bought much of this land in 1651 from the Indians. To facilitate transport between his farm, or *bouwerie*, and the urban market, he laid out a straight road now known as the **Bowery**.

Gateway to America – The first mass migration to the Lower East Side occurred with the arrival of Irish immigrants fleeing the Great Hunger of 1845 to 1852. From the 1880s until World War I, millions of southern and eastern Europeans arrived via Ellis Island and settled in the Lower East Side, where they could meet other recently arrived immigrants. The neighborhood swiftly became the most densely populated in the country.

Shopping in the Lower East Side

© Martha Cooper

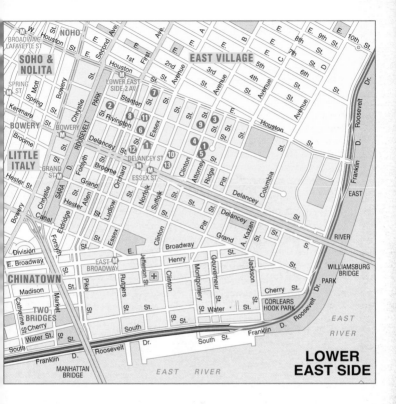

Eastern European Jews set down some of the strongest roots here, building synagogues and schools, publishing Yiddish newspapers, and opening Kosher delis. The Lower East Side was the original nosher's paradise, and for those in the know, it remains just that.

The Lower East Side Today – Today only 10 percent of Lower East Side residents are Jewish. The southern edge of the district is largely Chinese. Latinos still have a presence, but more prevalent—or at least visible—are the hordes of young Anglos who have transformed the once-gritty neighborhood into a free-spirited urban village.

Orchard Street between Canal and Houston streets is the district's spine; to the south it's lined with bargain stores; farther north (around Broome Street) trendy boutiques begin. Stanton and Rivington streets all the way east to Clinton Street are good for galleries, shops and cafes. A carnival atmosphere prevails at night on and around Ludlow Street between Houston and Delancey, where restaurants, bars and clubs stay full until the wee hours.

wd~50 ✿

Contemporary ✗✗

001

50 Clinton St. (bet. Rivington & Stanton Sts.)

Subway:	Delancey St	Mon – Sat 6pm - 11:30pm
Phone:	212-477-2900	Sun 6pm - 10:30pm
Fax:	212-477-7054	
Web:	www.wd-50.com	
Prices:	$$$	

wd~50/Robert Polidori

At wd~50, life, or at least the food part of it, most certainly imitates art. Award-winning chef Wylie Dufresne transforms simple plates into works of art by devising avant-garde, meticulously arranged compositions that taste as good as they look. At times it's debatable whether Dufresne, who trained under Jean-Georges Vongerichten (a co-owner of wd~50), is a chef or a mad scientist. Tender, rosy strips of pork belly resting on a bed of red Spaetzle in a Swiss cheese consommé is among the highly original and excellently prepared dishes.

This experimental style continues on the dessert menu, where you'll find ingredients not normally associated with dessert—parsnips for cake, miso for ice cream, olives for clafouti. Manchego cheesecake is a harmonious creation of creamy goat cheese, topped off with a thyme coulis, foamed pineapple and pieces of warm pear.

The dining room, with its custom-designed furnishings and deep tones of blue and brown, comes alive at night with a carnival atmosphere. And, in case you were wondering, the restaurant's name is composed of the chef's initials and the street number.

Appetizers

Pickled Beef Tongue, Fried Mayonnaise, Onion Streusel

Shrimp Couscous, Avocado, Papaya, Crispy Kaffir

Foie Gras, Candied Olives, Green Peas, Beet Juice

Entrées

Skate, Eggplant-Raisin Purée, King Oyster Mushroom, Fried Rice

Pork Belly, Sauerkraut Spaetzle, Swiss Cheese Consommé, Romaine

Rack of Lamb, Cranberry Beans, Parsley Root, Tamarind-Cashew

Desserts

Manchego Cheesecake, Foamed Pineapple, Quince

Braised Pineapple, Mustard Ice Cream, Coconut

Gelled Grapefruit, Black-Sesame Ice Cream, Tarragon Meringue

Ápizz

002

Italian ✗

217 Eldridge St. (bet. Rivington & Stanton Sts.)

Subway:	Lower East Side - 2 Av	Mon – Sat 6pm - 11pm
Phone:	212-253-9199	Closed Sun
Fax:	212-253-6130	
Web:	www.apizz.com	
Prices:	$$$	

A huge brick oven forms the focal point of Ápizz (say ah-BEETS), whose name derives from the Neapolitan word for pizza. The restaurant's concept, brought to you by the same duo—John LaFemina and Frank DeCarlo—who run Peasant in SoHo, is simple: "one room, one oven." This means that nearly all the dishes, from baked pastas to whole roasted fish, are fired in the wood-burning oven.

While the thin-crust pizzas go without saying, almost every dish that comes out of the wood-burning oven is worth attention here. The pastas especially sing with flavor. A meal in the dining room, which blends old and new between the rustic oven, the wood-beamed ceiling and the contemporary table settings, begins with an amuse-bouche of fresh ricotta and warm tomato sauce to eat with crusty country bread.

Chubo

003

Fusion ✗

6 Clinton St. (bet. Houston & Stanton Sts.)

Subway:	Lower East Side - 2 Av	Tue – Wed & Sun 6pm - 11pm
Phone:	212-674-6300	Thu – Sat 6pm - 11:30pm
Fax:	212-674-6340	Closed Mon
Web:	www.chubo.com	
Prices:	$$	

East meets West, and points in between, at Chubo, where the cuisine proves as eclectic as its chef/owner, Claude Chassagne. An American with a French father, a German-American mother and a Japanese wife, Chassagne can truly claim global influences.

So can his edgy cuisine, which borrows from his varied background and results in surprising combinations ("surf and turf" at Chubo translates into the likes of coriander-rubbed blue-fin tuna and oxtail white-truffle ravioli). The chef also offers intriguing ingredient-themed set-price tasting menus (such as soft-shell crabs in spring) from time to time. You're bound to find something out of the ordinary when you drop into Chubo, whose Japanese name means "professional kitchen."

Cube 63

004

63 Clinton St. (bet. Rivington & Stanton Sts.)

Subway: Delancey St
Phone: 212-228-6751
Fax: 212-228-6753
Web: www.cube63.com
Prices: $$

Sun – Thu 5pm - midnight
Fri – Sat 5pm - 1am
Closed Mon

Eclectic sushi is the name of the game at Cube 63, where the chef certainly thinks outside the box. He comes up with some pretty far-out combinations, such as the Mexican roll (white fish with jalapeño and spicy sauce) and the Puerto Rico roll (eel tempura and lobster salad with cucumber). Additionally, a wide selection of cooked items, from tempura to teriyaki, is also available.

You'll need to bring your own bottle if you want an alcoholic beverage at this little sushi joint; they don't have a liquor license yet. Not to worry, though, there's a liquor store just down the street, and the restaurant doesn't charge a corkage fee.

The crowd is trendy and the design is sparse and ultra-modern—check out the lime-green spotlights that illuminate the sushi bar.

Falai

005

68 Clinton St. (bet. Rivington & Stanton Sts.)

Subway: Lower East Side - 2 Av
Phone: 212-253-1960
Fax: 212-253-1961
Web: www.falainyc.com
Prices: $$

Mon – Thu 6pm - 11pm
Fri – Sun 6pm - 11:30pm

With its concentration of good restaurants, Clinton Street is already a destination for foodies. Falai and its bakery just makes it more so. This sliver of a spot, decorated with white-marble countertops and glittering crystal light fixtures, has an airy feel, even though the only window is at the front. Diners clamor for a table in the comfortable garden out back during warm months.

The Italian staff are welcoming and genuinely enthusiastic about the food—and for good reason. Creative fare at Falai is crafted with outstanding ingredients and expert techniques, so the assertive flavors shine through. Pasta stars, along with tantalizing desserts. It's a challenge to select between the many *dolci* on a full stomach, but it's worth saving room for the likes of *millefoglia* or polenta tortino.

Manhattan Lower East Side

'inoteca ☺

Italian ✗

006

98 Rivington St. (at Ludlow St.)

Subway:	Delancey St	Mon – Fri noon - 3am
Phone:	212-614-0473	Sat – Sun 10am - 3am
Fax:	212-614-0637	
Web:	www.inotecanyc.com	
Prices:	☙	

Big Sister to 'ino in the West Village, 'inoteca caters to the chic, young Lower East Side set. This wine bar owes its popularity in part to co-owner Joe Denton, who also has a hand in Lupa and Otto. True to its name (an *enoteca* is an Italian wine bar), the restaurant offers a superb selection of well-priced Italian wines—some 250 in all—from every region of Italy. Of these, 25 wines are available by the glass.

The menu emphasizes small plates and panini (stuffed with the likes of bresaola, fontina and arugula, or roasted vegetables and fresh ricotta); pick up a copy of the restaurant's cookbook to learn how to perfect the art of this Italian sandwich. If wine and cheese is your thing, you can choose assortments of 3, 5 or 7 different types of Italian cheeses to sample with your vino.

Katz's ☺

Deli ✗

007

205 E. Houston St. (at Ludlow St.)

Subway:	Lower East Side - 2 Av	Sun – Tue 8am - 10pm
Phone:	212-254-2246	Wed – Thu 8am - 11pm
Fax:	212-674-3270	Fri – Sat 8am - 3am
Web:	www.katzdeli.com	
Prices:	☙	

Established in 1888, Katz's is as much a New York institution as the Statue of Liberty. One of the few original Eastern European establishments remaining in the Lower East Side, Katz's attracts out-of-towners, residents and celebrities. In the never-ending debate over who serves the best pastrami, Katz's often tops the list.

For an authentic experience, queue up in front of the salty countermen, collect your meal, and head to a table. What to order? Matzo ball soup and a pastrami sandwich on rye (not toasted, please), with a side of fries.

Whatever you do, be sure to bring cash (that's the only form of payment they accept) and don't lose the ticket you get upon entering. It's your ticket out, and without it, you're going to want to crawl under a table and hide.

The Orchard

008

Contemporary ✗✗

162 Orchard St. (bet. Rivington & Stanton Sts.)

Subway:	Delancey St	Mon – Sat 6pm - 11pm
Phone:	212-353-3570	Closed Sun
Fax:	212-353-3572	
Web:	www.theorchardny.com	
Prices:	$$	

Creative and funky, modern and cool, The Orchard sparkles as a star on the Lower East Side. This delightful place celebrates contemporary style with its light woods and warm beige walls covered by strips of mirrors. From the young waitstaff to the diverse crowd of diners, The Orchard gives off a hip, unpretentious vibe. Great food and a small room make reservations hard to get.

The menu is Italian-inspired and upmarket, with an entire section devoted to crispy flatbreads, a specialty here and great for groups—if you can bring yourself to share. Entrées focus on inventive pastas like spaghettini with black tiger shrimp, crispy chorizo and panko oreganata.

Raid your cellar before arriving, since The Orchard is BYOB (they're hoping to soon be able to apply their creativity to a wine list).

Sachiko's On Clinton

009

Japanese ✗

25 Clinton St. (bet. Houston & Stanton Sts.)

Subway:	Delancey St	Tue – Wed & Sun 5:30pm - midnight
Phone:	212-253-2900	Fri – Sat 5:30pm - 1am
Fax:	212-253-2930	Closed Mon
Web:	www.sachikosonclinton.com	
Prices:	$$	

Opened in November 2004, Sachiko's is a survivor of the ever-changing landscape of the Lower East Side restaurant scene. This sushi and sake bar, as they bill themselves, is decorated with bright orange walls, blond woods and an intimate sushi counter where mounds of fresh raw fish are displayed.

The restaurant draws an international clientele who clamor for creative sushi, including some made with luxe ingredients such as caviar and lobster. *Kushiage* is the specialty: beef, chicken or vegetables are threaded on bamboo sticks (*kushi* in Japanese), breaded and deep-fried. Think of kushiage as Japanese kebobs—and be forewarned that they have way more fat calories than sushi. Even the cocktail menu has a Japanese focus, with sake making its way into cosmopolitans, margaritas and mojitos.

Manhattan **Lower East Side**

Schiller's Liquor Bar

European ✗

010

131 Rivington St. (at Norfolk St.)

Subway:	Delancey St	Mon – Wed 11am - 1am
Phone:	212-260-4555	Thu 11am - 2am
Fax:	212-260-4581	Fri 11am - 3am
Web:	www.schillersny.com	Sat 10am - 4pm & 6pm - 3am
Prices:	$$	Sun 10am - 4pm & 6pm - 1am

Founded by restaurateur Keith McNally (whose other ventures include Pastis and Balthazar) Schiller's fancies itself as a "low life" bar, but if this is how that other half lives, then lowbrow never looked so good. It's a lively, happening scene, decked out with subway tiles, antique mirrors and bare bistro tables; the noise level ratchets up higher and higher as the night goes on.

On the eclectic menu you'll find everything from steak frites to fish and chips to eggplant parmesan. For dessert, don't miss the sticky toffee pudding, a wonderful, creamy confection topped with vanilla ice cream. Schiller's serves a light supper menu until 3am on Friday and Saturday.

The wine list is divided into three sections: cheap, decent and good; according to the restaurant, "cheap" is the best.

The Stanton Social

Fusion ✗✗

011

99 Stanton St. (bet. Ludlow & Orchard Sts.)

Subway:	Lower East Side - 2 Av	Mon – Fri 5pm - 3am
Phone:	212-995-0099	Sat – Sun 11:30am - 3:30pm & 5pm - 3am
Fax:	212-995-0083	
Web:	www.thestantonsocial.com	
Prices:	$$	

Designed by the hip firm of AvroKO, Stanton Social fills a duplex with two floors of fun. The décor here honors the erstwhile haberdashers and seamstress shops of the Lower East Side with elements such as a wall of woven leather, vintage hand mirrors displayed in the upstairs bar, and wine shelves laid out in a herringbone pattern, inspired by a man's jacket.

Chef/owner Chris Santos' wildly eclectic and fun menu of small plates zigzags all over the globe, from England to China to Europe. Adorable little "sliders," filled with lobster, Kobe-style beef or barbecued pulled pork, are served on buttered brioche buns. Don't forget to bring some friends, since sharing is part of the deal. Weekend brunch is equal parts sweet and savory, and the Bloody Mary bar offers several thirst quenchers.

Suba

012 Contemporary Spanish ✗✗

109 Ludlow St. (bet. Delancey & Rivington Sts.)

Subway:	Delancey St	Sun – Thu 6pm - midnight
Phone:	212-982-5714	Fri – Sat 6pm - 4am
Fax:	212-982-3034	
Web:	www.subanyc.com	
Prices:	$$	

Hot, hot, hot. Designed by architect Andre Kikoski, Suba's three sleek levels fill a 1909 tenement from the ground-floor tapas lounge down the twisting steel staircase to the Grotto, where a polished-concrete dining island floats in a pool of water, and farther down still to the brightly painted Skylight Room for private dining.

All this high style comes at an equally high price. It's worth a splurge to sway to the Latin beat while you sip a mojito and sample ceviche before digging into signatures such as almond-crusted tuna, hanger steak with potato and mushroom gratin, or braised lamb and chickpea empanada.

Suba offers entertainment throughout the week, from "Dinner and a Movie" to Latin bands and Flamenco dancers. Check to see if one of their events ties in with your dining plans.

Tides

013 Seafood ✗

102 Norfolk St. (bet. Delancey & Rivington Sts.)

Subway:	Delancey St	Tue – Thu noon - 3pm & 5:30pm - 11pm
Phone:	212-254-8855	Fri noon - 3pm & 5:30pm - 11:30pm
Fax:	212-254-8866	Sat 5:30pm - 11:30pm
Web:	www.tidesseafood.com	Sun 11am - 3pm & 5:30pm - 10pm
Prices:	$$	Closed Mon

From anywhere in Tides' tiny 450-square-foot dining room, you can see the kitchen with its small staff hard at work. Above your head, tens of thousands of bamboo skewers are embedded in the back-lit ceiling, forming wavy patterns that suggest a grassy dune.

Lunch is an ultra-casual affair, with a limited menu (no dessert), plastic plates and cutlery, and a mix of table service and serve-yourself. At dinner, Tides displays a more stylish veneer, switching to contemporary serving pieces, all with an Asian flair. No matter when you dine here, you'll catch fabulously fresh seafood. The enthusiastic owners—who alternately play the role of waiter, sommelier and manager—refuse to skimp on quality, and the kitchen prepares seafood with a talented hand.

Midtown East & Murray Hill

A bustling business district, the swatch of land east of Fifth Avenue—contains some of the city's finest office buildings, from the Art Deco **Chrysler Building** to the modernist **Lever House**, as well as the spectacular Beaux-Arts **Grand Central Terminal**. All the way east, at the river, you'll find the headquarters of the United Nations. Tucked among these landmarks are historic hotels, posh shops lining Madison and Fifth avenues, and, last—but far from least—a plethora of restaurants to suit every taste.

A Bit of History – The area bounded by Fifth Avenue and the East River, between East 30th and 60th streets, was not always the tony place it is today. In the early 19th century, steam-powered locomotives chugged down Park Avenue all the way to a depot on 23rd Street, bringing with them noise and dirt. Residents complained, and in 1854 an ordinance was passed banning trains south of 42nd Street. That helped pave the way for downtown development, but did nothing to improve the lot of those in Midtown East, whose tenements surrounded a sooty railyard that spread from 42nd to 56th Street.

Underground Railroad – Enter railroad magnate "Commodore" Cornelius Vanderbilt (1794–1877), who opened the first Grand Central depot in 1871 on the present site of the Grand Central Terminal. Shortly thereafter, he began lowering the tracks feeding into it below street level, reducing some of the noise pollution. But smoke was still a big problem, and in 1889 the city demanded that the railroad electrify the trains or leave the city. To finance the electrification process, the Vanderbilts sunk the entire railyard fronting the depot below ground and sold the land above it to developers, who soon lined Madison and Park avenues with exclusive apartment buildings. The Grand Central Terminal you see today, which now houses a gourmet market and a sprawling dining concourse, was completed in 1913.

Midtown Street Scene

© Martha Cooper

Onward and Upward – After World War II, many of the apartment houses along Madison, Park and Lexington avenues in Midtown were replaced by high-rise office towers. Today the area claims an eclectic mix of old and new, including the residential enclave of opulent mansions, elegant brownstones and converted 19th-century carriage houses known as **Murray Hill** (between 40th & 30th Sts.). In quiet Murray Hill, foodies will discover a world of cuisines, from sophisticated sushi and Indian curries to hearty steak.

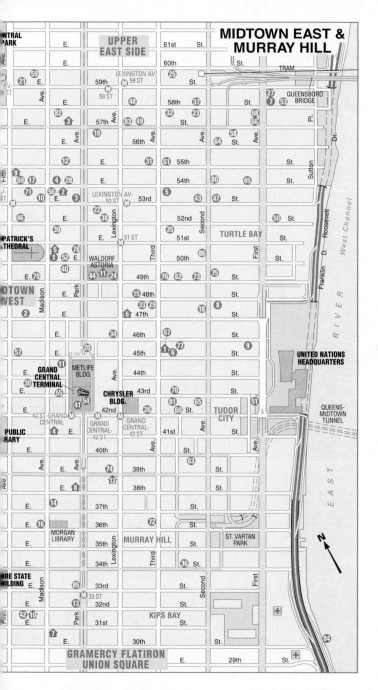

Kurumazushi ❀

002

7 E. 47th St. (bet. Fifth & Madison Aves.)

Subway: 47-50 Sts - Rockefeller Ctr
Phone: 212-317-2802
Fax: 212-317-2803
Web: N/A
Prices: $$$$

Mon – Sat 11:30am – 2pm
& 5:30pm – 10pm
Closed Sun & major holidays

George Rosmer III

Located on an unassuming Midtown block on the second floor of an office building, Kurumazushi offers some of the best sushi in town. The décor is typically Japanese in its simple, clean design, and the restful ambience allows the outstanding fish to sparkle. The team behind the red and black-lacquer sushi bar will shout a welcome in Japanese to you as you enter this tiny place, and an equally energetic greeting will be issued when you leave.

Settle in and prepare to be wowed by sushi master Toshihiro Uezu. Incredibly fresh sushi and sashimi (toro, Japanese yellowtail, shimi aji, Japanese red snapper, sea eel and more) are all sliced perfectly and have a sweet buttery flavor. Even the rice here is expertly prepared. Quality doesn't come cheaply at this restaurant, which is preferred by those dining on expense accounts.

If you sit at the sushi bar, consider asking for a menu, especially if cost is a concern. Otherwise, go for broke (the price of an omakase feast here can add up fast) and allow the chef to create a delectable multicourse meal for you.

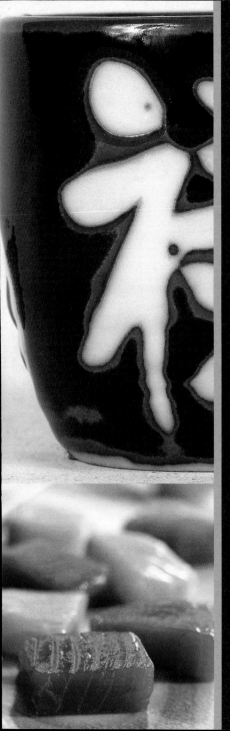

APPETIZERS

Russian King Crab Legs Marinated with Special Vinegar Sauce

Toro Caviar: Very Fatty Tuna Tartare with Russian Beluga, or Russian or Iranian Osetra Caviar

Seared Toro: Very Fatty Tuna Seared with Special Sauce

ENTRÉES

Omakase with Master Chef's Selected Sushi and Sashimi

DESSERTS

Yokan: Traditional Japanese Red-Bean Cake

Seasonal Fruit

Ice cream: Green Tea or Vanilla Flavor, with or without Red-Bean Sauce

JAPANESE

Lever House ✿

Contemporary

003

390 Park Ave. (enter on E. 53rd St. bet. Madison & Park Aves.)

Subway:	Lexington Av - 53 St	Mon – Thu 11:45am - 2:30pm
Phone:	212-888-2700	& 5:30pm - 11pm
Fax:	212-888-2740	Fri 11:45am - 2:30pm & 5:30pm - 11:30pm
Web:	www.leverhouse.com	Sat 5:30pm - 11:30pm
Prices:	**$$$**	Sun 5pm - 10pm

If you fancy retro-modern design, make a beeline for this podlike dining room, where Mark Newsen's honeycomb motif, repeated in everything from the carpet and the light fixtures to the hexagonal cubbyholes for wine bottles, grabs the eye. The rounded corners of the dining room, lit by a honey-toned glow, complement the angular tower of green-blue glass and steel that is the landmark Lever House building, designed by Gordon Bunshaft in 1952 as Park Avenue's first glass-clad tower. Its Midtown location among banks and office buildings makes it a natural choice for power lunches.

The buzz about the food here is well deserved. Chef Dan Silverman, whose culinary resume includes stints at Chez Panisse in Berkeley, California, as well as at New York's Le Bernardin and Union Square Café, knows how to pick excellent ingredients. Tastes of the seasons illuminate the modernized American food here, encompassing tuna tartare mixed with celery-root confit and topped with trout roe, roasted poussin with tarragon jus, and delicate sesame-crusted halibut. For dessert, the Tin Roof sundae made with rich peanut-butter ice cream and dark-chocolate sauce will appeal to your decadent side.

Appetizers

Fluke Tartare with Jalapeño, Orange and Scallion

Lobster Tempura with Tartar Sauce

Watercress Soup with Maine Baby Shrimp and Lemon-Ginger Crème Fraîche

Entrées

Sesame-crusted Halibut with Baby Bok Choy and Herb Nage

Long Island Duck Breast with Farro, Toasted Almonds, and Apricots

Colorado Rack of Lamb with Spicy Lamb Sausage, Parsley, Bulghur and Mint

Desserts

Peanut-Butter Bombe with Fudge and Peanut-Butter-Swirled Ice Cream

Grapefruit-Caramel Meringue Pie with Grapefruit Sorbet

Steamed Chocolate Cake with Dried-Fruit Compote and Armagnac Ice Cream

CONTEMPORARY

Oceana ✿

004

55 E. 54th St. (bet. Madison & Park Aves.)

Subway:	5 Av – 53 St
Phone:	212-759-5941
Fax:	212-759-6076
Web:	www.oceanarestaurant.com
Prices:	$$$$

Mon – Fri noon – 2:30pm
& 5:30pm – 10:30pm
Sat 5pm – 10:30pm
Closed Sun

Welcome aboard! You'll think you're on the high seas instead of the East 50s when you step into Oceana. Both the name and the décor suggest a luxury ocean liner, complete with blue-gray leather banquettes and faux windows painted with murals of the glittering sea and passing ships. Culinary Institute of America grad Cornelius Gallagher captains this enterprise, having learned French technique at the Waldorf=Astoria. His resume includes time in the kitchens of Lespinasse, Daniel and Bouley, as well as study in France.

At Oceana, Gallagher pairs simple seafood with flavors that spark the natural taste of fresh fish and shellfish; loup de mer, for example, might be served en croûte, over a bed of basmati rice with coconut-milk emulsion and tamarind coulis. Lunch and dinner are popular with neighborhood power brokers, and the bar features a short menu of oysters, cheeses and sashimi perfect for after-work noshing.

The wine list is extensive, with more than 25,000 bottles in the cellar, and three- and six-course tasting menus feature exclusive pairings. For dessert, Oceana's elegant version of sticky toffee pudding rivals that of the best British gastropub.

Appetizers

Etouffée of East Coast Oysters

Black Forest Ham, Celery,
Hon-Shimeji Mushrooms,
Razor-Clam Chowder

Panaché of Chilled Smoked
Sable, with Artichoke, Olive,
Basil, Radish and Piquillo

Pavé of Foie Gras with
Mountain Huckleberry Gelée,
Marcona Almond Coffee
Brittle

Entrées

Australian Swordfish with
Cashew and Pepperberry,
Mustard, Endive and
Roasted Salsify Purée

Striped Bass in the style
of Venice, with Sopressata,
Homemade Sage Orecchiette,
Kale, Plum Tomato, and
Fennel-Seed Sausage Broth

Alaskan Black Cod with
Tamaki Gold Rice, Long
Beans, Spiced Papaya, and
Calamansi-Soy Dressing

Desserts

Warm Sticky Toffee Pudding
with Black-Walnut Ice Cream

Cactus Pear and Lychee Granité
Salad with Vanilla Custard

Sicilian Pistachio Sundae with
Milk-Chocolate Feuillentine
Crunch

Vong ❀

Contemporary Asian ✗✗

200 E. 54th St. (bet. Second & Third Aves.)

Subway: Lexington Av - 53 St
Phone: 212-486-9592
Fax: 212-980-3745
Web: www.jean-georges.com
Prices: $$$

Mon – Fri noon - 2:30pm
& 5:30pm - 11pm
Sat 5:30pm - 11pm
Sun 5:30pm - 10:30pm

♿

Jean-Georges Management

One of the nation's foremost chefs, Jean-Georges Vongerichten has made his mark on American cuisine with a galaxy of restaurants (just under 20 at last count) and three cookbooks to his credit.

You'll get your first clue about the culinary concept at Vong (which opened in 1992) as you enter the dining room, where bowls of aromatic spices decorate a long table. The Alsatian-born chef fuses Thai flavors—and 150 different herbs and spices—with French technique here. It was a natural evolution for Vongerichten, who began cooking in France, then spent several years working in Bangkok. In Thailand he developed an appreciation for Asian foods, particularly, bold spices such as curry powder, cardamom and coriander. The lobster and daikon appetizer epitomizes the chef's masterful technique and artful presentation, while the Peking duck with sticky sesame sauce, served with baby bok choi and fried rice, consistently wins raves.

From the Thai silks and louvered wooden panels in the dining room to the tabletop's bamboo flatware and metal-accented serving pieces, Asian details permeate the design.

APPETIZERS

Crab Spring Rolls, Tamarind Dipping Sauce

Prawn Satay, Fresh Oyster Sauce

Chicken and Coconut Milk Soup, Galangal and Shiitake Mushrooms

ENTRÉES

Spiced Cod Fish, Curried Artichokes and Tamarind Ketchup

Lobster Thai Herbs

Chicken with Lemongrass, Asian Long Beans and Sweet Rice in Banana Leaf

DESSERTS

Roasted Asian Pear Licorice Ice Cream and Sableuse Cake

Coconut Sticky Rice, Mango, and Coconut Reduction

Passion Fruit Soufflé, Passion Fruit Ice Cream

Aburiya Kinnosuke

006

213 E. 45th St. (bet. Second & Third Aves.)

Subway:	Grand Central - 42 St	Mon – Fri noon - 2pm & 6pm - midnight
Phone:	212-867-5454	Sat 6pm - 11pm
Fax:	N/A	Sun 5:30pm - 10:30pm
Web:	N/A	
Prices:	$$$	

New York offers the world, and at Aburiya Kinnosuke, patrons are treated to an insider's view of Japan. From its mostly Japanese clientele to the extensive menu not often found outside Japan, this restaurant is every bit the real thing.

Guests are invited to take part in the action here, where sochu cocktails involve citrus to be hand-squeezed, and grilled dishes require cooking over a small tabletop charcoal grill. Yawarakani, a kind of Japanese comfort food involving ground-chicken mini-meatloaves cooked over open charcoal is one of the highlights of the menu. Ingredients are top-notch and the attention to detail from the chefs in the open kitchen is superb.

Aburiya Kinnosuke requires advance booking, but once you're in, you won't be rushed through your meal by the cordial and competent staff.

Aja

007

1068 First Ave. (at 58th St.)

Subway:	59 St	Sun – Wed 5pm - midnight
Phone:	212-888-8008	Thu – Sat 5pm - 1am
Fax:	212-888-8588	
Web:	N/A	
Prices:	$$$	

Inside Aja's windowless stone façade you'll discover a dark and sultry temple-like décor constructed with stone walls, water elements, and a giant Buddha at the back of one of the small rooms. Loud contemporary music fills the space and raises the volume of conversations, seemingly of little concern to the mix of young bankers and their dates, posh Upper East Siders, and well-to-do Sutton residents who shun the sushi bar in favor of tables by the Buddha and side-by-side banquettes.

Strikingly fresh sushi, sashimi and maki split menu space with original Pan-Asian entrées and combination platters. Flashy presentations have an Asian flair, with flaming rocks and colorful cocktails traveling to tables past admiring guests. You'll pay for the show, but high prices don't put a damper on the party.

The Alamo

Mexican ✗✗

304 E. 48th St. (bet. First & Second Aves.)

Subway: 51 St
Phone: 212-759-0590
Fax: 212-759-4619
Web: www.thealamorestaurant.com
Prices: $$

Mon – Fri noon - 11pm
Sat 5pm - 11:30pm
Closed Sun

Its façade suggesting the real Alamo in Texas, this restaurant reopened in spring 2005, after a three-year hiatus (the restaurant first opened in 1985). Bright primary colors, red tabletops with fresh roses, and tile floors contribute to the room's lively vibe.

Tasty Mexican specialties ranging from fajitas to chicken mole to paella (a nod to Spain) bring fans back for more. The menu also features an array of unusual combinations, like dorado with chipotle-chile guajillo vinaigrette. Don't miss the tequila bar, where the extensive list of spirits is divided into *blanca* (showcasing the pure spirit of the blue agave), *reposado* (aged in French oak), or *anejo* (aged for 1 to 10 years). Across from the bar, note the colorful mural depicting famous Mexican figures from politics and the arts.

Alcala

Spanish ✗✗

342 E. 46th St. (bet. First & Second Aves.)

Subway: Grand Central – 42 St
Phone: 212-370-1866
Fax: 212-370-3583
Web: www.alcalarestaurant.com
Prices: $$

Mon – Thu noon - 2:30pm
& 5:30pm - 10pm
Fri noon - 2:30pm & 5:30pm - 11pm
Sat 5:30pm - 11pm
Sun 5:30pm - 9pm

In its former incarnation, this restaurant served Basque cuisine as Marichu; now as Alcala, the place has broadened its horizons to include regional fare from across the entire country of Spain. Located just across from the United Nations complex, Alcala serves tapas and other Spanish specialties in its rustic, red-brick, wood-beamed dining room.

At Alcala, the kitchen concentrates on Spanish home-style cooking, using traditional recipes and giving them a modern twist. Sized for two, the paella can be topped with seafood or chicken and beef. Appetizers run from salted codfish salad to shrimp in sizzling garlic sauce. Here you can enjoy a quiet conversation over a pitcher of fruity sangria.

Alto

Contemporary ✂✂✂

010

520 Madison Ave. (enter on 53rd St. bet. Fifth & Madison Aves.)

Subway:	5 Av - 53 St	Mon – Thu noon - 2:15pm
Phone:	212-308-1099	& 5:30pm - 10:15pm
Fax:	212-308-3573	Fri noon - 2:15pm & 5pm - 11pm
Web:	www.altorestaurant.com	Sat 5pm - 11pm
Prices:	$$$	Closed Sun

Opened in April 2005, Alto is the second restaurant by chef Scott Conant and his partners from L'Impero. The food takes its inspiration (and the restaurant its name) from the Alto Adige region of northeastern Italy. This area's proximity to Austria influences many of the menu items, including smoked ocean trout with horseradish and trout roe, herbed Spaetzle with slow-braised rabbit, and house-made pastas.

A large piece of the Berlin Wall serves as an impressive entrance to the restaurant. The dining space is swanky, with red-velvet chairs and huge windows. The floor-to-ceiling wall of wine bottles is for display purposes only, but oenophiles will certainly find something to suit their palates in the basement cellar filled with a staggering 12,000 bottles.

Ammos Estiatorio

Mediterranean ✂✂

011

52 Vanderbilt Ave. (at 45th St.)

Subway:	Grand Central - 42 St	Mon – Fri 11:30am - 11pm
Phone:	212-922-9999	Sat – Sun 4pm - 11pm
Fax:	212-922-3544	
Web:	www.ammosnewyork.com	
Prices:	$$$	

Conveniently located in the shadow of Grand Central Terminal, Ammos Estiatorio opened its Manhattan branch (the original is in Astoria, Queens at 20-30 Steinway St.) in November 2005. True to its name ("sand" in Greek), the open, airy restaurant sports a modern décor that adheres to a Greek island theme. Hand-blown glass fishing buoys and canvas market umbrellas add to the décor, while weathered stone and wood beams provide rustic touches.

Chef/partner Christos Christou landed here after cooking in Avra Estiatorio and Molyvos. His menu, which zeros in on seafood, offers his signature meze (think braised octopus with tomatoes, onions and Mediterranean herbs) from different regions of Greece, plus a short list of entrées and a good selection of whole grilled fish, served by the pound.

Aquavit

012

Scandinavian

65 E. 55th St. (bet. Madison & Park Aves.)

Subway:	5 Av - 53 St	Open daily noon - 2:30pm
Phone:	212-307-7311	& 5:30pm - 10:30pm
Fax:	212-265-8584	
Web:	www.aquavitrestaurant.com	
Prices:	$$$	

Everything about Aquavit is Scandinavian; its design, its cuisine, its chef. Named for the Scandinavian spirit that figures prominently on its beverage menu, Aquavit moved in early 2005 from the West Side to the ground floor of the Park Avenue Tower. There's a casual cafe and bar area up front; the more refined contemporary dining room, softened by beige tones and varnished woods, lies beyond.

Chef/owner Marcus Samuelsson's take on Scandinavian food is contemporary as well. Born in Ethiopia and raised in Sweden, Samuelsson excels at pairing unexpected textures and flavors, such as the hot-smoked trout with salsify purée, geoduck clam, asparagus salad and apple-horseradish broth. The restaurant even makes its own Aquavit, flavored with everything from pineapple to pumpkin.

Artisanal

013

French XX

2 Park Ave. (enter on 32nd St. bet. Madison & Park Aves.)

Subway:	33 St	Mon – Thu 11:45am - 11pm
Phone:	212-725-8585	Sat 5pm - midnight
Fax:	212-685-0183	Sun 11am - 11pm
Web:	www.artisanalcheese.com	
Prices:	$$	

Say cheese. That's the focus of Terrance Brennan's Artisanal restaurant, which celebrates cheese from around the world. Opened in 2001, Brennan's Murray Hill brasserie, with its high ceilings, burgundy-colored walls and velour banquettes serves cheese in many forms: fondue, macaroni and cheese, puffy gougères and cheese ravioli, to name a few. In fact, there's even a separate cheese menu, offering tastings of some 250 types of artisanal cheese. Choose your beverage from the equally dizzying list of more than 150 wines by the glass. Don't like cheese? Never fear, Artisanal offers a wide selection of classic French fare, such as escargots, trout amandine, and lamb cassoulet.

Check out the tempting cheese display in the back of the dining room (you can even buy some to take home with you).

Asia de Cuba

014

237 Madison Ave. (bet. 37th & 38th Sts.)

Subway:	Grand Central - 42 St	Mon – Fri noon - 11pm
Phone:	212-726-7755	Sat 5:30pm - midnight
Fax:	212-726-7575	Sun 5:30pm - 10pm
Web:	www.chinagrillmgt.com	
Prices:	$$$	

A trendy venue in the Morgans Hotel in residential Murray Hill, Asia de Cuba still packs in a chic crowd, despite the fact that it's no longer new (a lesser restaurant would have been demoted to has-been status long ago). Designer Philippe Starck fitted the striking bi-level interior with gauzy drapes lining the soaring walls, a 25-foot-high hologram of a flowing waterfall and a 50-foot-long, alabaster communal table running the length of the downstairs room.

Generously sized dishes marry elements of Asian and Latin cuisines in signatures such as tunapica (tuna tartare picadillo style), calamari salad, and *ropa vieja* of duck. Round up a few gorgeous friends who like to share, and order from the family-style menu. Don't overlook sides like panko-crusted crispy plantains or Thai coconut sticky rice.

Avra Estiatorio

015

141 E. 48th St. (bet. Lexington & Third Aves.)

Subway:	51 St	Mon – Fri noon - 4pm & 5pm - midnight
Phone:	212-759-8550	Sat – Sun 11am - 4pm & 5pm - midnight
Fax:	212-751-0894	
Web:	www.avrany.com	
Prices:	$$$	

This lively taverna-style eatery recalls the Mediterranean with its limestone floors, faux-stone walls and arched doorways. You can choose to sit inside or out, or you can compromise with a table near the large doors that open onto the terrace in warm weather.

Fresh fish nets the most attention here, and you can view a display of the day's catch on ice in the front dining room. Flown in fresh from Europe or purchased from New York's relocated Fulton Fish Market, fish and shellfish are brushed with olive oil and grilled whole over charcoal. Your choice will be priced per pound, so beware if your eyes tend to be bigger than your stomach. Avra's specialty appetizers make an authentic and delicious way to start a meal here.

Available on weekends, the set lunch menu offers good prices.

Barbès

016

21 E. 36th St. (bet. Fifth & Madison Aves.)

Subway:	33 St	Open daily 11:30am - midnight
Phone:	212-684-0215	
Fax:	212-684-6131	
Web:	N/A	
Prices:	$$	

A sparkling diamond in an otherwise unpolished neighborhood rife with generic delis and overpriced Italian restaurants, Barbès glows with its friendly staff and traditional French-Moroccan fare. Brick walls and a beamed ceiling create a rustic mood in the cozy dining room, while the infectious Moroccan music lends an exotic note.

Here, the menu presents diners with a wide choice of items; dishes have a decidedly North African bent but with heavy Mediterranean influences (the names of the dishes—*moules à la Marocaine, crevettes aux pistou, couscous Marocaine traditionneles*—are all in French). The manager's presence ensures the warm quality of the service; he employs the requisite flourish when pouring mint tea into small Moroccan-style glasses.

Bice

017

7 E. 54th St. (bet. Fifth & Madison Aves.)

Subway:	5 Av - 53 St	Mon – Sat 11:30am - midnight
Phone:	212-688-1999	Sun 11:30am - 11pm
Fax:	212-752-1329	Closed Christmas Day
Web:	www.bicenewyork.com	
Prices:	$$$	

Opened in 1987, Bice New York forms part of a chain of some 40 Italian restaurants that reaches around the world. Bice was founded in Milan in 1926 by Beatrice ("Bice") Ruggeri. Her sons, Roberto and Remo, later opened additional branches, first in Italy, and in 1987, on East 54th Street in New York City—the first location in North America.

The Manhattan outpost owes its oh-so-cool, yet elegant custom-designed Art Deco interior to Adam Tihany, who has done work for many big-name chefs. Northern Italian fare makes up the menu (veal Milanese, risotto, hearty homemade pasta), and Midtown's chic set dines at Bice on a regular basis. Even fashionistas save room for dessert here, where the enticing menu includes tiramisu, panna cotta and gelato, among other selections.

Manhattan Midtown East & Murray Hill

Blair Perrone

018

Steakhouse ✗✗

885 Second Ave. (bet. 47th & 48 Sts.)

Subway:	51 St	Mon – Fri 11:30am - 10:45pm
Phone:	212-796-8000	Sat 5pm - 10:45pm
Fax:	N/A	Closed Sun
Web:	www.blairperrone.com	
Prices:	$$$	

Partners Charlie Blair (a Peter Luger alumnus) and Joe Perrone set up shop in this former Ruth's Chris Steakhouse on the ground floor of an imposing residential building in Midtown. The dining area splits into two large rooms, both classy contemporary settings of warm woods, comfortable seating, and floor-to-ceiling windows, equally à propos for a business dinner or a nice evening out.

U.S.D.A. Prime dry-aged Porterhouse comes in cuts for two, three or four people. Steaks and chops are perfectly cooked to order, the meat juicy and flavorful. And a list of seafood dishes makes non-carnivores feel like they're part of the club. Save room for the creamy New York-style cheesecake, served with a dollop of Schlag.

BLT Steak

019

Steakhouse ✗✗✗

106 E. 57th St. (bet. Lexington & Park Aves.)

Subway:	59 St	Mon – Fri 11:45am - 2:30pm
Phone:	212-752-7470	& 5:30pm - 11pm
Fax:	212-752-7420	Sat 5:30pm - 11:30pm
Web:	www.bltrestaurants.com	Closed Sun
Prices:	$$$$	Closed Thanksgiving & Christmas Day

Why would a French chef name his restaurant after an American sandwich? He would, if he fancied his restaurant to be a contemporary bistro (B) and his name was Laurent Tourondel (LT). In fact, Bistro Laurent Tourondel is not a French bistro at all, but a Frenchman's vision of an American steakhouse. Sleek décor, with its Macassar ebony tables, café-crème-colored banquettes and sepia-toned photographs of New York, smacks of big-city sophistication.

For dinner, naturally-aged, corn-fed Certified Angus beef is served with your choice of side dish and sauce; the latter range from béarnaise to red wine caper brown butter. (And, yes, there are fish selections, too.) Sides, like shoestring fries, sautéed potatoes and grilled asparagus, are served in cute cast-iron pans.

Bobby Van's Steakhouse

020

230 Park Ave. (at 46th St.)

Subway:	Grand Central - 42 St	Mon – Sat 11:45am - 11pm
Phone:	212-867-5490	Closed Sun
Fax:	212-867-3350	
Web:	www.bobbyvans.com	
Prices:	$$$$	

Bobby Van's owes its first Manhattan location to Leona Helmsley, who cajoled the owners into opening an outpost here (the original Bobby Van's is in Bridgehampton on Long Island). This is clearly an Atkins-diet paradise, catering to business people on expense accounts. As you'd imagine, it's a clubby, old-boy kind of place, with lots of wood and mirrors in the spacious dining room.

Expect to pay rather dearly for huge portions of meltingly tender beef and well-cooked seafood (lobster is priced by the pound, and you can order the USDA Prime Porterhouse for two, three or four people.)

You'll find other Bobby Van's locations in Midtown East (131 E. 54th St.), in Midtown West (135 W. 50th St.), and in the Financial District (25 Broad St.).

Bottega del Vino

021

7 E. 59th St. (bet. Fifth & Madison Aves.)

Subway:	5 Av - 59 St	Mon – Fri 8am - 11pm
Phone:	212-223-2724	Sat 9am - midnight
Fax:	212-223-3608	Sun 10am - 11pm
Web:	www.bottegadelvinonyc.com	
Prices:	$$$	

From Verona comes not two, but one gentleman, Severini Barzan, who opened the New York outpost of his Italian wine bar in November 2004. The words painted on a beam along this charming restaurant's wall sum up his philosophy: *Dio mi guardi da chi non beve vino* ("may God protect me from those who do not drink wine"). Indeed wine steals the show here, with bottles displayed on shelf after shelf in the dining room, and a cellar that stocks some 2,800 different labels. Barzan has even designed his own line of hand-blown stemware to highlight the taste of each individual wine.

Wine, of course, influences the food, and many of the wonderful dishes are wine-focused or include wine in the preparation. Hailing from the Veneto region, the "antica bottega" creations are the house signatures.

Brasserie

022

Contemporary French ✗✗

100 E. 53rd St. (bet. Lexington & Park Aves.)

Subway:	Lexington Av - 53 St
Phone:	212-751-4840
Fax:	212-751-8777
Web:	www.rapatina.com/brasserie
Prices:	$$$

Mon – Thu 11:30am - midnight
Fri 11:30am - 1am
Sat 4:30pm - 1am
Sun 4:30pm - 10pm

The original concept of a brasserie as a brewery that provided food for hungry travelers has come a long way to this modern interpretation, redecorated after a fire in 1995. Today the Brasserie's retro design employs white-leather chairs and small plastic-topped tables, with pear wood panels lining the ceiling in a sort of wave.

Features on the short menu are American, but many are rendered with a European touch (steak frites, whole fish with *herbes de Provence*). For a sweet finish, try the chocolate beignets.

Brasserie is more suited for a group of friends or a business meal than a romantic date. Seating is close, and the appealing menu and attractive space make this a lively and popular spot. The long bar serves tasty snacks and is a sophisticated lair for an adult beverage.

Bruno

023

Italian ✗✗

240 E. 58th St. (bet. Second & Third Aves.)

Subway:	59 St
Phone:	212-688-4190
Fax:	212-688-4342
Web:	www.brunosnyc.com
Prices:	$$$

Mon – Sat noon - midnight
Closed Sun

Bruno Selimaj must be doing something right; his eponymous eatery has been around since 1978. A roster of classic Italian dishes fills the menu here, with selections like osso buco Milanese (served with saffron risotto), grilled branzino, and ravioli made in-house with a different filling every day. Meat is also well-represented here, with selections such as porcini-rubbed ribeye steak, grilled veal chop and rack of lamb. Service is casual in the Art Deco-style dining room, where, as if to inspire diners, a colorful corner mural depicts a crowd of well-dressed revelers.

Four nights a week (Wednesday to Saturday from 9pm to 1am), a pianist tickles the ivories for patrons' entertainment in the bar area.

Bull and Bear

024

S t e a k h o u s e ✕✕

301 Park Ave. (bet. 49th & 50th Sts.)

Subway:	51 St	Mon – Fri noon - 11:30pm
Phone:	212-872-4900	Sat – Sun 5pm - 11:30pm
Fax:	212-872-1266	
Web:	www.waldorfastoria.com	
Prices:	$$$	

Picture an elegant English pub set about with mahogany wood, brass and crystal chandeliers, wine cabinets, cushy banquettes and plenty of mirrors, and you've got the Bull and Bear. Located on the ground floor of the legendary Waldorf=Astoria *(see hotel listings)*, this bar/restaurant takes its moniker from the bronze bull and bear statues—representing the rise and fall of the stock market—that lord over the elegant mahogany bar.

The place is popular with brokers and Wall Street types, who come for the signature martinis, the dry-aged Prime Angus beef and the classy men's-club ambience. Beef may be the focal point, but seafood is given equal attention here. Don't try wearing jeans and sneakers, though; the Bull and Bear's "elegant casual" dress code forbids them.

Canaletto

025

I t a l i a n ✕✕

208 E. 60th St. (bet. Second & Third Aves.)

Subway:	Lexington Av - 59 St	Open daily noon - 3pm & 5pm - 10:30pm
Phone:	212-317-9192	
Fax:	212-317-2855	
Web:	N/A	
Prices:	$$	

Attention Bloomingdale's shoppers: this neighborhood Italian spot, a half-block down 60th Street from Bloomie's, makes a great place for a lunch if you're looking to take a break from riffling through the racks.

A meal at classy, comfortable Canaletto begins with a plate of Italian salamis and aged parmesan cheese. Then move on to a pasta such as penne all'arabiatta, cooked perfectly al dente with spicy homemade tomato sauce. As for entrées, head towards the meat dishes, where the best flavors lie. It's easy to get your daily serving of olive oil and greens when you add on a side of the garlicky spinach or broccoli rabe.

You'll feel like part of the family here, where you'll find patient, cheerful service, along with prices that are very reasonable for the neighborhood.

The Capital Grille

026

Steakhouse XXX

155 E. 42nd St. (bet. Lexington & Third Aves.)

Subway:	Grand Central - 42 St	Mon – Fri 11:30am - 3pm & 5pm - 11pm
Phone:	212-953-2000	Sat 5pm - 11pm
Fax:	212-953-0244	Sun 5pm - 10pm
Web:	www.thecapitalgrille.com	Closed major holidays
Prices:	$$$$	

Here's an address that's well located for Midtown business lunchers. Two blocks east of Grand Central Terminal, the clubby Capital Grille occupies the ground floor of the seven-story Trylon Towers, part of the complex that includes the famed Chrysler Building. The Atlanta, Georgia-based chain made its New York debut in summer 2004, and Manhattanites are glad it did.

Here you can dine on juicy dry-aged steaks and chops, hand-cut and grilled precisely to your liking, or, if you prefer, there's broiled lobster and a selection of fresh fish. As far as wine goes, the inventory of 400 labels includes a Captain's List of rare vintages to round out your meal. Highly professional service from an amiable waitstaff completes the enjoyable experience here.

Casa La Femme North

027

Egyptian X

1076 First Ave. (bet. 58th & 59th Sts.)

Subway:	Lexington Av - 59 St	Sun – Wed 5pm - midnight
Phone:	212-505-0005	Thu – Sat 5pm - 3am
Fax:	212-505-3062	
Web:	www.oasisgroupny.com	
Prices:	$$	

Here's a place for a romantic interlude. Gauzy tents provide privacy for the tables lining the walls, creating the perfect setting in which to steal a kiss or make a proposal (note that the only dining option available at the tented tables is the prix-fixe menu). Formerly located on Prince Street in SoHo, Casa La Femme North brings its exotic mix to sometimes stuffy Midtown.

Not in the mood for romance? That's okay, you'll still enjoy the restaurant's foreign feel, with its hanging lanterns, curving banquettes and leafy palm trees. At dinner, a belly dancer shimmies her way around the room—did someone say "Take me to the Casbah?" Tasty North African cuisine, such as tagines served with fluffy homemade couscous, and baked whole fish, will vie with the dancer for your attention.

Cellini

028

Italian ✗

65 E. 54th St. (bet. Madison & Park Aves.)

Subway:	Lexington Av - 53 St	Mon – Sat noon - 3pm
Phone:	212-751-1555	& 5:30pm - 10:30pm
Fax:	212-753-2848	Closed Sun
Web:	www.cellinirestaurant.com	
Prices:	$$$	

Rustic and homey, that's Cellini. Indeed, you'll feel like family at this warm and welcoming restaurant, two blocks from the south end of Central Park. The dimly lit dining room is simply decorated with wood wainscoting, and wrought-iron chandeliers and wall sconces. Folk art and crockery plates enliven the otherwise plain walls, while the beamed ceiling is draped with cheery red fabric.

Like the décor, the food is not complicated; regional Italian dishes here are interpreted with a careful touch and prepared using high-quality ingredients. Specials might include homemade ravioli filled with grilled beets and sage in a four-cheese reduction, or veal martini, crusted with parmesan and sautéed in Absolut vodka and dry vermouth.

Chiam

029

Chinese ✗✗

160 E. 48th St. (bet. Lexington & Third Aves.)

Subway:	51 St	Sun – Fri 11:30am - 11pm
Phone:	212-371-2323	Sat 5pm - 11pm
Fax:	212-935-0012	
Web:	N/A	
Prices:	$$	

Don't confuse Chiam with the neighboring noodle joints. Chiam may not have the neighborhood authenticity of Chinatown, or the chi-chi star appeal of Mr Chow, but it does have serious Chinese cuisine and top-notch service. Think of this place, with its elegant dining room, fine china, lacquer chopsticks, and well-heeled clientele, as a place for a special occasion or for that expense-account business dinner.

Presented with flair, Hong Kong-style dishes are prepared using quality products and a refined technique that includes a soup-çon of European flavor. Dishes such as the Grand Marnier prawns tend to be challenging to finish, but accompaniments like sautéed watercress provide a welcome bitter foil to the richness. The impressive wine list is carefully selected to match the food.

Chikubu ☺

030

12 E. 44th St. (bet. Fifth & Madison Aves.)

Subway:	Grand Central - 42 St	Mon – Fri 11:30am - 2pm
Phone:	212-818-0715	& 5:30pm - 10pm
Fax:	N/A	Sat 5:30pm - 10pm
Web:	N/A	Closed Sun & major holidays
Prices:	**$$**	

Expect to find a line out the door of this authentic little Japanese spot at lunchtime most days. What's the attraction? A wide selection of Kyoto-style items, including sushi, sashimi, tempura, rice and noodles dishes. Specials include *hitsuma bushi* (served Monday through Thursday only), broiled eel in eel sauce ladled over rice mixed with scallions. The dish is presented in a heated bowl on a hot stone; the additional sauce is meant to be stirred into the rice. After all the ingredients are mixed up together, the serving is placed into a smaller bowl, where you can season it with the wasabi and extra broth provided.

Kimono-clad waitresses provide polite assistance to those diners who may not be familiar with Japanese dining traditions.

Da Antonio

031

157 E. 55th St. (bet. Lexington & Third Aves.)

Subway:	Lexington Av - 53 St	Mon – Fri noon - 3pm & 5pm - 11pm
Phone:	212-588-1545	Sat 5pm - 11pm
Fax:	212-588-1547	Closed Sun
Web:	www.daantonio.com	
Prices:	**$$**	

Father and son team Antonio and Mario Cerra preside over the dining room at this animated restaurant, located a few steps down from the street level. Fresh flowers and oil paintings festoon the space, which is crowded with white-clothed tables.

From the kitchen come wonderful pastas and well-prepared seafood, poultry and meat dishes, all made with fresh ingredients. The lunch and dinner menu is the same, and a pre-theater menu, with choice of appetizer, entrée and dessert, is offered nightly. Ignore the occasional flaws in the service, which makes up for in sincerity what it might lack in execution.

The bar scene here is a vibrant one, enlivened by nightly entertainment on the piano—you'll hear everything from oldies to jazz to show tunes, depending on who's playing.

Däwat

032

Indian ✗✗

210 E. 58th St. (bet. Second & Third Aves.)

Subway:	59 St	Mon – Thu 11:30am - 3pm
Phone:	212-355-7555	& 5:30pm - 11pm
Fax:	212-355-1735	Fri – Sat 11:30am - 3pm & 5:30pm - 11:30pm
Web:	www.restaurant.com/dawat	Sun 5pm - 10:30pm
Prices:	$$	

It's not every restaurant whose chef started out as an actor, but that's exactly what Madhur Jaffrey did. The Delhi native came to Däwat by way of the stage in England, and then to America, where she wrote articles about food to help support her family. Those articles led to a series of cookbooks about Indian cuisine, and well, the rest is history, as they say.

With a string of some ten titles to her credit, Jaffrey designed the menu at Däwat, where tandoori, curries and kebabs, as well as a host of vegetarian specialties, are as authentic as they are delicious. In addition to the comprehensive menu, guests can choose to sample Jaffrey's tasting menus, prepared for the entire table. Come on, dig in. How can you go wrong at a restaurant whose name means "invitation to feast?"

Diwan

033

Indian ✗

148 E. 48th St. (bet. Lexington & Third Aves.)

Subway:	51 St	Mon – Thu 11:30am - 2:30pm
Phone:	212-593-5425	& 5pm - 10:30pm
Fax:	212-593-5732	Fri 11:30am - 2:30pm & 5:30pm - 11pm
Web:	www.diwanrestaurant.com	Sat 11:30am - 3pm & 5:30pm - 11pm
Prices:	$$	Sun 11:30 - 3pm & 5pm - 10:30pm

The bounteous, inexpensive lunch buffet draws diners here at midday for a rich and varied selection of traditional dishes. Set out in front of the windows looking into the busy kitchen, the buffet is a good way to sample the regional fare of India, encompassing biriyani, vegetables spiced by Diwan's own special blend of masala, and curries accompanied by sweet-hot chutneys. At dinner, you can order from the pricier and well-edited à la carte menu, which is careful not to list too many items. Spice levels are toned down for an American palate, while many dishes get a modern, lighter interpretation.

Attractive rich fabrics and low lighting give the room warmth (though the leather chairs sit very low to the table), and a lively mix of locals and tourists lends the place a lived-in feel.

Django

034

480 Lexington Ave. (at 46 St.)

Subway:	Grand Central - 42 St
Phone:	212-871-6600
Fax:	212-871-6163
Web:	www.djangorestaurant.com
Prices:	$$$

Mon – Fri 11:30am - 2pm
& 5:30pm - 10:30pm
Sat 6pm - 10pm
Closed Sun

In the bohemian spirit of jazz guitarist Django Reinhardt, who wowed Paris audiences in the 1930s with his improvisational riffs, this restaurant embraces the carefree soul of a gypsy. Done by David Rockwell, the eclectic interior exudes an ethnic ambience with bright banquettes backed by cushy pillows, and a Murano glass chandelier to light the room. High ceilings and large windows lend an openness not often found in city dining rooms.

From the kitchen comes sunny "Riviera cuisine," which can include anything from bouillabaisse to spiced Angus beef tagine. Five- and eight-course dinner tasting menus show off inspired combinations by chef Andrew Karasz. To get in the mood, start with the house cocktail—the Djangito—a potent blend of Stoli Ohranj, yuzu juice and a dash of Cointreau.

Dona

035

208 E. 52nd St. (bet. Second & Third Aves.)

Subway:	51 St
Phone:	212-308-0830
Fax:	212-308-9190
Web:	www.donanyc.com
Prices:	$$$

Mon – Fri noon - 2:30pm
& 5pm - 10:30pm
Sat 5pm - 11pm
Closed Sun

Everything Donatella Arpaia (Ama, Davidburke & Donatella) touches seems to turn to gold, and Dona is no exception. Located in the former Bellini space, gorgeous Dona dresses in refreshing white, yellow and black with ultra-flattering low lighting and a mod, stylish vibe. Well-heeled, deep-pocketed patrons, many of whom were regulars at Bellini, flock here for inventive Mediterranean-influenced cuisine served by an amiable, attentive waitstaff.

Cumin-spiced tuna served over bulgar tossed with feta cheese hints of Greece, while shredded-veal-stuffed cannelloni highlight the chef's Italian mood. Detail-oriented, the ambitious kitchen plates meals with pride. The wine list presents a variety of unusual wines from Spain, Portugal and Greece, hospitably explained by the charming sommelier.

El Parador 😊

036

325 E. 34th St. (bet. First & Second Aves.)

Subway:	33 St	Open daily noon - 11pm
Phone:	212-679-6812	Closed Sun June - September
Fax:	212-889-1223	
Web:	www.elparadorcafe.com	
Prices:	$$	

Everything about El Parador is old-fashioned, but in the best possible way. Don't let the windowless façade turn you away; inside, the upbeat ambience and retro Mexican décor attract a grown-up crowd who enjoy animated conversation and killer margaritas at the bar.

While the cuisine balances traditional fare—like mole poblano, the national dish of Mexico—with Americanized dishes, all the food bursts with flavor and good-quality ingredients. A line on the bottom of the menu sums up the restaurant's attitude: "Please feel free to ask for any old favorite dish that you like." This may be very un-New York, but it's a charming offer and one you don't often see. Plus it speaks volumes about the service style here, which is warm, attentive and completely focused on the customer.

Felidia

037

243 E. 58th St. (bet. Second & Third Aves.)

Subway:	Lexington Av - 59 St	Mon – Fri noon - 3pm & 5pm - 11pm
Phone:	212-758-1479	Sat 5pm - 11:30pm
Fax:	212-935-7687	Sun 4pm - 10pm
Web:	www.lidiasitaly.com	
Prices:	$$$	

Lidia Bastianich is no stranger to the restaurant business. The empire of this TV personality and cookbook author currently includes eight establishments, four of them in New York City, but Felidia remains her flagship. In the bi-level dining room, sunny colors, towering flower arrangements and hardwood wine racks set a refined palette on which to present competent northern Italian cooking.

Whole-grilled Mediterranean sea bass and bitter-chocolate pappardelle with wild boar ragu are just a sampling of what you might find on the seasonal menu. Pastas are expertly prepared and topped with a variety of sauces, and Lidia's famous homemade cheesecake with caramelized pears guarantees a sweet finish. The award-winning wine list cites some 1,400 selections, most of them Italian.

The Four Seasons

American XXXX

038

99 E. 52nd St. (bet. Lexington & Park Aves.)

Subway:	51 St	Mon – Fri noon - 2:30pm & 5pm – 10pm
Phone:	212-754-9494	Sat 5pm - 11pm
Fax:	212-754-1077	Closed Sun
Web:	www.fourseasonsrestaurant.com	
Prices:	$$$$	

The moneyed, the powerful, the chic all frequent the Four Seasons, where they blend right in with the opulent setting. Designed by Mies van der Rohe and Philip Johnson, the restaurant boasts hand-loomed carpets, custom-designed tableware and original artwork by Picasso.

A serene white-marble pool forms the centerpiece of the Pool Room, while the Grill Room sports an appealing bar with an expert staff and a power-lunch scene to match. You've really made it in New York when Julian assigns you a regular lunch table in the Grill Room.

The kitchen updates classics (Chateaubriand, Dover sole), while respecting the traditional dishes patrons have been paying sizeable sums for since 1959. Dramatic floral displays add to the ambience—there's nothing like cherry blossom season by the pool here.

Fresco by Scotto

Italian XXX

039

34 E. 52nd St. (bet. Madison & Park Aves.)

Subway:	5 Av - 53 St	Mon – Fri 11:30am - 11pm
Phone:	212-935-3434	Sat 5pm - 11pm
Fax:	212-935-3436	Closed Sun
Web:	www.frescobyscotto.com	
Prices:	$$$	

You never know what familiar faces you might see here. Known as the "NBC Commissary" (check out the photographs of *Today Show* newscasters by the staircase), this lively Italian place has long attracted media moguls and politicos, whose expense accounts accommodate the upscale prices. The Scotto family established their restaurant in Midtown in 1993, not far from Rockefeller Center. Here, Marion Scotto warmly welcomes customers to the bright dining room, decorated with sunny scenes of the Italian landscape.

Hearty entrées include grilled Italian sausage filled with cheese and parsley, or a plate of fettucine with parmesan and black-truffle cream sauce. For those who don't have time for a sit-down lunch, adjacent Fresco by Scotto On The Go offers Scotto-quality food for home or office.

Giambelli 50th

040

Italian ✕✕

46 E. 50th St. (bet. Madison & Park Aves.)

Subway:	5 Av - 53 St
Phone:	212-688-2760
Fax:	212-751-6290
Web:	www.giambelli50.com
Prices:	$$$

Open daily noon - midnight

There's something to be said for consistency, and you can count on Frank Giambelli for that. Over the years since he opened his Gotham restaurant in 1960, Giambelli has fed mayors and minions, politicos and pundits—and even the Pope when he visited New York City. The draw? Consistently good, home-style Italian food, cooked to order. From the rolls to the desserts, everything here is made in-house. The menu presents a dizzying array of homemade pastas, tender meat dishes and fresh seafood.

Be sure to take a look at the collection of portraits by members of the Bachrach family, who, beginning with Bradford Bachrach, has photographed every American president since Abraham Lincoln in 1868. You'll find the photographs hanging on the walls in both the downstairs and upstairs dining rooms.

Grand Central Oyster Bar

041

Seafood ✕

Grand Central Terminal (Park Ave. & 42nd St.)

Subway:	Grand Central - 42 St
Phone:	212-490-6650
Fax:	212-949-5210
Web:	www.oysterbarny.com
Prices:	$$

Mon – Fri 11:30am - 9:30pm
Sat noon - 9:30pm
Closed Sun

&

Snag a seat at the counter here and prepare for a quintessential New York experience: oysters Rockefeller and clam chowder at the Oyster Bar. Located on the lower level of Grand Central Terminal, the historic Oyster Bar is a popular place, especially with regulars from the business-lunch brigade. Commuters waiting for their trains often pop in for a bite, too.

The restaurant, which opened in 1913, sports ceiling vaults tiled by Raphael Guastavino—making for a beautiful, but cacophonous, setting. The raw bar menu reads like an ode to the oyster, with dozens of varieties from Long Island's Blue Point to Oregon's Yaquina. Oysters are the clear winners here, but there's also a long list of other offerings, including the day's grilled fresh catch, seafood salads, and a lobster roll.

HanGawi

Korean ✗✗

042

12 E. 32nd St. (bet. Fifth & Madison Aves.)

Subway:	33 St	Mon – Fri noon - 10:30pm
Phone:	212-213-0077	Sat – Sun noon - 10:15pm
Fax:	121-689-0780	
Web:	www.hangawirestaurant.com	
Prices:	$$	

Don't worry about wearing your best shoes to HanGawi; you'll have to take them off at the door before settling in at one of the restaurant's low tables. In the serene space, decorated with Korean artifacts and soothed by meditative music, it's easy to forget you're in Manhattan.

The menu is all vegetarian (many of the dishes conform to vegan diets), in keeping with the restaurant's philosophy of healthy cooking to balance the yin and yang—or um and yang in Korean. You can quite literally eat like a king here; the emperor's roll and steamboat soup (on the prix-fixe menu) were once cooked in the royal kitchen.

Of course, all good things must end, and eventually you'll have to rejoin the rat race outside. Still, it's nice to get away from the pulsing vibe of the city . . . now and Zen.

Il Nido

Italian ✗✗✗

043

251 E. 53rd St. (bet. Second & Third Aves.)

Subway:	Lexington Av - 53 St	Mon – Sat noon - 3pm & 5pm - 11pm
Phone:	212-753-8450	Closed Sun
Fax:	212-224-0155	
Web:	www.ilnidonyc.com	
Prices:	$$$	

Patrons who enjoy dressing for dinner and being known by name flock to Il Nido. This old-school restaurant, with its outdated décor and established staff, treats diners to a classic formality not often seen anymore. Continental-style service from tuxedo-wearing waiters who fuss over diners like mother birds (*il nido* means "the nest") becomes theater here. From the owner's effusive greeting when you arrive to the staff's culinary show on tabletop gas stoves in the dining room, Il Nido is slightly over the top.

Old World northern Italian fare like linguine with clam sauce, spaghetti carbonara and swordfish sautéed with sun-dried tomatoes and capers are part and parcel of the menu, but the staff gladly handles guests making amendments or special off-the-menu orders.

Inagiku

044

111 E. 49th St. (bet. Lexington & Park Aves.)

Subway: 51 St
Phone: 212-355-0440
Fax: 212-888-3735
Web: www.inagiku.com
Prices: $$$

Mon – Fri noon - 2pm & 5:30pm - 10pm
Sat – Sun 5:30pm - 10pm

&

Tucked into a remote corner of the Waldorf=Astoria hotel, Inagiku owes its city-slick digs to renowned interior designer Adam Tihany. Traditional and contemporary elements play off each other in the same space here: whimsical representations of rice grains appear in custom-designed wall sconces; the paisley shape of the yin/yang symbol is etched on glass panels; and wooden slats undulate across the ceiling.

Like the design, the food pairs old with new. First courses are categorized by "cold" and "warm," and "classic little dishes" (think of them as Japanese tapas) give diners the opportunity to fashion their own meal from a number of small courses. Japanese ingredients, such as sweet red beans and green tea, flavor Inagiku's unique versions of desserts.

Jubilee

045

347 E. 54th St. (bet. First & Second Aves.)

Subway: Lexington Av - 53 St
Phone: 212-888-3569
Fax: 212-755-0614
Web: www.jubileeny.com
Prices: $$

Mon – Fri noon - 3pm & 5:30pm - 11pm
Sat 5:30pm - 11pm
Sun noon - 3pm & 5pm - 10pm
Closed Sun July & August

Your mother was right when she told you never to judge a book by its cover. From the outside, this little building may not look like much, but inside lies a pleasant space with soft lighting, a pressed-tin ceiling and neat rows of tables and banquettes lining the long, narrow room.

Prince Edward Island mussels are the signature dish here; they're prepared five different ways, and served Belgian-style with frites, or with a green salad for calorie counters. Otherwise, the menu has decided French leanings, with such classics as roasted chicken with mashed potatoes, leg of lamb, and escargots. Some dishes have a modern touch, like tuna tartare paired with ginger and guacamole. Desserts, including molten chocolate mousse cake, profiteroles and warm apple tart, are memorable.

La Grenouille

French XXXX

046

3 E. 52nd St. (bet. Fifth & Madison Aves.)

Subway:	5 Av - 53 St	Tue – Sat noon - 2:30pm
Phone:	212-752-1495	& 5:30pm - 11pm
Fax:	212-593-4964	Closed Sun & Mon
Web:	www.la-grenouille.com	Closed August
Prices:	$$$$	

Opened in 1962, La Grenouille manages to remain, all these years later, the Masson family's bastion of traditional high-priced French cuisine in Midtown. Charles and Gisèle Masson founded this establishment; today Charles junior oversees the enterprise his parents started. A high coffered ceiling, silk wall coverings and stunning arrangements of fresh flowers—a signature of the late Charles Masson the elder—characterize the lovely dining space, which is worthy of a special occasion. Style reigns at La Grenouille, which acts as a high-class cafeteria of sorts for those who still properly dress up for meals.

Menu selections might include simply prepared fish, meats braised in red wine, and, of course, the house signature—les *cuisses de grenouilles* (frogs legs prepared Provençal-style).

La Mangeoire

French XX

047

1008 Second Ave. (bet. 53rd & 54th Sts.)

Subway:	Lexington Av - 53 St	Sun – Thu noon - 3pm
Phone:	212-759-7086	& 5:30pm - 10:30pm
Fax:	212-759-6387	Fri – Sat noon - 3pm & 5:30pm - 11pm
Web:	www.lamangeoire.com	
Prices:	$$	

The countryside of southern France comes to mind when you enter this sunny restaurant. Copper cookware ornaments the walls, dried herbs and flowers hang from the beams, and rustic lanterns dangle from the vaulted ceiling. During warmer months, guests can also dine outdoors at the sidewalk tables.

Despite what you see, the cuisine here is not limited to the South of France—though the five-course Flavors of the Côte d'Azur tasting menu does focus on Provence. Entrées (rabbit legs simmered in mustard, herb-grilled baby lamb chops, sautéed diver scallops) are offered in both small and regular-size portions, so you can tailor the size of your meal to your appetite. Kick off the set-price Sunday brunch with a mimosa or a Bloody Mary before digging into egg dishes, salads and sandwiches.

Le Cirque

048

Contemporary ✗✗✗✗

151 E. 58th St. (bet. Lexington & Third Aves.)

Subway: 59 St
Phone: 212-644-0202
Fax: 212-644-0388
Web: www.lecirque.com
Prices: $$$$

Mon – Sat 11:45am - 2:30pm
& 5:30pm - 11pm
Sun 5:30pm - 10pm

Like many of its loyal ladies-who-lunch, the grand dame of New York restaurants, Le Cirque 2000, needed some time off to rest and revamp. After closing its doors in the New York Palace Hotel, the newest Le Cirque has recently reopened in the stylish Bloomberg Building. This incarnation is truly a masterpiece of design. Huge curving windows introduce a modern air, while the distinguished feel of past incarnations of Le Cirque remains with an impressive canopied ceiling and elegant deep burgundy carpets detailed with rich gold patterns.

Sirio Maccioni keeps a tight leash on his latest heir. It still draws one of the best power scenes in the city, with a mix of masters of the universe and socialites, who come here as much to be seen as they do for steamed branzino, Muscovy duck and pot au feu.

Le Colonial

049

Vietnamese ✗✗

149 E. 57th St. (bet. Lexington & Third Aves.)

Subway: 59 St
Phone: 212-752-0808
Fax: 212-752-7534
Web: www.lecolonialnyc.com
Prices: $$$

Mon – Fri noon - 2:30pm
& 5:30pm - 11pm
Sat – Sun 5:30pm - 11pm
Closed major holidays

New Yorkers can enjoy the vibrant cuisine of South Vietnam at Le Colonial. The kitchen's excellent interpretations of Vietnamese food include *bo bia*, soft vegetable-filled rolls served with a thick, sweet bean sauce; *pho*, an aromatic oxtail broth filled with noodles and chunks of beef tenderloin; and *ca chien Saigon*, crisp-seared whole red snapper. Diners may order à la carte or enjoy the prix-fixe menus at lunch and dinner.

The dining room, with its lazy ceiling fans, dark wood furnishings, tropical plants and historic black-and-white photographs, will transport you back to the turn of the century, when Vietnam was a French colony, then known as Indochina. Whether you're waiting for a table or just stopping by for a drink, you'll find a thriving scene at the upstairs bar.

Manhattan Midtown East & Murray Hill

Le Périgord

French

050

405 E. 52nd St. (off First Ave.)

Subway:	51 St
Phone:	212-755-6244
Fax:	212-486-3906
Web:	www.leperigord.com
Prices:	$$$

Open daily noon - 3pm & 5pm - 10pm

Just a few short blocks from the United Nations in leafy Sutton Place, Le Périgord wraps diners in luxury under its coffered ceiling, amid period chairs covered in willow-green fabric, Limoges china, crystal stemware and fresh flowers in pastel hues. This is a jacket-and-tie kind of place, where waiters in white waistcoats or black tuxedos provide formal service, and the lunch crowd consists largely of diplomats from the U.N.

Le Périgord is one of the few remaining old-fashioned French restaurants in New York City, and the classic entrées, from rack of lamb to sole meunière, bear testament to the tried and true. For the pièce de résistance, desserts are rolled to your table on a cart; count on a mouth-watering selection of homemade seasonal fruit tarts being among the choices.

L'Impero

051

Contemporary Italian

45 Tudor City Pl. (bet. 42nd & 43rd Sts.)

Subway:	Grand Central - 42 St
Phone:	212-599-5045
Fax:	212-599-5043
Web:	www.limpero.com
Prices:	$$$

Mon – Thu noon - 2:30pm
& 5:30pm - 10:30pm
Fri noon - 2:30pm & 5pm - 11:30pm
Sat 5pm - 11:30pm
Closed Sun & major holidays

You'll find L'Impero on the ground floor of one of the structures of Tudor City, a complex of 12 Tudor-style apartment buildings completed in 1928. This is the domain of chef/owner Scott Conant, also of Alto in Midtown East *(520 Madison Ave.).*

The kitchen staff adheres to Italian culinary tradition by using the best quality seasonal products they can find. This practice pays off in contemporary signature dishes like rich duck and foie gras agnolotti (all pastas are handmade in-house), marinated Pacific yellowtail and roasted Vermont *capretto* (pasture-raised baby goat).

Tables tend to be cramped in the elegant dining room, with its pale gray-green leather chairs and dark fabric banquettes fashioned by renowned designer Vicente Wolf.

Maloney & Porcelli

052

37 E. 50th St. (bet. Madison & Park Aves.)

Subway: 51 St
Phone: 212-750-2233
Fax: 212-750-2252
Web: www.maloneyandporcelli.com
Prices: $$$

Open daily noon – 11:30pm

No wonder lawyers frequent this restaurant; it's named after the owner's law firm. Torts are no doubt discussed in the attractive, bi-level dining room with its varnished woods and copper accents. Whether you have a law degree or not, you'd best bring a big appetite (and a big wallet) to dine on mammoth portions of grilled rib steaks and veal chops here.

The signature dish, the much-ordered crackling pork shank, is first deep-fried, then slow-roasted to hold in the juices. This hearty chunk of meat comes with jalapeño-pepper-spiked "firecracker" apple sauce. Side dishes (fresh-cut French fries, creamed spinach, whipped potatoes) are sized for sharing. Saturday brunch brings out well-dressed neighborhood residents.

March

Contemporary

053

405 E. 58th St. (bet. First Ave. & Sutton Pl.)

Subway: 59 St
Phone: 212-754-6272
Fax: 212-838-5108
Web: www.marchrestaurant.com
Prices: $$$

Open daily 5:30pm - 10:30pm

Once you enter this enchanting Sutton town house, through the brick-lined courtyard, you'll be immersed in a romantic aura, enhanced by a working fireplace, Limoges china, antique Persian carpets and Lalique vases.

The staff may initially overwhelm you with food choices, but relax—all you need to do is decide the number of courses you want (three, four, five or six) and select your dishes. Then sit back and put yourself in the creative and capable hands of the kitchen staff, whose elegant cuisine underscores New York's diverse culinary heritage. There is often a superb lobster entrée on the menu, and the hirame sashimi is a well-balanced starter.

Weather permitting, you can dine alfresco on the rooftop terrace, overlooking the 59th Street Bridge and the Bridgemarket complex.

Manhattan Midtown East & Murray Hill

Métrazur

054

American 🍴🍴

Grand Central Terminal (42nd St. at Park Ave.)

Subway:	Grand Central - 42 St	Mon – Fri 11:30am – 3pm
Phone:	212-687-4600	& 5pm - 10:30pm
Fax:	212-687-5671	Sat 5pm - 10:30pm
Web:	www.charliepalmer.com	Closed Sun
Prices:	$$$	

Métrazur takes every advantage of its spectacular location on the east balcony of Grand Central Terminal. The sleek design of the two large dining rooms plays against the opulence of the station's cavernous main concourse. Prime seats allow guests to view the intricate architectural details, and the acoustics are very conducive to conversation.

Owned by famed chef Charlie Palmer, Métrazur is named for a train that once traveled France's Côte d'Azur on its way to Monaco. Indeed, you'll find that flavors of the Mediterranean infuse seasonally changing dishes like tapenade-brushed halibut and ravioli filled with pulled oxtail meat and served in a heady porcini broth topped with frizzled leeks. The large bar that wraps around the dining space provides a prime spot for a pre-train cocktail.

Michael Jordan's

055

Steakhouse 🍴🍴

Grand Central Terminal (corner of Park Ave. & 42nd St.)

Subway:	Grand Central - 42 St	Mon – Fri noon - 11pm
Phone:	212-655-2300	Sat 5pm - 11pm
Fax:	212-271-2324	Sun 5pm - 10pm
Web:	www.theglaziergroup.com	
Prices:	$$$	

There's no denying that dining in Grand Central Terminal affords one of the best views in the city—indoor views, anyway. From Michael Jordan's on the west balcony, you can gaze up to see the constellations of the zodiac painted on the soaring vaulted ceiling; its 12-story height would dwarf even "His Airness" himself.

At dinner, generous servings of Prime dry-aged Angus beef are what you can expect here. Sides are heavy on the carbs (potatoes come mashed, baked or as French fries). Lunch adds lighter salads (Cobb; Maine lobster; breast of chicken) for those who don't want to lapse into a food-induced stupor during that afternoon meeting. Oenophiles will want to book a dinner or cocktail party in the wine salon.

The elliptical mahogany bar is a chic setting for a happy-hour beverage.

Monkey Bar

056

Steakhouse ✗✗✗

60 E. 54th St. (bet. Madison & Park Aves.)

Subway: 5 Av - 53 St
Phone: 212-838-2600
Fax: 212-838-4595
Web: www.theglaziergroup.com
Prices: $$$

Mon – Fri 11:30am - 2:30pm
& 5:30pm - 11pm
Sat 5:30pm - 11pm
Closed Sun

Former haunt of actors Tallulah Bankhead and Marlon Brando, baseball great Joe DiMaggio and playwright Tennessee Williams, the Elysée Hotel's *(see hotel listings)* Monkey Bar was the place to be in the 1930s. Today it's still a popular, albeit pricey, watering hole. You'll feel like you're on the set of an old Hollywood movie, set about by walls covered in burgundy fabric, Art Deco chandeliers and glass panels separating the cushy banquettes.

And while a horde of simians may frolic on the restored hand-painted murals in the 1930s bar, there's no monkeying around when it comes to the food. Order your favorite cut of meat, from New York strip to double-cut lamb T-bone, along with a side of crispy fried onions or black truffle creamed spinach, and settle back to take in the scene.

Morton's

057

Steakhouse ✗✗✗

551 Fifth Ave. (enter on 45th St. bet Fifth & Madison Aves.)

Subway: 5 Av
Phone: 212-972-3315
Fax: 212-972-0018
Web: www.mortons.com
Prices: $$$

Mon – Fri 11:30am - 11pm
Sat 5pm - 11pm
Sun 5pm - 10pm

Part of a chain that started in Chicago and now extends across the U.S. and into Canada and the Far East, Morton's reigns as a well-respected chophouse. The Fifth Avenue location lies within easy walking distance of Grand Central Terminal and Times Square. In the often crowded dining space, the soaring ceiling leaves room for a mezzanine overlooking the first floor. Clubby, masculine décor incorporates mahogany paneling, booths lining the wall, and imposing chandeliers.

The menu, which is the same in all Morton's locations, centers on USDA Prime aged beef, but also features crab cakes and lobster— all at rather beefy prices. California vintages are the focus of the extensive wine list. Morton's convenient Midtown location makes it popular with area business people and tourists alike.

Mr Chow

Chinese ✗✗

058

324 E. 57th St. (bet. First & Second Aves.)

Subway:	59 St	Open daily 6pm - midnight
Phone:	212-751-9030	
Fax:	212-644-0352	
Web:	www.mrchow.com	
Prices:	$$$	

Actor, artist, interior designer and restaurateur, Michael Chow did the design for all four of his establishments (two of the others are in Southern California; the fourth is in London). A striking mobile fashioned of red fabric hangs above the bustling and oh-so-hip black and white dining room, where even the waiters have trouble moving between the closely spaced tables.

Diners don't seem to mind the cramped quarters, though; Mr. Chow lures a high-profile crowd night after night. It's not cool to ask for a menu here; it's expected you'll allow your waiter to order for you (though they will grudgingly bring a menu if you insist). Downtown residents need not venture north for Chow; a location at 121 Hudson Street in TriBeCa is now open, and it's sure to be an equally trendy address.

Nicole's

American ✗✗✗

059

10 E. 60th St. (bet. Fifth & Madison Aves.)

Subway:	5 Av - 59 St	Mon – Sat noon - 4pm
Phone:	212-223-2288	Closed Sun
Fax:	212-233-5112	
Web:	www.nicolefarhi.com	
Prices:	$$	

Food follows fashion at Nicole's, the eponymous restaurant located in the basement of Nicole Farhi's Midtown boutique. When you need a break from rifling through the racks of chic men's and women's clothing created by the Britain-based designer, just follow the staircase down to the sleek, 4,000-square-foot restaurant. While you're deciding what to order, you can check out the action in the kitchen, housed in an ice-blue illuminated glass cube.

Here, a talented cooking team prepares seasonal dishes with a Cal-Med spirit. The menu, which changes daily, incorporates an array of premium ingredients ranging from local organic produce to fine imported food items.

Just a stone's throw away from the boutiques on Fifth and Madison avenues, Nicole's attracts a steady stream of ladies who lunch.

Osteria Laguna

060

Italian ✗

209 E. 42nd St. (bet. Second & Third Aves.)

Subway:	Grand Central - 42 St	Mon – Fri 11:30am - 11pm
Phone:	212-557-0001	Sat – Sun 5pm - 11pm
Fax:	212-692-0473	
Web:	www.osteria-laguna.com	
Prices:	$$	

♿

Convenient to Grand Central Terminal and the United Nations, Osteria Laguna is tucked into the ground floor of a redbrick office building. Surprisingly charming for this stretch of 42nd Street, the dining space is separated into two rooms: a sunny, high-ceilinged front room, lit by large windows and wrought-iron chandeliers; and a more intimate back room, with white-clothed tables and black banquettes lining the walls. Large posters and Palio-style banners add a colorful note.

For the most part warm and pleasant, the waitstaff delivers authentic fare such as homemade pasta, pizza and risotto to your table. Other entrées run the gamut from roasted branzino to veal saltimbocca. Rustic food is complemented by a casual, laid-back style, and the prices are easy on the wallet.

P.J. Clarke's

061

Gastropub ✗

915 Third Ave. (at 55th St.)

Subway:	Lexington Av - 53 St	Open daily 11:30am - 4am
Phone:	212-317-1616	
Fax:	212-317-2043	
Web:	www.pjclarkes.com	
Prices:	⌒⌒	

Named for Patrick Joseph Clarke, who purchased the place in 1904, this saloon remains a slice of old New York, despite its change of ownership in 2002.

Pub fare still reigns at this former haunt of Frank Sinatra and Jackie O: big burgers, shepherd's pie and a long list of beers on tap. The bar scene, usually packed four deep with one of the city's best happy-hour crowds, overshadows the food, but this doesn't faze the good-looking young professionals who come to meet and greet. If you have to wait for a table (the restaurant doesn't take reservations), the bar is the place to be.

The latest additions to the family include P.J. Clarke's on the Hudson *(Four World Financial Center at Vesey St.)*, and P.J. Clarke's at Lincoln Center *(W. 63rd St. at Columbus Ave.)*.

Manhattan Midtown East & Murray Hill

Pampano

062

209 E. 49th St. (bet. Second & Third Aves.)

Subway:	51 St	Mon – Wed 11:30am - 2:30pm
Phone:	212-751-4545	& 5pm - 10:30pm
Fax:	212-751-0800	Thu – Fri 11:30am - 3pm & 5pm - 11pm
Web:	www.modernmexican.com/pampano	Sat 5pm - 10:30pm
Prices:	$$$	Sun 5pm - 10pm

Here's an unlikely marriage: opera star Placido Domingo and Acapulco-born chef Richard Sandoval. It's not a literal marriage, of course, but a business partnership; both are co-owners of Pampano. Here, Sandoval uses European techniques to bring the vivid flavors of Mexico to life.

The airy dining room, with its crisp white walls, sand-colored banquettes and light pouring in from the loft-style glass ceiling, evokes sun-bleached shores. Accordingly, fish takes top billing on the menu, appearing in seafood tacos, empanadas, tamales and quesadillas, as well as forming the focus of the ceviche tastings. Traditional sides include fried plantains, and black beans and rice. Top it all off with a perfect margarita, and it's almost like being by the beach in Acapulco.

Phoenix Garden ☺

063

242 E. 40th St. (bet. Second & Third Aves.)

Subway:	Grand Central - 42 St	Open daily 11:45am - 10:30pm
Phone:	212-983-6666	
Fax:	212-490-6666	
Web:	N/A	
Prices:	⌘⌘	

You'll find this gem of a Chinese place not in Chinatown, but tucked into a modest brick building in Murray Hill. Inside, there's nothing remarkable about the décor, but authentic Cantonese specialties keep locals coming back for more and more.

The extensive menu cites some 200 different choices, but it's worth requesting input from the friendly staff to assist in narrowing down your options. Don't miss the steamed chive dumplings, pepper and salty shrimp and pea shoots with crabmeat sauce. In addition, the daily specials on the blackboard in the entryway usually list entrées like Peking duck and steamed whole fish. The menu is meant for sharing, so bring as many friends as you can.

Prices can't be beat, especially considering that you can BYOB (Phoenix Garden doesn't serve alcohol).

Picasso

064

303 E. 56th St. (bet. First & Second Aves.)

Subway: 59 St
Phone: 212-759-8767
Fax: 212-759-8801
Web: www.restaurantpicasso.com
Prices: $$

Mon – Fri noon - 11pm
Sat – Sun 1pm - 11pm

Posters of toreadors and flamenco dancers evoke sunny Spain here, as does the long bar lined with giant jars of olives, legs of *jamón* and pork, and an enormous tortilla on a pedestal. Authentic fare from paella to *tortilla a la Espanola* draw Spanish ex-patriots who come here to chat up the bartender or catch up with *El País*.

A variety of seafood, meats and poultry fills the menu; many entrées are served tableside from their cast-iron cooking pots. If you're not up for a big meal, tapas are listed, Spanish-style, on the wall: *jamón Serrano*, chorizo, beef empanadas and croquetas are just a sampling. Then take your pick from the list of full-bodied Riojas and other regional Spanish wines. The hospitable waitstaff adds to the convivial atmosphere, animated by a lively clientele.

Pietro's

065

232 E. 43rd St. (bet. Second & Third Aves.)

Subway: Grand Central - 42 St
Phone: 212-682-9760
Fax: 212-682-4379
Web: www.pietros.com
Prices: $$$

Mon – Sat noon - 3pm & 5:30pm - 10pm
Closed Sun

Trendy it's not. Inexpensive? Not with a Midtown address in the shadow of the Chrysler Building. Founded in 1932 by Pietro Donini and his brother Natale, Pietro's is an old-fashioned Italian eatery. The plain dining room sports a patriotic (for Italy) red, green and white color scheme, and the food will certainly be familiar: minestrone, chicken Parmigiana, spaghetti with meatballs, veal Marsala, shrimp scampi, along with steaks and chops. Your Italian grandmother probably didn't even cook food this good, but Pietro won't tell.

Pietro's may not have a chic décor or a fancy menu, but don't overlook this tried-and-true place. The service is good and preparations are rendered using excellent, fresh ingredients and homemade pasta—now that's Italian!

Raffaele

066

1055 First Ave. (bet. 57th & 58th Sts.)

Subway:	Lexington Av - 59 St	Mon – Fri noon - 3pm & 5pm - midnight
Phone:	212-750-3232	Sat 5pm - midnight
Fax:	212-750-0077	Closed Sun
Web:	www.raffaele.citysearch.com	
Prices:	$$	

Owner Raffaele Esposito, the restaurant's namesake, greets customers personally here. A former chef at Rome's Grand Hotel, Esposito now manages his own Southern Italian eatery in Midtown. The attractive dining room is done with bright-red walls, a green ceiling and black and white floor tiles. Photographs of Italy line the walls, while small bunches of dried red chiles adorn the white-clothed tables.

Traditional Italian fare fills the menu, along with daily specials (and a frequently changing roster of desserts). Pasta and risotto dishes are always a sure bet, and chicken, meat and seafood are prepared in a variety of delicious ways. If you fall in love with Raffaele's sauce after a meal here, you can buy it by the pint before you leave.

Riingo

067

205 E. 45th St. (bet. Second & Third Aves.)

Subway:	Grand Central - 42 St	Mon – Wed noon - 2:30pm
Phone:	212-867-4200	& 5:30pm - 10:30pm
Fax:	212-867-1700	Thu – Fri noon - 2:30pm & 5:30pm - 11pm
Web:	www.riingo.com	Sat 5:30pm - 11pm
Prices:	$$	Sun 11am - 3pm

Derived from the Japanese word for "apple" (as in the Big Apple), Riingo features Scandinavian chef Marcus Samuelsson's interpretation of Japanese and American dishes. The stylish, contemporary restaurant, just off the lobby of the Alex Hotel *(see hotel listings)*, incorporates ebony wood, bamboo floor planks and thoughtful touches such as custom-made ceramic sake sets. Located in the lounge, a bar complements the small (40 seats) downstairs dining room and is a popular place for an after-work cocktail.

In addition to the creative kitchen menu and extensive raw-bar selection, Riingo offers a full range of sushi and maki of impressive quality. Open for all-day dining, Riingo and its original menu rise a cut above your typical hotel restaurant.

Rosa Mexicano

068

1063 First Ave. (at 58th St.)

Subway:	59 St	Mon – Thu 5pm - 10:30pm
Phone:	212-753-7407	Fri – Sun 4pm - 11:30pm
Fax:	212-753-7433	
Web:	www.rosamexicano.com	
Prices:	$$	

Rosa Mexicano promises good food and a good time and it always delivers. While outposts have popped up in New York *(61 Columbus Ave. at W. 62nd St.; 9 E. 18th St., between Fifth Ave. & Broadway)* and other cities, this East Side location is the original.

With its terrific pomegranate margaritas and guacamole made to order, the bar is usually packed three deep and is the place to wait for a table or unwind after work. The waitstaff is as lively as the scene, which feels like a continuous party. Reservations are difficult to secure at the last minute, so plan ahead—especially on weekends.

Decadent entrées like *budin Azteca* (multi-layer tortilla pie), and *salmon en Manchamanteles* (crusted with blue corn and served with a Manchamanteles mole) display elements of both upscale and comfort food.

Rothmann's

069

3 E. 54th St. (bet. Fifth & Madison Aves.)

Subway:	5 Av - 53 St	Mon – Fri 11:30am - 11pm
Phone:	212-319-5500	Sat 4pm - 11pm
Fax:	212-319-5540	Sun 5pm - 10pm
Web:	www.rothmannssteakhouse.com	Closed major holidays
Prices:	$$$	

It all started in 1907, when Charles and Franziska Rothmann purchased a little cafe in Brooklyn and an inn on Long Island. Now, Rothmann's reigns as a Manhattan meat lovers' heaven.

Colorado lamb chops, Prime dry-aged Porterhouse steaks, roasted pork loin chops and bone-in ribeyes are all served in a comfortable and upscale atmosphere of rosy carpets, mahogany wood and banquettes covered with soft beige leather. The sommelier can help decipher the extensive wine list; with some 600 different selections from around the globe, you might just need some assistance narrowing down your choices. Don't expect any bargains, though—remember that you're in Midtown.

For succulent steak on Long Island, visit Rothmann's in East Norwich.

Manhattan Midtown East & Murray Hill

Sakagura

070

211 E. 43rd St. (bet. Second & Third Aves.)

Subway:	Grand Central - 42 St	Mon — Thu noon - 2:30pm
Phone:	212-953-7253	& 6pm - 11:45pm
Fax:	212-682-1957	Fri noon - 2:30pm & 6pm - 12:45am
Web:	www.sakagura.com	Sat 6pm - 12:45am
Prices:	$$$	Sun 6pm - 10:45pm

It's all about sake at Sakagura. Although the restaurant is located in the basement of a Midtown office building (enter the lobby and walk down the back stairs), this is as authentic a sake den as you'll find in the city. Here, you'll be transported to Tokyo with traditional Japanese décor, secluded booths and tables filled with Japanese businessmen.

More than 200 kinds of sake are exquisitely presented in imported serving sets carefully selected by the helpful staff. The menu plays a supporting role, designed to complement the sake list (no sushi is served, only sashimi, to best enjoy the sake). Other than that, the tremendous menu does not skimp on variety, authenticity or quality. Share a few small plates at a time as part of a lengthy ritual of nibbling and sake sipping.

San Pietro

Italian

071

18 E. 54th St. (bet. Fifth & Madison Aves.)

Subway:	5 Av - 53 St	Mon — Sat noon - 2:45pm
Phone:	212-753-9015	& 5pm - 10:30pm
Fax:	212-371-2337	Closed Sun
Web:	www.sanpietro.net	
Prices:	$$$	

At San Pietro, the chef imports more than three-quarters of his ingredients, including cheeses and fish, from southern Italy (a practice, as you'd expect, that comes at a price). The three Bruno brothers run this traditional restaurant, where ancient recipes from Rome and Campania are revived and revitalized.

Vegetables figure prominently on the generous, seasonally changing menu: fresh fava beans are flavored with pecorino cheese and black truffles, broccoli rabe is sautéed in olive oil and garlic. Sure, there are pastas and risotto, but the signature dish is Pesce San Pietro, John Dory braised in garlic sauce scented with thyme and served with baked fennel and toasted hazelnuts.

Ceramic murals, decorative odes to the owners' native region of Campania, enhance the elegant dining area.

Sarge's

072

548 Third Ave. (bet. 36th & 37th Sts.)

Subway:	33 St	Open daily 24 hours
Phone:	212-679-0442	
Fax:	212-545-1540	
Web:	www.sargesdeli.com	
Prices:	🍪	

Opened many moons ago by former NYPD sergeant Abe Katz, Sarge's is a classic New York deli that pulls in a steady stream of locals. Pastrami is king here, but you can't go wrong with any of the choices, which range from blintzes to matzoh ball soup. If you can squeeze in dessert after a triple-decker sandwich or a deli Wellington (a diet-busting combination of corned beef, pastrami and potatoes baked in a puff-pastry shell), Sarge's serves a mean cheesecake.

Abe is no longer on hand to chat up the customers, but the chipper waitstaff makes everyone feel like a regular, and children are always welcome. Still run by the Katz family, Sarge's is a Murray Hill must for a real New York deli experience.

For Long Island-bound commuters, Sarge's has a location in Syosset *(236 Jericho Tpk.)*.

Seo

073

249 E. 49th St. (bet. Second & Third Aves.)

Subway:	51 St	Mon – Fri noon - 2:30pm
Phone:	212-355-7722	& 5:30pm - 10:30pm
Fax:	212-355-6940	Sat – Sun 5:30pm - 10:30pm
Web:	N/A	
Prices:	$$	

Seo is the lovely sort of neighborhood spot you'd like to be a regular at, so you could enjoy their authentic Japanese cuisine all the time. It's an understated place, located on a residential block near the United Nations, The Japan Society and the "Dag." In a neighborhood rich with Japanese eateries, Seo stands out for its excellent light dishes, such as miso-marinated cod, sake-steamed clams and squid, and eel and cucumber vinaigrette. They serve sushi and sashimi too, but don't let these dominate your meal or you'll miss out on the menu's variety.

Seo offers a good selection (given the restaurant's size) of sakes and beers to match the food. Sit at the sushi bar, or claim a table in the serene little dining room that overlooks a traditional Japanese garden behind the town house.

Manhattan Midtown East & Murray Hill

Shaburi

074

125 E. 39th St. (bet. Lexington & Park Aves.)

Subway:	Grand Central - 42 St
Phone:	212-867-6999
Fax:	212-867-7435
Web:	www.shaburi.com
Prices:	$$$

Mon – Thu noon - 3pm & 5:30pm - 11pm
Fri 5:30pm - midnight
Sat 5pm - midnight
Sun 5pm - 11pm

In an age where everything is interactive, Shaburi fits right in with hands-on dining. Both the communal bar and individual tables are equipped with electric burners for making shabu shabu, the house specialty. Just order the ingredients that appeal (Matsuzaka beef, Kurobuta pork, seafood, veggies) and simmer them in hot broth at your table. While you're at it, you can use the tabletop burners to stir-fry bite-size pieces of meat or tofu, marinated in sugar or soy, for sukiyaki (served over rice or udon).

Especially at night, it's lots of fun for a group of friends—and a great ice-breaker for that awkward first date. Wet your whistle with a sake, a house cocktail or Kirin on tap (not often found in New York). The first American outpost of a Taiwanese chain, Shaburi opened in 2004.

Sip Sak

075

928 Second Ave. (bet. 49th & 50th Sts.)

Subway:	51 St
Phone:	212-583-1900
Fax:	212-583-1777
Web:	www.sip-sak.com
Prices:	🍴

Open daily noon - midnight
Closed Sun in Summer

Turkish native and talented chef Orhan Yegen is notorious for loving and leaving the restaurants he opens. His current flame is Sip Sak, a homey place where a young Turkish waitstaff welcomes a crowd of international neighborhood residents.

The chef's manic personality pervades the room, as he seems to have a hand in every table while overseeing the take-out orders and the kitchen. He may be peripatetic, but he produces some outstanding Turkish food—which is an excellent value, to boot. The best ingredients, handled with traditional Turkish techniques, yield tasty and well-balanced dishes including meze, kebabs and zesty grilled lamb meatballs.

Will Yegen stay with Sip Sak? That remains to be seen, but with any luck, this romance will last a long time.

Smith & Wollensky

076

S t e a k h o u s e ✗✗✗

797 Third Ave. (at 49th St.)

Subway:	51 St	Open daily 11:45am - 2am
Phone:	212-753-1530	
Fax:	212-751-5446	
Web:	www.smithandwollensky.com	
Prices:	$$$	

Part of a well-known chain with locations in 10 other U.S. cities, Smith & Wollensky's 390-seat New York flagship opened in 1977 and still reigns as one of the city's most celebrated steakhouses. (Oddly, the restaurant's name is not related to its owners; founder Alan Stillman picked the two surnames randomly from the phone book).

USDA Prime beef, which is dry-aged on the premises, accounts for Smith & Wollensky's fine reputation. The décor is old-school steakhouse, with wood floors, dark green painted over white on the walls, and accents of brass throughout the room.

For night owls, adjoining Wollensky's Grill (the restaurant's separate bar/lounge) serves a less-expensive menu of light fare until 2am, complete with a rowdy post-work party at the bar.

Sparks Steak House

077

S t e a k h o u s e ✗✗

210 E. 46th St. (bet. Second & Third Aves.)

Subway:	Grand Central - 42 St	Mon – Thu noon - 11pm
Phone:	212-687-4855	Fri – Sat noon - 11:30pm
Fax:	212-557-7409	Closed Sun
Web:	www.sparksnyc.com	
Prices:	$$$	

With seating for 687 people, Sparks is well equipped to handle crowds. Indeed, it has drawn hordes of expense-account types for years. The bi-level dining space feels even more gigantic on an evening when the place is jamming. There's a raucous, masculine vibe, enhanced by dark woods, large tables, and 19th-century landscapes of the Hudson River Valley lining the wainscoted walls.

Unlike many New York steakhouses, Sparks doesn't offer a Porterhouse, but thick cuts of Prime sirloin and filet mignon will satisfy your beef cravings (for seafood lovers, lobsters weigh in from 3 to nearly 6 pounds). Appetizers lean toward classics like shrimp cocktail and tomato-onion salad.

Waiting for a table here is de rigueur, but speedy bartenders will shake a frosty martini for you in the meantime.

Sushi-Ann

Japanese ✗✗

078

38 E. 51st St. (bet. Madison & Park Aves.)

Subway:	51 St	Mon – Fri noon - 2:45pm & 6pm - 10pm
Phone:	212-755-1780	Sat 5:30pm - 9:30pm
Fax:	212-755-1788	Closed Sun & major holidays
Web:	www.sushiann.com	
Prices:	$$	

Located just around the corner from Saks (in case you need a break from shopping), Sushi-Ann is a refreshingly unpretentious haven with its L-shaped sushi bar and blond varnished-wood tables, all adorned with fresh roses. This place next to the New York Palace Hotel is a good choice for a traditional sushi experience. Not to be overlooked, Sushi-Ann competes with the best sushi bars in the city.

Uniformed waiters cater to a casual clientele that includes business types as well as tourists, who all enjoy the excellent quality and variety of the sushi, sashimi and hand rolls served here. Those in the know take a seat at the sushi bar (there's a $30 minimum at the sushi counter) for individualized selections from the friendly and talented chefs.

Though pricey, the sake list highlights a number of good selections.

Sushiden

Japanese ✗✗

079

19 E. 49th St. (bet. Fifth & Madison Aves.)

Subway:	5 Av - 53 St	Mon – Fri & Sun 11:45am - 2:15pm
Phone:	212-758-2700	& 5:30pm - 10pm
Fax:	212-644-2942	Closed Sat & major holidays
Web:	www.sushiden.com	
Prices:	$$$	

Inside Sushiden's windowed façade you'll find a long sushi bar, behind which several chefs work their magic, preparing raw fish with a legerdemain that proves the old saying that the hand is quicker than the eye. Each piece of fresh fish is sized perfectly over its tiny bed of rice, so the taste of one ingredient doesn't overwhelm the others (regulars recommend the toro, a fatty and flavorful cut of tuna taken from the fish's belly). As at many Japanese restaurants, a good selection of fixed-price meals are also offered, all at a good value. Young women in kimonos attend to customers in an efficient and pleasant manner.

The restaurant is closed on Saturdays, but is a good bet for weekday sushi. If you're on the West Side, there's a second Sushiden at 123 West 49th Street.

Sushi Ichimura

080

Japanese ✗✗

1026 Second Ave. (bet. 54th & 55th Sts.)

Subway:	Lexington Av - 53 St	Open daily 6pm - 11:30pm
Phone:	212-355-3557	
Fax:	N/A	
Web:	N/A	
Prices:	$$$$	

This sliver of a Japanese restaurant hides behind a façade of frosted glass. Inside, the place sparkles with refined settings of lacquerware, hand-thrown ceramics, and unique sake sets. The main focus of Ichimura, however, is the food. Choice products star in courses like sake-marinated broiled king salmon, and monkfish liver served with yuzu compote. Visible at all times from the dining room, the talented kitchen staff takes incredible care in preparing each dish and arranging the food simply but artfully on the plate; chef Ichimura's doting presence assures perpetual quality.

An upscale clientele lingers over their plates, savoring sushi cut from fish that is flown in from Tokyo several times a week, while the warm and remarkably attentive staff tends to their every need.

Sushi Yasuda

081

Japanese ✗✗

204 E. 43rd St. (bet. Second & Third Aves.)

Subway:	Grand Central - 42 St	Mon – Fri noon - 2:15pm
Phone:	212-972-1001	& 6pm - 10:15pm
Fax:	212-972-1717	Sat 6pm - 10:15pm
Web:	www.sushiyasuda.com	Closed Sun
Prices:	$$$$	

Discreetly tucked away in the corridor between Grand Central Terminal and the United Nations, Sushi Yashuda appears almost Scandinavian with its blond woods and contemporary style. But look again: the walls, tables, ceiling and floor are all wrapped in solid bamboo planks. Even the sushi bar, the domain of Japanese chef Naomichi Yasuda, is made of unfinished bamboo.

Yasuda, whose twenty years of experience include gigs in Tokyo and New York City, is a stickler for purity and simplicity. His raw fish offerings change daily, depending on the most pristine products available. Sushi and rolls are traditional edo style, served in small pieces specifically seasoned to enhance the flavor of each. Between the deft sushi chefs and the friendly servers, Sushi Yasuda knows how to please.

Manhattan Midtown East & Murray Hill

Tao

082

42 E. 58th St. (bet. Madison & Park Aves.)

Subway:	59 St	Mon – Tue 11:30am - midnight
Phone:	212-888-2288	Wed – Fri 11:30am - 1am
Fax:	212-888-4148	Sat 5pm - 1am
Web:	www.taorestaurant.com	Sun 5pm - midnight
Prices:	$$$	

Asia's tastiest dishes star at this former movie theater, built in the 19th century as a stable for the Vanderbilt family. It's hard to imagine catching a flick in this space today, outfitted as it is with a Chinese scroll draped across the ceiling and a 16-foot-high statue of Buddha towering over a reflecting pool in the main dining room. The theater's former balconies now accommodate diners, too—some 300 of them on three levels.

The menu spotlights mainly Hong Kong Chinese, Japanese and Thai dishes, from Thai seafood hot pots to Tao lo mein with roast pork. Perfect for sharing, a host of small plates offers everything from dragon-tail spare ribs to lobster wontons. On weekend nights, the scene becomes a real show, as Manhattan's young and restless turn out in droves.

Teodora

Italian

083

141 E. 57th St. (bet. Lexington & Third Aves.)

Subway:	Lexington Av - 59 St	Mon – Sat noon - 11pm
Phone:	212-826-7101	Sun noon - 10:30pm
Fax:	212-826-7138	
Web:	www.teodoranyc.com	
Prices:	$$	

It's a pleasant surprise to discover this dark, cozy restaurant on 57th Street, one of Midtown's busiest commercial thoroughfares. Providing a respite from the buzz just outside, the long, narrow dining room recalls a typical bistro with its wood bar, Belle Époque-style light fixtures and shelves lined with bottles of wine and carafes of vinegar.

Chef/owner Giancarlo Quadalti, who, with his partner, Roberta Ruggini, also owns Celeste on the Upper West Side, hails from the Emilia-Romagna area of Italy. Accordingly, the menu emphasizes northern Italian dishes that use staples from his native region, such as Parmigiano Reggiano and aged balsamic vinegar. Specials listed on the blackboards are particularly enjoyable.

If you're in the Village, visit sister Bianca (*5 Bleecker St.*).

The Water Club

Seafood ✗✗✗

084

E. 30th St. (at the East River)

Subway:	33 St	Mon – Sat noon - 3pm & 5pm - 11pm
Phone:	212-683-3333	Sun 11am - 3pm & 5:30pm - 10pm
Fax:	212-646-4099	
Web:	www.thewaterclub.com	
Prices:	$$	

Set on an elegant barge on the East River, the Water Club boasts the perfect ambience for a romantic night out in Murray Hill. With floor-to-ceiling windows overlooking the river, and water views from every table, the restaurant provides a respite from the crowded city streets. Marine signal flags hanging from the ceiling and a waitstaff dressed as a ship's crew complete the nautical theme.

The menu celebrates American dishes and spotlights seafood such as Maryland-style she-crab soup and Maine lobster. A few meat dishes like Colorado rack of lamb are added to please those pesky landlubbers. Water Club features live piano music nightly, and in summer (May to October), the Crow's Nest on the restaurant's upper deck offers outdoor dining and a casual menu.

Wolfgang's Steakhouse

Steakhouse ✗✗

085

4 Park Ave. (at 33rd St.)

Subway:	33 St	Mon – Thu noon - 10:30pm
Phone:	212-889-3369	Fri noon - 11:30pm
Fax:	212-889-6845	Sat – Sun 5pm - 10:30pm
Web:	www.wolfgangssteakhouse.com	
Prices:	$$$	

Wolfgang Zwiener worked for 41 years as a headwaiter at Brooklyn's Peter Luger steakhouse. Just as he was planning to retire, he got sidetracked into starting his own restaurant in Manhattan with his son and several other former waiters from Luger's. Opened in 2004, Wolfgang's occupies the main dining room of the 1912 Vanderbilt Hotel. What sets this space apart is its gorgeous vaulted and tiled ceiling, crafted by 19th-century artisan Rafael Guastavino.

It's all about meat here—strapping portions of Porterhouse (sized for two, three or four) served on the bone (for fish fans, there's a three-pound lobster). Wolfgang's hand-selects and even dry-ages the meat in-house. Side dishes are à la carte, so you'll pay more to add the decadent creamed spinach or the signature German potatoes.

Manhattan Midtown East & Murray Hill

Zarela

086

953 Second Ave. (bet. 50th & 51st Sts.)

Subway:	51 St	Mon – Thu noon - 3pm & 5pm - 11pm
Phone:	212-644-6740	Fri noon - 3pm & 5pm - 11:30pm
Fax:	212-980-1073	Sat 5pm - 11:30pm
Web:	www.zarela.com	Sun 5pm - 10pm
Prices:	$$	

Every day's a fiesta in this boisterous bistro, hung with bright paper garlands and flowers, ceremonial masks, puppets and other Mexican artifacts. Zarela Martinez sees to that. The chef opened her restaurant here in 1987, and it's still perpetually packed. Her secret recipe for fantastic, but powerful, margaritas is just one of the reasons.

A native of Mexico, Zarela courts a carnival ambience with lively music and food that's served family-style for sharing. In the evenings, the place teems with people who often spill out onto the sidewalk while they wait to dig into flavorful regional Mexican fare such as chicken braised in tequila, slow-cooked pork shoulder marinated in achiote and sour oranges, and *pastel de cocoa*, a traditional cake made with unsweetened chocolate and almonds.

A WATER THAT BELONGS ON THE WINE LIST.
ACQUA PANNA STILL FROM S.PELLEGRINO.

Midtown West

When you think of Midtown West, Times Square probably comes to mind. True, brash **Times Square**, at Broadway and 42nd Street, demands your attention with its blazing marquees, but the neighborhood that runs from Fifth Avenue west to the Hudson River is so much more than that. Here you'll also find picturesque **Bryant Park**, the **Empire State Building**, and **Rockefeller Center**, home to NBC studios and the city's famous skating rink. For shoppers, **Macy's** anchors a frenetic shopping hub *(on Sixth Ave. at 34th St.)*, and **Diamond and Jewelry Way** *(W. 47th St., between Fifth & Sixth Aves.)* ranks as the world's largest district for diamonds and other precious stones.

If it's dining that interests you, look no further. Midtown West holds a dense concentration of eateries, from Restaurant Row (as the block of West 46th Street is known) to the Time Warner Center (on Columbus Circle), home to some of New York's most celebrated new restaurants.

A Bit of History – In the colonial era, this slice of Midtown belonged to the city but was actually the country, as New York's population was concentrated well below Canal Street. By the mid-19th century, the area was covered with brownstone town houses, home to upper-middle-class families who couldn't afford a mansion on Fifth Avenue. Upon the completion of the Sixth Avenue "El" (elevated railway) in 1878, a majority of these residents deemed the quarter too noisy and dirty, and, with their Fifth Avenue neighbors, began moving uptown.

The construction of **Rockefeller Center** between 1930 and 1940 permanently changed the character of the neighborhood. More than 225 buildings, mostly brownstones, were demolished to make room for the original 12 buildings of the complex, and the residential population was dispersed to other parts of the city. But with that loss came significant gain. The center was hailed as an architectural triumph. Rockefeller's insistence that early tenants be

affiliated with the television and radio industries soon attracted other media outlets to the district, boosting its worldwide visibility.

The Dividing Line – Although Fifth Avenue officially separates the east and west sides of Manhattan, it is the Avenue of the Americas (still known as Sixth Avenue to locals, though it was officially renamed in 1945) that actually feels like the dividing line. In part, that's because its neighbors are so distinct. One block east, the department stores of **Fifth Avenue** ooze gentility. One block west, the fabled **Theater District** (spreading north from Times Square along Broadway) teems with performance venues and restaurants, the latter touting their pre- and post-theater menus.

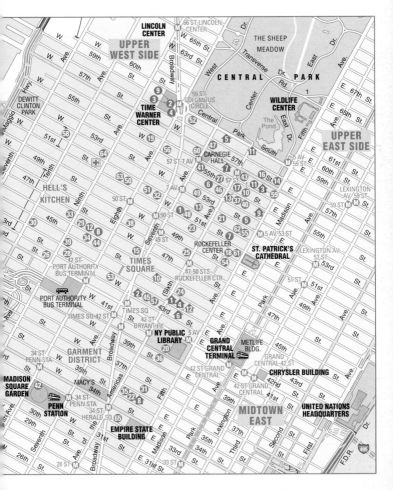

Le Bernardin ✿✿✿

Le Bernardin/Shimon & Tammar Photography

Seafood 🍴🍴🍴🍴🍴

001

155 W. 51st St. (bet. Sixth & Seventh Aves.)

Subway:	47-50 Sts - Rockefeller Ctr	Mon – Thu noon - 2:30pm
Phone:	212-554-1515	& 5:15pm - 10:30pm
Fax:	212-554-1100	Fri noon - 2:30pm & 5:15pm - 11pm
Web:	www.le-bernardin.com	Sat 5:15pm - 11pm
Prices:	$$$$	Closed Sun & major holidays

In a city where chefs seem to change at the drop of a toque, it's remarkable that Le Bernardin has been under the same ownership since 1986, and that chef Eric Ripert has ruled the kitchen since 1994. Such stability shines through in the effortlessly efficient way that this celebrated restaurant operates. The extensive use of teak in the furnishings and the coffered ceiling gives Le Bernardin its grandeur, while an extensive art collection belonging to owner Maguy Le Coze, and elegant tables topped with Limoges porcelain and fine crystal add to the opulence.

At lunch, a business clientele tends to rush through their meals; at dinnertime, the ambience is leisurely, with more focus on the food. Ripert is a master in the treatment of fish and his cuisine spotlights the bounty of the sea. The prix-fixe menu is divided into sections of "almost raw" (fluke ceviche), "barely touched" (poached lobster in lemon miso broth) and "lightly cooked" (baked codfish in a salt crust); chef's tasting menus are also available. Sauces here obtain their depth of flavor from ingredients imported from around the globe.

Appetizers

Layers of Thinly Pounded Yellowfin Tuna, Foie Gras and Toasted Baguette, Shaved Chives and Extra Virgin Olive Oil

Progressive Tasting of Marinated Fluke: Four different Ceviches, from simple to complex combination

Iranian Osetry Caviar on a Nest of Tagliolini, with Quail Egg and Bacon Carbonara Sauce

Entrées

A Tribute to Gaudí: Pan-roasted Monkfish with Confit Peppers and Fiery Patatas Bravas, Chorizo-Albariño Emulsion

Baked Lobster with Braised Endive, Enoki and Black Trumpets, and Bourbon Black-Pepper Sauce

Masala-spiced Crispy Black Bass with Peking Duck and Green Papaya Salad in a rich Ginger-Cardamom Broth

Desserts

Dark-Chocolate, Cashew and Caramel Tart, Red-Wine Reduction, Banana, and Malted Rum Milk-Chocolate Ice Cream

Passion Fruit Cream Enrobed in White Chocolate, with Ginger Caramel and Mandarin Sorbet

Slow-baked Apple Confit, Armagnac-soaked Golden Raisins, Almond Wafer, Crème Fraîche Sorbet, and Warm Apple Broth

SEAFOOD

Per Se ✿✿✿

Contemporary 🍴🍴🍴🍴🍴

002

10 Columbus Circle (in the Time Warner Center)

Subway:	59 St - Columbus Circle	Mon – Thu 5:30pm - 10pm
Phone:	212-823-9335	Fri – Sun 11:30am - 1pm
Fax:	212-823-9497	& 5:30pm - 10pm
Web:	www.perseny.com	
Prices:	$$$$	

Per Se

Having built his reputation at the storied French Laundry in Napa Valley, California, Thomas Keller took his talents to New York in 2004 with Per Se. The restaurant's luxe Adam Tihany design is characterized, in part, by the fabulous views of Central Park from its fourth-floor aerie in the Time Warner Center.

Precision reigns, from the choreographed service (distinguished by details such as little ottomans for ladies' handbags) to the superlative cuisine. Diners here are treated to a series of original small bites (choose from a five- or a nine-course prix-fixe menu), and while the portions are diminutive, these tiny servings pack a serious gastronomic punch. Minimalist presentations amount to modern art on the plate, arranged with contrasting shapes, colors and textures. Wine pairings are pricey, but exceptional and worth the splurge.

With only 16 tables, Per Se plays hard-to-get with its reservations. They only accept bookings two months in advance, so practice your speed-dialing—and your patience. Once you experience Keller's sublime cuisine, any frustration you may have felt will melt away like a chocolate truffle.

Appetizers

"Oysters and Pearls": Sabayon of Pearl Tapioca with Island Creek Oysters and Russian Sevruga Caviar

Terrine of Hudson Valley Moulard Duck Foie Gras with Poached Washington State Rhubarb, Spiced Shortbread, Field Mizuna, Rhubarb Mignonnette and Toasted Tellicherry Pepper Brioche

Hot-smoked Columbia River Sturgeon with Celeriac "Fondant," Celery Branch and Whole-Grain-Mustard Emulsion

Entrées

Snake River Farm's *Calotte de Boeuf Grillée* with Crispy Bone Marrow, Haricots Verts, Yellow Wax Beans, Morel Mushrooms, and *Pommes Écrasées* with Sauce Bordelaise

Fricassée of Nova Scotia Lobster "Mitts" with Caramelized Red Endive, Cara Cara Orange Suprêmes, Rucola Leaves and Sauce Maltaise

Sirloin of Hallow Farm's Rabbit wrapped in Applewood-smoked Bacon, with Ramp-Top Subric and Fondue of Ramps with Rabbit Jus

Desserts

Tentation au Chocolat, Noisette et Lait: Milk-Chocolate Crémeux, Hazelnut Streusel with Condensed-milk Sorbet, *Pain au Lait* Sauce and Sweetened Salty Hazelnuts

Vacherin Fribourgeois: Sour Cherry Clafoutis, Pickled Sunchokes and Cherry Syrup

Pink Guava Sorbet: Yogurt Bavarois, Yuzu-scented Génoise and "Compressed" Pineapple

Masa ❀ ❀

J a p a n e s e ✕✕

003

10 Columbus Circle (in the Time Warner Center)

Subway:	59 St - Columbus Circle
Phone:	212-823-9800
Fax:	212-823-9809
Web:	www.masanyc.com
Prices:	$$$$

Mon 6pm - 9pm
Tue – Fri noon - 1:30pm & 6pm - 9pm
Sat 6pm - 9pm
Closed Sun & December 24 – January 8

Masa/Mikiko Kikayama

Before you go to Masa, you should know that the price they charge for a meal here will bust any normal budget (the omakase will set you back $350). Indeed, many diners make their decision to go or not to go on this point alone (and you will need to decide in advance, since the restaurant doesn't accept walk-ins).

What can you expect for your money here? Expect the finest sushi you are ever likely to eat. This memorable culinary festival begins with 4 to 5 little appetizers (perhaps a purée of toro with a generous spoonful of caviar, or sea urchin risotto sweetened with corn) to gently tease the taste buds. Then come 15 to 20 courses of the most exquisite sushi (from squid to sea breem, and flounder to fluke), all flown in fresh from Japanese waters. Pick one of the 10 seats at the sushi counter if you want to interact with master sushi chef Masa Takayama.

Tucked inside the Time Warner Center, 26-seat Masa is truly a temple of serenity. From the bamboo garden and pond behind the sushi counter to the stunning Hinoki cypress flown in from Japan, the interior calls to mind the simple beauty of nature.

SEASONAL FEATURES

Uni Risotto with Seasonal Truffles

Toro Tartare with Caviar

From November to February, Fugu fish is on the menu, prepared as a Sashimi Salad, as a Fried Karaage, and as Sushi.

From May to August, Hamo fish is featured on the menu as a seasonal item.

JAPANESE

Café Gray ✿

Contemporary ✗✗✗

004

10 Columbus Circle (in the Time Warner Center)

Subway:	59 St - Columbus Circle
Phone:	212-823-6338
Fax:	212-823-6221
Web:	www.cafegray.com
Prices:	$$$

Mon – Wed noon - 2pm
& 5:30pm - 9:30pm
Thu – Fri noon - 2pm & 5:30pm - 11pm
Sat 5pm - 11pm
Closed Sun in Spring & Summer

Café Gray

The impersonal vibe of the Time Warner Center disappears as you walk through the book-lined, paneled hallway into the entrancing third-floor world of Café Gray. While the dining room sparkles with its mirrored columns and circular banquettes, its most eye-catching feature is the open stainless-steel kitchen, situated near the window wall that boasts spectacular Central Park panoramas. The kitchen's location and view makes you wonder how the chefs concentrate so intently on their job, but concentrate they do.

Chef Gray Kunz's clever cuisine reflects his global background. He grew up in Singapore and worked in Europe and Asia before settling in New York, where he earned respect from industry insiders and food lovers alike during his years at legendary Lespinasse (now closed).

Faced with all the offerings on the extensive à la carte menu available at lunch and dinner, you may have trouble deciding between entrées such as coconut-coated red snapper with crabmeat and papaya, and seared foie gras and quail with pickled ramps, Asian pears and hazelnuts. For a sweet finale, desserts like the blackberry baked Alaska with *vin santo* and sour cream are truly works of art.

Appetizers

Velouté of Artichokes, Langoustines and Olive Oil

Steak Tartare Tenderloin Carpaccio and Ketjap Manis

Risotto Mushroom Fricassée

Entrées

Coconut-coated Red Snapper with Crabmeat and Papaya

Skate Schnitzel with Parsnips, Pumpkin Seeds and Preserved Lemon

Braised Short Rib of Beef, with Soft Grits and Meaux Mustard

Desserts

Chocolate Soufflé with Raspberry Coulis

Caramelized Key Lime Pie with Vanilla Schlag

Sorbets and Ice Creams Café Gray

The Modern ❁

9 W. 53rd St. (bet. Fifth & Sixth Aves.)

Subway:	5 Av - 53 St	Mon – Thu noon – 2pm
Phone:	212-333-1220	& 5:30pm - 10:30pm
Fax:	212-408-6326	Fri noon - 2pm & 5:30pm - 11pm
Web:	www.themodernnyc.com	Sat 5:30pm – 11pm
Prices:	$$$	Closed Sun

The Modern/Sara Beth Turner

It's not easy to compete with priceless works of art by Giacometti and Picasso, but that's the challenge that Alsatian-born chef Gabriel Kreuther faces at The Modern. Operated by Danny Meyer (Gramercy Tavern, Union Square Cafe) and housed in the boldly renovated Museum of Modern Art, this restaurant overlooks the 31 works displayed in the Abby Aldrich Rockefeller Sculpture Garden. The warm, light-filled dining room fits the atmosphere with its huge window wall, Danish-designed furnishings and 46-foot-long marble bar.

You can order à la carte at lunch; at dinner there's a three-course prix-fixe menu. Either way, you'll relish dishes like foie gras terrine marbled with roasted artichokes, chorizo-crusted cod and a Napoleon filled with rich layers of lemon cream. The wine list, with over 900 selections, has an impressive collection of Alsatian vintages

The Dining Room has a separate street entrance, and when you come in this way, prepare to wade through the crowds in the Bar Room —a more informal space (walk-ins accepted) with its own identity and menu of small and large plates of rustic Alsatian cuisine.

Appetizers

Tartare of Yellowfin Tuna and Diver Scallops seasoned with Yellowstone River Caviar

Chilled Maine Lobster Salad with Green Asparagus *en Chartreuse* and Lobster Essence

Escargots and Potato *Gâteau* with Pearl Onions, Shiso and Celeriac Froth

Entrées

Squab and Foie Gras *Croustillant* with Caramelized Ginger Jus and Farm Vegetables

Chorizo-crusted Chatham Cod with White-Coco-Bean Purée and Harissa Oil

Wheat-Beer-Poached Monkfish, Granny Smith Apples and Morcilla Sausage

Desserts

Lemon Napoleon, Exotique *Brunoise* and Fromage Blanc Sorbet

Modern Chocolate Tart, Chocolate *Crémeux* and Chocolate Sorbet

Citrus *Craquelin*, Pistachio Dacquoise and Mandarin Sorbet

CONTEMPORARY

Abboccato

006

136 W. 55th St. (bet. Sixth & Seventh Aves.)

Subway:	57 St
Phone:	212-265-4000
Fax:	212-265-4007
Web:	www.abboccato.com
Prices:	$$$

Mon noon - 3pm & 5:30pm - 10pm
Tue – Sat noon - 3pm & 5:30pm - 11pm
Sun 4pm - 10pm

Brought to you by the Livanos family, whose stable includes Molyvos and Oceana, Abboccato bears the hallmarks of these experienced restaurateurs. The menu eschews the ubiquitous offerings found in many Italian eateries and instead provides more unusual fare, such as half-moon pasta filled with beets and Gorgonzola dolce, suckling pig cooked in milk and hazelnuts, and *Vaniglia e Cioccolato* (vanilla-scented braised veal cheeks served with soft polenta and chunks of wild boar braised in red wine accented with bitter chocolate). If you're dining with someone special, the menu also includes a section dedicated to dishes prepared tableside for two.

The 75-seat dining room has an understated elegance with its chic, modern styling, and the 20-seat terrazzo opens onto the sidewalk, creating a sense of alfresco dining.

Acqua Pazza

007

36 W. 52nd St. (bet. Fifth & Sixth Aves.)

Subway:	5 Av - 53 St
Phone:	212-582-6900
Fax:	212-245-5211
Web:	www.acquapazzanyc.com
Prices:	$$$

Mon – Fri noon - 3pm & 5pm - 10pm
Sat 5pm - 10pm
Closed Sun

The name Acqua Pazza (Italian for "crazy water") recalls a practice of fishermen in southern Italy, who would douse their catch of the day with a little olive oil and bake the fish whole in seawater. Indeed, the kitchen at this stylish Midtown establishment takes much of its epicurean inspiration from the coastline of Italy, although meat and pasta lovers will find selections aplenty to satisfy them, too. Diners fearing carbs will appreciate the reduced-carbohydrate pastas topped with tender seafood.

Surroundings here are crisp and sophisticated without any undue pomp and circumstance, which is why the atmosphere remains so convivial. Smartly attired in blue shirts, the staff provides prompt and efficient service.

Barbetta

008

Italian ✗✗✗

321 W. 46th St. (bet. Eighth & Ninth Aves.)

Subway: 50 St (Eighth Ave.)
Phone: 212-246-9171
Fax: 212-246-1279
Web: www.barbettarestaurant.com
Prices: $$$

Tue – Sun noon - midnight
Closed Mon

In 2006 Barbetta will celebrate its 100th birthday, still under the ownership of the Maioglio family who founded it. Inside the four 19th-century Maioglio-Astor town houses, you'll be transported to the heyday of 1950's continental dining in an ornate room decorated with 18th-century Piemontese furnishings and an antique crystal and gilded-wood chandelier.

The ample seasonal menu, featuring the specialties of Italy's Piemonte region—including some wonderful pastas—lists the date on which a particular dish first made its appearance. Pair your meal with one of the more than 1,700 different labels on the tremendous wine list.

Scented by gardenias, oleander and jasmine, the secluded garden is an oasis in the heart of the Theater District.

Bar Masa

009

Japanese ✗

10 Columbus Circle (in the Time Warner Center)

Subway: 59 St - Columbus Circle
Phone: 212-823-9800
Fax: 212-823-9809
Web: www.masanyc.com
Prices: $$$

Mon & Sat 6pm - 9pm
Tue – Fri noon - 1:30pm & 6pm - 9pm
Closed Sun & Dec 25 - Jan 8

If you want upscale ingredients with elegant preparations served in a serene setting, head to Bar Masa. Adjacent to its pricey relative, Masa, Bar Masa features a long, thin dining room, with a bar on one side and a line of tables on the other. Japanese limestone tiles and dark woods lend an earthy element to the room, while a gauzy burgundy curtain separates the tables from the bar, allowing for more peaceful dining (the bar accommodates both diners and those just stopping by for a drink).

The structured seasonal menu provides a wide choice of appetizers, rolls, sushi, noodles and other entrées. Dessert choices range from refreshing grapefruit granité to rich chocolate rainbow cake. And while it's nowhere near the experience of Masa next door, prices here are certainly easier to swallow.

Bay Leaf

Indian ✕✕

010

49 W. 56th St. (bet. Fifth & Sixth Aves.)

Subway:	57 St	Open daily noon - 3pm & 5pm - 11pm
Phone:	212-957-1818	
Fax:	N/A	
Web:	N/A	
Prices:	$$	

In a sea of ethnic restaurants on a busy Midtown street, Bay Leaf stands out for its classic Indian cooking and enjoyable setting. This Indian eatery is popular at lunch with the business crowd who frequents the restaurant for its well-priced buffet, but it's also a sure bet for dinner with a diverse assortment of à la carte items, including traditional curries and Tandoori dishes. Expertly managed, the service is smooth from start to finish, and the staff helps guests navigate the many choices.

Bay Leaf shies away from the predictable décor with an elegant display of rich paneled woods, framed black-and-white photography and discreet Indian music. Service is also available on the terrace during warmer months.

Beacon

American ✕✕

011

25 W. 56th St. (bet. Fifth & Sixth Aves.)

Subway:	57 St	Mon – Thu noon - 2:30pm
Phone:	212-332-0500	& 5:30pm - 10pm
Fax:	212-262-4787	Fri noon - 2:30pm & 5:30pm - 10:30pm
Web:	www.beaconnyc.com	Sat 5pm - 10:30pm
Prices:	$$$	Sun 10am - 2:30pm & 5pm - 9pm

Open-fire cooking is the theme at Beacon, where a wood-burning oven, rotisserie and grill are the preferred means of cooking. The reason it works so well is that chef and co-owner Waldy Malouf uses the best-quality raw ingredients he can get his hands on. Whether it's a sophisticated suckling pig or a wood-roasted Catskill trout, there's something on the menu to appeal to most any appetite—and bringing your appetite is de rigueur here, since the portions of American cuisine are generous.

For those who want to enjoy the view of the bustling dining room, the mezzanine is the best place to sit; diners who consider cooking to be a spectator sport should grab one of the ringside seats by the open kitchen. The bar's sexy spirit and exciting cocktail menu always draws a crowd.

Becco

012

355 W. 46th St. (bet. Eighth & Ninth Aves.)

Subway:	42 St - Port Authority Bus Terminal	Sun – Mon noon - 10pm
Phone:	212-397-7597	Tue, Thu & Fri noon - midnight
Fax:	917-206-0026	Wed & Sat 11:30am - midnight
Web:	www.becconyc.com	Closed Christmas Day
Prices:	$$	

If you're seeking a quick bite before a show, this Restaurant Row town house in the Theater District can get you in and out with time to spare before the curtain rises. If you have a free evening, come later to appreciate the hearty Italian cooking in less frenetic surroundings. Hanging copper pots, Italian landscapes and shelves full of country knickknacks dress the three separate dining spaces here, lending a homey air to this casual homestyle Italian restaurant.

Owned by Lidia Bastianich and her son, Joseph, Becco features a varied menu augmented by a list of specials. For those with big appetites, the *sinfonia di pasta* offers an abbondanza of unlimited portions of the chef's three daily pasta creations—just make sure your pants have an elastic waist.

Ben Benson's

013

123 W. 52nd St. (bet. Sixth & Seventh Aves.)

Subway:	5 Av - 53 St	Mon – Thu 11:45am - 11pm
Phone:	212-581-8888	Fri 11:45am - midnight
Fax:	212-581-1170	Sat 5pm - midnight
Web:	www.benbensons.com	Sun 5pm -10pm
Prices:	$$$$	

If you grimace at the mere thought of fusion cooking, then this is the place for you. Since 1982, Ben Benson's has been serving Prime cuts of USDA meats and other classic American fare to its contented macho clientele of power brokers and politicians. (It's easy to tell the regulars—their names are emblazoned on brass plaques set in the wainscoting). The menu is huge, including the usual suspects like sirloin steaks and veal chops, yet Southern fried chicken and crab cakes earn equal billing.

The high-ceilinged dining room is airier than many of the wood-paneled steakhouses in town. Refreshingly, this New York steakhouse remains stubbornly independent from chain ownership. For those who favor alfresco dining, the spacious sidewalk terrace provides a pleasant setting in nice weather.

BG

754 Fifth Ave. (at 58th St.)

Subway:	5 Av - 59 St	Mon – Fri 11:30am - 7pm
Phone:	212-872-8977	Sat 11:30am - 6pm
Fax:	212-872-8886	Sun noon - 5pm
Web:	www.bergdorfgoodman.com	
Prices:	$$$	

Located on the seventh floor of Bergdorf Goodman, BG is destined to be the new top spot for the ladies who lunch. In December 2005, Bergdorf's closed their old restaurant in favor of this sleek salon, decorated in haute Parisian style by Los Angeles interior designer Kelly Wearstler. Soft shades of blue, green and yellow create a feminine elegance in the airy, natural-light-filled room, which with its hand-painted wallpaper and 18th-century-inspired chairs is appropriately posh for the champagne-sipping set.

While the menu includes the standard salads and sandwiches, the list also enumerates sophisticated entrées and desserts that are on par with many fine-dining establishments in the city. The wine list is well-selected and concise, and the chef displays a talented hand in the kitchen.

Blue Fin

015

1567 Broadway (at 47th St.)

Subway:	49 St	Sun – Mon 11:30am - 4pm
Phone:	212-918-1400	& 5pm - midnight
Fax:	212-918-1300	Tue – Thu 11:30am - 4pm
Web:	www.brguestrestaurants.com	& 5pm - 12:30am
Prices:	$$$	Fri – Sat 11:30am - 4pm & 5pm - 1am

You'd think it would be easy to spot this two-tier 400-seat restaurant on Times Square, but Blue Fin seductively conceals itself behind its glass-front bar. Connected to the W Hotel Times Square, the restaurant adds another notch to restaurateur Steve Hanson's belt. Downstairs, the dazzling, nightclub-like design incorporates ocean-blue walls, polished mirrors reflecting glittering light, and a fanciful mobile of fish that seem to swim above the diners. Follow the floating staircase upstairs, where the mood turns sultry in the jazz club.

The extensive menu celebrates all creatures from the sea, from herb-crusted black bass to sesame-crusted big-eye tuna— including a selection of fresh oysters, clams, sushi, sashimi and seafood towers from the raw bar.

Brasserie 8 1/2

016

9 W. 57th St. (bet. Fifth & Sixth Aves.)

Subway:	57 St	Mon – Thu 11:30am - 3pm
Phone:	212-829-0812	& 5:30pm - 10pm
Fax:	212-829-0821	Fri 11am - 3pm & 5:30pm - 11pm
Web:	www.brasserie8andahalf.com	Sat 5:30pm - 11pm
Prices:	$$$	Sun 11am - 3pm & 5:30pm - 9pm

Brasserie 8½'s individual style meshes contemporary dash with a hint of the fabulous Fifties. Get ready to make a theatrical entrance down the red-carpeted spiral staircase to gain access to the dining room. At the foot of the stairs, you'll find a circular lounge. A few more steps down, the brasserie is a big, bold contemporary affair, with a white-tile floor, brown-leather banquettes and a striking glass mural walling off the kitchen.

Well-executed dishes are elegantly plated and range from steamed red snapper en croûte with ginger-glazed bok choy to truffle-crusted loin of lamb. Lunch is particularly busy, but with more than 200 seats, the restaurant copes easily. Service is speedy, ideal for those who need to get back to the office, or go home to practice their grand entrances.

Brasserie LCB

017

60 W. 55th St. (bet. Fifth & Sixth Aves.)

Subway:	57 St	Sun – Thu noon - 3pm & 5pm - 10:30pm
Phone:	212-688-6525	Fri – Sat noon - 3pm & 5pm - 11:30pm
Fax:	212-258-2102	Closed Sun in Summer
Web:	www.jjrlcb.com	
Prices:	$$	

Formerly La Cote Basque, this Belle Époque-style brasserie has been reinvented by its venerable chef and owner Jean-Jacques Rachou. In its present incarnation, LCB turns away from the pomp and circumstance of La Cote Basque and replaces it with a more casual ambience of black leatherette banquettes, large framed mirrors, tulip-shaped light fixtures and a mosaic-tile floor.

A varied menu respects the regional French terroir with specialties such as a traditional and tasty choucroute Alsacienne, Dover sole meunière, cassoulet with duck confit, and Prime steak au poivre. The lunch menu du jour, with a choice of three courses, represents a good balance of quality and price. When appropriate, artistic elements are incorporated onto the plates here.

Brasserie Ruhlmann

French XX

018

45 Rockefeller Plaza (bet. Sixth & Seventh Aves.)

Subway:	47-50 Sts - Rockefeller Ctr
Phone:	212-974-2020
Fax:	212-974-3331
Web:	www.brasserieruhlmann.com
Prices:	$$

Mon – Fri 11am - 3pm & 5:30pm - 11pm
Sat 11:30am - 3pm & 5:30pm - 11pm
Sun 11:30am - 3pm

The right address is everything in Manhattan, and Brasserie Ruhlmann enjoys one of the city's most prestigious locations in the heart of Rockefeller Center. The convenient Midtown venue draws a steady supply of executives and Fifth Avenue shoppers. The Art Deco influence pays homage to the owners' fascination with that period and is emphasized in the textured, lacquered-wood walls, red fabric seating, and delightful bistro-style tables covered with crisp white linens.

Brasserie Ruhlmann showcases French-influenced continental cuisine. Listing breakfast, lunch and dinner, the menu was revamped after the restaurant's rocky opening in early 2006, and now focuses on appealing bistro dishes that are ideal for a power meal. The wine list is primarily domestic, and the by-the-glass pours are plentiful.

Bricco

Italian XX

019

304 W. 56th St. (bet. Eighth & Ninth Aves.)

Subway:	57 St - 7 Av
Phone:	212-245-7160
Fax:	212-245-6085
Web:	www.bricconyc.com
Prices:	$$

Mon – Thu noon - 11pm
Fri noon - midnight
Sat 4pm - midnight
Sun 4pm - 11pm
Closed major holidays

Amore comes to mind when you see the rose-red walls and autographed lipstick kisses that cover the ceiling in this romantic Italian place. The dining space spreads over two floors, with the upstairs room being the sunnier and more tranquil of the two. If it's action you want, stick to the first floor, where chefs fire pizzas in the wood-burning oven and waiters scurry around the room, skillfully managing to keep the dishes coming without rushing diners. The two Italian owners play host and professional flirt to a bevy of regulars, many of them women, who come for the warmth and personal touch.

The strength of this straightforward Italian menu lies in its wide selection of light and flavorful homemade pastas. You usually won't go wrong if you choose from the abundant daily specials.

Bryant Park Grill

020

American ✗✗

25 W. 40th St. (bet. Fifth & Sixth Aves.)

Subway:	42 St - Bryant Pk
Phone:	212-840-6500
Fax:	212-840-8122
Web:	www.arkrestaurants.com
Prices:	$$$

Mon – Fri 11:30am - 3:30pm
& 5pm - 11pm
Sat – Sun 11:30am - 3:30pm
& 5pm - 11pm

Overlooking Bryant Park, the grill enjoys an enviable location adjacent to the stately, Beaux-Arts New York Public Library. The restaurant takes its design cues from the park, with abundant natural light and a colorful, wall-length bird mural.

Lunch and dinner menus are similar, with pastas, grilled meat and fish entrées; a few extra salad selections are available at midday. A new feature, the children's fixed-price weekend brunch menu (for ages 12 and under), includes favorites like scrambled eggs, blueberry pancakes and grilled cheese sandwiches.

A favorite post-work and warm-weather outdoor lunch spot for the young business crowd, Bryant Park Grill is always full, so reservations are advised. Ask for a window table for the best park views, or dine on the pleasant terrace in summer.

China Grill

021

Asian ✗✗

60 W. 53rd St. (bet. Fifth & Sixth Aves.)

Subway:	5 Av - 53 St
Phone:	212-333-7788
Fax:	212-581-9299
Web:	www.chinagrillmgt.com
Prices:	$$$

Mon – Wed 11:45am - 10:45pm
Thu – Fri 11:45am - 11:45pm
Sat 5:30pm - 11:45pm
Sun 5:30pm - 10pm

If ever a restaurant represented Midtown and all its corporate machismo, it's China Grill. Set within the CBS Building, the cavernous space, with its 30-foot ceilings, acres of black marble and open kitchen can get awfully noisy, but that doesn't seem to dissuade the large numbers of corporate diners who crowd the place every day for lunch.

The grill bills their food as "world cuisine," which translates to appetizers and entrées that take their influences from across Asia, and desserts that bear assorted European accents. Enormous portions of dishes like barbecued salmon with Chinese mustard sauce or grilled Szechuan beef with sake and soy are perfect for sharing.

China Grill's recipe works, since the restaurant has gone global with locations in Miami, Las Vegas and Mexico City.

Manhattan Midtown West

Cho Dang Gol 🎭

Korean 🍴

022

55 W. 35th St. (bet. Fifth & Sixth Aves.)

Subway: 34 St - Herald Sq
Phone: 212-695-8222
Fax: N/A
Web: www.chodanggolny.com
Prices: 😋😋

Open daily 11:30am - 10pm

Named after a village in South Korea that's famed for its tofu, this unassuming eatery in Koreatown offers something different from the host of surrounding places that all seem to serve Korean barbecue.

Tofu, or soybean curd (*doo boo* in Korean) is the house specialty at Cho Dang Gol. Made fresh here each day, tofu forms the basis of many of the dishes; it absorbs the flavors of the spices or sauces it is cooked in, and is said to have many health benefits. Dishes are family size and meant to be shared. An order of the *kalbi* or *bulgogi* are easily big enough for several people, and appetizers can feed a hungry crowd. An abundance of plum wine, sake and *soju* will liven up your meal in no time.

The friendly staff caters to a largely Korean clientele in the modest dining room.

Cité

Steakhouse 🍴🍴🍴

023

120 W. 51st St. (bet. Sixth & Seventh Aves.)

Subway: 50 St (Broadway)
Phone: 212-956-7100
Fax: 212-956-7157
Web: www.citerestaurant.com
Prices: $$$

Mon – Thu noon - 2pm & 5pm - 10pm
Fri noon - 2pm & 5pm - 11:30pm
Sat 5pm - 11:30pm
Sun 5pm - 10pm

Cité's Midtown location ensures that many deals are made over meals here, and the restaurant enjoys a lively buzz. It's no secret why: after 8pm on weeknights (and after 5pm on Sundays), Cité's popular wine dinners are available. For a set price, you get your choice of three courses (entrées include fish, chicken and meat) and unlimited wine to go with them—a terrific value any way you look at it.

The surroundings themselves are also partly responsible for the diners' purr of satisfaction; the room is done in a striking Art Deco style highlighted by hand-painted tiles and wrought-iron grillwork, and the staff caters to diners with a watchful eye.

If it's a lighter menu you crave, the Cité Grill next door offers an informal setting where you can nosh on burgers, sandwiches and salads.

DB Bistro Moderne

024

Contemporary ✕✕

55 W. 44th St. (bet. Fifth & Sixth Aves.)

Subway:	5 Av	Mon noon - 2:30pm & 5:15pm - 11pm
Phone:	212-391-2400	Tue – Sat noon - 2:30pm
Fax:	212-391-1188	& 5:15pm - 11:30pm
Web:	www.danielnyc.com	Sun 5pm - 10pm
Prices:	$$$	Closed major holidays

More moderne than bistro, Daniel Boulud's classy Midtown restaurant blends the freshest American ingredients with French recipes in a way that would make the UN proud.

A glass bar divides the space into two dining rooms; the more informal front room boasts deep-red, rubbed-plaster walls hung with large, lustrous floral photographs that are reflected in the mirrors on the opposite wall.

Arranged by category (shellfish, asparagus, red meat, tuna), the impressive menu singles out the house specialties—Boulud's smoked salmon, tomato tarte Tatin, *Baeckeoffe* of escargots— as well as the dishes of the day. Boulud's irreverent takes on standards, like the hamburger stuffed with foie gras and black truffles, wins him rave reviews. Effortlessly efficient service adds to this dining experience.

Del Frisco's

025

Steakhouse ✕✕✕

1221 Sixth Ave. (at 49th St.)

Subway:	47-50 Sts - Rockefeller Ctr	Mon – Fri 11am - midnight
Phone:	212-575-5129	Sat 5pm - midnight
Fax:	212-575-5491	Sun 5pm - 10pm
Web:	www.delfriscos.com	
Prices:	$$$	

This sprawling bi-level Midtown steakhouse, with its wraparound floor-to-ceiling windows, exudes a strong aura of corporate muscle. Located on the ground level of the McGraw Hill Building (diagonally across from Radio City Music Hall), Del Frisco's attracts a suited clientele who all look like they know their way around a balance sheet.

Start with a classic wedge of iceberg lettuce or shrimp cocktail. Then it's straight to the Prime aged, corn-fed steaks from the Midwest, in portions that would make a Texan proud. In fact, Del Frisco's has locations in the Lone Star state, as well as in Colorado, Florida and Las Vegas. After delivering your steak, the waiter will remain at your side until you have carved into it and determined that it's cooked to your satisfaction.

Manhattan Midtown West

Esca

Italian 𝑋𝑋𝑋

026

402 W. 43rd St. (bet. Ninth & Tenth Aves.)

Subway: 42 St - Port Authority Bus Terminal
Phone: 212-564-7272
Fax: N/A
Web: www.esca-nyc.com
Prices: $$$

Mon noon - 2:30pm & 5pm - 10:30pm
Tue – Sat noon - 2:30pm
& 5pm - 11:30pm
Sun 4:30pm - 10:30pm

Esca translates as "bait" in Italian, and the fish are indeed biting at this establishment headed by chef/partner David Pasternack, in league with Mario Batali and Joseph Bastianich. Placed in a less crowded part of Midtown, Esca boasts a bright, yellow-tone décor.

On the daily changing menu, Italian-style seafood, such as the crispy skate with its perfect golden crust, nets the starring role. Pasta dishes are cooked al dente in the southern Italian way (firm to the bite) and are tossed with clams, scallops and other fruits of the sea. From the raw bar, crudo tastings are great for a group.

Wine appears prominently displayed in shelves around the room. About ten selections from the all-Italian wine list are available by the quartino (approximately one-third of a bottle).

Estiatorio Milos

Greek 𝑋𝑋𝑋

027

125 W. 55th St. (bet. Sixth & Seventh Aves.)

Subway: 57 St
Phone: 212-245-7400
Fax: 212-245-4828
Web: www.milos.ca
Prices: $$$

Mon – Fri noon - 2:45pm
& 5pm - 11:30pm
Sat 5pm - 11:30pm
Sun 5pm - 10:45pm

It's not nice to fool Mother Nature, and at Milos, they don't try—when you use carefully sourced organic ingredients, you don't need to do much to improve on them. The concept here is simple: you choose your fish (there are a few meat selections, too) from the fresh-from-the-sea array displayed at the counter, decide which weight you want, and specify how you want it to be cooked—charcoal-grilled or baked in sea salt. Soon, it will appear at your table, adorned with olive oil and lemon sauce. The Milos Special is absolutely the best starter, and deliriously sweet baklava makes the perfect ending.

The cacophonous dining room melds industrial modern with Greek taverna in a setting so bright you'll want to wear shades. Prices can be high, but it's still cheaper than a trip to the Greek Islands.

Etcetera Etcetera

028

352 W. 44th St. (bet. Eighth & Ninth Aves.)

Subway:	42 St - Port Authority Bus Terminal
Phone:	212-399-4141
Fax:	212-399-4899
Web:	www.etcrestaurant.com
Prices:	$$

Tue & Thu — Sat 5pm - 11:15pm
Wed noon - 2:30pm & 5pm - 11:15pm
Sun noon - 2:30pm & 5pm - 10pm
Closed Mon & major holidays

ViceVersa's little sister opened in 2005, and shares the same combination of stylish surroundings and confident, affable service. Like its older sibling, Etcetera Etcetera's menu is Italian, but here they add Mediterranean accents such as feta cheese, preserved lemons and Serrano ham. Ravioli filled with veal, raisins and amaretti, and potato and squid-ink gnocchi are melt-in-your-mouth good.

Philippe Starck designed the molded plastic chairs in pastel colors to complement the ebony woodwork and the gray ceramic-tile wall in the dining room; modern artwork and sculptures complete the picture. Located just two blocks from The Great White Way, Etcetera Etcetera makes a convenient and pleasant place for a pre- or post-theater meal. The large room upstairs is perfect for private parties.

Firebird

✕✕✕

029

365 W. 46th St. (bet. Eighth & Ninth Aves.)

Subway:	42 St - Port Authority Bus Terminal
Phone:	212-586-0244
Fax:	212-957-2983
Web:	www.firebirdrestaurant.com
Prices:	$$$

Tue & Thu – Fri 5pm - 11pm
Wed & Sat 11:45am - 2:30pm
& 5pm - 11pm
Sun 5pm - 9pm
Closed Mon

Dramatic décor marks this "pre-Revolutionary" Russian establishment on Restaurant Row (as this block of West 46th Street is popularly known). Drama befits the place, though, standing as it does so near the theater district. The dining room is nearly as intricate as a Fabergé egg, every inch of it set about with Russian art, rare Russian books, plush fabrics and wall sconces dripping with crystals.

As you'd expect, the menu lists Russian specialties such as borscht, beef Stroganov, and an extensive selection of caviar. In addition to the à la carte selections, three- and seven-course tasting menus are available at lunch and dinner. The staff, costumed in Cossack garb, provides well-orchestrated formal service—just don't expect the check to come in rubles.

Manhattan Midtown West

44 & X Hell's Kitchen

030

Contemporary ✗

622 Tenth Ave. (at 44th St.)

Subway: 42 St - Port Authority Bus Terminal
Phone: 212-977-1170
Fax: 212-977-1169
Web: www.44andx.com
Prices: $$

Mon – Fri 5:30pm - midnight
Sat – Sun 11:30am - 3pm
& 5:30pm - midnight

This restaurant's striped awning and white flower boxes brighten up the intersection of Tenth Avenue and 44th Street (The "X" in the name refers to Tenth Avenue) in the now edgy Hell's Kitchen neighborhood of Midtown.

Inside, white and cream tones, molded chairs and leather banquettes create a cool, contemporary vibe. A mix of theatergoers and neighbors from the 'hood makes for a lively atmosphere. In keeping with their motto that this place is "a little bit of heaven in Hell's Kitchen," the young staff sports T-shirts emblazoned with "Heaven" on the front and "in Hell" on the back.

American classics take on a 21st-century twist here (for example, buttermilk fried chicken comes with a chive waffle, and macaroni and cheese is given a sophisticated oomph with Vermont cheddar).

Frankie & Johnnie's

031

Steakhouse ✗✗

32 W. 37th St. (bet. Fifth & Sixth Aves.)

Subway: 34 St - Herald Sq
Phone: 212-947-8940
Fax: 212-629-5952
Web: www.frankieandjohnnies.com
Prices: $$$

Mon – Thu noon - 2:30pm
& 4pm - 10:30pm
Fri noon - 2:30pm & 4pm - 11pm
Sat 4pm - 11pm
Closed Sun

The fourth location of Frankie & Johnnie's steakhouse empire (the first was established in 1926 on West 45th Street) offers diners a little bit of history in the heart of the Garment District. The renovated town house in which it is set was once the home of John Drew Barrymore. In fact, Barrymore's library, with its coffered ceiling and original fireplace, forms part of the masculine, wood-paneled main dining room on the second floor.

Diners with booming baritone voices feel no need to tone down their bonhomie while chowing down on some serious cuts of Prime dry-aged beef here. No one seems to mind, though; the all-male brigade of waiters has seen it all before. Service is especially accommodating, and the restaurant even has a limousine service to shuttle guests anywhere in Midtown.

Gallagher's

032

Steakhouse 🍴

228 W. 52nd St. (bet. Broadway & Eighth Ave.)

Subway: 50 St (Broadway) Open daily noon - midnight
Phone: 212-245-5336
Fax: 212-245-5426
Web: www.gallaghersnysteakhouse.com
Prices: $$$

Gallagher's, as they say, is "New York City to the bone." Established in 1927 next door to what is now the Neil Simon Theater, Gallagher's satisfies carnivores with beef, beef and more beef. From the outside, you'd think you were in front of a butcher's shop; all you can see in the window are rows of assorted cuts of beef hanging in the meat locker. Past that, you enter a wood-paneled dining room where the waiters wear gold-trimmed blazers, and the walls are lined with photographs of Broadway stars, politicians and athletes of both the human and equine varieties.

While it doesn't come cheap, the beef shows a quality that really stands out. Surf and Turf, with its 10-ounce filet mignon and 8-ounce lobster tail, always wins raves.

Hell's Kitchen

033

Contemporary Mexican 🍴

679 Ninth Ave. (bet. 46th & 47th Sts.)

Subway: 50 St (Eighth Ave.) Sun – Mon 5pm - 11pm
Phone: 212-977-1588 Tue 11:30am - 3pm & 5pm - 11pm
Fax: 212-871-0927 Wed – Fri 11:30am - 3pm
Web: www.hellskitchen-nyc.com & 5pm - midnight
Prices: $$ Sat 5pm - midnight

As any New Yorker can tell you, this restaurant's name speaks to the 19th-century moniker for the surrounding neighborhood (the area between 34th and 59th streets, west of Eighth Avenue). At this hip Mexican eatery, the only thing devilish can be the wait you sometimes have to endure to get a table.

The "progressive Mexican" menu avoids the bland and the predictable in favor of dishes that are robust, yet possess a delicacy of execution and a true understanding of textures and flavors. Tamarind-marinated filet mignon chalupas and duck confit empanadas are light years away from the usual.

Bolstered by the unflappable staff, a convivial atmosphere prevails in the narrow room, where tables line one side, and a bar lines the other. Check out the cool chandeliers made from glass bottles.

Manhattan Midtown West

Joe Allen

034

American 🍴

326 W. 46th St. (bet. Eighth & Ninth Aves.)

Subway:	50 St (Eighth Ave.)	Mon, Tue & Thu noon - 11:45pm
Phone:	212-581-6464	Wed 11:30am - 11:45pm
Fax:	212-265-3383	Fri – Sat noon - midnight
Web:	www.joeallenrestaurant.com	Sun 11:30am - 11:45pm
Prices:	$$	

This chain sensibly applies the principle "if it ain't broke, don't fix it" to their New York City operation on Midtown West's restaurant row. Opened in 1965 and named for its owner, the 46th Street location is the original; since then, branches have sprouted up in Florida, Maine and as far afield as Europe. As is typical of many eateries in this neighborhood near the Theater District, Joe Allen's walls are covered with old Playbills. But wait, look closer: these aren't Broadway hits—these are the shows that bombed!

Luckily the menu of tried-and-true American dishes is successful, and for late risers, Joe Allen even offers omelets and frittatas until 4pm every day. The large menu, with a huge assortment of appetizers, salads, sandwiches and entrées, certainly has something for everyone.

Keens Steakhouse

035

Steakhouse 🍴🍴🍴

72 W. 36th St. (bet. Fifth & Sixth Aves.)

Subway:	34 St - Herald Sq	Mon – Fri 11:45am - 3pm
Phone:	212-947-3636	& 5:30pm - 10:30pm
Fax:	212-594-6371	Sat 5pm - 10:30pm
Web:	www.keens.com	Sun 5pm - 9pm
Prices:	$$$	

This macho palace of steaks and single-malt Scotch has been around since 1885, the lone survivor of the erstwhile Herald Square Theater District. A palpable sense of history pervades the restaurant, which enforced a strict men-only rule until 1901. That's the year British actress Lillie Langtry challenged Keens' discriminatory policy in court, and won. Look up on the ceiling to see the restaurant's collection of clay smoking pipes, another vestige of its men's-club days.

Efficient waiters clad in bow ties present hearty steaks and Keens' legendary mutton chops, in portions large enough to satisfy the hungriest carnivores. Or, straddle land and sea and order the surf and turf selection, served with a steamed Maine lobster and filet mignon.

Koi

Contemporary Japanese ✗✗

40 W. 40th St. (bet. Fifth & Sixth Aves.)

Subway:	42 St - Bryant Pk
Phone:	212-921-3330
Fax:	212-921-3360
Web:	www.koirestaurant.com
Prices:	$$$

Mon – Fri noon - 2:30pm
& 5:30pm - 11:30pm
Sat 5:30pm - 11:30pm
Sun 6pm - 10pm

This New York offshoot of the über-trendy flagship in West Hollywood opened in March 2005 in the Bryant Park Hotel, and it's always packed with the young, the restless and the affluent. The first thing you'll notice is the enormous white lattice canopy that dominates the dining room; underneath it, many of the elements of feng shui have been incorporated into the eye-popping design (with the exception of the pulsating music at night).

The menu is equally à la mode: an extensive choice of sushi and sashimi, as well as Pan-Asian fare with some original combinations. From the black-clad waitstaff and the chic plating to the A-list crowd, cool is the operative word at Koi. For a hipster's night out on the town, visit the equally trendy Cellar Bar before or after dinner.

La Bonne Soupe

036

French ✗

48 W. 55th St. (bet. Fifth & Sixth Aves.)

Subway:	57 St
Phone:	212-586-7650
Fax:	212-765-6409
Web:	www.labonnesoupe.com
Prices:	$$

Open daily 11:30am - 11pm

A reference to a line in the eponymous 1950's French play by Félicien Marceau, the phrase *la bonne soupe* has come to mean the "good life," one abounding in health, happiness and wealth. That's the image that owners Jean-Paul and Monique Picot promote in their Midtown West bistro. Convenient to Fifth Avenue shopping and a brace of Midtown hotels, this spot provides out-of-towners—and residents—with a good meal at a reasonable price.

In the long, narrow dining room, tables with checkered cloths cluster along the walls. The kitchen does indeed whip up good soup here, as well as a satisfying selection of savory crêpes, salads, omelets, and *plats du jour* such as steak frites and *poulet au citron*.

Manhattan Midtown West

La Masseria

038

Italian ✗✗

235 W. 48th St. (bet. Broadway & Eighth Ave.)

Subway:	50 St (Eighth Ave.)	Mon – Sat noon - 3pm & 5pm - midnight
Phone:	212-582-2111	Sun noon - 10:30pm
Fax:	212-582-2420	
Web:	www.lamasserianyc.com	
Prices:	$$	

With its wrought-iron chandeliers, beamed ceiling and walls plastered with an array of antique farming implements, La Masseria's décor takes its cue from the ancient farmhouses of Puglia. The overall effect creates a warm country feel in the dining room, which retains a hint of intimacy despite its large size—especially the space at the back, with its own mezzanine.

The cooking adds another delightfully rustic note with dishes such as rabbit slowly roasted and served in an earthenware pot, and homemade stuffed fresh mozzarella—a house specialty. Italian comfort food, such as braised short ribs, and rigatoni with traditional "Sunday Grandmother's sauce," really hits the spot.

If you're looking for a relaxed meal, La Masseria operates at a less frenetic pace than many places in this neighborhood.

Marseille

French ✗✗

039

630 Ninth Ave. (at 44th St.)

Subway:	42 St - Port Authority Bus Terminal	Mon 11:30am - 3pm & 5:15pm - 11pm
Phone:	212-333-2323	Tue – Fri 11:30am - 3pm
Fax:	212-333-4488	& 5:15pm - midnight
Web:	www.marseillenyc.com	Sat 11am - 3pm & 5:15pm - midnight
Prices:	$$	Sun 11am - 3pm & 5:15pm - 11pm

As vibrant and bustling as the southern French city for which it is named, Marseille boasts a brasserie feel with its wicker chairs, handmade Art Deco floor tiles, stained glass, green-trimmed arches and zinc bar. The menu features cooking from the southern Mediterranean with Franco-Moroccan overtones. Appetizers include assorted meze, while lamb tagine and bouillabaisse number among the entrées.

Owing to Marseille's proximity to theaters (the restaurant is two blocks west of Times Square), it's busy almost constantly, often with out-of-towners. The waitstaff handles the crowds with visible ease, though.

Downstairs, the dimly lit lounge hints at something both secretive and alluring; while you're down there, check out the wine cellar—it's housed in a former bank vault.

Michael's

040

24 W. 55th St. (bet. Fifth & Sixth Aves.)

Subway:	57 St
Phone:	212-767-0555
Fax:	212-581-6778
Web:	www.michaelsnewyork.com
Prices:	$$$

Mon – Fri noon – 2pm
& 5:30pm – 10:30pm
Sat 11:30am – 2pm & 5:30pm – 10:30pm
Closed Sun & major holidays

East Coast expense accounts meet West Coast cooking at this busy Midtown institution. California style infuses the interesting array of American dishes here. Chef/owner Michael McCarty, who founded the original Michael's near the beach in Santa Monica in 1979, developed his market-driven menu way before using fresh seasonal fare was fashionable. Enjoy dishes like pan-roasted salmon and dayboat monkfish tails at lunch or dinner.

In the airy dining room, light pours in from a wall of windows, illuminating the artwork on the peach-tone walls. Favored by media moguls, Michael's gets mobbed at lunchtime, and the waitstaff has to run at a big-city pace. The fact that everyone seems to be a regular here is proof enough that the brigade is up to the task.

Molyvos

041

871 Seventh Ave. (bet. 55th & 56th Sts.)

Subway:	57 St - 7 Av
Phone:	212-582-7500
Fax:	212-582-7502
Web:	www.molyvos.com
Prices:	$$

Mon – Thu noon – 3pm
& 5:30pm – 11:30pm
Fri noon – 3pm & 5:30pm – midnight
Sat noon – 3pm & 5pm – midnight
Sun noon – 11pm

An attractive Greek storefront façade beckons diners to Molyvos, named for the Greek village on the island of Lesvos, homeland of owner John Livanos. Inside, Greek artifacts, ceramics and family photographs dream up a homey ambience in the roomy dining space. Molyvos has been a Midtown staple for years, yet its quality and charm have never faltered. Close to Carnegie Hall, the restaurant makes a terrific pre- or post-performance gathering place.

Chef/partner James Botsacos designed the menu based on Greek home-style dishes, which he reproduces with contemporary flair and delicious consistency. Many dishes are cooked in the wood-fired oven, and everything, including the phyllo dough, is made on the premises. Begin your meal with a round of shared meze, followed with a glass of ouzo.

Manhattan Midtown West

Nick & Stef's

042

Steakhouse ✗✗

9 Penn Plaza (bet. Seventh & Eighth Aves.)

Subway:	34 St - Penn Station	Mon – Fri 11:30am - 3pm & 5pm - 10pm
Phone:	212-563-4444	Sat 5pm - 10pm
Fax:	212-563-9184	Closed Sun
Web:	www.rapatina.com/nickStef	
Prices:	$$$	

Sports fans going to Madison Square Garden to catch a Knicks or a Rangers game will no doubt appreciate the succulent cuts of Prime beef served at Nick & Stef's, while evening revelers tend to celebrate with the unique bison-grass vodka cocktails. Food portions are hefty but you can still choose sides, from macaroni and cheddar to asparagus, to go with your steak (of course, they also offer the requisite baked potatoes and creamed spinach). You'll find fresh seafood on the menu, too, in the form of Maine lobster, meaty crab cakes, shrimp scampi and more.

What sets this steakhouse apart is its contemporary feel. With its large windows, angled pine ceiling and warm tones, the Patina Group's version of a steakhouse—named for Joachim Splichal's twin sons—is less masculine than many others in the city.

Nobu Fifty-Seven

043

Contemporary Japanese ✗✗✗

40 W. 57th St. (bet. Fifth & Sixth Aves.)

Subway:	57 St	Mon – Fri 11:45am - 2:15pm
Phone:	212-757-3000	& 5:45pm - 11:15pm
Fax:	212-757-6330	Sat 5:45pm - 11:15pm
Web:	www.noburestaurants.com	Sun 5:45pm - 10:15pm
Prices:	$$$$	

Chef Nobu Matsuhisa has done it again with his new Midtown palace. Nobu Fifty-Seven's entrance may be sandwiched between two office buildings, but David Rockwell's sleek interior design incorporates sake jugs hanging above the bar, exotic woods and rattan wall coverings. Low lighting creates a sultry mood—not an easy feat in a place as large and busy as this one.

The restaurant pulls in a stylish business crowd whose expense accounts can handle the hefty prices. House specialties include rock shrimp tempura (a plate of plump, crispy, batter-fried shrimp bathed in a creamy and piquant chile sauce), and black cod with miso, a dish that made Nobu famous.

Creative à la carte offerings feature great variety, but you can always opt to let the chef decide—the omakase starts at about $100.

Orso

044

Italian ✗✗

322 W. 46th St. (bet. Eighth & Ninth Aves.)

Subway: 42 St - Port Authority Bus Terminal
Phone: 212-489-7212
Fax: 212-265-3383
Web: www.orsorestaurant.com
Prices: $$

Open daily 11:30am – 11:45pm
Closed major holidays

A respected member of the Restaurant Row dining fraternity, Orso concentrates on what it does well, and does it with aplomb. As at its two other branches, in Los Angeles and London, the restaurant offers diners a wide choice of Italian fare, running the gamut from pizza to pork chops. Entrées include roasted hot Italian sausages with polenta, grilled lamb or pork chops and sautéed calf's liver.

The dining room, done in warm pastel shades, accommodates those who come in for a quick meal before the theater, as well as diners who are making an evening of it. Star gazers will be interested to know that the later you dine, the more likely you are to see an actor from one of the neighboring theaters catching a post-performance bite to eat.

Osteria Al Doge

045

Italian ✗

142 W. 44th St. (bet. Broadway & Sixth Ave.)

Subway: Times Sq - 42 St
Phone: 212-944-3643
Fax: 212-944-5754
Web: www.osteria-doge.com
Prices: $$

Mon – Thu 11:30am - 11:30pm
Fri 11:30am - midnight
Sat 4:30pm - midnight
Sun 4:30pm - 10:30pm

Set amid the hustle and bustle of Times Square, Osteria Al Doge presents an inviting, Mediterranean-style ambience enhanced by wrought-iron chandeliers, Italian ceramics and fresh flowers. This elegant Venetian-inspired restaurant is a terrific choice in an area filled with overpriced tourist traps.

Homemade green pappardelle with lamb ragu, and tortellini filled with Atlantic salmon and goat cheese exemplify the authentic pasta dishes here. They are complimented by a good selection of fish and meat entrées—all served by a smiling and efficient staff of waiters. There's even a list of pizzas if you don't feel like bothering with multiple courses.

Staying in the Times Square area? Call in your order and the restaurant will deliver it.

Osteria Del Circo

Italian ✗✗

046

120 W. 55th St. (bet. Sixth & Seventh Aves.)

Subway:	57 St	Mon – Fri noon - 10:30pm
Phone:	212-265-3636	Sat – Sun 5pm - 10:30pm
Fax:	212-265-9283	Closed Sun in Summer
Web:	www.osteriadelcirco.com	
Prices:	$$$	

From the Maccioni family, who brought you the famous Le Cirque (now reopened in the Bloomberg Building), comes this less formal but exuberantly decorated Italian restaurant. Here the circus motif dominates, from the big-top tent billowing from the ceiling to the trapeze that swings down over the bar. Clown and monkey figurines abound, and a sculptural acrobat overlooks diners from his lofty platform. With such a spirited décor, it's little wonder that the atmosphere always buzzes, too.

The menu offers a wide choice of attractively presented Northern Italian fare, along with daily changing specials (come Monday for tripe, Thursday for osso buco). Yummy pizzas make a great shared appetizer or a light main course. As you leave, you can purchase a copy of the *Maccioni Family Cookbook*.

Petrossian

French ✗✗✗

047

182 W. 58th St. (at Seventh Ave.)

Subway:	57 St - 7 Av	Open daily 11:30am - 10:30pm
Phone:	212-245-2214	
Fax:	212-245-2812	
Web:	www.petrossian.com	
Prices:	$$$	

You'll want to linger on the sidewalk to marvel at the ornate Renaissance-style 1907 Alwyn Court Building that frames the entrance to Petrossian. Opened in the 1980s, this is the New York sister to Petrossian Paris, which has been delighting French diners since the 1920s. It was then that the two Petrossian brothers from Armenia made caviar the toast of the town in Paris, and founded the company that now ranks as the premier importer of Russian caviar—the restaurant's specialty.

Located a block from Carnegie Hall, Petrossian showcases ingredients that are as luxurious as its surroundings, which are decked out with Lalique crystal wall sconces, etched Erté mirrors and Limoges china. The contemporary French menu, peppered with caviar and foie gras, is perfect for lunch, brunch or dinner.

Piano Due

048

Italian 🍴🍴🍴

151 W. 51st St. (bet. Sixth & Seventh Aves.)

Subway:	49 St
Phone:	212-399-9400
Fax:	N/A
Web:	www.pianoduenyc.com
Prices:	$$$

Mon – Thu 11:45am - 3pm & 5pm - 10pm
Fri 11:45am - 3pm & 5pm - 11pm
Sat 5pm - 11pm
Closed Sun

Piano Due and Palio Bar represent the perfect yin and yang, with dazzling bursts of color in one setting and soothing tones in another. The first floor Palio Bar (which survived after Palio restaurant closed) dazzles the eye with its riotous reds and oranges, while Sandro Chia's powerful frescoes dominate the design. Whereas Palio sets the scene with its energetic spirit, Piano Due sports a luscious design upstairs with off-white hues punctuated by red jewel tones.

Tasting menus offer an excellent way to sample several dishes of Piano Due's contemporary Italian cuisine, though an à la carte menu is also available. The signature dish is soft egg-yolk ravioli filled with fluffy ricotta cheese and spinach, topped with a decadent shaving of black truffles.

Remi

049

Italian 🍴🍴🍴

145 W. 53rd St. (bet. Sixth & Seventh Aves.)

Subway:	7 Av
Phone:	212-581-4242
Fax:	212-581-5948
Web:	www.remi.citysearch.com
Prices:	$$

Mon – Fri noon - 4pm & 5pm - 11pm
Sat 5pm - 11:30pm
Sun 5pm - 9:30pm

Dreams of Venice come to mind when you enter this perennially busy Italian restaurant. Between the Venetian-glass chandelier, the 120-foot-long mural of Venice that covers one wall, and the bright sunlight streaming in through the large front windows, there's much to suggest that lovely city. Indeed, *remi* means "oars" in Italian, a reference to the famous canals of Venice.

In keeping with this theme, the food derives much of its influence from the Veneto region. Dishes such as sautéed calf's liver, and ravioli stuffed with tuna are just two of Remi's signature dishes. Homemade pastas are particularly good, but be sure to leave room for *dolci* such as tiramisu and white-chocolate hazelnut semifreddo. Managers run the dining room with a watchful eye.

René Pujol

050

French ✗✗

321 W. 51st St. (bet. Eighth & Ninth Aves.)

Subway:	50 St (Eighth Ave.)
Phone:	212-246-3023
Fax:	212-245-5206
Web:	www.renepujol.com
Prices:	$$$

Tue – Thu noon - 2:30pm & 5pm - 10pm
Fri – Sat noon - 2:30pm & 5pm - 11pm
Sun 11:45am - 2:30pm & 4:30pm - 6:30pm
Closed Mon
Closed Sun in Summer

In a city where the trendy establishments of the moment seems to eclipse other eateries, René Pujol stands out as a 30-year veteran in the Theater District. A loyal clientele often bring their offspring with them to ensure the restaurant's continued success with the next generation.

What's the draw? They all come for the classic French cuisine (flounder meunière, cassoulet, snails in garlic, parsley and tomato butter), which remains true to its roots by respecting Gallic culinary tradition.

Normally, there's a calm atmosphere in the carpeted dining room, with its lace curtains and working brick fireplace. The pre-theater rush can be a little overwhelming for newcomers, but the mature waitstaff handles it all with practiced proficiency.

Russian Samovar

051

Russian ✗

256 W. 52nd St. (bet. Broadway & Eighth Ave.)

Subway:	50 St (Broadway)
Phone:	212-757-0168
Fax:	212-765-2133
Web:	www.russiansamovar.com
Prices:	$$

Tue – Thu 5pm - midnight
Fri – Sat 5pm - 1am
Sun 5pm - 11pm
Closed Mon

It is no surprise that Russian Samovar borders the theater district; this restaurant, with its flashy mix of Russian celebrities, bigwigs and hockey players, provides enough entertainment to rival Broadway. The crowd is lively and the vodka is strong here, and guests can sample many varieties of house-infused vodka available by the shot, carafe or bottle. The décor is one part Old World and one part Russian grandmother, but this restaurant knows how to entertain its often-raucous crowd.

It's strictly business at Russian Samovar, where the staff can seem standoffish but are helpful even so. Authentic favorites, such as crisp chicken Kiev, rich beef Stroganoff, hearty *pelmeni*, and perfectly prepared blini, provide a taste of Moscow in the middle of Manhattan.

San Domenico NY

052

Italian ✗✗✗

240 Central Park South (bet. Broadway & Seventh Ave.)

Subway:	59 St - Columbus Circle
Phone:	212-265-5959
Fax:	212-397-0844
Web:	www.restaurant.com/sandomenicony.com
Prices:	$$$

Mon – Fri noon - 2:30pm
& 5:30pm - 11pm
Sat 5pm - 11:30pm
Sun 11:30am - 3pm & 5pm - 10pm

There's no denying that San Domenico has a lot going for it: its enviable location across from Central Park; its sumptuous ambience, given a facelift by designer Adam Tihany; and its memorable Italian cuisine. Opened by restaurateur Tony May (formerly of the Rainbow Room) in 1988, San Domenico shows off a style that is matched by its well-heeled patrons and its team of waiters in ties and waistcoats. Tihany's redesign displays leather-wrapped columns, fabric-covered light "boxes" and furnishings imported from Italy.

Elegant Italian food is spotlighted here, and house-made pastas shine with a delicacy and lightness all their own. In season, you can even partake in dishes luxuriously made with white truffles. If you're watching your wallet, go for the set-price lunch.

Sardi's

053

American ✗✗

234 W. 44th St. (bet. Broadway & Eighth Ave.)

Subway:	Times Sq - 42 St
Phone:	212-221-8440
Fax:	212-302-0865
Web:	www.sardis.com
Prices:	$$$

Tue – Sat 11:30am - 11:30pm
Sun noon - 8pm
Closed Mon

Grand dame of New York's theater-district restaurants, Sardi's has been serving patrons of the Great White Way since the 1920s. Stage-curtain red is the color scheme in the dining room, from the walls to the leather banquettes to the jackets worn by the mature brigade of waiters. And, of course, no self-respecting show-biz star can claim to have made it on Broadway until they see their caricature hanging among the framed portraits that paper Sardi's walls.

Exemplified by signature dishes like cannelloni au gratin and shrimp Sardi (sautéed in garlic sauce), the American fare here provides ample (as in large portions) sustenance to get you through a show. If you prefer to dine post-theater, Sardi's even has a late supper seating.

Manhattan Midtown West

The Sea Grill

Seafood XX

054

19 W. 49 St. (bet. Fifth & Sixth Aves.)

Subway:	47-50 Sts - Rockefeller Ctr
Phone:	212-332-7610
Fax:	212-332-7677
Web:	www.rapatina.com/seaGrill
Prices:	$$$

Mon – Fri 11:30am - 2:30pm
& 5pm - 10pm
Sat 5pm - 10pm
Closed Sun

You'll descend in an elevator like a deep-sea diver down to this Rockefeller Center seafood emporium, where the blues and beiges of the stylish décor capture the colors of the sand and sea. In winter, you can enjoy the Sea Grill's magical setting overlooking the famed Rock Center skating rink (open October to April). Large windows peer out over the ice, where golden lights sparkle at night. In summer, the rink's space is crowded with umbrella-shaded tables.

Offerings include everything from oysters and clams from the seafood bar to roasted whole fish and seafood prepared *a la plancha* (on a traditional cast-iron griddle). Whatever you choose, you'll savor a daily changing selection of fish and shellfish, fresh off the boat. Sides are sized for sharing.

Soba Nippon

Japanese X

055

19 W. 52nd St. (bet. Fifth & Sixth Aves.)

Subway:	5 Av - 53 St
Phone:	212-489-2525
Fax:	212-489-0326
Web:	www.sobanippon.com
Prices:	$$

Open daily noon - 3pm & 5:30pm - 10pm

This sushi and noodle restaurant in Midtown West always seems to pack in the crowds—everyone from Japanese businessmen to shoppers wandering through the neighborhood. They jostle for seats at counters, tables and bars that curve through the center of the dining room—all spaces that are jammed during the lunchtime crush.

An offshoot of Nippon in Midtown East *(155 E. 52nd St.)*, Soba Nippon focuses on soba and udon dishes, with the addition of sushi as well. Like its sister, the restaurant prides itself on making soba noodles from buckwheat grown on the restaurant's own farm in Canada. The menu lists both hot and cold soba noodle dishes, as well as soba salads, pleasing plates mounded with noodles and garnished with vegetables and greens.

Sugiyama

056

Japanese ✗

251 W. 55th St. (bet. Broadway & Eighth Ave.)

Subway:	57 St - 7 Av	Tue – Sat 5:30pm - 11:45pm
Phone:	212-956-0670	Closed Sun & Mon
Fax:	212-956-0671	
Web:	www.sugiyama-nyc.com	
Prices:	$$$	

♿

When you walk into Sugiyama, the first thing you'll notice is the cloud of smoke rising from the red-hot stones on the tabletops, where beef or seafood are cooking. Welcome to the world of *kaiseki*, a traditional Japanese dining experience that ignites your taste buds with a parade of small dishes and broths with an amazing richness and depth of flavor. If there's a time to splurge, this is it. Put yourself in chef Nao Sugiyama's hands and allow him to wow you with his talent.

Waiters will explain the dishes and the concept; all you have to do is decide how many courses your appetite or wallet can accommodate. Reserve a space at the counter, where you can interact with the personable chefs and take in all the action. This is unquestionably the best seat in the house.

Sushi Zen

057

Japanese ✗✗

108 W. 44th St. (bet. Broadway & Sixth Ave.)

Subway:	42 St - Bryant Pk	Mon – Fri noon - 2:45pm
Phone:	212-302-0707	& 5:30pm - 10pm
Fax:	212-944-7710	Sat 5pm - 10pm
Web:	www.sushizen-ny.com	Closed Sun
Prices:	$$$	

♿
🍵

Chef/owner Toshio Suzuki creates delicately textured sushi and sashimi, which, while it certainly tastes good, is also good for you (that's the Zen part). There's a wealth of different menus here. If you're new to raw fish, try the Introduction to Sushi from the sushi bar. Teriyaki, hand rolls, sashimi and more are all available à la carte, but you can also choose among three fixed-price tasting menus. The latter provide a good way to experience the kitchen's expertise, and you can sample the impressive sake selection to accompany your meal. The helpful staff will happily guide you through the menu.

As the restaurant's name implies, decoration is minimal, albeit bright and comfortable. Grab a seat at one of the outdoor tables on a nice day and watch the hustle and bustle of Midtown.

Taboon

Middle Eastern ✗

058

773 Tenth Ave. (at 52nd St.)

Subway:	50 St (Eighth Ave.)
Phone:	212-713-0271
Fax:	212-713-0491
Web:	N/A
Prices:	$$

Mon – Fri 5pm - 11pm
Sat 5:30pm - 11:30pm
Sun 5pm - 10pm

Tenth Avenue in Midtown, with its car dealerships and industrial spaces, may lack the personality of many other New York neighborhoods, but it's worth visiting just for a meal at Taboon. This unique Middle Eastern restaurant, with its crackling wood-burning brick oven (or *taboon*), adds character to an otherwise barren street in Hell's Kitchen.

Weathered flooring, whitewashed furniture, and windows dressed with white linen panels lend a Mediterranean look to this inviting place. Meals begin with heavenly flatbreads, slathered with olive oil, sprinkled with rosemary and sea salt, and brought to the table still warm from the oven; freshly made tzatziki serves as a sparkling accompaniment. Middle Eastern accents enliven delicious dishes, from dough-wrapped sweetbreads to lamb osso buco.

Town

Contemporary ✗✗✗

059

15 W. 56th St. (bet. Fifth & Sixth Aves.)

Subway:	57 St
Phone:	212-582-4445
Fax:	212-582-5535
Web:	www.townnyc.com
Prices:	$$$

Mon – Thu noon - 2:30pm
& 5:30pm - 10:30pm
Fri noon - 2:30pm & 5:30pm - 11pm
Sat 5:30pm - 11pm
Sun 11am - 2pm & 5:30pm - 10pm

At the Chambers Hotel *(see hotel listings)*, "a night on the town" translates as a meal at the property's stylish restaurant, located downstairs from the lobby bar. The discreetly understated yet hip décor, designed by David Rockwell in blond woods and cascades of beads, appeals to Gotham fashionistas and well-heeled tourists. Town opened in 2001 as the first independent venture of chef Geoffrey Zakarian, who recently opened Country in Gramercy.

Zakarian prides himself on his modern and healthy cuisine. Market availability influences the menu selections, which could include grilled sea bass served over artichoke leaves or fresh asparagus salad. Many of the dishes are presented in a colorful neo-Californian style. Service is well-timed and courteous at this serious restaurant.

Trattoria Dell'Arte

060

900 Seventh Ave. (bet. 56th & 57th Sts.)

Subway:	57 St - 7 Av	Mon – Sat 11:45am – 11:30pm
Phone:	212-245-9800	Sun 11am - 10:30pm
Fax:	212-265-3296	
Web:	www.trattoriadellarte.com	
Prices:	$$	

The nose knows. Take your cue from the much-larger-than-life nose sculpture that tops the entrance to Trattoria Dell'Arte. Designed as an idiosyncratic artist's studio, the interior exhibits unfinished paintings, sculptural body parts and a gallery of works depicting Italian noses. The trattoria, which is bigger than it first appears, sits opposite Carnegie Hall, a location that assures the restaurant is constantly abuzz.

A long antipasto bar teems with assorted seafood, cured meats, and cheeses, while the menu offers a substantial selection of Italian favorites from pappardelle to panettone. Delicious pizza choices include the aragosta, topped with a one-pound lobster, tomatoes and zucchini. Confident service adds to the contagiously exuberant air of the place.

Tuscan Square

061

16 W. 51st St. (at Fifth Ave.)

Subway:	47-50 Sts - Rockefeller Ctr	Mon – Fri 11:30am - 3:30pm
Phone:	212-977-7777	& 5pm - 10pm
Fax:	212-977-3144	Sat noon - 10pm
Web:	www.tuscansquare.citysearch.com	Closed Sun
Prices:	$$	

All things Tuscan infuse this restaurant with the ambience of the Italian countryside, starting with the warm yellow and green walls in the 200-seat dining room. Bright plates, tile floors, and sideboards set with dried flowers and bottles of olive oil add rustic touches.

From osso buco to lobster Fra Diavolo, the menu offers authentic Italian staples; be sure to sample a bottle of robust Tuscan red wine. This jack-of-all-trades restaurant also features an espresso bar, a bakery and a market downstairs, all showcasing the best products Tuscany has to offer. Downstairs, those on the go can take out everything from panini to pizza and whole cakes to calzones.

After a meal here, you'll be booking a flight to Italy.

Manhattan Midtown West

21 Club

062

21 W. 52nd St. (bet. Fifth & Sixth Aves.)

Subway:	5 Av - 53 St
Phone:	212-582-7200
Fax:	N/A
Web:	www.21club.com
Prices:	$$$

Mon – Fri noon - 2:30pm
& 5:30pm - 9:30pm
Sat 5:30pm - 11pm
Closed Sun
Closed Sat in Summer

A dowager among New York City restaurants, the 21 Club started as a speakeasy during the Prohibition era. In the 1950s, the club debuted in its first film, *All About Eve*. Since then, the restaurant has starred in a multitude of movies, as well as playing host to a galaxy of stars, including Humphrey Bogart, Frank Sinatra and Helen Hayes.

With its dim lighting and once-secret wine cellar (in a basement vault in the building next door), 21 Club still exudes a clandestine air. It's clearly a place for power brokers, and the presence of a Bloomberg terminal in the lounge reminds guests that in New York, money is a serious business.

Cuisine here sticks to the tried and true; 21 Classics, including the burger favored by Aristote Onassis, provide the best traditional experience.

ViceVersa

063

325 W. 51st St. (bet. Eighth & Ninth Aves.)

Subway:	50 St (Eighth Ave.)
Phone:	212-399-9291
Fax:	212-399-9327
Web:	www.viceversarestaurant.com
Prices:	$$

Mon – Fri noon - 2:30pm & 5pm - 11pm
Sat 5pm - 11pm
Closed Sun & major holidays

Run by the experienced team of three Italian men who cut their teeth at San Domenico on Central Park South, ViceVersa (pronounced VEE-cha versa) celebrates *la dolce vita*. The restaurant fashions an urbane ambience in its earth-tone dining space, highlighted by a zinc bar and softly lit wall alcoves displaying antique classical urns. Locals love the enclosed terrace at the back for summer dining.

Approachable fixed-price menus complement extensive à la carte offerings, all of which come to the table in artful presentations. Pasta dishes are consistently good, while entrées, like rack of lamb and sesame-coated salmon, show a deft hand. Be sure to leave room for the irresistible desserts like the rich, dark-chocolate cake, served warm beside a scoop of vanilla gelato.

Xing

064

785 Ninth Ave. (bet. 52nd & 53rd Sts.)

Subway:	50 St (Eighth Ave.)	Mon – Fri 5pm - 11pm
Phone:	212-289-3010	Sat – Sun 11am - 3pm & 5pm - midnight
Fax:	212-289-3014	
Web:	www.xingrestaurant.com	
Prices:	$$	

♿

True to its name ("star" in Chinese), Xing has been shining bright in the developing West Side neighborhood of Hell's Kitchen since the restaurant opened in early 2005. The front space sports a cool cafe style, done in blond woods and bright bamboo green. If you continue through to the back room, you'll find the mood turns sultry with deep-red velvet-covered walls and banquettes, sobered by black furnishings. The Asia-meets-Las Vegas look attracts an equally hip crowd of area denizens.

Xing (say "shing") recently underwent a complete cuisine and kitchen overhaul, and the result is a more elegant menu of upscale, modernized fusion dishes with a Chinese touch. Various Asian ingredients make secondary appearances, and the cocktail list cites an imaginative assortment of concoctions.

Yang Pyung Seoul 😊

065

43 W. 33rd St. (bet. Broadway & Fifth Ave.)

Subway:	34 St - Herald Sq	Open daily 24 hours
Phone:	212-629-5599	
Fax:	N/A	
Web:	N/A	
Prices:	😊	

Hard by the Empire State Building in the area known as Little Korea, Yang Pyung Seoul brings an authentic slice of Korea to this section of Midtown. What draws many people from New York's Korean community to this nondescript little place, which is open 24 hours a day, is the quality and authenticity of its cuisine.

Don't worry if your Korean is a little rusty; the menu includes helpful photographs of the various dishes. *Banchan*, complimentary offerings that are served before your meal, are tasty as well as generous in size. Specialties of the house here include the rich and robust broths, particularly the *hae jang gook*, which is reputed to stave off winter colds and even cure hangovers. Finish it all off with a "shot" of sweet liquid yogurt.

Manhattan **Midtown West**

SoHo & NoLIta

The heart of Manhattan's downtown fashion scene, SoHo—short for South of Houston—is New York at its trendiest and most colorful. Visitors throng the district *(bounded by West, Houston, Lafayette and Canal streets)* on weekends, making even walking down the sidewalk difficult—especially given the proliferation of sidewalk tables full of purses and jewelry, sunglasses and scarves, and "outsider" art. The restaurant scene is a lively one here, as eclectic as SoHo itself. You'll find everything from designer-decorated, high-end restaurants to tiny, decidedly untrendy eateries.

NoLIta (for North of Little Italy), Little Italy's über-fashionable sister, actually sits within that district's former boundaries; four blocks long and three blocks wide, it stretches from Kenmare to Houston streets on Mulberry, Mott and Elizabeth streets. The moniker NoLIta came courtesy of real-estate developers, who in the 1990s wanted to distinguish it from the red-sauce joints of the old neighborhood. Today NoLIta is chock-a-block with chic cafes that are ideal for people-watching.

A Bit of History – Site of the first free black community in Manhattan, SoHo was settled in 1644 by former slaves of the Dutch West India Company, who were granted land for farms. In the early 19th century, Broadway was paved and a number of prominent citizens, including *Last of the Mohicans* author James Fenimore Cooper, moved in, bringing cachet to the district. In the late 1850s, stores such as Tiffany & Co. and Lord & Taylor were joined on Broadway by grand hotels. Theaters, casinos and brothels entertained visitors—and drove respectable middle-class families uptown. The exodus made room in the late 1800s for a slew

Shopping in SoHo

© *Martha Cooper*

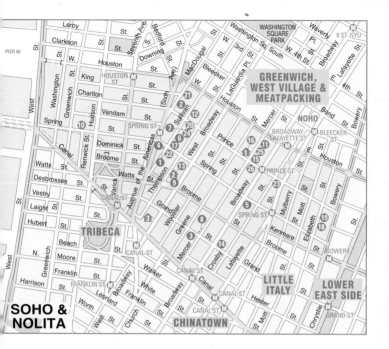

of new warehouses and factories, many built with ornamented cast-iron façades, which looked like carved stone. The area thrived as a commercial center until the 1890s, when fashionable businesses began relocating to Fifth Avenue.

Art Brings a New Start – By the late 1950s the neighborhood was a slum known as "Hell's Hundred Acres," and city planners slated it for demolition to make room for an expressway until residents objected. Often in violation of building codes, painters and sculptors converted vacant warehouses into studios, galleries and living quarters. An underground art scene took root and thrived until the early 1980s, when uptown galleries, boutiques and affluent professionals began to push out the very artists who'd made the neighborhood so desirable in the first place.

Today few artists can afford to live or work in SoHo, and the migration of galleries northward to Chelsea continues. Locally owned boutiques have been largely supplanted by international couturiers, making SoHo a Mecca for moneyed fashionistas. Overflowing with traffic, pedestrians and sidewalk vendors, **Broadway** is SoHo at its most commercial. The west end of Broadway ranks as the neighborhood's premier corridor for fashion and art as well as dining.

Fiamma Osteria ✿

Italian 🍴🍴🍴

001

206 Spring St. (bet. Sixth Ave. & Sullivan St.)

Subway:	Spring St (Sixth Ave.)	
Phone:	212-653-0100	
Fax:	212-653-0101	
Web:	www.brguestrestaurants.com	
Prices:	$$$	

Mon – Thu noon - 2:30pm
& 5:30pm - 11pm
Fri noon - 2:30pm & 5:30pm - midnight
Sat 5:30pm - midnight
Sun 5pm - 10pm

Manhattan SoHo & NoLIta

Fiamma Osteria/Eric Laignel

The jewel in SoHo's culinary crown, Fiamma Osteria resulted from a partnership between renowned chef Michael White and Steven Hanson, head of the B.R. Guest Restaurant Group. A glass elevator whisks guests—who have included a veritable Who's Who of Hollywood stars—to the upper two of three distinct dining levels (the third is reserved for private dining). Rich brown and fawn hues, warm ambient lighting from large, hanging lanterns, and elegantly laid tables set a seductive tone.

In keeping with the restaurant's name, which is Italian for "flame," tantalizing and artfully presented dishes will spark your taste buds using premium regional Italian ingredients, such as aged prosciutto di Parma, lentils from Castelluccio, truffled pecorino cheese and fragrant Tuscan olive oil. The branzino, with its two nice fillets of pan-roasted sea bass over colored couscous with shrimp and calamari, particularly sparkles. Pasta dishes offer tremendous flavor, and the dessert menu showcases delightfully creative concoctions.

282 - Manhattan

Appetizers

Misticanza: Mixed Baby Lettuces, Roasted Beets, Red-Wine Bacon Vinaigrette and Ricotta Salata

Capesante: Seared Diver Scallops, Braised Wild Mushrooms, Brown-Butter Truffle Vinaigrette

Fonduta: White-Truffle Robiola Cheese, Soft Targna Polenta, Piemontese Fonduta

Entrées

Garganelli: Imolese Quill Pasta, San Daniele Prosciutto, Treviso Truffle Butter, Parmigiano

Branzino: Pan-roasted Black Sea Bass, Sicilian Almond Couscous, Shrimp, Calamaretti

Brasato: Red-Wine-braised Beef Short Rib, Root Vegetables, Celery-Root Purée, Grated Horseradish

Desserts

Semifreddo: Honey-Nougat Parfait, Caramelized Bananas, Passion Fruit, Almond Cake

Budino: Meyer Lemon Custard, Huckleberry Guazzetto, Sicilian Pistachios, Meyer Lemon Granita

Crocchette: Crispy Winter-spiced Beignets, Maple, Chocolate and Butterscotch Sauce

Ama

Italian ✕

002

48 MacDougal St. (bet. Houston & Prince Sts.)

Subway: Spring St (Sixth Ave.)　　　　　　　Open daily noon - 3pm & 5pm - 11pm
Phone: 212-358-1707
Fax: 212-358-1238
Web: www.amanyc.com
Prices: $$

How appropriate that a restaurant whose name derives from the Italian word for love should open on Valentine's Day (2005). Passers-by are drawn here by the warm glow coming from within. Once inside, one finds a narrow room balanced by mirrors and an impressionistic painting on the ceiling; tables cluster close together, adding to the intimate feel.

The menu avoids run-of-the-mill Italian fare in favor of cooking that takes its influences from Puglia. Ingredients, in dishes like quail filled with pancetta and served on polenta with cardoncelli mushrooms, are first-rate. Unusual creations, such as the mushroom-and-blueberry-filled pasta, are the standard at Ama. After a meal here, being attended to by the charming waitstaff, you're bound to leave feeling a little bit better about the world.

Antique Garage

Turkish ✕

003

41 Mercer St. (bet. Broome & Grand Sts.)

Subway: Canal St (Broadway)　　　　　　　　　Open daily noon - midnight
Phone: 212-219-1019
Fax: 212-219-1828
Web: www.antiquegaragesoho.com
Prices: ⊜

The name of this place tells you just what to expect: it's set in a former auto-repair garage converted to an antique store/restaurant. Filled with antique tiles, furniture, china and light fixtures—many of which are for sale—the cozy dining room feels more like a little roadside restaurant in the country than a chic SoHo eatery. Seating is at tiny tables, or on low antique sofas, with coffee tables between them.

Oddly, the food is the only thing notably Turkish here, and it's quite authentic and packed with flavor. Eggplant salad, grilled Turkish meatballs made with ground lamb and beef, and Mediterranean shrimp could be ordered as a meze selection to share or as progressive courses. Mint lemonade is freshly squeezed, and they brew an excellent cup of heady Turkish coffee.

Aquagrill

Seafood ✗✗

004

210 Spring St. (at Sixth Ave.)

Subway:	Spring St (Sixth Ave.)
Phone:	212-274-0505
Fax:	212-274-0587
Web:	www.aquagrill.com
Prices:	$$

Mon – Thu noon - 3pm & 6pm - 10:45pm
Fri noon - 3pm & 6pm - 11:45pm
Sat noon - 4pm & 6pm - 11:45pm
Sun noon - 4pm & 6pm - 10:30pm
Closed major holidays

From the staggering selection of oysters at the raw bar to simple grilled fish, Jeremy and Jennifer Marshall's establishment aims to please all seafood lovers. The husband-and-wife team divides up the work here: Culinary Institute of America-trained chef Jeremy keeps watch over the kitchen and Jennifer oversees the dining room, set about by lamps and pictures made from seashells.

The chef treats his fresh supplies with due deference, adding subtle Asian accents to enhance the preparations. Clever combinations, like falafel-crusted salmon, are a hallmark of Aquagrill. Brunch is a real treat on weekends and lunch is always busy, but it's at dinner that the kitchen staff really struts their stuff. Service is smoothly choreographed, and an air of professionalism pervades the whole operation.

Balthazar

French ✗

005

80 Spring St. (bet. Broadway & Crosby St.)

Subway:	Spring St (Lafayette St.)
Phone:	212-965-1414
Fax:	212-343-1274
Web:	www.balthazarny.com
Prices:	$$$

Mon – Thu 7:30am - 12:30am
Fri 7:30am - 1:30am
Sat 8am - 1:30am
Sun 8am - 12:30am

What sets this establishment apart is its authentic ambience, constantly animated by lively conversation. All the requisite décor elements are here (red leatherette banquettes, mosaic tile floor, mirrors bearing extracts of the menu), conjuring up late-19th-century Paris. Part of Keith McNally's empire, which also includes Pastis, Balthazar is where the cool crowd hangs.

There's nothing surprising about the menu, either, but the products are fresh and the dishes are well-prepared. Specials correspond to the day of the week (come Friday for bouillabaisse), and the restaurant gets its baguettes and pastries from its own bakery. Like any self-respecting brasserie, Balthazar offers a late-night supper menu, which runs from salad Niçoise to poached eggs and boudin noir.

Manhattan SoHo & NoLita

Blue Ribbon

006

97 Sullivan St. (bet. Prince & Spring Sts.)

Subway:	Spring St (Sixth Ave.)	Open daily 4pm - 4am
Phone:	212-274-0404	
Fax:	N/A	
Web:	www.blueribbonrestaurants.com	
Prices:	$$$	

♿

Simple comforts here create a convivial atmosphere that makes you feel like a SoHo insider, although the closeness of the tables means that conversation is rarely private. Denizens of late-night New York will appreciate the fact that the restaurant serves until 4am.

The kitchen turns out an eclectic but winning array of dishes that range from all-American (fried chicken, hamburgers) to Mediterranean (paella, sautéed skate). Blue Ribbon's success has spawned several offspring over the years, with a Blue Ribbon Sushi just a few doors down, Blue Ribbon Bakery a few blocks west, and a sister to Blue Ribbon *(280 Fifth Ave.)* and Blue Ribbon Sushi *(278 Fifth Ave.)*, both in Park Slope. None of the Blue Ribbon locations take reservations for parties of less than five.

Blue Ribbon Sushi

007

119 Sullivan St. (bet. Prince & Spring Sts.)

Subway:	Spring St (Sixth Ave.)	Open daily noon - 2am
Phone:	212-343-0404	
Fax:	N/A	
Web:	www.blueribbonrestaurants.com	
Prices:	$$	

A few doors down from its sister restaurant Blue Ribbon, the equally popular Blue Ribbon Sushi bears a sign so discreet that you'd think they were trying to keep the place a secret. Inside the cozy, compact room, you'll find wooden booths and a sushi counter behind which the chefs jostle for space to prepare their specialties.

Divided into sections by ocean (Atlantic and Pacific), the extensive menu of sushi can appear bewildering at first glance, but what sets it apart are unusual offerings such as jellyfish and spicy lobster with egg wrapper. The requisite cooked dishes are also available, as is a tempting array of seasonal specials. If you're going for dinner, be sure to get there early; the no-reservations policy means the restaurant fills up quickly in the evening.

Cendrillon

008

45 Mercer St. (bet. Broome & Grand Sts.)

Subway: Canal St (Broadway)
Phone: 212-343-9012
Fax: 212-343-9670
Web: www.cendrillon.com
Prices: $$

Tue – Sun 11am - 10pm
Closed Mon

All too often, fusion cuisine merely reflects where the chef took his last vacation, but at this roomy SoHo restaurant, a real understanding of Asian culinary culture underscores the cooking. With Filipino cooking at its core, Cendrillon surprises diners with zesty and vivacious flavors, guaranteed to cheer the most sullen taste buds. Noodle dishes and Asian barbecue compete with tantalizing entrées, like grilled oxtail and salt-roasted duck. Although portion size is on the generous side, you'll definitely want to leave room for dessert. Check out the impressive selection of exotic Asian teas to complement your meal.

This place is typical SoHo, incorporating the requisite exposed brickwork and vent shafts, with the brightest spot at the back, past the open kitchen.

Downtown Cipriani

009

376 West Broadway (bet. Broome & Spring Sts.)

Subway: Spring St (Sixth Ave.)
Phone: 212-343-0999
Fax: 212-925-3610
Web: www.cipriani.com
Prices: $$$

Open daily noon - midnight

Part of the Cipriani restaurant group, a rapidly expanding hospitality (and now real-estate) empire in Manhattan, the Downtown satellite seems right at home in its oh-so-SoHo surroundings. On sunny days, the Euro crowd is in top form outside, where sidewalk tables afford great people-watching. Don't be surprised if you recognize some faces among the well-heeled regulars; this place attracts a high-profile clientele.

With its laid-back atmosphere, Downtown Cipriani features an equally casual menu of hearty Italian fare. Be sure to try a bellini (prosecco with peach purée), the cocktail created by Giuseppe Cipriani at the famed Harry's Bar in Venice. Siblings include Cipriani Dolci *(West Balcony, Grand Central Terminal)*, and Harry Cipriani, in the Sherry Netherland hotel *(781 Fifth Ave.)*.

Manhattan SoHo & NoLita

Giorgione

010

307 Spring St. (bet. Greenwich & Hudson Sts.)

Subway:	Spring St (Sixth Ave.)
Phone:	212-352-2269
Fax:	212-352-8734
Web:	N/A
Prices:	$$

Mon – Thu noon - 3pm & 6pm - 11pm
Fri noon - 3pm & 6pm - midnight
Sat 6pm - midnight
Sun noon - 4pm & 5pm - 11pm

All the buzz occurs inside rather than outside Giorgione, since it is situated in a relatively quiet spot in SoHo. Giorgio DeLuca, one of Dean & DeLuca's founders, owns this lively place, which you enter via the sleek bar. Follow the narrow space toward the back, and the room widens into the main dining area, where chrome-topped tables, boxy light fixtures, white-leather seating and ice-blue walls contribute to the cool vibe.

A party-hearty crowd drops in for a select menu of oven-fired pizzas, pastas, risottos and the fresh catch from the oyster bar. After dinner, you'll find it difficult to resist the temptations of the dessert trolley when it's rolled to your table.

Just around the corner at 508 Greenwich Street, Giorgione 508 serves one of the most delicious roasted-tomato soups ever.

Honmura An

011

170 Mercer St. (bet. Houston & Prince Sts.)

Subway:	Broadway - Lafayette St
Phone:	212-334-5253
Fax:	212-334-6162
Web:	N/A
Prices:	$$$

Tue 6pm - 10pm
Wed – Thu noon - 2:30pm & 6pm - 10pm
Fri – Sat noon - 2:30pm & 6pm - 10:30pm
Sun 6pm - 9:30pm
Closed Mon

Buckwheat noodles, called soba, are the specialty at this second-floor Japanese restaurant, whose flagship is in Tokyo. Serene, simple interiors set the tone here, but the food takes center stage. Chefs learn the art of preparing delicate soba noodles in practically the same time it takes to become an architect, so when you see the chefs at work behind the glass wall of the kitchen, you should appreciate their skill.

While you can order handmade noodles cold or hot, it's the latter, swathed in salty broth, that really stand out—slurping from your bowl is expected. For a non-noodle house specialty, try the giant prawn tempura. Small tasting plates are designed for sharing any time of day, and the set menu at lunchtime gives newcomers the soba experience without breaking the bank.

Jean Claude

012

137 Sullivan St. (bet. Houston & Prince Sts.)

Subway:	Spring St (Sixth Ave.)	Open daily 6pm - 11pm
Phone:	212-475-9232	
Fax:	N/A	
Web:	N/A	
Prices:	$$	

Just add a plume of Gauloise smoke, and this little French bistro could be on the Left Bank in Paris instead of planted in the heart of SoHo. Simply decorated with bottles and assorted Gallic-themed posters, the dining room sports a lively, yet romantic, atmosphere. Brown-paper-covered tables here snuggle so close together that if you like the looks of your neighbor, it wouldn't be difficult to start up a conversation about the tasty, classic French fare, which includes grilled foie gras, roasted monkfish and seared sea scallops.

Newcomers may be deterred by the fact that Jean Claude doesn't take credit cards, but if you don't mind coming early, you won't need oodles of cash to afford the inexpensive fixed-price menu, offered from 6pm to 7:30pm.

Kittichai

013

60 Thompson St. (bet. Broome & Spring Sts.)

Subway:	Spring St (Sixth Ave.)	Sun – Wed 7am - 11pm
Phone:	212-219-2000	Thu – Sat 7am - midnight
Fax:	212-925-2991	
Web:	www.kittichairestaurant.com	
Prices:	$$$	

Located in the fashionable Sixty Thompson Hotel *(see hotel listings)*, this sensual SoHo newcomer offers subtly spiced Thai cooking, thanks to chef Ian Chalermkittichai, who came to New York from the Four Seasons Hotel in Bangkok.

The food is as appealing as the exotic setting here, where orchids float in bottles on lighted shelves, lush silk fabrics and Thai artifacts adorn the walls, and a reflecting pool forms the centerpiece of the dining room. Appetizers and entrées are modern and approachable, balancing European technique with New York accents and Thai inflections. Black-clad waiters can help you sort out which is which.

At times, the food seems more fusion than Thai, as the chopsticks on the table and the sashimi-style appetizers suggest.

L'Ecole

French ✕✕

014

462 Broadway (at Grand St.)

Subway:	Canal St (Broadway)	Mon – Wed 12:30pm - 2pm & 6pm - 9:30pm
Phone:	212-219-3300	Thu – Sat 12:30pm - 2pm
Fax:	212-334-4866	& 5:30pm - 9:30pm
Web:	www.frenchculinary.com	Sat 5:30pm - 9:30pm
Prices:	$$	Closed Sun

If you want to be a guinea pig, this is the place to do it. The restaurant of New York's French Culinary Institute provides the opportunity for its students to show off what they've learned—and that's a lot. They've certainly mastered the first rule of good cooking: use the best quality ingredients you can find and don't mess around too much with a good thing.

The kitchen earns top marks for its four- or five-course dinner menus, and the prix-fixe lunch menu is a great—and inexpensive—way to sample the flavorful regional French fare, which changes every six weeks (be sure to make reservations). A conscientious student waitstaff caters to customers in a soothing yellow room decorated with photographs depicting the frenetic world of a restaurant kitchen.

Lure Fishbar

Seafood ✕✕

015

142 Mercer St. (bet. Houston & Prince Sts.)

Subway:	Prince St	Mon – Thu 11:30am - 11pm
Phone:	212-431-7676	Fri 11:30am - midnight
Fax:	212-925-4018	Sat 5:30pm - midnight
Web:	www.lurefishbar.com	Sun 5:30pm - 11pm
Prices:	$$$	

If your credit card's not maxed out from visiting the Prada shop above this restaurant, Lure Fishbar makes a great place to drop anchor. The seafaring-themed restaurant recently re-opened after a fire destroyed the interior last year. It's decked out in a fantastic tiki-trendy style with angular porthole windows, teak paneling and tropical-print fabrics, reminiscent of a luxury ocean liner. The only thing missing from the maritime motif is the sound of waves crashing and the feel of sand between your toes.

Have a seat at the sushi bar and order a sushi-sashimi combo, or sit at the raw bar to share a shellfish plateau. In the main dining room, you can choose among the fresh catches, which are as pleasing to the eye as they are to the palate. Just one visit and you'll be hooked.

Mercer Kitchen

016

99 Prince St. (at Mercer St.)

Subway:	Prince St	Sun – Thu noon - 3pm & 6pm - midnight
Phone:	212-966-5454	Fri – Sat noon - 3pm & 6pm - 1am
Fax:	212-965-3855	
Web:	www.jean-georges.com	
Prices:	$$	

When it opened in the basement of SoHo's Mercer Hotel (see hotel listings) in 1998, Mercer Kitchen took a position at the vanguard of the culinary new wave. Today the restaurant, which owes its existence to wunderkind Jean-Georges Vongerichten, remains fiercely fashionable. This is the quintessential SoHo experience: a Prada-clad crowd, eccentric décor (think hanging umbrellas) and a staff all dressed in—what else?—black.

In the subterranean dining room, with its arched brick entryways and open kitchen, you'll be treated to cooking that has roots in France but travels to faraway locales for inspiration. Raw tuna and wasabi dress up pizza; salmon is given a boost with lime and cucumber. If you want to make a new friend, take a seat at one of the communal tables overlooking the kitchen.

Mezzogiorno

017

195 Spring St. (at Sullivan St.)

Subway:	Spring St (Sixth Ave.)	Mon – Fri noon - 3:30pm
Phone:	212-334-2112	& 6pm - midnight
Fax:	212-941-6294	Sat – Sun noon - midnight
Web:	www.mezzogiorno.com	Closed Christmas Day
Prices:	$$	

A SoHo veteran established more than 12 years ago by Vittorio and Nicola Ansuini, Mezzogiorno (the name means "midday") recreates the warm, vibrant atmosphere of the owners' native Florence. More than 100 Italian artists were asked to interpret the restaurant's logo, a smiling sun; their collection of collages, paintings and small objets d'art are displayed at one end of the room.

The Florentine theme continues in the menu of seasonal dishes, which includes a host of fresh products imported from Italy. An extensive collection of pastas, including risotto and ravioli of the day, proves enticing, while veal and meat dominate the main courses. Outside, the attractive raised terrace provides a great vantage point for people-watching when the weather is fine.

Peasant

Italian

018

194 Elizabeth St. (bet. Prince & Spring Sts.)

Subway:	Spring St (Lafayette St.)	Tue – Sun 6pm - 11pm
Phone:	212-965-9511	Closed Mon
Fax:	212-965-8471	
Web:	www.peasantnyc.com	
Prices:	$$	

Chef Frank DeCarlo named his restaurant for his cooking style. Opened in 2000, Peasant emphasizes honest, Italian country fare, much of which is cooked in the wood-burning brick oven at the back of the room and served in terra-cotta pots.

Comforts are simple here, too, with church-pew seating, exposed brick walls and tabletop candles providing the main source of light. (Okay, the restaurant is dark, but who doesn't look good in dim, romantic candlelight? Besides, the menu is entirely in Italian, so you can always use the lack of light as an excuse to ask for a translation.) Rustic entrées include lamb with polenta, gnocchi with meaty wild mushrooms and steak Florentine. Pizza, with pepperoncini and soppressata or mortadella, among other toppings, is a sure-fire hit.

Public

Fusion

019

210 Elizabeth St. (bet. Prince & Spring Sts.)

Subway:	Spring St (Lafayette St.)	Mon – Thu 6pm - 11:30pm
Phone:	212-343-7011	Fri 6pm - 12:30am
Fax:	212-343-0918	Sat 11am - 4pm & 6pm - 12:30am
Web:	www.public-nyc.com	Sun 11am - 4pm & 6pm - 10:30pm
Prices:	$$$	

Here's your chance to sample Tasmanian sea trout, grilled kangaroo or New Zealand venison, complemented by a good selection of boutique wines from Down Under. Public's kitchen takes its cue from London restaurant The Providores (owned by the same pair of chefs who founded Public) in creating a unique style of cooking that fuses Australian and New Zealand ingredients with influences that span the globe. Brunch is eye-opening, with selections ranging from coconut pancakes to grilled chorizo and salad.

Designed by AvroKO, this bright, airy NoLIta spot incorporates salvaged pieces of public buildings into the erstwhile muffin factory it occupies, adding whimsical touches like shelves of library books and vintage card catalogs, and bronze post office boxes in which regulars can stash wine.

Raoul's

020

180 Prince St. (bet. Sullivan & Thompson Sts.)

Subway:	Spring St (Sixth Ave.)	Open daily 5pm - 1am
Phone:	212-966-3518	
Fax:	212-966-0205	
Web:	www.raouls.com	
Prices:	$$$	

For any restaurant to survive for thirty years in this fickle business, they must be doing something right—and Raoul's does a lot of things right. The restaurant boasts authentic bistro charm, its walls covered with an assortment of artwork.

Waiters here have mastered the stereotypic Gallic insouciance, and the kitchen turns out good classic French food, from roast duck with confit and morels to goat cheese soufflé with green-tomato marmalade; the menu is presented on small, individual blackboards. You can't help but be caught up in the energetic atmosphere in the dimly lit main dining room, but if you're seeking a calmer spot for a quiet conversation, try the bright upstairs space or the tiny garden room.

Salt

021

58 MacDougal St. (bet. Houston & Prince Sts.)

Subway:	Spring St (Sixth Ave.)	Mon – Thu 6pm -11pm
Phone:	212-674-4968	Fri – Sat 6pm - midnight
Fax:	212-529-9111	Closed Sun & major holidays
Web:	www.saltnyc.com	
Prices:	$$	

The term "neighborhood restaurant" is bandied about on a fairly casual basis these days, but Salt genuinely deserves this moniker. Here diners are encouraged to sit at one of three communal tables in the middle of the room, where they can rub elbows with the locals—and maybe even eavesdrop on some juicy SoHo gossip.

From salt-crusted venison loin and Alaskan King salmon to grilled Newport steak, this menu is a showpiece of contemporary American cooking. Short but interesting, it contains a section called "Protein + 2," which is perfect for South Beach dieters, since it allows you to choose your entrée and pair it with any two side items (most of which are vegetables). You'd do equally well to trust the kitchen, though; the chef's selections are always fresh and seasonal.

Savore

Italian ✖✖

022

200 Spring St. (at Sullivan St.)

Subway: Spring St (Sixth Ave.)
Phone: 212-431-1212
Fax: 212-343-2605
Web: www.savoreny.com
Prices: $$

Open daily noon - midnight
Closed December 25 - 26

SoHo certainly claims its fair share of jam-packed eateries where the dictates of fashion override any serious thought of the cuisine. Fortunately for those who put food first, there's Savore. Bang in the middle of SoHo, this restaurant with its sunny atmosphere provides a comforting haven for those seeking refuge from the terminally hip.

Warm yellow hues and architectural drawings provide a soothing backdrop for savoring solid Northern Italian cooking, complemented by a good selection of Tuscan wines. Grilled baby octopus or lobster and asparagus salad whet the appetite, while pastas tossed with vegetables, meat or seafood are consistently flavorful. All this plus courteous attentive service will make you want to linger a while before braving the bustling neighborhood outside.

Savoy

Contemporary ✖

023

70 Prince St. (at Crosby St.)

Subway: Prince St
Phone: 212-219-8570
Fax: N/A
Web: www.savoynyc.com
Prices: $$

Mon – Thu noon - 10:30pm
Fri – Sat noon - 11pm
Sun 4pm - 10pm

If this restaurant wasn't so successful, locals would gladly keep Savoy as their own little secret. This charmer is as unpretentious as it is relaxed, and it makes an ideal respite from the stresses of the day.

Peter Hoffman and his wife, Susan Rosenfeld, opened Savoy in 1990 with the idea of creating memorable meals from the best local ingredients. To that end, they have developed relationships with local growers and producers so that the food you eat here quite literally has roots in the community. Items like sausage and bread are made in-house, and such entrées as braised leg of rabbit and aïoli-glazed blackfish exemplify elegant country cooking.

The restaurant takes up two floors of an 1830s Federalist-style town house, where wood-burning fireplaces add charm to each floor.

Snack 😊

024

105 Thompson St. (bet. Prince & Spring Sts.)

Subway: Spring St (Sixth Ave.)
Phone: 212-925-1040
Fax: 212-925-0696
Web: N/A
Prices: $$

Mon – Wed noon - 10pm
Thu – Sat noon - 11pm
Sun noon - 9pm
Closed major holidays

Don't blink, or you're liable to walk right past Snack. Seating just ten people at five lime-green tables, this sweet little Greek place offers a refreshing antidote to SoHo's über-trendy temples of gastronomy. Enveloped by sepia-toned photographs of Hellenic landmarks and shelves of Mediterranean grocery items, you'll feel transported to sunnier climes.

Indeed, when you taste the fresh, authentic Greek cuisine, you'll half expect to feel sand between your toes. The friendly staff is more than willing to advise diners trying to choose from the delectable array of meze, sandwiches and savory pies (the list of offerings is scrawled on a blackboard).

If you're craving souvlaki or stuffed grape leaves while in the West Village, visit the Snack with bigger digs at 63 Bedford Street.

Woo Lae Oak

025

148 Mercer St. (bet. Houston & Prince Sts.)

Subway: Prince St
Phone: 212-925-8200
Fax: 212-925-8232
Web: www.woolaeoaksoho.com
Prices: $$

Sun – Thu noon - 11pm
Fri – Sat noon - 11:30pm

Want to go out to cook tonight? Each of the marble-topped tables in stylish Woo Lae Oak contains a built-in griddle for customers to barbecue anything from tuna loin and tiger prawns to shiitake mushrooms and free-range chicken breast. For those whose idea of cooking is making reservations, the restaurant also offers Korean specialties (beef short ribs; stuffed, braised chicken breast) prepared with a flair for depth of flavor.

It's not just the cooking that sets this place apart from more traditional eateries in Koreatown; it's the attractive dining space, too, with its roomy, open floor plan and glam downtown crowd. Woo Lae Oak may not be the most authentic Korean experience, but for the less adventurous, it provides a good introduction to this type of cuisine.

Zoë

026

90 Prince St. (bet. Broadway & Mercer St.)

Subway:	Prince St	Mon noon - 3pm
Phone:	212-966-6722	Tue – Thu noon - 3pm & 6pm - 10:30pm
Fax:	212-966-6718	Fri noon - 3pm & 6pm - 11pm
Web:	www.zoerestaurant.com	Sat 11:30am - 3pm & 5:30pm - 11:30pm
Prices:	$$	Sun 11:30am - 3pm & 5:30pm - 10pm

With its terra-cotta columns, rich colors and mosaic tile, Zoë's bold surroundings have been packing 'em into this 19th-century landmark since 1992. The prime location on SoHo's Prince Street, with its high-end stores and intriguing galleries, simply can't be beat. The cuisine is American at heart, but it roams from the Far East to the Mediterranean for its inspiration. Fish is a popular menu staple here, and Zoë offers more than 35 wines by the glass as accompaniment. Just be sure to leave room for such goodies as caramelized banana tart and cappuccino cheesecake.

Clad in matching blue suits, the waitstaff boasts the courteous and unflustered manner that comes from being proficient at working a busy room. As a whole, the operation possesses the confidence of a well-oiled machine.

**Not every atlas comes with
a legend like this.**

We put the same quality and reliability into our atlases that we put into
our tires. The innovative design makes for easy navigation, allowing you to
travel with confidence. To learn more, visit michelintravel.com.

TriBeCa

An intriguing wedge of warehouses, loft residences, art galleries and oh-so-chic restaurants, TriBeCa was named in the 1970s by a real-estate agent hoping to create a hip identity for the area. The acronym—which stands for Triangle Below Canal—stuck, and true to expectations, TriBeCa has become a trendy place. So far, it has not been commercialized nearly to the extent that SoHo has, despite being home to dozens of celebrities, most notably actor Robert DeNiro. For paparazzi-dodging starlets, that is precisely its appeal.

Technically, TriBeCa is not a triangle but a trapezoid. Its boundaries are *(clockwise from north)* Canal Street, Broadway, Murray Street, and the Hudson River. Greenwich and Hudson streets are the main thoroughfares for dining and nightlife; art and interior-design stores are scattered throughout the district.

A Bit of History – Once used as farmland by Dutch settlers, the area now known as TriBeCa was included in a large tract granted to Trinity Church in 1705. In the ensuing century, wealthy families built elegant residences around Hudson Square (now the Hudson River Tunnel traffic rotary). A fruit and produce market opened in 1813 at the western edge of the neighborhood, but the quarter remained primarily residential until the mid-19th century, when the shipping and warehousing industries formerly located at the South Street Seaport moved to deepwater piers on the Hudson River. Five- and six-story "store and loft" buildings were built around the district to accommodate the new trade. By 1939, Washington Market, as the area along Greenwich Street came to be known, boasted a greater volume of business than all the other markets in the city combined.

TriBeCa

© Martha Cooper

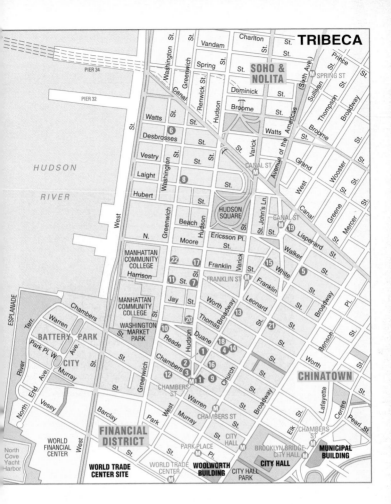

In the 1960s, city planners approved urban-renewal projects that called for the demolition of many buildings along the waterfront. Luckily, enough of the old commercial warehouses remained to attract artists pushed out of SoHo and others seeking cavernous industrial living space. Today, those same artists would be hard-pressed to afford such a space in TriBeCa; loft-apartment prices now start at around $1 million.

Trendy TriBeCa – Catering as they do to a local clientele of creative types, TriBeCa is a cool place to eat. You can splurge on a meal here in expensive restaurants whose reputations precede them, or go for more modest fare. If it's a sunny day, snag an umbrella-shaded table outside—TriBeCa's wide sidewalks accommodate lots of them.

Bouley ✿ ✿

001

120 West Broadway (at Duane St.)

Subway:	Chambers St (West Broadway)	Open daily 11:30am - 3pm
Phone:	212-964-2525	& 5pm - 11:30pm
Fax:	212-693-7490	
Web:	www.davidbouley.com	
Prices:	$$$$	

Bouley/Tobias Everke

David Bouley's culinary skill reflects two different cultures. Born and raised in Connecticut, Bouley gained his love of cooking at the stove of his French grandmother. After stints in a number of U.S. restaurants, the chef went to France, where he worked with some of Europe's finest chefs.

At Bouley, two vaulted-ceilinged rooms cosset diners: the intimate red room, with its claret-colored Venetian-plaster walls; or the airy white room, accented by an antique French fireplace. The menu reflects the chef's travels to Japan, along with his strong grounding in French technique. Innovatively prepared and presented, dishes exhibit a festival of flavors (think Japanese yellowtail with Cavaillon melon and hon shimeji mushrooms). Tasting menus allow diners to sample a treasure trove of culinary delights, and the flurry of little extras from the kitchen rounds out the progression of courses. Whether your tastes lean more toward tart fruits or decadent chocolates, the dessert menu has something extraordinary to suit your fancy.

Across the street, Bouley's three-level food emporium houses the Upstairs dining room (open 6pm – 11:30pm; no reservations), Bouley Bakery/Café, and Bouley Market.

Appetizers

Young Maine Skate steamed with Fresh Chamomile, Organic Pineapple, Capers, Globe Basil and Jerez Vinegar Dressing

Phyllo-crusted Florida Shrimp, Cape Cod Baby Squid, Scuba-Dived Sea Scallop, Sweet Maryland Crabmeat in an Ocean Herbal Broth

Organic Connecticut Farm Egg steamed with Black Truffle, Serrano Ham, Parmigiano Reggiano, and 25-year-old Balsamic Dressing

Entrées

New Zealand Venison Crusted with Pink Peppercorns, Jerusalem Artichoke and Young-Garlic Confit, Roasted Brussels Sprouts Leaves

Organic Pennsylvania Lamb: Rack baked in a Black-Truffle Crust, Loin steamed in New England Wild Ramps with Jumbo White Asparagus

Pennsylvania All-Natural Chicken baked in Buttermilk, with Seasonal Rapini and Roasted Maitake

Desserts

Warm Tahitian Vanilla Nishiki Rice Pudding, Coconut-Orange Tuile, Meyer Lemon Sorbet

Chocolate Frivolous: Toasted Hazelnut Dacquoise, Chocolate Brûlé and Chocolate Soufflé, Chocolate Cointreau Cake and Espresso Ice Cream

Roquefort Brûlé with Bartlett Pears and Burnt Black Mission Fig Jam

Danube ✿

Austrian ✗✗✗

30 Hudson St. (bet. Duane & Reade Sts.)

Subway:	Chambers St (West Broadway)	Mon – Sat 5:30pm - 11pm
Phone:	212-791-3771	Closed Sun
Fax:	212-693-7490	
Web:	www.davidbouley.com	
Prices:	$$$	

Danube/Tobius Everke

Named for the river that flows through Vienna, Danube represents chef David Bouley's Austrian fantasy, as realized by designer Jacques Garcia and architect Kevin White. Have a seat in the stately dining room (located just around the corner from Bouley), and you'll be immersed in the luxury of late-19th-century Vienna. Here, plush sofas stand in for banquettes, ceilings are covered in Venetian plaster, and dark drapes dress tall, arched windows. Stunning paintings, inspired by the work of Austrian artist Gustav Klimt, line the walls.

À la carte menus include weekly market choices, an Austrian menu, and a "modern eclectic" menu. There's also a prix-fixe five-course tasting. All blend Austrian ingredients or preparations with contemporary and even Asian elements. Japanese yellowtail makes a frequent appearance, as do classics like Wiener Schnitzel, Spaetzle and Kavalierspitz. The tasting menu weaves together a delicious symphony of flavors and styles, and is an easy way to sample the chef's favorites. Of course, dessert is de rigueur here, with updated versions of Austrian pastry, and a cheese course, if you so desire. The interesting wine list spans Austria, France and the U.S.

Appetizers

Diver Sea Scallop and New England Crabmeat with Paradeiser Coriander and Fresh Lemon-Thyme Sauce

Freshly harpooned Sashimi-quality Bluefin and Hamachi Tuna, Key Lime Pickled Onion, Pumpkin-Seed Oil and Sesame Mustard Dressing

Warmed Smoked Wild Salmon, Austrian Potato Salad with New York State Watercress Dressing

Entrées

Japanese Yellowtail with Austrian Crescent Potato, Leaf Spinach, Belvedere Vodka and Caviar

Gently heated Wild King Salmon with Styrian Wurzelgemüse, Apple Rosemary Purée and Horseradish Chive Sauce

Veal Wiener Schnitzel with Austrian Crescent Potatoes, Cucumber Salad, Mixed Greens and Lingonberries

Desserts

Crisp Caramel Strudel with Bartlett Pears, Aged Balsamic and Moscato d'Asti Ice Cream

Topfenpalatschinken: Warm Wild Huckleberry Crêpes, Huckleberry Sour-Cream Sorbet and Topfen Ice Cream

Austrian Chocolate Hazelnut Soufflé with Raspberry Sauce, Lychees and Chocolate-Chip Ice Cream

Acappella

Italian ✗✗✗

003

1 Hudson St. (at Chambers St.)

Subway: Chambers St (West Broadway)
Phone: 212-240-0163
Fax: 212-240-0271
Web: www.acappella-restaurant.com
Prices: $$$

Mon – Sat noon - 11pm
Closed Sun & July 2 - 13

If this restaurant looks familiar, it may be because you saw it in the first episode of the popular HBO series *The Sopranos*, part of which was filmed here. A reproduction of the imposing portrait of Federico da Montefebre, erstwhile Duke of Urbino, dominates the brick wall of the dining room (the original, painted by Piero della Francesca in 1645, is on display in Florence). The rest of the lovely room boasts stately columns, antique tapestries and large curtained windows in front.

Overseen by chef/owner Sergio Acappella, the kitchen turns out carefully prepared northern Italian dishes, including homemade pastas. In winter, the menu is peppered with the likes of wild boar and buffalo meat. At the end of your meal, enjoy a complimentary glass of grappa alongside your dessert.

Blaue Gans

Austrian ✗

004

139 Duane St. (bet. Church St. & West Broadway)

Subway: Chambers St (West Broadway)
Phone: 212-571-8880
Fax: 212-571-8883
Web: www.wallse.com
Prices: $$

Open daily 8am - midnight

Taking over the space formerly occupied by Le Zinc, chef Kurt Gutenbrunner may have saved the long zinc bar and the vintage film and art posters of the former tenant, but he has turned the menu upside-down with his Austro-German cooking.

Open for three meals as well as brunch and late-night noshing, the restaurant focuses on Austrian specialties, including an entire section devoted to sausages. The chef eschews the heavy hand often used in this style of cooking and instead offers delicate preparations of Austrian classics like Wiener Schnitzel, with each ingredient perfectly represented—down to the fresh-grated horseradish.

The dessert list is to die for; apple strudel, chocolate-hazelnut cake and Salzburger Nockerl are a few of the lip-smacking-good selections.

Bread Tribeca

005

301 Church St. (at Walker St.)

Subway:	Canal St (Sixth Ave.)
Phone:	212-334-8282
Fax:	212-334-3272
Web:	www.breadtribeca.com
Prices:	$$

Mon – Thu 11:30am - 11pm
Fri – Sat 10:30am - midnight
Sun 10:30am - 11pm

Inside this windowed façade on the corner of Church and Walker streets, you'll find a simple, contemporary décor trumped by good Italian cuisine that's a pleasure to eat any time of the day. As you'd guess from the name, Bread Tribeca specializes in a variety of tasty sandwiches, with fillings such as Sicilian sardines, homemade mozzarella and prosciutto di Parma stuffed between crusty ciabatta bread or baguettes.

But wait, there's more. The menu also cites an impressive collection of non-sandwich items at lunch, brunch and dinner. Don't overlook the fresh salads, pastas, seafood entrées and thin-crust pizzas cooked in the wood-burning oven. And be sure to leave room for the delicious caramelized banana tart, served with vanilla ice cream.

Capsouto Frères

006

451 Washington St. (at Watts St.)

Subway:	Canal St (Sixth Ave.)
Phone:	212-966-4900
Fax:	212-925-5296
Web:	www.capsoutofreres.com
Prices:	$$

Mon 6pm - 11pm
Tue – Thu noon - 3:30pm & 6pm - 11pm
Fri – Sat noon - 3:30pm & 6pm - midnight
Sun noon - 3:30pm & 6pm - 11pm

Before you enter Capsouto Frères, be sure to stop and take a gander at the striking 1891 landmark structure in which the restaurant is housed. A handsome mix of Romanesque and Flemish Revival styles, this brick and stone building on the corner of Watts Street once held a shoe factory. Inside the ground-floor restaurant, the owners have preserved the building's old-fashioned charm.

Since 1980, Capsouto Frères has been pleasing diners at lunch, brunch and dinner with the likes of sole meunière, duck confit and cassoulet. Light-as-air soufflés, a house specialty, are the best choice if your sweet tooth is crying for dessert, while savory soufflés, like wild mushroom and spinach and cheese varieties, make a satisfying snack or a light meal.

Manhattan TriBeCa

Chanterelle

007

Contemporary French ✗✗✗

2 Harrison St. (at Hudson St.)

Subway:	Franklin St
Phone:	212-966-6960
Fax:	212-966-6143
Web:	www.chanterellenyc.com
Prices:	$$$$

Mon – Wed 5:30pm - 10:30pm
Thu – Sat noon - 2:30pm
& 5:30pm - 10:30pm
Sun 5:30pm - 10:30pm

It's not easy to keep a restaurant going for more than 20 years, but owners Karen and David Waltuck have managed to do it, and do it well. Set within the 19th-century New York Mercantile Exchange, the Art Nouveau-style dining room reflects Karen's feminine touch in its peach tones, sheer balloon shades, fresh flowers and the menu's sprawling handwritten script.

The menu offers David's take on French cuisine with a light contemporary touch. While the seasonal selections change monthly, the signature grilled seafood sausage is the only dish that is available at any time.

Be sure to check out Chanterelle's collection of menu covers near the reception desk; Keith Haring, Roy Lichtenstein and Louise Nevelson number among the famous artists who have designed covers for the restaurant.

Dylan Prime

008

Contemporary ✗✗

62 Laight St. (at Greenwich St.)

Subway:	Canal St (Varick St.)
Phone:	212-334-4783
Fax:	212-334-2276
Web:	www.dylanprime.com
Prices:	$$$

Mon – Thu noon - 2:30pm
& 5:30pm - 11pm
Fri noon - 2:30pm & 5:30pm - midnight
Sat 5:30pm - midnight
Sun 5pm - 10pm

Dylan Prime lies a bit off the beaten track from the heart of TriBeCa's action, but you won't regret the detour. The menu is contemporary American with an emphasis on meat: Prime cuts of filet mignon, aged prime rib and a man-size 32-ounce Porterhouse are all served with your choice of sauces (from herb Béarnaise to foie gras butter). Then there's the Carpetbagger steak, the chef's creation of an 11-ounce filet mignon stuffed with Blue Point oysters. You'll also find a few seafood entrées, but the meat's the main reason to come here.

Low, moody lighting provides an intimate vibe, and a window wall affords diners a look at the impressive wine selection, which consists mainly of California vintages. The new "Pie-tini" list entices with apple pie, lemon-meringue and mud-pie cocktails.

Fresh

009

Seafood ✗✗

105 Reade St. (bet. Church St. & West Broadway)

Subway:	Chambers St (West Broadway)	Mon – Fri 11:30am - 2:30pm
Phone:	212-406-1900	& 5pm - 10:30pm
Fax:	212-406-4814	Sat 5pm - 10:30pm
Web:	www.freshrestaurantnyc.com	Sun 4pm - 9pm
Prices:	$$	

It's easy to ensure that your restaurant serves the freshest seafood possible when you own your own seafood company. That's the case with Eric Tevrow, the proprietor of Fresh. His company is the sole provider of fish to Fresh, so it's no wonder that this sea-themed dining room nets a steady stream of loyal fish lovers.

As you'd expect, the menu changes every day to spotlight the daily catch, which might include the likes of Maine peekytoe crab, Nantucket striped bass and Florida Keys grouper. Simply grilled entrées are delicious, while everything from soy-ginger dressing to orange-ponzu sauce tops the daily specials. The lobster roll and the New England clam chowder embody American simplicity at its best; they're both prepared authentically with an elegant hand.

Gigino Trattoria

010

Italian ✗✗

323 Greenwich St. (bet. Duane & Reade Sts.)

Subway:	Chambers St (West Broadway)	Sun – Thu 11:30am - 11pm
Phone:	212-431-1112	Fri – Sat 11:30am - midnight
Fax:	212-431-1294	
Web:	www.gigino-trattoria.com	
Prices:	$$	

Picture a little trattoria in Italy. When you walk in, you receive a warm greeting from the staff; the décor is unpretentious, but cheery, with a wood-beamed ceiling, glowing yellow walls and a wood-burning oven. This is the ambience you'll find at Gigino, hidden away in lower TriBeCa.

With an extensive list of reasonably priced dishes ranging from oven-fired pizzas to hearty entrées to the signature pasta—spaghetti del Padrino, made with beets, escarole, garlic and anchovy-flavored olive oil—Gigino works at satisfying the appetites of every member of the family. The menu reads like a collection of favorite family recipes, yet the artful plating is far from ordinary.

In the Financial District, Gigino at Wagner Park *(20 Battery Place)* boasts an outdoor terrace with harbor views.

Manhattan TriBeCa

The Harrison

Contemporary XXX

011

355 Greenwich St. (at Harrison St.)

Subway:	Franklin St	Mon – Sat 5:30pm - 11pm
Phone:	212-274-9310	Sun 5pm - 10pm
Fax:	212-274-9376	Closed major holidays
Web:	www.theharrison.com	
Prices:	$$	

Chef/owner Jimmy Bradley has a magic touch creating warm, welcoming restaurants—like The Red Cat in Chelsea *(227 Tenth Ave.)*—with widely appealing food. He's done it again at The Harrison, which opened at the corner of Harrison and Greenwich streets in 2001.

At The Harrison, the professional team is always ready to help; the staff keeps a constant lookout around the rustic-chic dining room to make sure their customers have everything they want. From the kitchen here comes contemporary American cuisine that doesn't take itself too seriously; the menu always looks to the seasons with a wink of fun.

Desserts, like chocolate-filled beignets or strawberry-rhubarb crisp, are worth the wait. To top off your meal, choose a wine by the glass or a selection from the 300-bottle wine list.

Kitchenette

American X

012

156 Chambers St. (bet. Greenwich St. & West Broadway)

Subway:	Chambers St (West Broadway)	Mon – Fri 7:30am - 11pm
Phone:	212-267-6740	Sat – Sun 9am - 11pm
Fax:	212-732-1334	
Web:	www.kitchenettenyc.com	
Prices:	😋	

For a taste of home, visit Kitchenette. This casual cafe brings the taste of Mom's kitchen to the heart of trendy TriBeCa. Affordable and appealing, this luncheonette-style restaurant with its kitschy-cool country appeal has attracted a loyal following of area residents for over ten years. Guests are met by the heady scent of fresh baked goods upon entering, and those in the know save room for a slice of one of the scrumptious pies or cakes.

The soul of traditional American cooking is alive and well here, where meatloaf, chili and blue-plate specials number among the most requested dishes. Far from fancy, Kitchenette's meals are stick-to-your-ribs good and perfect for lunch, weekend brunch or weeknight dinner. And kids are welcome, an asset in adult-oriented Manhattan.

Landmarc

013

French ✗✗

179 West Broadway (bet. Leonard & Worth Sts.)

Subway: Franklin St
Phone: 212-343-3883
Fax: 212-343-3890
Web: www.landmarc-restaurant.com
Prices: $$

Mon – Fri noon - 2am
Sat – Sun 11am - 2am

Established by chef Marc Murphy and his wife, Pamela, in spring 2004, Landmarc brings innovative bistro-style fare to TriBeCa. As the son of a diplomat, Murphy grew up traveling in France and Italy, a heritage that is reflected in the restaurant's menu and well-priced wine list.

Landmarc is a rare treat, offering adults the chance to sample upscale cuisine like grilled quail or rock-shrimp risotto while their little ones munch on kid-friendly food. Be sure to try dessert here; kids can have an ice-cream cone while, for one low set price, you can sample every sweet on the menu.

With its exposed brick walls, sleek booths and contemporary artwork, the bi-level dining room blends well with the neighborhood's trendy ambience. Reservations are not accepted for parties of less than six people.

Megu

014

Japanese ✗✗✗

62 Thomas St. (bet. Church St. & West Broadway)

Subway: Chambers St (West Broadway)
Phone: 212-964-7777
Fax: 212-964-7776
Web: www.megunyc.com
Prices: $$$

Mon – Wed 11:30am - 2:30pm
& 5:30pm - 10:15pm
Thu – Fri 11:30am - 2:30pm & 5:30pm - 11:15pm
Sat 5:30pm - 11:15pm
Sun 5:30pm - 10:15pm

For an awe-inspiring experience, follow the kimono-clad hostess downstairs to the two-story space Megu reserves for diners. Ultra-sleek design meets traditional Japanese elements in this capacious room, which centers on an ice carving of Buddha floating over a rose-petal-strewn pool. Above the Buddha hangs a huge *bonsho*, an exact replica of Japan's largest temple bell. White porcelain columns, made from rice bowls and sake vases, line the room's upper tier.

The progression of courses in Megu's different tasting menus may include skewered meat or fish grilled over special bincho-tan charcoal, as well as meat seared on hot Japanese river stones.

Megu's new Midtown location in the posh Trump World Tower *(845 UN Plaza)* is equally impressive, but caters to more of an expense-account crowd.

Montrachet

Contemporary French ✗✗✗

015

239 West Broadway (bet. Walker & White Sts.)

Subway:	Franklin St	Mon – Thu 5:30pm - 10:30pm
Phone:	212-219-2777	Fri noon - 2:15pm & 5:30pm - 11pm
Fax:	212-274-9508	Sat 5:30pm - 11pm
Web:	www.myriadrestaurantgroup.com	Closed Sun
Prices:	$$	

If you're looking for a great restaurant for wine in New York City, look no farther. Named for the much-celebrated white Burgundy from France's Côte de Beaune, Montrachet offers a superb wine list numbering some 1,000 bottles. The roster includes, of course, a huge selection of Burgundies.

Customers here can order from the à la carte menu or several different chef's tasting menus highlighting French-accented contemporary American cuisine. Monday is BYOB night, when patrons are welcome to bring a bottle of their own choosing, and the restaurant will waive the usual corkage fee.

Part of Drew Nieporent's Myriad Restaurant Group, which also includes Nobu and Tribeca Grill, Montrachet has been around since 1985, a fact that qualifies it as one of TriBeCa's first fine-dining restaurants.

Nam

Vietnamese ✗

016

110 Reade St. (bet. Church St. & West Broadway)

Subway:	Chambers St (West Broadway)	Mon – Thu noon - 2pm & 5:30pm - 10pm
Phone:	212-267-1777	Fri noon - 2pm & 5:30pm - 11pm
Fax:	212-267-3781	Sat 5:30pm - 11pm
Web:	www.namnyc.com	Sun 5:30pm - 10pm
Prices:	$$	

Nam attracts hosts of diners who come for generous, tasty and inexpensive Vietnamese cooking that balances yin and yang in its serene dining space. The likes of chile-lime sauce, coconut, curry powder, and fresh herbs flavor the delicate dishes. Classic starters are light and flavorful, but don't pass up the *Bun* dishes (various ingredients served over rice vermicelli) as an entrée. To end your meal, toasted coconut and banana bread is a warm, satisfying treat.

Efficient service by a young staff, and a simple but pleasant atmosphere, filled with bamboo trees and black-and-white photographs of Vietnam, are a few more reasons to like this place. If Chelsea is more convenient for you, visit Nam's sister, Omai *(158 Ninth Ave.)*.

Nobu

017

105 Hudson St. (at Franklin St.)

Subway:	Franklin St	Mon – Fri 11:45am - 2:15pm
Phone:	212-219-0500	& 5:45pm - 10:15pm
Fax:	212-219-1441	Sat – Sun 5:45pm - 10:15pm
Web:	www.myriadrestaurantgroup.com	
Prices:	$$$$	

In partnership with Drew Nieporent and actor Robert DeNiro, celebrity chef Nobu Matsuhisa opened Nobu in 1994 to a large fanfare, and the restaurant continues to enjoy success today. Architect David Rockwell imagined the Japanese countryside in Nobu's dining room, replete with stylized birch trees and a wall of black river stones (although the décor looks a bit tired these days).

Nobu is best known for its seductive sushi and sashimi, but don't pass up Matsuhisa's signature miso-glazed black cod, or monkfish pâté with caviar. Sharing several dishes is the best way to "do" Nobu. Nobu Next Door offers similar food in a simple ambience (reservations not accepted). In Midtown, try Nobu Fifty-Seven (40 W. 57th St.), which opened in summer 2005.

The Odeon

018

145 West Broadway (at Thomas St.)

Subway:	Chambers St (West Broadway)	Mon – Fri noon - 1am
Phone:	212-233-0507	Sat – Sun 9am - 2am
Fax:	212-406-1962	
Web:	www.theodeonrestaurant.com	
Prices:	$$	

A red neon marquee above the door marks The Odeon, a TriBeCa hot spot since the 1980s. Now as then, you can still catch a glimpse of big-name entertainers and artists here, but regular folks are welcome, too.

The Art Deco-style space uses Formica-topped tables, wood paneling and 1930s light fixtures to suggest a casual Parisian bistro, and the kitchen interprets American dishes with a discreet French flair (moules frites, lamb chops, roast chicken). Check out the weekday fixed-price menu for lunch; it's the perfect way to snag unpretentious, refined cuisine at reasonable prices.

If you're out partying late, drop by for croque monsieur sandwiches, French onion soup or crispy calamari available on the brasserie menu of light fare, served every night beginning at midnight.

Pepolino

019

281 West Broadway (bet. Canal & Lispenard Sts.)

Subway:	Canal St (Sixth Ave.)	Open daily noon - 4pm
Phone:	212-966-9983	& 5:30pm - midnight
Fax:	212-966-3858	
Web:	www.pepolino.com	
Prices:	$$	

A variety of thyme that grows wild in the hills of Tuscany, pepolino makes a fitting namesake for this rustic Italian eatery on TriBeCa's northern edge.

Indeed, herbs play a big part in the cooking here, and pepolino is the favorite of owner Patrizio Siddu, who shares the kitchen with partner Enzo Pezone. Both chefs grew up in Italy, where they mastered the nuances of regional Italian cooking before opening Pepolino in 1999. Their homemade spinach and ricotta gnocchi tossed with butter and sage melts in your mouth.

Charming country décor complements reasonably priced Tuscan recipes enhanced by extra-virgin olive oil, aged balsamic vinegar and fresh ricotta and mozzarella. Weekend brunch brings favorites from frittatas to panini.

Scalini Fedeli

020

165 Duane St. (bet. Greenwich & Hudson Sts.)

Subway:	Chambers St (West Broadway)	Mon 5:30pm - 10pm
Phone:	212-528-0400	Tue – Thu noon - 2:30pm & 5:30pm - 10pm
Fax:	212-587-8773	Fri noon - 2:30pm & 5:30pm - 11pm
Web:	www.scalinifedeli.com	Sat 5:30pm - 11pm
Prices:	$$$	Closed Sun

In the space formerly occupied by Bouley, Scalini Fedeli has a seductive, old-fashioned Tuscan ambience embellished with graceful vaulted ceilings and light yellow hues.

Chef/owner Michael Cetrulo trained in several big-name restaurants in Italy and Monaco, and his imaginative menu proves it. Diners here have a choice of three different fixed-price menus, all showcasing recipes from northern Italy with a personalized flair. If the sound of wild striped bass with spicy white bean and rosemary stew, or pappardelle with a game sauce made with venison and hare, finished with Barolo wine and bitter chocolate makes your mouth water, make tracks for Scalini Fedeli. For chocoholics, there's a separate dessert menu that just lists chocolate sweets. (Hint: If you're on a budget, go for lunch.)

66

021

Chinese ✕✕

241 Church St. (at Leonard St.)

Subway:	Franklin St
Phone:	212-925-0202
Fax:	212-925-5440
Web:	www.jean-georges.com
Prices:	$$

Mon – Wed 5:30pm - 11pm
Thu – Sat 5:30pm - midnight
Sun 5:30pm - 10:30pm

♿

Celebrated chef-cum-entrepreneur Jean-Georges Vongerichten has long been fascinated with the Orient, based on his many years of work and travel in that part of the world. Contemporary is the key word here, from the sleek décor to the modern interpretations of traditional Chinese dishes. At 66, red cloth banners festooned with Chinese characters drape like flags in a line above the communal table, and curving frosted-glass panels divide the dining space. One of the areas even has a view of the kitchen through an aquarium stocked with exotic fish.

Entrées run from steamed cod with caramelized onions, ginger and scallions to stir-fried Niman Ranch pork. If you're staying in the area, go beyond the standard, humdrum take-out fare and order delivery from 66.

Tribeca Grill

022

Contemporary ✕✕

375 Greenwich St. (at Franklin St.)

Subway:	Franklin St
Phone:	212-941-3900
Fax:	212-941-3915
Web:	www.myriadrestaurantgroup.com
Prices:	$$$

Mon – Thu 11:30am - 3pm
& 5:30pm - 11pm
Fri – Sat 5:30pm - 11:30pm
Sun 11:30am - 3pm & 5:30pm - 10pm

♿
🍽
✒
🍇

Another venture by Drew Nieporent and Robert DeNiro, Tribeca Grill burst on the scene in 1990. One of the first restaurants to cement TriBeCa's reputation as a gourmet destination, it still draws crowds nightly. The building that now serves as the headquarters for the grill as well as DeNiro's TriBeCa film company housed the Martinson Coffee factory in the early 1900s. Recalling its industrial origins, pipes and brickwork are left exposed in the dining room.

Today the first two floors pay homage to wine. More like a tome, the wine list cites 1,700 labels at prices starting as low as $30; selections include more than 250 vintages of Châteauneuf-du-Pape. The kitchen treats regional ingredients (peekytoe crab, Hudson Valley foie gras) with a light hand to showcase their natural flavors.

Manhattan TriBeCa

Upper East Side

An enclave for the wealthy and fashionable, the Upper East Side represents a broad cross section of New York neighborhoods and contains an impressive concentration of restaurants. In the area that stretches from Fifth Avenue to the East River, and from 60th Street to 97th Street, you'll find food to please every palate, from Austrian cuisine to vegetarian fare.

Rimming the east edge of Central Park, the Metropolitan Museum of Art, the Guggenheim Museum, the Jewish Museum, the Whitney Museum of American Art, the Frick Collection, the Neue Galerie, and the Cooper-Hewitt National Design Museum are collectively known as **Museum Mile**. An impressive concentration of galleries, along with elegant shops, upscale restaurants, clubs, exclusive private schools and fabulous residences grace this area as well. East of Lexington Avenue, where there's a significant population of single people, the atmosphere becomes more casual. Here, modern high-rise apartment buildings dominate, sharing space with a variety of pubs, sports bars and pizza joints.

A Bit of History – In the late 19th century, rich industrialists including Andrew Carnegie and Henry Clay Frick began building mansions on the large lots along Fifth Avenue, abutting Central Park. One of the first sections to be developed was around East 86th Street, where several prominent families of German descent, including the Schermerhorns, the Astors and the Rhinelanders, built country estates. Yorkville, as it was known, soon moved east past Lexington Avenue and became a suburb of middle-class Germans, many of whom worked in nearby piano factories and breweries—although hardly a rathskeller survives today. In the 1950s, waves of immigrants from Hungary and Eastern Europe established their own communities, only to disappear as gentrification set in a couple of decades ago.

Upper East Side

© Brigtta L. House / MICHELIN

Over the years, the posh East Side has been a magnet for celebrities—Greta Garbo, Andy Warhol, Richard Nixon and Woody Allen among them. Today, **Fifth Avenue** remains the neighborhood's most impressive thoroughfare, **Madison Avenue** is chock-a-block with chi-chi shops and art galleries; and **Park Avenue** is an elegant residential boulevard.

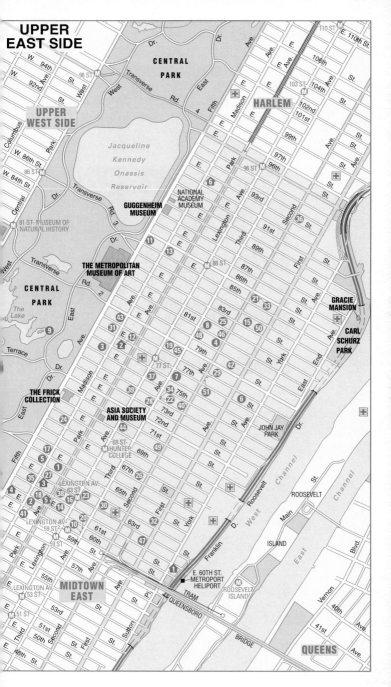

UPPER
EAST SIDE

Daniel ✿✿

Contemporary French 🍴🍴🍴🍴🍴

001

60 E. 65th St. (bet. Madison & Park Aves.)

Subway:	68 St - Hunter College	Mon – Thu 5:45pm - 11pm
Phone:	212-288-0033	Fri – Sat 5:45pm - 11:30pm
Fax:	212-737-0612	Closed Sun
Web:	www.danielnyc.com	
Prices:	$$$$	

Daniel/Peter Medilek

Raised on a farm outside Lyon, France, Daniel Boulud worked with some of the best chefs in France before landing in the United States. Here, he worked as executive chef of Le Cirque for seven years, and launched Daniel in 1993. His eponymous restaurant now occupies the ground floor of the former Mayfair Hotel—the space once filled by Le Cirque.

Daniel has become something of an Upper East Side institution, drawing a steady clientele of area denizens and well-heeled foreigners. An arched colonnade defines the Italian Renaissance-style dining room, designed with an 18-foot-high coffered ceiling and a bronze chandelier with alabaster globes that seem to float above the room.

It is in this palatial setting that Boulud turns the best domestic and imported seasonal products into artful dishes prepared in the French tradition. The chef and his talented team add a soupçon of American flair to such entrées as cassoulette of Louisiana crayfish with chanterelles, and Maine sea scallops with black truffle in golden pastry. On the other hand, dishes like rabbit terrine with porcini confit and fricassée of Dover sole are decidedly French.

Appetizers

Rabbit Foie Gras Terrine with Confit, Porcini, Baby Leeks, Frisée and Mustard Vinaigrette

Braised Beef-Cheek Ravioli with Fenugreek, Wilted Mustard Leaves and an Orange-Carrot Emulsion

"Timbale" of Louisiana Crayfish with Oregon Morels, Fiddlehead Fern, Cockscomb and Shaved Asparagus

Entrées

Lotte and Lobster wrapped in Apple-smoked Bacon, Celery Confit, Porcini and *Matelote* Sauce

Pigeon *à la Marocaine*: Cinnamon Skewered Breast *a la plancha*, with Glazed Brussels Sprouts, and Leg and Foie Gras Pastilla with Marcona Almonds

Colorado Rack of Lamb with Meyer Lemon Crust, Satur Farms Glazed Radishes, and Avocado-Mint Chutney

Desserts

Warm Griotte Black Forest with Vanilla Sorbet, Whipped Cream and Bittersweet Chocolate

Warm Grapefruit Tatin with Chilled Pomegranate, Green-Tea Soup and Fromage Blanc Sorbet

Champagne Mango Vacherin with Black-Sesame Meringue, *Île Flottante* and Lemon-Thyme Anglaise

Aureole ⌘

Contemporary XXXX

34 E. 61st St. (bet. Madison & Park Aves.)

Subway: 5 Av – 59 St
Phone: 212-319-1660
Fax: 212-755-3126
Web: www.charliepalmer.com
Prices: $$$$

Mon – Fri noon – 2:30pm
& 5:30pm – 11pm
Sat 5:30pm – 11pm
Closed Sun

Aureole/Vitaly Agibalov

Housed in a 1920s brownstone, this Upper East Side beauty belongs to Charlie Palmer's restaurant kingdom (there's a second Aureole in the Mandalay Bay Resort and Casino in Las Vegas). The refined atmosphere of the bi-level dining room goes hand in hand with the prestigious neighborhood. Fronted by a two-story window wall, the restaurant is filled with hanging ferns, honey-colored woodwork and burgundy-leather banquettes. If you were admiring the contemporary artwork on the walls, you're in luck—it's for sale through the nearby Pace Prints Gallery.

Artisanal food items and products from small local farms form the basis of what the restaurant bills as "progressive American" cuisine. Atlantic salmon in a phyllo crust with goat cheese and hazelnut emulsion, cumin honey-glazed duck and baked black sea bass stuffed with rock shrimp and corn-and-fava-bean succotash are just a few of the available choices. In addition to the three-course prix-fixe menu, the chef also whips up wonderful creations for his six-course market and vegetarian tastings. The computerized wine list cites more than 800 global selections.

Appetizers

Port-glazed Tuna and Foie Gras Terrine

Fluke Sashimi with House-made Coppa and Celery Variations

Rosemary Roasted Calamari with Black Cavatelli and Heirloom Tomatoes

Entrées

48-hour-braised Kobe-style Beef Cheeks with Gremolata, Sunchoke Purée and Mustard Greens

Potato-Crusted Striped Long Island Bass with Pickled Ramps and Vegetable Confetti

Lobster-Butter-Poached Skate Wing with English Peas and Pistachio Gratin

Desserts

Warm Bittersweet-Chocolate and Hazelnut Pyramid with Bombay Chai Gelato and Caramelized Puff Pastry

Hawaiian Mango and Key Lime Tart with Almond-Milk Sorbet and Candy Spiced Almonds

White-Chocolate Mousse and Carrot Torte with Ginger Cream-Cheese Ice Cream and Carrot Semifreddo

CONTEMPORARY

Café Boulud ✿

Contemporary French

003

20 E. 76th St. (bet. Fifth & Madison Aves.)

Subway: 77 St
Phone: 212-772-2600
Fax: 212-772-7755
Web: www.danielnyc.com
Prices: $$$

Sun – Mon 5:45pm - 11pm
Tue – Sat noon - 2:30pm
& 5:45pm - 11pm

Café Boulud/R. Manville

Set in the Surrey Hotel, Café Boulud brings a taste of the Old Country to the heart of the oh-so-posh Upper East Side. Operated by famed French chef Daniel Boulud, this restaurant pays homage to the cafe that Boulud's family owned just outside Lyon in France.

Boulud's food exhibits a controlled creativity and an intelligent marriage of ingredients. Two- and three-course prix-fixe lunch menus offer nice selections and quality, while four dinner menus appeal to different moods. If you're feeling old-fashioned, choose La Tradition, made up of French country classics (frisée salad with lardoons, smoke-roasted duck). If you want to dine according to the season, try La Saison. For vegetarians, there's Le Potager, which follows what's fresh at the market. Armchair travelers will favor Le Voyage, a menu inspired by global cuisine (as in a meal based on chiles from around the world).

Recalling 1930s Paris, the dining room is done in earth tones, with custom-designed mahogany chairs. Café Boulud functions as a club of sorts to a sophisticated Upper East Side crowd of ladies who lunch and soigné Europeans. Service can be a bit stiff, but is always polished and professional.

Appetizers

Peekytoe Crab Salad: White Asparagus, Ginger, Lime, Pistachio Oil

Peruvian Seafood Salad: Shrimp, Fluke, Lobster, Calamari, Pineapple, Aji Panca

Simply Shaved Porcini Salad: Porcini, Icicle Radish, Aged Balsamic, Almond Oil

Entrées

Australian Lamb Trio with Fennel Purée, Pearl Onions and Turnips

Roasted Atlantic Monkfish with Root Vegetables, Swiss Chard, and Basil-Thyme Jus

Sheep's-Milk-Ricotta Ravioli with Pea Mint Purée, Cubeb Black Pepper, Pea Shoots

Desserts

Champagne Mango: Basil Floating Island, Mango Sorbet

Blood Orange and Passion Fruit Meringue Bowl with Banana Sorbet

Bittersweet-Chocolate Mousse with Peanut Caramel, Spiced-Tea Ice Cream

Etats-Unis ✿

004

242 E. 81st St. (bet. Second & Third Aves.)

Subway:	77 St	Open daily 6pm - 11pm
Phone:	212-517-8826	
Fax:	212-517-8742	
Web:	N/A	
Prices:	$$$	

Etats-Unis

If you've ever felt that a restaurant's décor upstaged its food, you'll appreciate Etats-Unis. Delightful food here comes without pretentious surroundings. The little shoebox of a dining room is done in an industrial-chic style with bare light bulbs hanging from the ceiling, molded plastic chairs and uncovered varnished-wood tables. The open kitchen and the warm, family-run atmosphere combine to make dining here feel a bit like an intimate dinner party in your own home, but without all of the work.

Conceived by owner Tom Rapp, the limited menu changes daily to reflect the market. Simply prepared, without the fussy style often prevalent in this upper-crust neighborhood, the food here defines approachable gourmet cuisine. Flavors stand out in the balanced dishes, and the homey yet sophisticated desserts are a worthy excuse for decadent calorie consumption.

Etats-Unis is a place you'll want to come back to, but if you can't get a table, the charming Bar at Etats-Unis across the street offers the same menu.

Appetizers

Twice-risen Shropshire Blue Cheese Souffléd Pudding with Chopped Chives

Old-fashioned Scalloped Blue Point Oysters baked to order with Fresh-Grated Horseradish, Sautéed Onions, Crumbled Saltines, and a Touch of Cream

Mixed Green Salad with Warm Caramelized Pears, Crumbled Stilton Cheese, Toasted Hazelnuts, and a Drizzle of Balsamic-Vinegar Reduction and Hazelnut Oil

Entrées

Short Ribs of Beef braised all afternoon in Beer with Garlic, Onions, Roasted Tomatoes, and Fresh Herbs; served with Fluffy whipped-to-order Horseradish Mashed Potatoes

Charcoal-grilled Atlantic Halibut with a Celery-Root and Parsnip Purée; served with Roasted Granny Smith Apples and Steamed Haricots Verts

Charcoal-grilled Rack of Lamb, served au Jus with a Fresh Mint Pesto, and Crispy Oven-roasted Potatoes and Baby Artichokes

Desserts

Baked-to-order Date Pudding with a Caramelized Rum Sauce and a dollop of Freshly Whipped Cream

Baked-to-order Chocolate Soufflé with a Warm Molten Center

Old-fashioned Light and Fluffy Lemon Pudding Cake with a dollop of Freshly Whipped Cream

La Goulue ✿

005

746 Madison Ave. (bet. 64th & 65th Sts.)

Subway:	Lexington Av - 63 St	Open daily noon - 11:15pm
Phone:	212-988-8169	
Fax:	212-396-2552	
Web:	www.lagoulerestaurant.com	
Prices:	$$$	

La Goulue

Few places in Gotham say "Paris" more than this venerable bistro, opened in 1972. Named for the shameless 19th-century Moulin Rouge dancer immortalized in paintings by Henri de Toulouse-Lautrec, La Goulue re-creates La Belle Époque with framed vintage posters, brass-railing-topped banquettes backed by large mirrors, lace cafe curtains, and a light fixture signed by Art Nouveau furniture designer Louis Majorelle.

A steady supply of celebrities and well-heeled New Yorkers frequent this place, and the closely spaced bistro tables make eavesdropping particularly enjoyable (though they also make you feel a bit squeezed). From spring to fall, the highly coveted sidewalk tables are the perfect place to indulge in some serious people-watching.

The menu respects time-honored traditions with well-rendered classics. Succulent skate wing is seared golden and sauced with lemon butter and capers; profiteroles are filled with vanilla ice cream and drizzled with chocolate sauce perfumed with orange zest. Oh-so-French waiters, dressed in waistcoats and ties, deliver professional and efficient service. Just remember that the restaurant requires each guest to order at least an entrée.

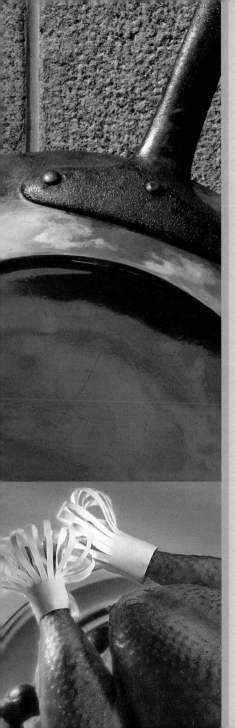

Appetizers

Tuna Tartare, Croutons of Tempura, Wasabi and Sesame

Baked Artichoke Heart with Corsican Cheese

Smoked-Duck Salad with Frisée Greens

Entrées

Steak au Poivre, La Goulue Fries

Roasted Corn-fed Chicken, Truffle Mashed Potatoes, Aged Balsamic Vinaigrette

Grilled Whole Royal Sea Bream, served boneless on Fennel Salad

Desserts

Profiteroles, Vanilla Ice-Cream Puffs, Hot Chocolate Sauce, Orange Zest

Crème Brûlée Maison

Tarte Tatin, Apple-Mango Tart, Vanilla Ice Cream

Sushi of Gari ✿

Japanese ✕

006

402 E. 78th St. (bet. First & York Aves.)

Subway:	77 St
Phone:	212-517-5340
Fax:	212-288-9235
Web:	N/A
Prices:	$$$

Tue – Sat 5pm - 10:45pm
Sun 5pm - 9:45pm
Closed Mon

Michelin

Nestled on a quiet street near First Avenue, Sushi of Gari is named for its genius chef, Masatoshi "Gari" Sugio, who also owns Gari on the West Side *(370 Columbus Ave.)*, as well as a third restaurant in Tokyo. Sushi connoisseurs, including devoted regulars, think that the wide choice of innovative Japanese fare—rich with ingredients flown in from Japan—is well worth a detour.

For a piece of the action, belly up to the sushi bar to sample Gari's fantastic and distinctive creations. Here, the expert sushi chefs will explain each ingredient and tailor your omakase (tasting menu) to your liking. If the sushi bar isn't your speed, there are tables, too. Though there's a lot less to see, as the two small dining rooms are sparsely furnished with a sober and rather bland style. Diners come here to have their taste buds—not their eyes—dazzled.

If you choose the omakase, be prepared to spend a bundle for an enchantment of the palate. Rest assured though, from the squid in salmon egg sauce to the lobster topped with seaweed salt, a succession of unusually original signature dishes will delight your senses. The chefs will feed you, piece by piece, until you say "uncle."

APPETIZERS

Tuna Tartare Special

SIGNATURE SUSHI

Bluefin Tuna with Creamy Tofu Sauce

Salmon with Sautéed Tomato and Onion Sauce

Miso-marinated Kanpachi with Daikon, Mint Paste and Garlic

Torched Yari-Squid with Creamy Sea Urchin Sauce

"Shabu Shabu" Snow Crab with Yuzu Sauce

Herb-marinated Lobster with Mo-Jio

DESSERTS

Tempura Ice Cream with Strawberry Sauce

Yuzu Panna Cotta

Atlantic Grill

Seafood 🍴

007

1341 Third Ave. (bet. 76th & 77th Sts.)

Subway:	77 St
Phone:	212-988-9200
Fax:	212-452-1447
Web:	www.brguestrestaurants.com
Prices:	$$

Mon – Thu 11:30am - 4pm & 5pm - midnight
Fri 11:30am - 4pm & 5pm - 12:30am
Sat 11:30am - 4pm & 4:30pm - 12:30am
Sun 10:30am - 4pm & 4:30pm - 11pm

Atlantic Grill is another drop in the bucket of the B.R. Guest Restaurant Group, whose finny empire also includes Blue Water Grill on Union Square and Ocean Grill on the Upper West Side. The popular 200-seat restaurant, which sports different color schemes in each section, hooks a sophisticated East Side clientele (be sure to make reservations). One room is done in nautical blue and white; the other has a sunny aspect with cream-colored walls and potted palms. Outdoor seating is in high demand during the warmer months.

Despite the restaurant's name, seafood selections, including raw-bar and sushi offerings, come from both the Atlantic and the Pacific. For dinner, go with one of the chef's entrées or try the fresh catch (anything from wild King salmon to Alaskan halibut), simply grilled.

Beyoglu 😊

Mediterranean 🍴

008

1431 Third Ave. (at 81st St.)

Subway:	77 St
Phone:	212-650-0850
Fax:	212-650-0849
Web:	N/A
Prices:	🍴

Open daily noon - midnight

Small plates star at this Mediterranean meze house, where low prices and a casual, convivial atmosphere add to the appeal. The simple dining room with its bright walls and inlaid-tile tables sets the scene for sharing meze (the menu lists over 20 different types) from homemade yogurt with cucumber and garlic to stuffed grape leaves to pan-fried cubes of calf's liver. Most of the recipes come from Turkey, but there are Greek and Lebanese accents in items like char-grilled octopus and hummus.

If the idea of small plates doesn't float your boat, there's also a short list of daily specials, including meat kebabs and grilled fish. Your waiter will fill you in on the delightful desserts, such as baklava, and kadayif filled with almonds, pistachios and honey.

Boathouse Central Park

009

American 🍴🍴

The Lake at Central Park (E. 72nd St. & Park Dr. North)

Subway: 68 St – Hunter College
Phone: 212-517-2233
Fax: 212-744-3949
Web: www.thecentralparkboathouse.com
Prices: $$

Mon – Fri noon - 4pm & 5:30pm - 9:30pm
Sat – Sun 9:30am - 4pm & 6pm - 9:30pm

You couldn't dream up a more romantic setting for a first date or a special occasion. Nestled on the shore of the lake in the middle of Central Park, the Boathouse features peaceful water views through its floor-to-ceiling windows. Built in the 1950s, Loeb Boathouse replaced the original two-story Victorian structure designed by architect Calvert Vaux in the 1870s.

Today the Boathouse is the only place in Manhattan for a lakeside meal. And the American fare (jumbo lump crab cakes, house-made cavatelli) is another good reason to go.

On a sunny day, sit out on the deck (be sure to make a reservation) and watch the boats float by or toss a few crumbs to the eager turtles and ducks. After lunch, why not hit the water with a gondola ride (advance notice required) or a rowboat rental?

Cabana

010

Caribbean 🍴

1022 Third Ave. (bet. 60th & 61st Sts.)

Subway: Lexington Av - 59 St
Phone: 212-980-5678
Fax: 212-750-6470
Web: www.cabanarestaurant.com
Prices: $$

Sun – Thu 11:30am - 11:30pm
Fri – Sat 11:30am - 1am

In a vibrant room swathed in bright yellows and blues, Cabana celebrates what it calls "Nuevo Latino" cuisine. As far as the food is concerned, this can mean anything from Cuban to Caribbean, with a dash of Spanish flavor thrown in for good measure. From paella to *chicarrónes de pollo*, the kitchen honors dishes with a Latin soul; a daily trip to the fish market ensures that the day's catch will be the freshest possible.

The restaurant, which cultivates a carnival atmosphere with its lively (and loud) Latin music, feels like a vacation from the typical staid Upper East Side restaurant. Part of a small chain, Cabana has two other locations: one in the Financial District at South Street Seaport (Pier 17) and one in Forest Hills, Queens.

Manhattan Upper East Side

Café Sabarsky

011

1048 Fifth Ave. (at 86th St.)

Subway:	86 St (Lexington Ave.)
Phone:	212-288-0665
Fax:	212-645-7127
Web:	www.wallse.com
Prices:	$$

Mon, Wed, Thu 9am – 6pm
Fri — Sun 9am – 9pm
Closed Tue

Art alone is reason enough to visit the Neue Galerie, founded in 2001 by cosmetics mogul Ronald Lauder to display his collection of early 20th-century Austrian and German art, as well as the collection of his friend, art dealer Serge Sabarsky. Besides fine art, you'll find a real gem in this 1914 Beaux Arts mansion, in the form of Café Sabarsky.

Old World charm oozes from this cafe, modeled on a late 19th-century Viennese *Kaffeehaus*. In the superb dining room, adorned with reproductions of Josef Hoffmann sconces, Otto Wagner fabrics and a Bösendorfer piano, chef Kurt Guntenbrunner (of Wallsé in Greenwich Village and Blaue Gans in TriBeCa) offers fine Austrian cuisine. You'll find the likes of bratwurst and beef goulash here, but whatever you do, don't pass up the pastries!

The Carlyle

012

35 E. 76th St. (at Madison Ave.)

Subway:	77 St
Phone:	212-570-7192
Fax:	212-744-2819
Web:	www.thecarlyle.com
Prices:	$$$$

Open daily noon - 3pm & 6pm - 11pm

Few places say old New York like The Carlyle *(see hotel listings)*. Opulent and well-mannered, The Carlyle exudes refinement, and its dining room proves a perfect complement to the hotel's sophistication. Decorated by Mark Hampton, this handsome space pulls out all the stops as far as luxury goes, from the tuxedo-clad waitstaff to the Cartier dessert cart. Tones of mushroom and chocolate-brown, lush fabrics, fresh flowers and soft lighting make the restaurant an equally ideal spot for staging a romantic tête-à-tête, a ladies' lunch or a business deal.

Understated yet elegant, the traditional menu is as classy as the crowd. French-influenced favorites such as seared Hudson Valley foie gras with roasted Mission figs, Prime aged ribeye and simple fish dishes are all pristinely prepared.

Centolire

013

Italian ✗✗

1167 Madison Ave. (bet. 85th & 86th Sts.)

Subway:	86 St (Lexington Ave.)
Phone:	212-734-7711
Fax:	212-794-5001
Web:	www.centolire.citysearch.com
Prices:	$$

Sun – Fri noon - 3pm & 5:30pm - 10:30pm
Sat noon - 3pm & 5:30pm - 11pm
Closed Sat lunch July 4 - Labor Day
Closed Sun July 4 - Labor Day

With 100 (*cento* in Italian) lire, you can go to America, or so an old Italian song goes. Accordingly, Tuscan-born restaurateur Pino Luongo (also of Tuscan Square) opened Centolire in 2001 to honor those Italians who, like himself, came to America to start a new life. Two dining spaces present different options: the more cozy and quiet downstairs room or the larger, more colorful upstairs area, accessed via a glass elevator.

At lunch, Centolire proposes a three-course menu of appealing Italian fare at a price you just can't refuse. Dinner brings a range of well-prepared entrées from tender osso buco to Tuscan fish stew brimming with shrimp, clams, mussels, calamari and the fresh fish of the day. Before you leave, check out the cookbooks by Pino, which are displayed near the entrance.

Davidburke & Donatella

Contemporary ✗✗✗

014

133 E. 61st St. (bet. Lexington & Park Aves.)

Subway:	Lexington Av - 59 St
Phone:	212-813-2121
Fax:	212-486-2322
Web:	www.dbdrestaurant.com
Prices:	$$$

Mon – Fri 11:45am - 2:30pm
& 5pm - 11pm
Sat 5pm - 11pm
Sun 11am - 2:30pm & 4:30pm - 9pm

Opened in December 2003 by David Burke and Donatella Arpaia, this restaurant reconfigures a traditional town house with geometric patterns, ebony parquet floors and a playful palette that runs from chocolate brown to lipstick red. The place is constantly mobbed with a chi-chi cadre of diners.

Burke, who oversees the kitchen, describes his cooking style as "David Burke unplugged." You'll know what this means when you taste dishes such as day boat scallops "Benedict," a take on the popular egg dish (in Burke's version, scallops replace the eggs, chorizo stands in for the ham and a potato pancake masquerades as an English muffin). At lunch, the set menu is the best value.

Everyone from the coat check to the bus staff operate with noteworthy efficiency and grace.

Donguri

309 E. 83rd St. (bet. First & Second Aves.)

Subway:	86 St (Lexington Ave.)	Tue – Sun 5:30pm - 9:30pm
Phone:	212-737-5656	Closed Mon
Fax:	212-737-5656	
Web:	www.dongurinyc.com	
Prices:	$$$	

In May 2005, Ito En, a well-known Japanese tea company, which also owns Kai *(822 Madison Ave.)*, acquired Donguri. Despite the change in ownership, Donguri maintains its extensive menu of notably authentic Japanese cuisine. With only 24 seats, this nondescript little place fills up quickly with a grown-up crowd who can afford the prices and appreciate the light, flavorful food.

Try one of the fixed menus, which might start with miso soup and a delightful plate of assorted appetizers, followed by sashimi, then broiled Chilean sea bass scented with ginger. Other entrées include ribeye steak and vegetable or seafood tempura. Dinner may also be ordered à la carte, or go all out and order the chef's omakase (tasting menu). All products are ultra-fresh and selections change regularly.

Fig & Olive

Mediterranean

808 Lexington Ave. (bet. 62nd & 63rd Sts.)

Subway:	Lexington Av - 63 St	Open daily 11am - midnight
Phone:	212-207-4555	
Fax:	212-207-4477	
Web:	www.figandolive.com	
Prices:	$$	

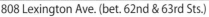

This Mediterranean restaurant and olive-oil shop is a great place to have a crisp salad topped with dressing made from fragrant extra virgin olive oil. Of course, your choices aren't limited to salads, though the menu does focus on olive oil, pairing a specific oil with each course. You'll find different flavors of oil from France, Italy and Spain here, and the wine list features bottles hand-selected from the same regions.

Settle into the pleasant dining room on a time-out from strenuous shopping at Bloomie's, and dig into salads, tartines, carpaccio, crostini, or a charcuterie platter brimming with prosciutto, bresaola, *jamón Iberico* and *saucisson sec*. The bright and balanced food will revive you for further shopping adventures without an expanded waistline.

Frederick's Madison

017

Mediterranean 𝕏𝕏

768 Madison Ave. (bet. 65th & 66th Sts.)

Subway: Lexington Av - 63 St
Phone: 212-737-7300
Fax: 212-737-7337
Web: www.fredericksnyc.com
Prices: $$$

Mon – Fri 8am - 4pm & 5:30pm - 11pm
Sat – Sun noon - 4:30pm
& 5:30pm - 11pm

Brothers Frederick and Laurent Lesort, known for Frederick's Bar & Lounge *(8 W. 58th St.)*, expanded their restaurant holdings in May 2005 with the opening of Frederick's Madison. The menu has expanded, too, from Asian-inspired small plates to contemporary Mediterranean fare. Signature dishes include foie gras chaud-froid, which comes seared, and in a cold terrine served with kumquat jam; open ravioli of braised rabbit; and slow-baked cod with clam nage. In the dining room, blond woods, brass wall sconces and claret-colored velour chairs create an elegant feel.

If you plan to get an early start on Madison Avenue shopping, you'll be glad to know that Frederick's is open for breakfast at 8am, while shoppers needing a midday snack will find an assortment of sweet and savory offerings.

Geisha

018

Contemporary Japanese 𝕏𝕏

33 E. 61st St. (bet. Madison & Park Aves.)

Subway: Lexington Av - 59 St
Phone: 212-813-1112
Fax: 212-813-1150
Web: www.geisharestaurant.com
Prices: $$$

Mon – Sat noon - 3:30pm
& 5:30pm - 11:30pm
Closed Sun & major holidays

Named for the sensuous world of the geisha, this restaurant is owned by the same team—Vittorio Assaf and Fabio Granato—who introduced Serafina to the New York dining scene. Four individually decorated dining spaces on two floors incorporate elements of Japanese costumes (silver beads like those used in geisha headdresses), Oriental flowers (cherry blossom light fixtures) and origami (a "3-D" wall of stacked, fabric-covered cubes).

The result is a cool, seductive space in which to savor the menu of French-accented Asian fare originally conceived by Eric Ripert of Le Bernardin. Coconut-marinated fluke, and hamachi and bluefin patchwork are two of the enticing selections. Sure, there's also sushi galore, but why not try something different, like grilled shrimp lollipops on sugarcane skewers?

Il Riccio

Italian

019

152 E. 79th St. (bet. Lexington & Third Aves.)

Subway:	77 St	Open daily noon - 3pm & 5pm - 11:30pm
Phone:	212-639-9111	
Fax:	212-639-9528	
Web:	N/A	
Prices:	$$	

Located four blocks from the Metropolitan Museum of Art, Il Riccio makes a great lunch spot when you've had your fill of fine art. A shiny brass door beckons you into the restaurant, which sits on a busy street, surrounded by boutiques and eateries. Two different dining rooms here offer a comfortable respite from trekking through museum galleries.

Diners are cosseted at Il Riccio, where the chef takes great care in preparing Italian classics. Although the menu is not extensive, it does offer a nice range of dishes—the emphasis here is on pasta, from spaghetti with crab meat and tomato to gnocchi with Taleggio cheese and radicchio—along with a roster of daily specials. The short wine list includes several fine venerable vintages of Italian wine.

Isle of Capri

Italian

020

1028 Third Ave. (at 61st St.)

Subway:	Lexington Av - 59 St	Mon – Sat 11:30am - 10pm
Phone:	212-223-9430	Closed Sun
Fax:	212-223-2705	
Web:	www.isleofcapriny.com	
Prices:	$$	

Tradition reigns in this stylish Upper East Side establishment, started in 1955 by Vincenzo and Maria Lammana, and still going strong. When the original owners died in the 1990s, Isle of Capri passed on to their two daughters, who run the restaurant today. There's a joyful air in the pleasant dining room, set about by Greco-Roman-style statues recalling the island where Roman emperors Octavian Augustus and Tiberius both had residences.

A table in the center of the dining room displays baskets full of seasonal and imported Italian products, hinting at the ingredients used in the time-honored dishes here. Excellent house-made pastas, broiled veal chops, shrimp scampi and *trippa alla Calabrese* (tripe braised in tomato sauce) are all authentic and satisfying.

Ithaka

021

Greek ✗✗

308 E. 86th St. (bet. First & Second Aves.)

Subway:	86 St (Lexington Ave.)	Mon – Fri 3pm - 11pm
Phone:	212-628-9100	Sat – Sun noon - 11pm
Fax:	212-734-6619	
Web:	www.ithakarestaurant.com	
Prices:	$$	

A Mediterranean-blue awning welcomes visitors to Ithaka, the way the sea would greet them in Greece. Inside, live music and an amiable staff makes Ithaka a vibrant and endearing spot.

This cozy place, with its beamed ceiling, brick walls and stone floors, presents an authentic Old World cuisine. Greek favorites like moussaka and pasticio share with *kalamari scharas* (grilled calamari) and *arni youvetsi* (baby lamb baked in a clay pot with orzo, tomato sauce and feta cheese). And perhaps best of all, the prices will leave some change in your pocket.

If you still have room for dessert after a hearty meal here, the creamy house-made yogurt (*yiaourti sakoulas*) is as good as any you'll get in Greece; here, it's drizzled with perfumed honey and topped with crunchy hazelnuts.

J.G. Mellon 🕸

022

American ✗

1291 Third Ave. (at 74th St.)

Subway:	77 St	Open daily 11:30am - 2:30am
Phone:	212-650-1310	
Fax:	N/A	
Web:	N/A	
Prices:	🕸🕸	

Preppies still wanting a taste of the college life haunt J.G. Mellon, where burgers and beers are the staples. The cheeseburger, cooked to order and served on a toasted English muffin, is arguably one of the best in the city, and the crispy, golden, cottage fries that accompany it perfectly round out the meal (literally, since the fries are round!). Cold nights bring customers begging for Mellon's chili.

This Upper East Side restaurant has been a New York institution for generations, and the place is always packed with neighborhood residents, including recent college graduates and young families with kids. Checkered tablecloths, wood floors and a long wooden bar give Mellon's an amiable local pub feel, while the old-school staff makes everyone feel like a regular.

Manhattan Upper East Side

JoJo

023

160 E. 64th St. (bet. Lexington & Third Aves.)

Subway:	Lexington Av - 63 St
Phone:	212-223-5656
Fax:	212-755-9038
Web:	www.jean-georges.com
Prices:	$$$

Mon – Thu noon - 2:30pm
& 5:30pm - 10:30pm
Fri noon - 2:30pm & 5:30pm - 11pm
Sat 5:30pm – 11pm
Sun noon - 2:30pm & 5:30pm - 10pm

JoJo will always be special to its "father," award-winning chef Jean-Georges Vongerichten. After all, this bistro was his first restaurant in New York, launched in 1991. Given the nickname that Vongerichten knew as a boy, JoJo got a major overhaul for its tenth birthday. Now the two-story town house drips with plush velvets, rich tapestries and fine silks. Low lighting from crystal chandeliers plays on the room's deep hues, casting a sultry glow.

In this sexy lair, the chef presents his modern version of French cuisine, in dishes like roasted cod with marinated vegetables in a fragrant sauce of olive oil and basil, or roast chicken with ginger, green olives and chickpea fries. JoJo's daytime small-plate menu is popular with the ladies who lunch.

Kai

024

822 Madison Ave. (bet. 68th & 69th Sts.)

Subway:	68 St - Hunter College
Phone:	212-988-7277
Fax:	212-570-4500
Web:	www.itoen.com
Prices:	$$$

Tue – Sat noon - 2:30pm
& 5:30pm - 9:30pm
Closed Sun & Mon

You'll find Kai hidden away on the second floor of the Upper East Side tea shop owned by Ito En, one of the best-known tea companies in Japan. A serene setting marked by clean lines and soothing tones creates just the right vibe in which to experience kaiseki cuisine.

Centuries ago, kaiseki originated in the temples of Kyoto as small dishes served during a traditional Japanese tea ceremony. Kai revives this tradition with a kaiseki menu that balances its offerings between land and sea. You can enjoy these dishes at lunch or dinner in the form of multicourse menus that change with the season (or there's always the selection of sushi and sashimi). With advance notice, the chef will create a special omakase, or tasting menu. Zen tea is served daily from noon to 4pm.

Kings' Carriage House

025

Contemporary ✗✗

251 E. 82nd St. (bet. Second & Third Aves.)

Subway:	86 St (Lexington Ave.)	Open daily noon - 10pm
Phone:	212-734-5490	
Fax:	212-717-2352	
Web:	N/A	
Prices:	$$	

This restored carriage house now holds an elegant restaurant and tea room for diners seeking a romantic getaway in the heart of the Upper East Side. Run by Elizabeth King and her husband Paul Farell (who hails from Dublin), Kings' Carriage House resembles an Irish country manor, set about with Chinese porcelains, antique furnishings and hunting trophies on the walls. Its lovely ambience is perfect for charming a loved one or friend, or impressing out-of-town guests.

There's nothing Old World about the food, though. American dishes are given a contemporary twist (roasted loin of lamb with blackberry-mint compote) on the daily changing fixed-price menu. The lunch menu is especially inexpensive, but if you can't make it for a meal, do drop 'round for afternoon tea.

L'Absinthe

026

French ✗✗

227 E. 67th St. (bet. Second & Third Aves.)

Subway:	68 St - Hunter College	Mon – Fri noon - 3pm & 5:30pm - 11pm
Phone:	212-794-4950	Sat 5:30pm - 11pm
Fax:	212-794-1589	Sun noon - 3pm & 5:30pm - 10pm
Web:	www.labsinthe.com	
Prices:	$$$	

Remember the good old days, when you sat around cafes all day, railing on the political system and sipping the mind-blowing liquor, absinthe, until you could no longer see?

Of course you don't—unless you happened to grow up in late-19th-century Paris. Though absinthe has long since been replaced by the gentler aperitif Pernod, the Art Nouveau age lives on at Jean-Michel Bergougnoux's brasserie. Chandeliers with tulip-shaped light fixtures, walls of large framed mirrors and sprays of bright flowers bring to mind Belle Époque Paris.

Meanwhile, the kitchen interprets timeless French dishes from cold pâté of quail to *choucroute Alsacienne*, for 21st-century patrons. Beef tartare and steamed mussels are featured at brunch, which also features a children's menu.

Manhattan Upper East Side

Le Bilboquet

027

25 E. 63rd St. (bet. Madison & Park Aves.)

Subway:	Lexington Av - 63 St	Open daily noon - 11:30pm
Phone:	212-751-3036	
Fax:	212-684-1659	
Web:	N/A	
Prices:	**$$**	

There's no sign indicating Le Bilboquet's presence, but this swanky French restaurant is populated nightly with a sexy international crowd. Once inside, you'll observe that most of the patrons (many of them are French) seem to know each other, adding to the private-club ambience. This hot spot, with its tight quarters and loud upbeat music, is not the place for a quiet conversation, but if you're looking for a party, it's an ideal place to be.

The kitchen turns out classic French bistro cuisine and leaves the modern interpretations and fussy presentations to the competition. Steak tartare, roast chicken, moules frites and salade Niçoise are among the most-requested dishes. An insouciant attitude pervades the service, but the crowd never seems to care.

Lenox Room

028

1278 Third Ave. (bet. 73rd & 74th Sts.)

Subway:	77 St	Mon – Fri noon - 2:30pm
Phone:	212-772-0404	& 5:30pm - 10:30pm
Fax:	212-772-3229	Sat 5:30pm - 10:30pm
Web:	www.lenoxroom.com	Sun 11:30am - 2:30pm & 5:30pm - 9pm
Prices:	**$$**	

Looking for good food in a cocoon-like ambience? You've come to the right place. Opened in 1995 by maitre d' Tony Fortuna and hotelier Edward Bianchini, the Lenox Room wraps diners in cozy comfort with its claret-red walls, cushy banquettes and warm, wood-paneled walls.

The updated American cuisine fits right in with this relaxed environment, and the service is pleasant and professional. Lunch brings salads, sandwiches and a short list of entrées; the three-course "I Love New York" menu is such a deal. At dinner, there's a nice balance of choices, including "Tiers of Taste," a combination of three small plates for a set price. Dinner entrées span the globe for inspiration; there's Wiener Schnitzel, rigatoni with duck sausage ragoût, and crisp-skin salmon.

Lusardi's

029

Italian ✗✗

1494 Second Ave. (bet. 77th & 78th Sts.)

Subway:	77 St
Phone:	212-249-2020
Fax:	212-585-2941
Web:	www.lusardis.com
Prices:	$$

Open daily noon - 3pm & 5pm - midnight

Both the décor and the service are warm at Lusardi's, an Upper East Side staple since Luigi and Mauro Lusardi founded the restaurant in 1982. Decorated with vintage Italian posters, the well-kept yellow dining room tends to be quiet at lunch; it comes alive in the evening, though, with a loyal following of diners who pack the place.

An ample choice of classic northern Italian fare attracts customers year-round, while special menus designed around white truffles or wild game are tuned to the season. Pasta lovers will find a wide range of alternatives, while fish and meat dishes are given equal face time. Lusardi's fans will be glad to know that they can purchase bottles of the family's own marinara sauce and extra virgin olive oil at the restaurant.

Mainland

030

Contemporary Asian ✗✗

1081 Third Ave. (at 64th St.)

Subway:	59 St
Phone:	212-888-6333
Fax:	212-888-9005
Web:	www.mainlandnyc.com
Prices:	$$$

Mon – Wed 11:30am - 2:30pm & 5pm - 10:30pm
Thu – Fri 11:30am - 2:30pm & 5pm - 11pm
Sat 5pm - 11:30pm
Sun 5pm - 10:30pm

You'll be impressed from the moment you enter Mainland and spy its gorgeous red and gold colors, bas-relief dragons, and antique Chinese ceramics. As you walk down from the bar to the inviting lounge, the first thing you'll see is the custom-made wood-burning oven behind a large glass wall. This is where Mainland's signature Peking duck is prepared and the expert chefs stand by, awaiting your order.

You can't go wrong with one of the bronze-skinned birds that hang behind the glass. Just know that the menu, divided into Raw & Iced, Lightly Cooked, Noodles & Dumplings, Seafood, Meat & Fowl, lists myriad other choices. The more friends you bring, the more dishes you can sample. Although the service isn't as sophisticated as the food, after a few cocktails you may find it less frustrating.

Mark's

031

Contemporary ✗✗✗

25 E. 77th St. (bet. Fifth & Madison Aves.)

Subway: 77 St
Phone: 212-879-1864
Fax: 212-744-2749
Web: www.themarkhotel.com
Prices: $$$

Open daily 11:30am - 2:30pm
& 6pm - 10pm
Closed New Year's Day

A half-block east of Central Park and three blocks south of the Metropolitan Museum of Art, The Mark Hotel claims a truly enviable location. Set off the lobby inside this elegant Upper East Side hostelry, you'll find Mark's to be a fitting culinary complement to the hotel. The restaurant, done up with stylish furnishings, fine linens and dark walls, features a bi-level dining room where breakfast, lunch, dinner and afternoon tea are served.

Decadent dishes with a light French touch include escargots with ramps and shallot confit, consommé of pheasant, and rack of lamb. The 10,000-bottle wine list really hits the mark with its combination of New and Old World selections, while the adjacent Mark's Bar is a favorite watering hole of Upper East Side notables.

Maya

032

Mexican ✗✗

1191 First Ave. (bet. 64th & 65th Sts.)

Subway: 68 St - Hunter College
Phone: 212-585-1818
Fax: 212-734-6579
Web: www.modernmexican.com
Prices: $$$

Sun – Mon 5pm - 10pm
Tue – Thu 5pm - 11pm
Fri – Sat 5pm - 11:30pm

Maya practically defines casual elegance. Few restaurants are able to carry off being informal enough for a weeknight while being upscale enough for a weekend, but Maya expertly straddles that line. This spirited Mexican restaurant's pastel walls and vibrant artwork make it feel like an elegant private home, and its lively, feel-good scene lures well-heeled Upper East Siders.

Far from the burrito-laden menus of the competition, Maya's comprehensive menu reads like a love letter to Mexico. Time-honored culinary traditions are updated with a contemporary twist in many of the dishes, and a seemingly limitless margarita menu complements the zesty creations from the devoted chef. Bursting with powerful flavors, the meals are plated in an eye-catching manner.

Maz Mezcal

033

Mexican ✕

316 E. 86th St. (bet. First & Second Aves.)

Subway: 86 St (Lexington Ave.)
Phone: 212-472-1599
Fax: 212-472-1498
Web: www.mazmezcal.com
Prices: $$

Mon – Thu 5pm – 11pm
Fri 5pm - midnight
Sat noon - 3pm & 5pm - midnight
Sun noon - 3pm & 4pm - 11pm
Closed Thanksgiving & Christmas Day

Simple Mexican food—and lots of it—leaves customers eager to return to Maz Mezcal, located on a busy restaurant block. Eduardo Silva now runs his family's Upper East Side stalwart (formerly El Sombrero); after he took the reins, he renamed the place Maz Mezcal, then expanded it several years ago.

From *arroz con pollo* to paella, dishes are tailored to mild palates, but if you prefer your food *picante*, the kitchen will be happy to spice things up. Takeout and delivery are also available if you're in the area.

With more than 50 different types of tequila, and its cousin, mezcal, available from the bar, you can count on a party atmosphere almost every night in the bright, terra-cotta-colored dining room. In warm weather, the party spills out to the backyard garden and the sidewalk seats.

Mezzaluna

034

Italian ✕

1295 Third Ave. (bet. 74th & 75th Sts.)

Subway: 77 St
Phone: 212-535-9600
Fax: 212-517-8045
Web: www.mezzalunany.com
Prices: $$

Open daily noon - 3:30pm & 6pm - 11:30pm

Mezzaluna is a restaurant that takes it name seriously. So much so, that they offered 20 meals to any artist (many of them Italian) who would agree to render his or her version of the restaurant's namesake crescent-shaped chopping knife. As you'll see, the 77 different artworks that paper the walls each depict a unique take on the this design and provide an eye-catching backdrop for well-prepared seasonal Italian dishes.

Founded by Aldo Bozzi (who previously headed Alfa Romeo in North America), the restaurant has been around since 1984. Antiques imported from Italy and tables nesting close together add to the simple comfort and convivial atmosphere. From black linguine topped with fiery tomato sauce to brick-oven pizza, it's easy to see why the crowds line up here.

Manhattan Upper East Side

Nello

035

696 Madison Ave. (bet. 62nd & 63rd Sts.)

Subway:	5 Av - 59 St	Open daily noon - midnight
Phone:	212-980-9099	
Fax:	212-980-3014	
Web:	N/A	
Prices:	$$$$	

It's all about the beautiful people at Nello. This place appeals to a moneyed, dress-to-impress clientele, who don't flinch at the restaurant's uptown prices. (After all, Nello needs to keep pace with neighbors Givenchy, Christofle, Hermès and Lalique.) Inside, black-and-white photographs of an African safari adorn the walls, and little crystal vases of fresh flowers brighten the tabletops. Tables are tight, but with this chic crowd, it's all the more pleasing.

Nello is worth the splurge, not only for the delectable Italian cuisine and the charming waitstaff, but for the opportunity to see how the "other half" lives. Before you leave, pause inside the entrance to check out photographs of the rich and famous patrons who have dined here in the past.

Nick's

036

1814 Second Ave. (at 94th St.)

Subway:	96 St (Lexington Ave.)	Open daily 11am - 11pm
Phone:	212-987-5700	
Fax:	212-987-5777	
Web:	N/A	
Prices:	🍸	

New York has long been known for its pizzerias, and this one takes the cake—or, rather, the pie. The Manhattan satellite of the Forest Hills (Queens) original, Nick's is everything you want a pizza place to be. The tin-ceilinged dining room is pleasant and cozy, the service is jovial and efficient, and you can watch the cooks hand-tossing the dough and firing your pizza in the wood-burning oven.

Pies here turn out thin and crispy, spread with a good balance of tomato sauce, herbs and your choice of toppings. On the list of pasta (properly called "macaroni" in the traditional Italian-American lexicon) and meat entrées, half portions accommodate those with less hearty appetites—but with food this good at such reasonable prices, you'll want to rethink your diet.

Orsay

037

1057 Lexington Ave. (at 75th St.)

Subway:	77 St	Open daily 11am - 11:30pm
Phone:	212-517-6400	Closed December 24 - 26
Fax:	212-517-3896	
Web:	www.orsayrestaurant.com	
Prices:	$$	

In true Parisian fashion, this smart brasserie at the corner of 75th Street overflows onto the sidewalk terrace through its large French doors. Inside, the Paris of the 1950s comes alive through the zinc bar, fan-patterned mosaic tile floor, mahogany paneling and brass accents. Arched walls and frosted-glass partitions add to the Art Nouveau stylings.

The chef takes a few liberties with modern preparations, but the origins are French to the core. Lamb navarin, escargots, and steak tartare speak to the classic technique, while the likes of citrus-cured hamachi, or wild Duclair duckling with blood-orange glaze show contemporary flair.

Ideal for business or pleasure, Orsay's attractive bar provides a comfortable spot for guests dining alone to enjoy a glass of wine and a bountiful shellfish platter.

Park Avenue Cafe

Contemporary ✗✗✗

038

100 E. 63rd St. (at Park Ave.)

Subway:	Lexington Av - 63 St	Mon – Thu 11:30am - 3pm
Phone:	212-644-1900	& 5:30pm - 10pm
Fax:	212-688-0373	Fri 11:30am - 3pm & 5:30pm - 11pm
Web:	www.parkavenuecafe.com	Sat 11am - 2:30pm & 5:30pm - 11pm
Prices:	$$$	Sun 11am - 2:30pm & 5:30pm - 10pm

Set on a tree-lined block at the intersection of prestigious Park Avenue, this comfortable neighborhood cafe (part of the Smith & Wollensky Restaurant Group) gives off an Upper East Side vibe with its attractive crowd of locals. Opened in 1992, the restaurant was refurbished in 2004 with cheery red-and-white-striped banquettes and crimson Venetian-plaster walls.

The kitchen turns a creative hand to dishes like goat cheese ravioli, and French fries with truffle mayonnaise. Pasta, bread, smoked meat and fish are all made in-house. Lunch lures a stylish crowd who come here for the East Side lobster roll and the grilled baby-chicken "BLT," served as a salad. To quench your thirst, the wine list offers some 250 selections.

Manhattan Upper East Side

Payard

Manhattan Upper East Side

French 🍴🍴

039

1032 Lexington Ave. (bet. 73rd & 74th Sts.)

Subway:	77 St	Mon – Sat noon – 3pm
Phone:	212-717-5252	& 5:45pm - 10:30pm
Fax:	212-717-0986	Closed Sun
Web:	www.payard.com	
Prices:	$$$	

Famous for its handmade chocolates and mouth-watering French pastries, Payard is also a restaurant. This elegant place brings a bit of Paris to the Upper East Side, and its windows filled with lacy confections are better than Macy's any day.

Since you have to walk past the cases of tempting sweets to reach the dining room, there's always the danger that you'll decide to forget the main course altogether. If you do resist (until the end of the meal, that is), you can expect classic French cuisine made with products such as farm-raised chicken, New York Black Angus sirloin and homemade gravlax.

And don't even think of leaving without a sweet souvenir—perhaps a box of French *macarons*, some champagne truffles or a selection of *pâtes de fruits*—to tide you over until breakfast.

Persepolis

Persian 🍴

040

1423 Second Ave. (bet. 74th & 75th Sts.)

Subway:	77 St	Open daily noon - 11:30pm
Phone:	212-535-1100	
Fax:	212-737-1155	
Web:	www.persepolisnyc.com	
Prices:	$$	

In 1990 Persian cuisine became accessible to New Yorkers, thanks to founder Kaz Bayati. His eatery bears the name of one of the ancient capitals of Persia, established in the late 6th century BC. (It also happens to be the name of the city where Bayati made a name for himself on the local soccer team in the 1970s.) The restaurant's new location accommodates a larger crowd of diners in its bright, spacious dining room.

Olive oil, lemon, garlic, saffron, cinnamon—and even a few secret ingredients—flavor tasty kebabs and vegetarian dishes here. Begin your meal with *khumus* or fresh feta cheese and market vegetables before tucking into saffron chicken or baby lamb barg—and be sure to order the sour cherry rice with any entrée.

Philippe

041

Chinese ✗✗

33 E. 60th St. (bet. Madison & Park Aves.)

Subway: 5 Av - 59 St
Phone: 212-644-8885
Fax: 212-644-8889
Web: www.philippechow.com
Prices: $$$

Open daily noon - midnight

When Rick Moonen closed RM in spring 2005, chef Philippe Chow seized this prime piece of real estate as an opportunity to go off on his own. After more than 25 years at Mr. Chow in Midtown, Chow opened Philippe in RM's appealing space. The main room now sports a clean, contemporary look, with leather banquettes lining the walls and vases of artfully arranged branches decorating the niches between the dining space and the bar.

Upscale Chinese cuisine ranges from striped bass Bejing to crispy duck. Entrées are sized—and priced—for two to three people (half-orders are available on some items). Noodles and dumplings merit a separate section on the menu; every evening at 8pm, you can watch the chef craft traditional noodle preparations at a station in the middle of the dining room.

Quatorze Bis

042

French ✗✗

323 E. 79th St. (bet. First & Second Aves.)

Subway: 77 St
Phone: 212-535-1414
Fax: N/A
Web: N/A
Prices: $$

Mon 5:30pm - 11pm
Tue – Sun noon - 2:30pm
& 5:30pm - 11pm

This French bistro has changed its location, but not its name—which refers to its former address on 14th Street (*quatorze* in French). The word "bis" was added to the title when the restaurant moved in 1989 (*bis* is French for "once again").

Regulars hope Quatorze Bis is on the Upper East Side to stay, so they can keep enjoying the likes of homemade pork terrine, bœuf Bourguignon, cassoulet, and cream-filled profiteroles right in their own backyard. Open for dinner nightly and lunch every day except Monday, Quatorze Bis is a gracious neighborhood restaurant.

The marble-topped bar, old French posters and cozy banquettes make for an inviting and oh-so-Parisian atmosphere. Be sure to check out the two caricatures of King Louis XIV of France that grace the wall.

Serafina Fabulous Pizza

043

1022 Madison Ave. (bet. 78th & 79th Sts.)

Subway:	77 St
Phone:	212-734-1425
Fax:	212-888-3899
Web:	www.serafinarestaurant.com
Prices:	$$

Open daily 11:30am - midnight

After browsing the tony boutiques of Madison Avenue, the beautiful people head for Serafina Fabulous Pizza. People-watching is fantastic at this trendy Italian spot, best known for specialties cooked in its wood-burning oven. The second-floor dining room has a lively and energetic feel, while the third level boasts a retractable roof for alfresco dining in warmer months.

Snagging a seat at this popular spot may prove difficult in the evening, but great pizzas, fresh pastas, and grilled meats and fish make it worth the wait. Fast-paced New Yorkers are expertly handled by the gracious staff, while those who prefer to linger are encouraged to sit back and enjoy a glass of the house sangria.

Four other Serafinas (all with the same menu) in Manhattan ensure that the party never ends.

Sette Mezzo

Italian ✕

044

969 Lexington Ave. (bet. 70th & 71st Sts.)

Subway:	68 St - Hunter College
Phone:	212-472-0400
Fax:	212-427-0986
Web:	N/A
Prices:	$$$

Open daily noon - 2:30pm
& 5pm -11:30pm

Celebrity appeal has always been a hallmark of this little trattoria. In fact, Oprah even declared the place, whose name refers to an Italian card game, to be her favorite restaurant in New York City. Whether they're famous or not, diners of all stripes crowd the long, narrow dining room here; they seem to be infatuated with the convivial atmosphere and the considerate waitstaff.

Not to mention the honest Italian cuisine, which respects its roots, even if it is a bit on the pricey side. In keeping with the ambience of this white-tablecloth establishment, plates of fresh fish and delicious pasta are elegantly presented.

Sette Mezzo's popularity means that the tables turn over quickly. When the bill comes, don't bother to offer your credit card—Sette Mezzo only accepts cash.

Manhattan Upper East Side

Shanghai Pavilion

045

1378 Third Ave. (bet. 78th & 79th Sts.)

Subway:	77 St	Open daily 11:30am - 10:30pm
Phone:	212-585-3388	
Fax:	212-288-9325	
Web:	N/A	
Prices:	⊜	

While so many of the Upper East Side's restaurants seem to tailor their prices to their upscale clientele, Shanghai Pavilion is a real gem if you're watching your wallet. For less than $25, you can dine well here on Eastern Chinese cuisine in a pleasing, contemporary setting. Served with two appetizers, a choice of soup and entrée, the lunch special is an incredible deal. For dinner, the generous menu covers all the bases, from vegetarian meals to the intriguing-sounding lion's head casserole (made with pork dumplings and vegetables).

If it's a Shanghai-style banquet you crave, call the day before to arrange it with the restaurant, then round up a group of friends for a multicourse feast. This isn't your average take-out joint—its food and its décor are far better than the standard.

Spigolo

046

1561 Second Ave. (at 81st St.)

Subway:	86 St (Lexington Ave.)	Sun – Mon 5:30pm - 10pm
Phone:	212-744-1100	Tue – Sat 5:30pm - 11pm
Fax:	212-744-1204	
Web:	www.spigolo.net	
Prices:	$$	

Even at the beginning of the week, this sliver of a dining room is packed. The draw? Upper East Siders want to be among the lucky few (the restaurant has less than 20 tables) to relish the inspired Italian cooking at Spigolo.

Husband-and-wife team Scott and Heather Fratangelo met at the Union Square Café before opening this popular establishment. Food and wine are like religion here, and Scott pays serious attention to quality. Unusual yet rustic presentations, such as hake *acqua pazza* (served in a tomato-and-fish-based broth made with garlic and hot chiles) are a sure bet, while more familiar dishes like light sheep's-milk-ricotta gnocchi with cream and pancetta are definite crowd pleasers. Heather plays the charming hostess when she's not whipping up delectable pastries.

Sushi Seki

047

Japanese ✗

1143 First Ave. (bet. 62nd & 63rd Sts.)

Subway:	Lexington Av - 59 St	Mon – Sat 5:30pm - 3am
Phone:	212-371-0238	Closed Sun & Aug 8 - 17
Fax:	N/A	
Web:	N/A	
Prices:	$$$	

Sushi Seki offers high quality for the price, making it a sure bet if you're looking for a good reason to go out for sushi. It's a tough reservation to get, as the restaurant is both popular and quite small, but it's worth the advance booking to sample the creations of the namesake chef, who formerly worked in the kitchen at Sushi of Gari.

In the modest, dimly lit dining room, the waitstaff keeps up a steady tempo, clearing plates and bringing more with equal finesse. Meanwhile, at the sushi bar, chefs craft fresh-from-the-boat products into tasty morsels. If you opt for Seki's omakase, you'll get the chef's choice of seafood air-shipped from the market in Tokyo.

The restaurant's late hours accommodate revelers who hanker for sushi after most places have closed.

Taste

048

Contemporary ✗✗

1411 Third Ave. (at 80th St.)

Subway:	77 St	Open daily 5:30pm - 10pm
Phone:	212-717-9798	
Fax:	212-737-5474	
Web:	www.elizabar.com	
Prices:	$$	

Youngest son of the founders of Zabar's, New York's landmark West Side deli, Eli Zabar launched his second fresh-food market, Eli's, in 1998. A recent adjunct to the market is Taste, a restaurant devised to pair small plates and daily changing entrées with Eli's favorite regional wines.

Drop in after work to sample affordable wines by the glass. Of course, you'll need something to nosh on, and small plates such as roasted eggplant and tomato tart, or baby burgers on brioche should do the trick. Dinner is full-service (at breakfast and lunch it's cafeteria-style), and has included items such as spit-roasted duck with garnet-yam purée, and a pork chop with slow-cooked cabbage. The food always represents the tasty, home-style fare Eli's is known for—cooked better at his place than yours.

Trata Estiatorio

049

1331 Second Ave. (bet. 70th & 71st Sts.)

Subway:	68 St - Hunter College	Open daily noon - midnight
Phone:	212-535-3800	
Fax:	212-535-9328	
Web:	www.trata.com	
Prices:	$$$	

Everything about this bright trattoria will remind you of the sea, from the crisp blue-and-white façade to the stone-washed white walls and the colorful mosaics of sea life above the bar. The chic design lures a fashionable clientele who also frequent its sister restaurant in the Hamptons.

With the Greek Islands as a theme and fresh seafood displayed on ice by the open kitchen, what else would you expect but a daily changing list of fish and shellfish? Whole fish are the house specialty; fresh catches like Arctic char, American snapper and barbouni from the Mediterranean Sea are charcoal-grilled and priced per pound. Go for lunch if you want a bargain.

Don't overlook the wine list here; there are numerous Greek varietals cited, along with nice descriptions of their characteristics.

Triangolo

Italian

050

345 E. 83rd St. (bet. First & Second Aves.)

Subway:	86 St (Lexington Ave.)	Mon – Sat 5pm - midnight
Phone:	212-472-4488	Sun 3pm - 10:30pm
Fax:	212-517-3256	
Web:	www.triangolorestaurant.com	
Prices:	$$	

Although it's tucked away in an Upper East Side neighborhood off the beaten track of upscale shops and world-class museums, Triangolo nonetheless keeps customers lining up outside the door. Why? Attentive service might be one reason. The warm décor in the simple dining room is another.

The greatest draw, though, is the generous menu of pastas, topped with hearty homemade sauces; *rotolo di pasta montanara* (rolled pasta filled with spinach, porcini and parmesan) is one of the signature dishes. Of course, you won't want to dive into the pastas without first sampling something from the long list of antipasti. And, by all means, save room for the tasty tiramisu.

Reasonable prices make one more reason why Triangolo might just be better than dining at your Italian grandmother's house.

Manhattan Upper East Side

Uva ☺

051

1486 Second Ave. (bet. 77th & 78th Sts.)

Subway: 77 St
Phone: 212-472-4552
Fax: 212-472-9776
Web: www.uvawinebarnewyork.com
Prices: $$

Mon – Fri 4:30pm - 3am
Sat – Sun noon - 3pm & 4:30pm - 3am

You'd never guess that this intimate little wine bar, with its mixed crowd, lively (as in loud) ambience, and impressive wine list (*uva* is Italian for "grape") was related to Lusardi's, an old-school Italian stalwart in the Upper East. In Uva's rustic, dimly lit dining room, the friendly Italian staff wends their way around the tightly spaced tables, delivering plates and happily offering advice about the wine and food.

Surprisingly good cuisine here is a far cry from the generic Italian-American standards. Instead, Uva's menu encompasses a creative selection of house-made pastas, entrées, cheeses and cured meats. And there always seems to be a crush at the bar, where patrons can taste more than 30 wines by the glass. Perhaps best of all, prices are reasonable and portions are generous.

Manhattan Upper East Side

Show the locals around.

Michelin® Green Guides will introduce you to a world of information on the history, culture, art, and architecture of a destination. You'll be so well informed, they'll never suspect you're a tourist. To learn more, visit michelintravel.com.

MICHELIN
A better way forward

Upper West Side

Great cultural institutions and good food are what you can expect from the Upper West Side, along with tidy rows of restored brownstones and stunning apartment buildings bordering Central Park. Reaching from Central Park West to the Hudson River between 59th Street and 116th Street, the Upper West Side is home to the **Lincoln Center for the Performing Arts**, the **American Museum of Natural History**, and the campus of **Columbia University**. This neighborhood is also where you'll run into some of the city's favorite food markets, such as Zabar's *(80th St. & Broadway)*, a family-run New York institution for more than 75 years.

A Bit of History – Development has been relatively recent in this neighborhood. In the late 19th century, shantytowns, saloons and stray goats populated the area. This all changed in 1884 when Henry Hardenbergh built New York's first luxury apartment house—the celebrated **Dakota**—at 1 West 72nd Street. With its eclectic turrets, Gothic gables and ornate finials, the Dakota made a fitting setting for the 1968 film *Rosemary's Baby*. Over the years, the Dakota housed many celebrities, including Leonard Bernstein, Lauren Bacall and John Lennon, who was shot outside the 72nd Street entrance by a crazed fan in 1980.

After the Dakota came the ornate **Ansonia Hotel** *(2101-2119 Broadway)* in 1904, the first to have a drive-in courtyard, and the elegant **San Remo** *(145 Central Park West)*, with its stunning Central Park views. These sumptuous digs appealed to bankers, lawyers and other well-to-do professionals, who were followed in the 1930s by prosperous Jewish families relocating from the Lower East Side. Gentrification of the older row houses has made the cross streets desirable, particularly among young professionals and college students. Today the Upper West Side's tree-lined residential blocks provide a quiet contrast to the bustle of Broadway, the area's commercial spine.

Zabar's Delicatessen

© Martha Cooper

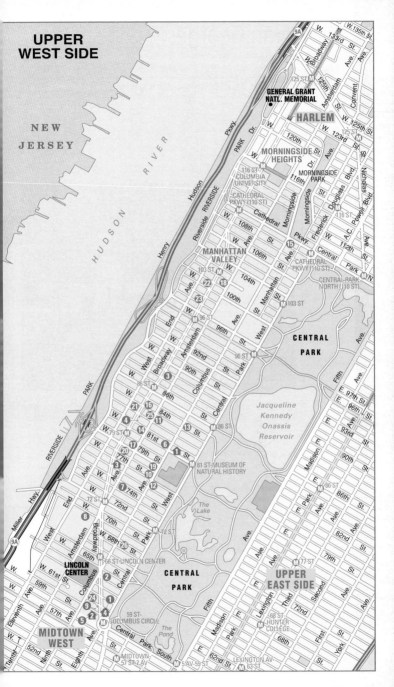

Jean Georges ✿✿✿

Contemporary 🍴🍴🍴🍴

001

1 Central Park West (bet. 60th & 61st Sts.)

Subway:	59 St - Columbus Circle
Phone:	212-299-3900
Fax:	212-299-3914
Web:	www.jean-georges.com
Prices:	$$$$

Mon – Fri noon - 2:30pm
& 5:30pm - 11pm
Sat 5:30pm - 11pm
Closed Sun

Jean-Georges Management

Jean-Georges Vongerichten owns a veritable galaxy of restaurants in New York City, but this one shines above the others. Premiering in 1997 on the ground floor of the Trump International Hotel, Jean-Georges wraps its space with huge window walls looking out on Columbus Circle. Adam Tihany sculpted the minimalist geometric motif, orchestrating the interior lighting to mimic natural light at different times of the day. Reservations are coveted at this award-winning restaurant consistently populated by a steady stream of notables.

The décor serves as a mere stage set for the main attraction here: the extraordinary cuisine. Unexpected combinations of flavors and textures surprise in the perfectly timed courses; meltingly tender morsels of duck might be topped with crunchy, caramelized almonds, or foie gras brulée sparked by kumquat marmalade and pink peppercorns. The prix-fixe lunch menu tempts diners with roasted squab and slow-baked salmon, while evening brings equally enchanting choices, such as black-trumpet-mushroom-dusted lamb or venison wrapped in cabbage. Whatever the menu, you can count on sublime ingredients transformed by the delicate hand of a master.

Appetizers

Bluefin Tuna Ribbons,
Avocado, Spicy Radish,
Ginger Marinade

Foie Gras Brûlé, Dried
Sour Cherries, Candied
Pistachios

Green Asparagus with
Morels, Asparagus Juice

Entrées

Scottish Cod, Purple-Potato
Fondant and Charred
Poblano

Black Sea Bass Crusted
with Nuts and Seeds,
Sweet and Sour Jus

Duck Breast Topped with
Cracked Jordan Almonds,
Honey Wine Jus

Desserts

Season: A Composition
of Four Different Seasonal
Desserts

Chocolate: A Composition
of Four Different Chocolate
Desserts

Exotic Fruit: A Composition
of Four Different Exotic Fruit
Desserts

Picholine ✿

French 🍴🍴🍴

002

35 W. 64th St. (bet. Broadway & Central Park West)

Subway:	66 St-Lincoln Center	Mon – Wed 5pm - 10pm
Phone:	212-724-8585	Thu – Fri 5pm - 11:45pm
Fax:	212-875-8979	Sat 11:45am - 2pm & 5pm - 11:45pm
Web:	www.artisanalcheese.com	Sun 5pm - 9pm
Prices:	$$$	Closed August

Picholine

Elegant older sister to Artisanal—chef/proprietor Terrance Brennan's Murray Hill brasserie—Picholine pulls in a cadre of smartly dressed regulars who come for Brennan's sophisticated French cuisine. Regulars here seem to have their preferred spot, in either the main dining room or in the smaller, intimate room behind it. The entire space was due for an update in late summer, so expect to see some changes in the fall.

The menu changes eight times a year to feature the best products (squab, pea shoots, blood oranges, Maine lobster) that each season has to offer. Picholine strikes gold with its French-inspired dishes like licorice-lacquered squab, olive-crusted saddle of lamb and wild mushroom and duck risotto. Desserts, such as cheesecake ice-cream sandwiches and pink-peppercorn funnel cake, are irreverently delicious. Don't pass up Picholine's cheese course—it's one of the best in the city. In 2003 Brennan opened his Artisanal Cheese Center, custom-designed with five caves for aging 300 types of cheese.

The restaurant's location close to Lincoln Center means that early evenings here can be frantic; if you're not rushing to catch a show, go later for a quiet dinner.

Appetizers

Warm Maine Lobster, Caramelized Endive, Kumquats and Vanilla Brown Butter

Sea Urchin Panna Cotta, Chilled Ocean Consommé and Osetra Caviar

Sautéed Veal Sweetbreads, Vegetables à la Grecque, and Mustard-Raisin Emulsion

Entrées

Olive-Crusted Saddle of Lamb, Basquaise Chutney, Romesco, and Garlic Chips

Millbrook Venison au Pondicherry Pepper, Parsnip "French Toast," Red-Cabbage Confit and Huckleberries

Roasted John Dory, Grapes, Chanterelles and Truffle Vinaigrette

Desserts

Warm Apple Pavé, Candied Walnuts and Brown-Sugar Ice Cream

Dark-Chocolate Soufflé, Fennel Ice Cream and Pine-Nut Nougatine

Celery Meringue, Peanut Crunch and Raisin Salad

Aix

003

2398 Broadway (at 88th St.)

Subway:	86 St (Broadway)	Mon – Thu 5:30pm - 10:30pm
Phone:	212-874-7400	Fri – Sat 5:30pm - 11pm
Fax:	212-874-7643	Sun 11:30am - 2:30pm
Web:	www.aixnyc.com	& 5:30pm - 9:30pm
Prices:	$$$	

To describe the cooking at Aix as Provençal would send any French culinary traditionalist crying into their copies of *Larousse Gastronomique*. Provençal cuisine is merely the jumping-off point for chef/owner Didier Virot's original, elaborate and playful takes on the dishes of southern France.

House-made pastas and sandwiches (peekytoe crab cake with aïoli and Napa cabbage slaw) share menu space with the likes of parmesan-crusted daurade and thyme-citrus-smoked brisket. Selections from the grill come with your choice of sauce and sides. The brunch menu retains a French accent, often including quiche, crêpes, and Gallic-infused egg dishes to start your Sunday on the right foot.

Ranging over two levels, the dining space reflects the warm orange, red, green and azure hues of Provence.

Artie's Deli

004

2290 Broadway (bet. 82nd & 83rd Sts.)

Subway:	79 St	Open daily 9am - 11pm
Phone:	212-579-5959	
Fax:	212-579-5958	
Web:	www.arties.com	
Prices:		

With its neon sign and no-frills décor, Artie's seems like something straight out of a *Seinfeld* episode. Opened in 1999, the restaurant may not have decades behind it, but it still manages to re-create the authentic feel of a 1930s Jewish deli. What the place lacks in history, it more than makes up for in its bright, shiny décor and helpful service.

All the deli classics are here—house-cured corned beef, handmade hot dogs, pastrami, chicken soup, chopped liver. And if you missed having turkey at grandma's house, Thanksgiving dinner is available here every day. Leave your diet behind and stop by for a sandwich piled high with deli meats and served, of course, with Kosher pickles. If you're hankering for a taste of old New York, Artie's will have you purring with nostalgic contentment.

Asiate

005

Contemporary Asian ✗✗✗

80 Columbus Circle (at 60th St.)

Subway:	59 St - Columbus Circle
Phone:	212-805-8881
Fax:	212-805-8884
Web:	www.mandarinoriental.com
Prices:	$$$$

Mon – Fri noon - 2pm & 5:30 - 10pm
Sat 11:30am - 2:30pm & 5:30pm - 11pm
Sun 11:30am - 2pm & 5:30pm - 8:30pm

Asiate reigns over the city from its 35th-floor aerie in the Mandarin Oriental *(see hotel listings)*. Wrap-around windows showcase breathtaking views of Central Park, making Asiate a top spot for view seekers. Thanks to designer Tony Chi, the dining room has a modern feel, capped off by a ceiling of transparent tubes representing stylized tree branches. Two walls by the entrance hold more than 1,300 bottles of wine.

Chef Noriyuki Sugie fashions adventurous cuisine with an exotic, yet approachable allure. A native of Japan who has cooked in kitchens all over the world, Sugie plates up courses such as black sea bass in broth infused with ginger and Thai basil, and roasted poussin with ginger-scallion chutney. Discreet servers cater equally well to business people, hotel guests and tourists.

Calle Ocho

006

Latin American ✗✗

446 Columbus Ave. (bet. 81st & 82nd Sts.)

Subway:	81 St - Museum of Natural History
Phone:	212-873-5025
Fax:	212-873-0216
Web:	www.calleochonyc.com
Prices:	$$

Mon – Thu 6pm - 11pm
Fri 6pm - midnight
Sat 5pm - midnight
Sun 11:30am - 3pm & 5pm - 10pm

Looking for good food and fun? You've come to the right place. Calle Ocho pulls in the partyers with its winning mix of pulsating salsa music, potent caipirinhas and mojitos, and zesty food—all borrowing influences from Argentina to Puerto Rico and from Cuba to Peru. Named for the bustling main drag in Miami's Little Havana neighborhood, Calle Ocho (Spanish for "Eighth Street") is always jumping, no matter which night you go.

The 200-seat dining room sets the tone for a good time with the vivid Cuban-themed mural that lines one wall, and the bold cuisine follows suit by balancing such ingredients as chipotle chiles, calabaza, yucca and plantains. Your taste buds will salsa after enjoying dishes like jerk pork chop, banana-leaf-wrapped snapper and panela-glazed salmon.

'Cesca

007

164 W. 75th St. (at Amsterdam Ave.)

Subway:	72 St (Broadway)
Phone:	212-787-6300
Fax:	212-787-1081
Web:	www.cescanyc.com
Prices:	$$$

Mon – Thu 5pm - 10:30pm
Fri – Sat 5pm - 11:30pm
Sun 5pm - 9:30pm
Closed major holidays

Bright and bold, 'Cesca is another venture by Godfrey Polistina, who enlivened the Upper West Side with this restaurant and its French sister, Ouest. ('Cesca is short for Francesca, Godfrey Polistina's daughter.)

Brown velvet covers the chairs and banquettes in the attractive dining room, with its custom-made iron chandeliers and stenciled ivory walls. Set daily specials complement the menu of modernized Italian dishes; on Sunday, 'Cesca features "Sunday Sauce," just like your *nonna* used to make. Items on the *per la tavola* (for the table) selection are ideal for munching while you sip that first glass of wine. Although the wine list does include a few American bottles, the focus is on Italian varietals, with many of Italy's wine-producing regions represented.

Compass

008

208 W. 70th St. (bet. Amsterdam & West End Aves.)

Subway:	72 St (Broadway)
Phone:	212-875-8600
Fax:	212-875-8400
Web:	www.compassrestaurant.com
Prices:	$$

Mon – Thu 5pm - 10pm
Fri – Sat 5pm - 11pm
Sun 11:30am - 2:30pm & 5pm - 9pm

Head north-northwest from Midtown and point yourself in the direction of the Upper West Side and the sophisticated surroundings of Compass and its popular bar. Slate-covered square pillars, marble floors, bright-red high-backed banquettes and vibrant, modern artwork combine with subtle, recessed lighting to create a décor that is at once confident and cool.

You can choose one of the chef's "Compositions" (think lamb with coco beans and piquillo peppers or buffalo with a ginger béarnaise) or order from the list of "Simply Roasted" entrées and pick your own side dish. Choose from two appetizers, three entrées and two desserts on the prix-fixe menu. The impressive wine collection, stored behind frosted glass, is well worth investigating.

Manhattan Upper West Side

Gabriel's

009

11 W. 60th St. (bet. Broadway & Columbus Ave.)

Subway:	59 St - Columbus Circle	Mon – Thu noon - 3pm & 5pm - 11pm
Phone:	212-956-4600	Fri noon - 3pm & 5pm - midnight
Fax:	212-956-2309	Sat 5pm - midnight
Web:	www.gabrielsbarandrest.com	Closed Sun
Prices:	$$$	

Despite this restaurant's enviable location opposite the Time Warner Center and near Lincoln Center, Gabriel's is much more than just a convenient place to catch a bite before the opera or after a day of shopping. Gabriel Aiello founded his eponymous eatery in 1991, and since then he has overseen every aspect of its management. Soft yellow and terra-cotta tones warm the dining room walls, which are brightened by vibrant paintings.

Against this sunny background, a crowd of locals, media moguls and celebrities enjoy everything from tagliatelle to wood-grilled trout to slow-roasted baby goat. Warm chocolate truffle cake, Italian-style rice pudding and fresh peach pie are among the dessert selections. A number of different wines are available by the glass.

Gari

010

370 Columbus Ave. (bet. 77th & 78th Sts.)

Subway:	81 St - Museum of Natural History	Mon – Thu 5pm - 11pm
Phone:	212-362-4816	Fri – Sat 5pm - 11:30pm
Fax:	N/A	Sun 5pm - 10pm
Web:	N/A	
Prices:	$$$	

As of January 2005, Upper West Side residents no longer need to taxi through the park to enjoy Masatoshi Sugio's trademark omakase. Gari, the better-dressed sister of Sushi of Gari (402 E. 78th St.), features a number of unique combinations from the sushi bar. At the chef's whim, raw salmon might be topped by grilled tomato or fatty tuna served with creamy tofu sauce. In addition to contemporary sushi and a traditional Japanese menu, there are also offerings like pan-roasted beef short ribs with yucca fries, or sea bass with sake-infused black beans. But to miss out on Gari's signature sushi is, after all, to miss the point.

The plain room has a convivial atmosphere, complemented by communal seating alongside, rather than facing, the sushi bar.

Good Enough to Eat

American ⚒

011

483 Amsterdam Ave. (bet. 83rd & 84th Sts.)

Subway: 79 St
Phone: 212-496-0163
Fax: 212-496-7340
Web: www.goodenoughtoeat.com
Prices: $$

Mon – Fri 8am - 10:30pm
Sat 9am - 11pm
Sun 9am - 10:30pm

Comfort food, home cooking: call it what you want, it still means food like Mom used to make. During the day, this cute little place is known for its bountiful breakfasts (they serve light lunches, too). At night it morphs into a cozy, full-service restaurant serving up ample portions of perennial favorites—meatloaf, pumpkin pie and turkey dinner with all the trimmings. When you're tired of trendy, this place hits the spot with its good old American cooking.

Sweet-natured servers deliver your order in a scene out of a Norman Rockwell painting, complete with folk art, quilts and antiques; there's even a white picket fence outside. The case of homemade cakes may remind you so much of home that, after a meal here, you'll be tempted to ask chef/owner Carrie Levin to adopt you.

Isabella's

Mediterranean ⚒⚒

012

359 Columbus Ave. (at 77th St.)

Subway: 79 St
Phone: 212-724-2100
Fax: 212-724-1156
Web: www.brguestrestaurants.com
Prices: $$

Mon 11:30am - 11:30pm
Tue – Thu 11:30am - midnight
Fri 11:30am - 1am
Sat 11am - 1am
Sun 10am - 11:30pm

A member of the B.R. Guest restaurant group (another one, Ocean Grill, sits across the street), Isabella's boasts a genuine neighborhood feel. It should—the restaurant has been attracting a loyal following on the West Side for more than fifteen years. One of the few places that's open for lunch in this part of town, Isabella's makes a great spot to take a break if you're touring the nearby Museum of Natural History. In summer, the airy bi-level dining space with its wicker chairs and French doors adds a pleasant outdoor terrace.

The menu is Mediterranean in tone, offering dishes like skewered chicken, pastas and assorted fish. Drop by Sunday for the popular, and delicious, brunch, or have a late lunch or early dinner daily from the sunset menu (served from 4pm to 5:30pm).

Jean-Luc

013

507 Columbus Ave. (bet. 84th & 85th Sts.)

Subway: 86 St (Central Park West)
Phone: 212-712-1700
Fax: N/A
Web: www.jeanlucrestaurant.com
Prices: $$

Mon – Fri 5:30pm - 11:30pm
Sat – Sun 11:30am - 3:30pm
& 5:30pm - 11:30pm

Jean-Luc provides West Siders with a stylish French bistro, done up in white tiles, red-velvet banquettes and Art Deco-inspired mirrors. For those who require a little more in the way of creature comforts, the raised dining section at the back of the restaurant is more formal and subdued.

Wherever you sit, you'll have access to the same menu, and it's one that showcases bistro staples as well as dishes of less Gallic persuasion (lobster and vegetable spring roll, pumpkin gnocchi)—all of which share the same degree of careful preparation. You can even order a little sushi before your coq au vin, or enjoy a salad or sandwich for dinner.

If you're headed to the Hamptons for the weekend, stop by one of Jean-Luc's two outposts—called JLX & Jean-Luc East—on Long Island.

Land Thai Kitchen

014

450 Amsterdam Ave. (bet. 81st & 82nd Sts.)

Subway: 79 St
Phone: 212-501-8121
Fax: 212-501-8123
Web: www.landthaikitchen.com
Prices: ⊜⊜

Mon – Thu noon - 10:30pm
Fri – Sat noon - 11pm
Sun noon - 10pm

Upper West Siders have taken quickly to this newcomer, which opened in early 2005. With seats for just thirty people, Land Thai Kitchen makes the most of its limited space, decorated with exposed brick on one wall, and on the other, a colorful fabric panel that diffuses the light behind it.

Executive chef and owner David Bank, who was born in Bangkok, creates high-quality Thai dishes that are just spicy enough for most palates. If you prefer your food with more of a kick, try one of the dishes indicated with an asterisk on the menu. The chef's specials include pan-seared duck breast and crispy, boneless, whole red snapper, both served with fragrant jasmine rice. The two-course prix-fixe lunch menu offered at just $8 is an unbelievably tasty bargain.

Miss Mamie's Spoonbread Too

015

366 W. 110th St./Cathedral Pkwy.
(bet. Columbus & Manhattan Aves.)

Subway:	Cathedral Pkwy (110 St)	Mon – Sat noon - 10:30pm
Phone:	212-865-6744	Sun 11am - 9pm
Fax:	212-865-0854	
Web:	www.spoonbreadinc.com	
Prices:	💳	

Columbia students in search of Southern-style cooking count on Miss Mamie's for finger-licking-good vittles. A country-diner décor highlighted by yellow Formica tables, yellow and red checkered floors, and vintage kitchen utensils takes guests back to the 1950s.

Southern fried chicken is a stand-out, its glistening, juicy meat covered in a crispy deep-fried coating, but don't overlook the daily specials posted on the blackboard. Side dishes include Dixie favorites like black-eyed peas and collard greens. Of course, you can't leave Miss Mamie's without a taste of the decadent red velvet cake slathered in white cream frosting—or a cup of dark, cinnamon-scented coffee, one of the best deals in town at only $1.

Check out Harlem sister, Miss Maude's, at 547 Lenox Avenue.

Nëo Sushi

016

2298 Broadway (at 83rd St.)

Subway:	86 St (Broadway)	Mon – Thu 5pm - 11:30pm
Phone:	212-769-1003	Fri – Sat 5pm - 12:30am
Fax:	212-769-1005	Sun 4pm - 10:30pm
Web:	www.neosushi.com	
Prices:	$$	

When you've finished checking out the photos of various celebrities who have dined here (which are displayed along with the menu on the outside of the restaurant's windows), step inside this minimally decorated space, lit by teardrop-shaped lanterns, and discover Japanese food for the New Age.

Modern takes on Japanese cuisine are organized according to "Nëo Fusion" sushi, and dishes "From the Kitchen." Whatever you order, don't expect to find soy sauce on the table; delicate and subtly flavored fare comes fully seasoned. You can't go wrong with one of the signature dishes, which include lobster mango salad, baby shrimp tempura bites, tuna tataki with garlic sauce and fluke with ponzu sauce. Can't decide? Leave it up to Nëo, and surrender to one of the multicourse tasting menus.

Nice Matin

017

201 W. 79th St. (at Amsterdam Ave.)

Subway: 79 St
Phone: 212-873-6423
Fax: 212-873-1832
Web: www.nicematinnyc.com
Prices: $$

Open daily 7am - midnight

Named after the daily newspaper published in the major city on France's Côte d'Azur, Nice Matin transports diners to the sun-drenched Mediterranean coast.

Niçoise dishes here exhibit as many vibrant colors as appear in the room's luminous décor. Done up as a French cafe, the place asserts its unique personality by avoiding all the decorative clichés you find in many faux-Gallic restaurants; lights dangle from the tops of high pillars that spread, umbrella-like, against the ceiling, and tables sport Formica tops.

The menu, like a tanned French lothario, is not just confined to the Riviera, but wanders the wider Mediterranean region for its inspiration. *Plats du jour* (*moules Provençal* on Monday, old-fashioned roast duck on Saturday) bring fans in on specific days of the week.

Noche Mexicana

018

852 Amsterdam Ave. (bet. 101st & 102nd Sts.)

Subway: 103 St (Broadway)
Phone: 212-662-6900
Fax: N/A
Web: N/A
Prices: 💰

Sun – Thu 10am - 11pm
Fri – Sat 10am - midnight

Tucked in between small restaurants and bodegas, Noche Mexicana is a great find. Bright and cheery, the restaurant's walls are papered with posters of artwork by Diego Rivera.

The dining room is small, but authentic Mexican food is the real focus here, where an engaging staff with a warm spirit attends to guests. The *taco de lengua* may be messy, but the tender, tasty beef tongue dressed with cilantro, onions and tomatoes, and wrapped in corn tortillas, is worth the laundry bill. You won't go wrong with the great tamales, tingas or the *taco cesina* (filled with preserved beef). If you like your food *caliente*, make sure to request it spicy.

Grab a seat in the back of the restaurant, where you can watch those delicious tamales being made.

Ocean Grill

Seafood XXX

019

384 Columbus Ave. (bet. 78th & 79th Sts.)

Subway:	79 St	Mon – Sat noon - midnight
Phone:	212-579-2300	Sun 10:30am - midnight
Fax:	212-579-0409	
Web:	www.brguestrestaurants.com	
Prices:	$$	

Set sail for a culinary adventure. Right across the street from the Museum of Natural History, Ocean Grill is one of the fleet of restaurants owned by the B.R. Guest group. You'll think you've just boarded an elegant ocean liner when you set foot inside the elegant room, bedecked with black-and-white photographs of the seashore and porthole windows peeking in on the kitchen.

You'll find something for every fish lover here, whether it's a plate of oysters from the raw bar, simply grilled fish, Maine lobster or the house maki rolls. And be sure to sample one of the scrumptious desserts. The "sunset menu" of light fare is served weekdays from 4pm to 5pm. Egg dishes, pancakes and French toast compete with crab cakes and caviar at the popular weekend brunch.

Onera

Contemporary Greek XX

020

222 W. 79th St. (bet. Amsterdam Ave. & Broadway)

Subway:	79 St	Sun – Thu 5pm - 10pm
Phone:	212-873-0200	Fri – Sat 5pm - 11pm
Fax:	212-873-6985	Closed Sun in Summer
Web:	www.oneranyc.com	
Prices:	$$	

Set on the bottom floor of a brownstone, Onera adds a bright note to the Upper West dining scene with its vivid blue walls and sparkling white paneling. Who cares that the tables are close together and competing conversations can create quite a din—you came here for the food, right?

In that regard you won't be disappointed, starting with the baguette brought to your table with roasted red pepper, kalamata olive, and chickpea spreads. From there, you'll have to choose among delectable fare like chilled roasted octopus salad, manti "reinvented" with bone marrow and chestnut-stuffed ravioli, and an "open" mousaka made with braised goat.

The bar is a nice spot for a pre- or post-dinner drink. Order a white wine from Santorini, sit back, and dream of sun-drenched afternoons in the islands.

Ouest

021

2315 Broadway (bet. 83rd & 84th Sts.)

Subway:	86 St (Broadway)
Phone:	212-580-8700
Fax:	212-580-1360
Web:	www.ouestny.com
Prices:	$$$

Mon – Thu 5pm - 11pm
Fri – Sat 5pm - midnight
Sun 11am - 2pm & 5pm - 10pm

If you find yourself Uptown, head *Ouest* (west) to discover this polished restaurant from chef Tom Valenti. Keep going past the perennially busy bar until you reach the large room at the back, which peers into the open kitchen. Bring some friends so you'll be more likely to snag one of the terrific circular booths covered in deep-red tufted leather. Low lighting makes this a romantic spot for dinner, or liven up your weekend with green-apple martinis and poached eggs with duck at brunch.

Behind the stoves, a veritable army of chefs riffs on American classics, resulting in dishes, such as skate with Yukon potato purée, celery and caperberries, which are high on originality and strong on presentation. Many bottles on the ample, well-balanced wine list are attractively priced.

PicNic Market & Café

022

2665 Broadway (bet. 101st & 102nd Sts.)

Subway:	103 St (Broadway)
Phone:	212-228-8222
Fax:	N/A
Web:	www.picnicmarket.com
Prices:	$$

Open daily 11:30am - 4pm & 6pm - 11pm

Close to Columbia University and Riverside Drive, this cafe grew out of a picnic-basket business that catered to Central Park concertgoers. Fans can now enjoy heartier meals in the pleasant, pea-green room, decorated with a colorful mural by Peter Marks. Daily specials augment the short menu of main courses such as coq au vin, steak au poivre, and pan-fried trout. Salmon tartare with ginger vinaigrette, and crostini topped with plump pieces of calamari make good places to start.

Everyone from Columbia professors to Upper West Side families gathers here, and the neighborhood regulars are chummy with the chef and the waitstaff. Charcuterie, cheese, and salad plates are still available to go, as are the oils, vinegars, coffees and teas displayed on shelves alongside the bar area.

Manhattan Upper West Side

Regional

023

Italian 🍴

2607 Broadway (bet. 98th & 99th Sts.)

Subway:	96 St (Broadway)
Phone:	212-666-1915
Fax:	N/A
Web:	N/A
Prices:	$$

Mon – Wed 5pm - 11pm
Thu – Fri 5pm - 11:30pm
Sat noon - 3pm & 5pm - 11:30pm
Sun noon - 3pm & 5pm - 10:30pm

The area above 96th Street is seeing more and more small, independent restaurants opening these days, and Regional makes a noteworthy addition to this artsy, academia-oriented neighborhood.

In keeping with its name, the restaurant spotlights specialties from all 20 regions of Italy. Recipes stay true to their geographical origins here, with honest fare like *involtini di vitello* (two scaloppini of veal stuffed with parmesan and Italian pork sausage) and *pasta al pesto di Trapani* (tossed with fresh tomatoes and a pesto made from almonds and basil) representing the best of each area.

Made in-house, desserts like the wonderful *torta di Capri* (an ultra-rich and moist flourless chocolate cake covered with molten chocolate sauce), are worth abandoning your diet for.

Sapphire

024

Indian 🍴

1845 Broadway (bet. 60th & 61st Sts.)

Subway:	59 St - Columbus Circle
Phone:	212-245-4444
Fax:	212-245-9145
Web:	www.sapphireny.com
Prices:	$$

Open daily noon - 3pm & 5pm - 10:30pm

Sapphire's location near Lincoln Center and the Time Warner Building assures it of having a lively crowd of notables, residents and shoppers from this busy neighborhood. Location aside, Sapphire serves satisfying Indian food in an upscale décor enriched by elaborately carved wood panels and embroidered silk panels that drape from the ceiling.

Recalling dishes from different regions of India, the food ranges from curries and kebabs to Tandoori specialties. Unusual appetizers include the delicately spiced chutney *idli* (steamed lentil cakes topped with coconut curry). Come for the delicious lunch buffet, where you can sample everything from tikka masala to tandoori dishes.

Even when they're busy, the helpful waiters are willing to take time to guide novices through the extensive menu.

Manhattan Upper West Side

Spiga

025

200 W. 84th St. (bet. Amsterdam Ave. & Broadway)

Subway:	86 St (Broadway)	Open daily 5:30pm - 11:30pm
Phone:	212-362-5506	
Fax:	N/A	
Web:	www.spiganyc.com	
Prices:	$$$	

Tucked away on a quiet Upper West Side block, this delightful restaurant feels like a well-kept secret with its satisfying food, tables nestling in every available nook, and a gracious owner who warmly welcomes each diner. The petit and peaceful dining room lies in stark contrast to the bustling vibe created by the kitchen.

The chef seduces diners with his original takes on Italian favorites. Lasagna, for example, is inventively retooled as squares of fresh pasta lined with sautéed wild mushrooms, gorgonzola cheese and truffle oil, while fennel salad appears as a rustic plate on which the licorice taste of fennel, the sweetness of oranges and the saltiness of black olives play off each other.

The short, Italian-focused wine list cites excellent offerings by the glass.

Telepan

026

72 W. 69th St. (bet. Central Park West & Columbus Ave.)

Subway:	66 St - Lincoln Center	Mon – Tue 5pm - 11pm
Phone:	212-580-4300	Wed – Thu 11:30am - 2:30pm & 5pm - 11pm
Fax:	212-580-4379	Fri 11:30am - 2:30pm & 5pm - 11:30pm
Web:	www.telepan-ny.com	Sat 11am - 2:30pm & 5pm - 11:30pm
Prices:	$$$	Sun 11am - 2:30pm & 5pm - 10:30pm

From décor to dishes, Telepan shows off all that is modern American. Located in an elegant town house, this newcomer is the culinary child of chef Bill Telepan, formerly of Midtown's JUdson Grill. Grass-green walls hung with small paintings and large-format photography set a simple tone for the dining room, where lack of space between the tables leaves little room for privacy.

Contemporary American cooking here has generated well-deserved interest. The menu spotlights the seasons with farm-fresh ingredients, made with little fuss and lots of flavor. The list of American wines, including some from Long Island, is extensive. Although the staff's attitude matches the cool ambience, fans line up at Telepan, glad to have a quality dining spot in this gastronomically barren neighborhood.

Manhattan Upper West Side

Washington Heights

Manhattan's northernmost neighborhood, Washington Heights reaches from West 145th Street to West 218th Street. This narrow neck of land is rimmed by water, the Hudson River on the west and the Harlem River on the east.

Attracted by the comparatively low rents and spacious apartments, young urban professionals are slowly adding to the ethnic mix in this neighborhood, thanks to a recent real-estate boom. The northwestern section of Washington Heights is dominated by the green spaces of Fort Tryon and Inwood Hill parks. Fort Tryon, the highest natural point in Manhattan, is home to the **Cloisters**. The main draw for visitors to this area, the re-created 12th-century monastery belongs to the Metropolitan Museum of Art and is fabled for its collection of medieval artifacts, including the 16th-century Unicorn tapestries.

Although you wouldn't necessarily think of Washington Heights as a dining destination, while you're visiting the Cloisters there are a few good restaurants to sample in this pleasant quarter.

A Bit of History – Wealthy New Yorkers sought rural sanctuaries near the water here in the late 18th and 19th centuries. One of these, the 130-acre estate where George Washington planned the battle of Harlem Heights in 1776, welcomes the public as the **Morris-Jumel Mansion** *(160th St. & Edgecombe Ave.)*. Lining the mansion's original cobblestone carriage drive, now called **Sylvan Terrace**, you can see some of the city's few remaining wood-frame houses.

Washington Heights and George Washington Bridge

© Martha Cooper

By the turn of the 20th century, the neighborhood was populated primarily by working-class Greek and Irish immigrants, followed by German Jews fleeing Nazi persecution in the late 1930s and 40s. Cubans and Puerto Ricans began to move to the neighborhood in the 50s, and a large influx of residents immigrated from the Dominican Republic in the late 70s. African-American luminaries such as jazz great Duke Ellington, Supreme Court Justice Thurgood Marshall, and historian W.E.B. Dubois, co-founder of the NAACP, all lived in this area at one time.

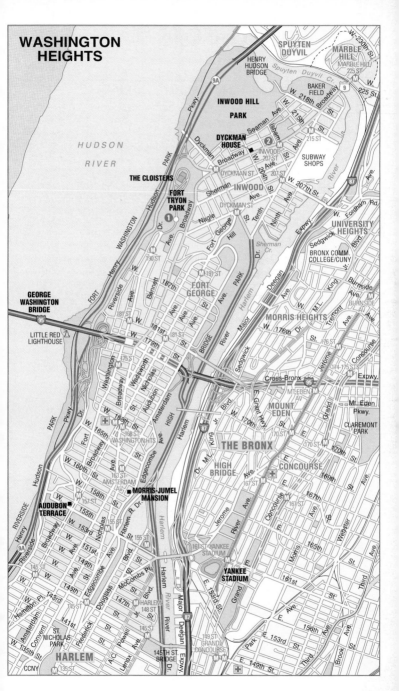

WASHINGTON HEIGHTS

SPUYTEN DUYVIL

MARBLE HILL

HENRY HUDSON BRIDGE

BAKER FIELD

INWOOD HILL PARK

SUBWAY SHOPS

DYCKMAN HOUSE

HUDSON RIVER

INWOOD

THE CLOISTERS

FORT TRYON PARK

UNIVERSITY HEIGHTS

BRONX COMM. COLLEGE/CUNY

FORT GEORGE

BURNSIDE

MORRIS HEIGHTS

GEORGE WASHINGTON BRIDGE

LITTLE RED LIGHTHOUSE

WASHINGTON HTS

Cross-Bronx Expwy.

MOUNT EDEN

CLAREMONT PARK

THE BRONX

HIGH BRIDGE

CONCOURSE

MORRIS-JUMEL MANSION

AUDUBON TERRACE

YANKEE STADIUM

HARLEM

CCNY

ST. NICHOLAS PARK

New Leaf Café

American ✗

001

1 Margaret Corbin Dr. (Fort Tryon Park)

Subway:	190 St
Phone:	212-568-5323
Fax:	212-923-3222
Web:	www.nyrp.org/newleaf
Prices:	$$

Tue – Sat noon - 3pm & 6pm - 10pm
Sun 11am - 4pm & 5pm - 9:30pm
Closed Mon

There are few better places to be on a summer's day than on the sunny terrace of this adorable little place in Fort Tryon Park. Housed in a 1930s-era stone building a few minutes walk from the Cloisters, the cafe offers a cozy getaway with arched windows overlooking the park. If the sun is shining, this place fills up fast at lunch, so be sure to make reservations. Otherwise, go for dinner and enjoy the luxury of on-site parking. Live jazz entertains diners on Thursdays.

At lunch the menu offers salads and sandwiches, while at dinner the kitchen shows off its more creative instincts, offering everything from fried rock shrimp and beef carpaccio to pan-roasted salmon and handmade pappardelle. Order freely, as all proceeds from the cafe go toward the upkeep of the historic park.

Park Terrace Bistro

Moroccan ✗

002

4959 Broadway (bet. 207th & Isham Sts.)

Subway:	Inwood - 207 St
Phone:	212-567-2828
Fax:	N/A
Web:	www.parkterracebistro.com
Prices:	$$

Tue – Thu 5pm - 10:30pm
Fri – Sat 5pm - 11pm
Sun 5pm - 10pm
Closed Mon

A slice of Morocco in Washington Heights, this sweet bistro sits just a couple of blocks east of Inwood Hill Park. Inside they've captured the essence of the Casbah with red and terra-cotta washed walls, paintings depicting Moroccan life, and an assortment of colorful glass lamps.

The cuisine of North Africa is celebrated here; traditional tagines are served with your choice of fish, chicken or lamb, or opt for a taste of history with the Fifteenth-Century couscous, a combination of seafood, almonds, apricots and cranberries in a light saffron cream sauce. French-influenced dishes include filet mignon and grilled pork chops. The Casablanca-born owner, Karim Bouskou, and his wife, Natalie Weiss, promote a convivial atmosphere, aided by the delightful waitstaff.

EVERYTHING YOU GET FROM MICHELIN TIRES NOW
IN A NEW RANGE OF AUTOMOTIVE ACCESSORIES.

TAKE THEM FOR A TEST DRIVE TODAY.

For over a hundred years, Michelin has developed products and services to make life on the road safer, more efficient and more enjoyable. And now Michelin offers an innovative collection of automotive accessories which epitomize its long-standing values of performance, dependability and safety. The collection includes inflation and pressure monitoring products, air compressors and air tools, emergency/breakdown assistance products, wiper blades, wheel and tire change equipment, wheel and tire care products, pressure washers, floor mats and air fresheners. **The** Michelin Automotive Accessories Collection is on the road right now.

The Bronx

New York Botanical Garden

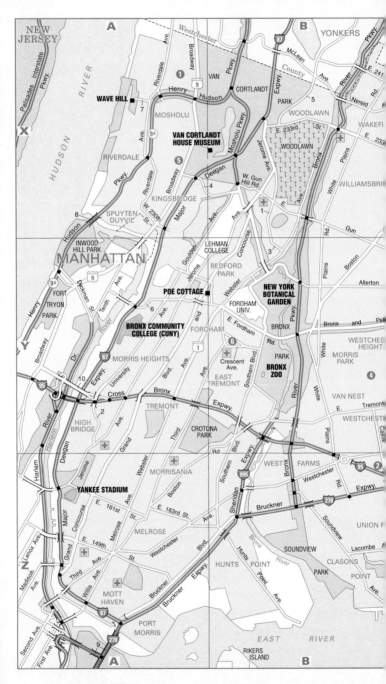

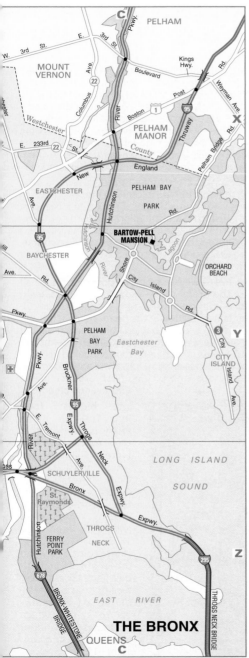

Allerton Ave.	BCY
Bainbridge Ave.	1 BX
Baychester Ave.	CX
Boston Rd.	AZCX
Broadway	AX
Bronx and Pelham Pkwy.	BCY
Bronx River Pkwy.	BXZ
Bruckner Blvd.	AZ
Bruckner Expwy.	AZCY
Castle Hill Ave.	BYZ
City Island Ave.	CY
City Island Rd.	CY
Crescent Ave.	BY
Cross Bronx Expwy.	AYCZ
Edw. L. Grant Hwy.	2 AY
E. Gun Hill Rd.	BXCY
E. Fordham Rd.	ABY
E. Tremont Ave.	BYCZ
E. 149th St.	AZ
E. 161st St.	AZ
E. 163rd St.	AZ
E. 204th St.	3 BY
E. 233rd St.	BCX
E. 241st St.	BX
Goulden Ave.	ABXY
Grand Blvd. and Concourse	ABXZ
Henry Hudson Pkwy.	ABXY
Hunts Point Ave.	BZ
Hutchinson River Pkwy.	CXZ
Jerome Ave.	AZBX
Major Deegan Expwy.	AZBX
Melrose Ave.	AZ
Mosholu Pkwy.	BX
Nereid Ave.	BX
New England Thruway	CX
Pelham Bridge Rd.	CX
Riverdale Ave.	AX
Sheridan Expwy.	BZY
Shore Rd.	CXY
Soundview Ave.	BZ
Southern Blvd.	BYZ
Third Ave.	ABYZ
Throgs Neck Expwy.	CYZ
University Ave.	AY
Van Cortlandt Park South	4 ABX
Van Cortlandt Park East	5 BX
Webster Ave.	ABXZ
Westchester Ave.	AZCY
W. Fordham Rd.	6 AY
W. 230th St.	AX
W. 252nd St.	7 AX
W. Gun Hill Rd.	BX
White Plains Rd.	BXZ
Willis Ave.	AZ

BRIDGES

Bronx-Whitestone Bridge	CZ
Henry Hudson Bridge	8 AX
Throgs Neck Bridge	CZ
Triborough Bridge	9 AZ
Washington Bridge	10 AY

The Bronx

The only borough attached to the mainland, the Bronx is marked by contrasts. Run-down apartment buildings and massive housing projects characterize the southern part of the borough, although, in recent years, funds have been allocated to make the area more livable. To the north, grand mansions and lush gardens fill prosperous sections such as Riverdale and Fieldston. Thanks to journalist John Mullaly, who led a movement in the late 1800s to buy inexpensive parcels of land and preserve them as parks, 25 percent of the Bronx today consists of parkland.

A Bit of History – Named after Jonas Bronck, a Swede who settled here in 1639, the borough developed in the late 1800s. In 1904, the first subway line connecting the Bronx to the island of Manhattan opened, causing significant migration to this outlying borough. Grand Art Deco apartment buildings sprang up along the wide tree-lined thoroughfare called the **Grand Concourse**, attracting Jews from Eastern and Central Europe; many of their descendents remain here to this day.

A Modern Melting Pot – Hispanics make up more than half of the population of the Bronx today. African-Americans, Irish-Americans, West Indies immigrants and others round out the cultural stew. A host of Italians settled in the Belmont area, though now they share their streets with Albanian immigrants. Located near the **Bronx Zoo** and **New York Botanical Gardens**, Belmont's main street, **Arthur Avenue**, lures diners from all over town, who come to eat authentic Italian fare, shop for salami and provolone at their favorite food shops, and pick up fresh produce in the mid-avenue arcade.

Along Arthur Avenue

© Martha Cooper

The biggest food news in the Bronx today is the fact that New York's venerable **Fulton Fish Market**, where most of the city's restaurateurs purchase their finny fare, has moved from Lower Manhattan (where it's been since 1869) to new digs in Hunts Point. Spanning the length of four football fields, the market facility boasts a state-of-the-art climate-control system, which maintains the indoor temperature at a constant 41°F.

The Bronx

Beccofino

001

Italian ✕

5704 Mosholu Ave. (at Fieldston Rd.)

Subway:	231 St (& bus BX7)	Open daily 5pm - 11pm
Phone:	718-432-2604	
Fax:	N/A	
Web:	N/A	
Prices:	$$	

Beccofino is a charming newcomer to the Riverdale section of the Bronx. Located on a quiet tree-lined street, Beccofino, with its quality Italian food and warm service, fits perfectly in the residential neighborhood.

There are less than 20 tables in this intimate restaurant, where exposed brick walls, terra-cotta floors and soft lighting add to the appealing rustic ambience. Locals and regulars cram this place for generous portions of tasty Italian creations like fettuccine topped with fresh peas, prosciutto and tomato in a cream sauce, and tender veal Forestier. Lemony ricotta cheesecake makes a perfect end to any meal here.

Beccofino doesn't accept reservations, but it charms customers with its friendly service, which makes even first-time visitors feel like regulars.

Brisas Del Caribe

002

Puerto-Rican ✕

1207 Castle Hill Ave. (bet. Ellis & Gleason Aves.)

Subway:	Castle Hill Av	Open daily 8am - 11:30pm
Phone:	718-794-9710	
Fax:	N/A	
Web:	N/A	
Prices:	⌾⌾	

Brisas Del Caribe delivers a good bang for the buck. This large and lively restaurant in a vibrant Latin neighborhood in the Bronx is always full with people waiting for tables (the restaurant doesn't take reservations) or grabbing take-out orders. While you're waiting, review the menu, posted on a large board above the counter.

Come armed with a big appetite to tackle huge portions of delicious Latin- and Caribbean-influenced food like *mofongo de cerdo*, a mashed plantain and pork dish that is accompanied by *pastel*, a smooth masa of cassava steamed in banana leaves.

It helps to know the language when dealing with the mostly Spanish-speaking staff, but their generous spirit will make anyone feel welcome. Brisas Del Caribe draws from all walks of life—you'll find everyone from bikers to babies here.

Le Refuge Inn

003

586 City Island Ave. (bet. Bridge & Cross Sts.)

Subway:	Pelham Bay Park (& bus BX29)	Tue – Sun 6pm - 10pm
Phone:	718-885-2478	Closed Mon
Fax:	718-885-3363	
Web:	www.lerefugeinn.com	
Prices:	$$	

City Island, an oasis of marinas, yacht clubs, fried-seafood restaurants and Victorian homes, forms the setting for Le Refuge. The inn, which overlooks the harbor, occupies a lovely white French Empire-style house, built for wealthy oysterman Samuel Pell c.1876.

While Le Refuge operates as a bed-and-breakfast inn, its charming restaurant is open to the public (lunch and brunch are served by reservation only). Several different rooms downstairs accommodate diners in Victorian style with antiques, crystal chandeliers, wood parquet floors and classic window treatments. On the plate, chef/owner Pierre Saint-Denis proffers a taste of France, from *mousse de foie gras* to *canard à l'orange*. All menus are prix-fixe, but modestly priced.

Upstairs, seven guestrooms are individually designed with comfort in mind.

Patricia's Pizza & Pasta

004

1080 Morris Park Ave. (bet. Haight & Lurting Aves.)

Subway:	Pelham Pkwy (& bus BX8)	Open daily 11am - 11pm
Phone:	718-409-9069	
Fax:	N/A	
Web:	N/A	
Prices:	🍝	

For a small-town feel in the heart of the Bronx, check out Patricia's Pizza and Pasta. This trattoria is tucked away in an Italian-American section of the Bronx, where neighbors congregate outdoors to catch up on local gossip while kids play baseball in the small playground down the street. Patricia's, with its laid-back style and good home cooking (and no-reservations policy), is a natural addition to this endearing area.

Seating is limited here, where, as the name suggests, pizza and pasta form the focus of the menu. Here you can expect old-fashioned Italian-American comfort food—in enormous quantities with hearty flavors—served by an efficient, no-nonsense waitstaff.

Visit Patricia's Bronx sibling, Nonno Tony's, at 554 West 235th Street.

The Bronx

Riverdale Garden

005

4576 Manhattan College Pkwy.
(bet. Broadway & Waldo Ave.)

Subway:	Van Cortlandt Park - 242 St	Mon 5pm - 11pm
Phone:	718-884-5232	Tue – Fri 11:30am - 2:30pm & 5pm - 11pm
Fax:	N/A	Sat – Sun 10:30am - 2:30pm & 5pm -11pm
Web:	www.theriverdalegarden.com	
Prices:	$$	

Close to Van Cortlandt Park in the Riverdale neighborhood, this restaurant sits on a quiet street adjacent to the subway station. Go on a warm, sunny day, when you can enjoy the lovely garden, filled with greenery, flowers and tile-inlaid tables.

Chef/owner Michael Sherman updates his menu daily, but favors game dishes in season (venison, quail, wild boar); his wife, Lisa, creates the luscious desserts. It's worth leaving Manhattan for entrées like ostrich filet with cheese grits and lime-poached bass with grilled plums. On weekends, the restaurant features "Blunch," the best of breakfast (apple-cranberry-ricotta pancakes, egg-white frittata) along with typical lunch entrées.

And if you just can't be without your laptop, Riverdale Garden offers wireless Internet access.

Roberto's

006

603 Crescent Ave. (at Hughes Ave.)

Subway:	Fordham Rd (Grand Concourse)	Mon – Fri noon - 2:30pm & 5pm - 11pm
Phone:	718-733-9503	Sat 4pm - midnight
Fax:	718-733-2724	Closed Sun
Web:	www.robertobronx.com	
Prices:	$$	

There are no American accents in the southern Italian cuisine at Roberto Paciullo's restaurant near Arthur Avenue, the epicenter for Italian food in the Bronx. This is traditional Italian fare, simply the best you can find in this borough. Many of the excellent house-made pastas, like the tubettini with porcini, are best eaten with a spoon—as the helpful staff will explain—in order to fully appreciate the aroma of the dish and scoop up the rich sauce. From grilled rabbit to veal scalloppine, you'll feel like you have died and gone to an Italian heaven here.

The dining room (which doesn't take reservations) mixes farmhouse tables with elegant chandeliers and a wine wall. And speaking of wine, the list proffers more than 550 labels, most of them ranging over the different regions of Italy.

The Bronx

Brooklyn

Carroll Gardens, Brooklyn

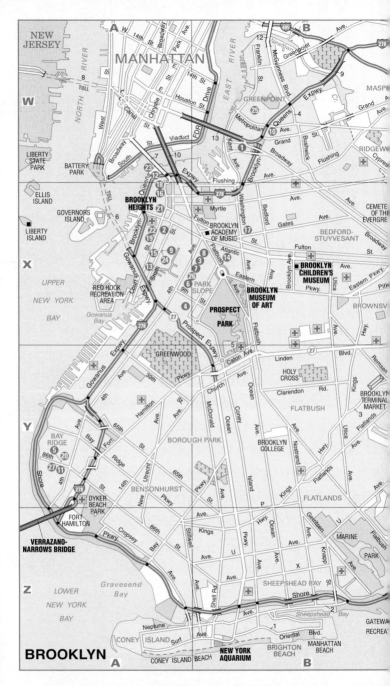

Atlantic Ave.	ACX
Avenue P	BYZ
Avenue U	BZCY
Avenue X	BZ
Bay Pkwy.	AZBY
Bay Ridge Pkwy.	AYZ
Beach Channel Dr.	CZ
Bedford Ave.	BX
Brighton Beach Ave.	**1** BZ
Broadway	BWCX
Brooklyn Ave.	BX
Brooklyn-Queens Expwy.	AXCW
Bushwick Ave.	BWX
Caton Ave.	BY
Church Ave.	BY
Clarendon Rd.	BY
Coney Island Ave.	BYZ
Court St.	AX
Cropsey Ave.	AZ
Eastern Pkwy.	BX
Emmons Ave.	**2** BZ
Flatbush Ave.	BXCZ
Flatlands Ave.	BCY
Flushing Ave.	BXCW
Foster Ave.	**3** BY
Franklin St.	BW
Fort Hamilton Pkwy.	ABY
Fulton St.	ACX
Gates Ave.	BX
Gerritsen Ave.	BZ
Gowanus Expwy.	AXY
Grand Ave.	BW
Grand St.	BW
Greenpoint Ave.	BW
Humboldt St.	**4** BW
Jamaica Ave.	CX
Kent Ave.	BW
Kings Highway	AZBX
Knapp St.	BZ
Linden Blvd.	BYCX
McDonald Ave.	BYZ
McGuinness Blvd.	BW
Metropolitan Ave.	BCW
Myrtle Ave.	AXCW
Neptune Ave.	ABZ
New Utrecht Ave.	AYZ
Nostrand Ave.	BYZ
Ocean Ave.	BYZ
Ocean Pkwy.	BYZ
Oriental Blvd.	BZ
Parkside Ave.	**5** BY
Pennsylvania Ave.	CXY
Pitkin Ave.	BCX
Prospect Expwy.	AXBY
Remsen Ave.	BXCY
Seaview Ave.	CY
Shell Rd.	BZ
Shore Pkwy.	ACYZ
Smith St.	AX
Stillwell Ave.	ABZ
Surf Ave.	ABZ
Utica Ave.	BXY
Washington Ave.	BX
4th Ave.	AYBX
9th St.	ABX
14th Ave.	AYZ
39th St.	AY
65th St.	AYBZ
86th St.	ABZ

BRIDGES

Brooklyn-Battery Tunnel	**6** AX
Brooklyn Bridge	**7** AW
Holland Tunnel	**8** AW
Kosciuszko Bridge	**9** BW
Manhattan Bridge	**10** AW
Marine Parkway Bridge	**11** CZ
Pulaski Bridge	**12** BW
Verrazano-Narrows Bridge	AZ
Williamsburg Bridge	**13** BW

Brooklyn

New York's most populous borough, with 2.5 million residents, Brooklyn sits on the western tip of Long Island. Its landmass extends from the East River to Coney Island and from the Narrows to Jamaica Bay. Although almost half a million Brooklynites commute to Manhattan, the borough retains a distinctive, country-village atmosphere in its eclectic mix of neighborhoods.

A Bit of History – Founded by the Dutch in 1636, the area now called Brooklyn was first christened Breuckelen ("broken land" in Dutch) after a small town near Utrecht. By the time it became part of New York City in 1898, Brooklyn was flourishing as a center of industry and commerce. Its first direct link to Manhattan came in 1883 in the form of the **Brooklyn Bridge**. Then came the Williamsburg Bridge (1903), the Manhattan Bridge (1909), and the first subway, in 1905. The 13,700-foot-long **Verrazano-Narrows Bridge**, completed in 1964, further facilitated travel between Brooklyn and the other boroughs.

A Taste of the Neighborhoods – A close look at Brooklyn reveals a patchwork of neighborhoods. Verdant **Park Slope**, a choice residential community, is the most recent haven for the diaper-and-stroller crowd. Staid **Brooklyn Heights** reigns as a wealthy enclave of narrow, tree-lined streets bordered by historic brownstones. Don't miss a walk along the riverside **Esplanade**, which affords stunning views of Lower Manhattan.

Brooklyn Bridge

Brigitta L. House/MICHELIN

Traditionally an Italian, Hispanic and Hasidic Jewish neighborhood, hipster **Williamsburg** now welcomes an influx of young artists, who have created their own community called DUMBO (Down Under the Manhattan Bridge Overpass). Bedford Avenue is where you'll find hip art galleries, boutiques and cafes. Brooklyn's Little Italy, **Bensonhurst** boasts a proliferation of pizza joints and pasta restaurants.

Brooklyn

© Martha Cooper

Downtown Brooklyn

You can't ignore **Coney Island**. A bit faded since its mid-20th-century heyday, this place still brings crowds to its boardwalk for Coney Island hot dogs—not to mention the wide expanse of beach. Less than a mile east of Coney Island, **Brighton Beach** is a thriving Russian neighborhood; this is where you want to go for authentic blinis and borscht.

Peter Luger ✿

001

178 Broadway (at Driggs Ave.)

Subway:	Marcy Av	Open daily 11:45am – 10:45pm
Phone:	718-387-7400	
Fax:	718-387-3523	
Web:	N/A	
Prices:	$$$	

Brooklyn

Peter Luger

Don't be fooled by the beer-hall ambience; Peter Luger serves some of the best steaks in the country. Famed for its velvety USDA Prime beef, dry-aged on the premises, this Williamsburg institution has been catering to carnivores since 1887. Brooklyn factory-owner Sol Forman purchased the restaurant in the 1940s, after namesake Peter Luger passed away. Today the Forman family hand-selects every cut of meat.

Service can be brusque, but who cares, when you can have steak this good? Sharing is de rigueur, and the menu offers Porterhouse steak for 2, 3 or 4 people (there's a steak for one if you're dining alone). Creamed spinach, served in a crock big enough to feed two people, is a Luger tradition, along with French fries for one or two. Creamy cheesecake with a perfect graham-cracker crust and a generous dollop of Schlag is the way to end your feast. If you can't get that steak out of your mind, order some online for delivery to your door.

On any given day at Luger's, you might rub elbows with local politicians, FDNY cronies, and young couples in from the "island," all of whom come for hearty steakhouse fare that has been satisfying diners generation after generation.

APPETIZERS

Jumbo Shrimp Cocktail

Sizzling Canadian Bacon

Sliced Salad of Tomatoes
and Onions, served with
Peter Luger Steak House
Old-fashioned Sauce

ENTRÉES

Dry-aged, family-selected,
USDA Prime Porterhouse
Steak (for two)

Broiled Lamb Chops

DESSERTS

Cheesecake with
homemade Schlag

Pecan Pie with
homemade Schlag

Holy Cow Sundae with
homemade Schlag

Saul ❀

Contemporary ✗✗

140 Smith St. (bet. Bergen & Dean Sts.)

Subway:	Bergen St	Open daily 5:30pm - 10:30pm
Phone:	718-935-9842	
Fax:	718-532-1399	
Web:	www.saulrestaurant.com	
Prices:	$$$	

Saul/Ellen Wallop

Saul Bolton named his restaurant after himself, and in this case, the vanity is well deserved. The chef honed his skills in the kitchens of no less than Eric Ripert and David Bouley before setting out on his own in Brooklyn's Boerum Hill. The 35-seat dining room, with its exposed brick walls and tin ceiling tiles, is a magnet for the area's cosmopolitan mix of intellectuals, professionals and young families. Though informal in spirit and style, the staff is highly competent and knowledgeable.

Bolton offers top-quality seasonal ingredients sourced from local markets and New England farms. Dishes such as seared day boat scallops with organic polenta, pan-roasted Vermont-raised veal with spring garlic and fava beans, and the signature baked Alaska—served over a dark-chocolate cookie drizzled with caramel sauce—illustrate his considerable prowess in the kitchen. À la carte selections are always a sure bet, but the prix-fixe menu, offered at $30 for two choices per course, is a bargain. Carefully selected wines are featured on the concise, value-conscious list.

Appetizers

Terrine of Hudson Valley Foie Gras Wrapped in Prosciutto studded with Pistachios and served with Quince Jelly

Warm Fall Salad of Grilled Leeks, Roasted Wild Mushrooms, and Haricots Vert with Chaput Bouc Emissaire Cheese and a warm Hazelnut Vinaigrette

Tartare of Japanese Hamachi layered with Avocado Purée, pickled Yellow Beets, Wasabi-infused Flying Fish Roe and Crispy Red Beets

Entrées

Three Corner Fields Farm Lamb Tasting: Braised Shoulder Wrapped in Socca, Homemade Merguez Sausage, Pan-roasted Chop and Liver served with Black Lentils and Curried Spinach

Broken Arrow Ranch Axis Venison with Roasted Porcini Mushrooms, Cardamom-scented Cashew Purée, and Gingered Pear Chutney

Caramelized Maine Diver Scallops with Green Kale braised with Ham Hocks, a Purée of Cannelini Beans, Roasted Hen-of-the-Wood Mushrooms, and a Toasted Pine-Nut, Currant and Preserved-Lemon Vinaigrette

Desserts

Gratin of Valrhona-Araguani Chocolate with Cinnamon-scented Buttercup-Squash Ice Cream and Banyuls Sauce

Three Corner Fields Farm Sheep's-Milk Panna Cotta with Sauterne-soaked Apricots

Rosemary-scented Pine-Nut Tart with Chestnut-Honey Ice Cream

Al Di Lá

003

248 Fifth Ave. (at Carroll St.)

Subway:	Union St	Mon & Wed – Thu 6pm - 10:30pm
Phone:	718-783-4565	Fri 6pm - 11pm
Fax:	718-783-4555	Sat 5:30pm - 11pm
Web:	www.aldilatrattoria.com	Sun 5pm - 10pm
Prices:	$$	Closed Tue

In a world of laminated menus, it's always a joy to find a daily changing bill of fare that actually bears the day's date. At this perennially busy Park Slope trattoria, husband-and-wife team Emiliano Coppa and Anna Klinger offer diners a balanced selection of fresh and seasonal Italian dishes that are both robust in flavor and generous in size. New Yorkers, a breed not often known for their patience, wait quietly just to taste Klinger's risotto.

The high-ceilinged room boasts a certain faded chic, with its church-pew seats and eccentric touches, such as the coffee pots hanging from the walls. If you have questions about the menu, the knowledgeable staff can offer sound advice. Plan to get here early, though, since Al Di Lá's no-reservations policy means it fills up quickly.

Applewood

004

501 11th St. (bet. Seventh & Eighth Aves.)

Subway:	7 Av	Tue – Sat 5pm - 11pm
Phone:	718-768-2044	Sun 10am - 3pm
Fax:	718-768-2032	Closed Mon
Web:	www.applewoodny.com	
Prices:	$$	

Park Slope real-estate agents hoping to convince Manhattanites to make the big move across the river should bring them to Applewood. Set within a turn-of-the-century house, this place is a real neighborhood jewel, where everyone seems to know each other. Experienced duo David and Laura Shea run the restaurant along with help from family and friends.

The pretty dining room is done in shades of lime green, with a bar at one end and a fireplace to warm diners in winter. A changing exhibit of works by local artists gives the place a homespun, funky feel. In the kitchen the best local organic produce, hormone-free meats and wild fish are transformed into main courses, like braised suckling pig, and pan-roasted dayboat cod, that are well-balanced and full of flavor.

Brooklyn

Areo

005

Italian ✗✗

8424 Third Ave. (bet. 84th & 85th Sts.)

Subway:	86 St	Tue – Wed & Sun noon - 10pm
Phone:	718-238-0079	Thu – Sat noon - midnight
Fax:	718-238-1189	Closed Mon
Web:	N/A	
Prices:	$$	

With its large windows and attractive façade, this Bay Ridge Italian eatery packs in diners in the evening, while lunch is a more subdued affair. The bar divides the two dining rooms, which come decorated with dried flowers and Roman-themed wall stencils. Although the tables are well separated, the din at dinnertime rules out any hope of whispered conversation.

Prices seem more Manhattan than Brooklyn, but that doesn't deter the crowds that flock here for their favorite Italian dishes. So settle back and enjoy the complimentary plate of bruschetta, olives and salami while you consider the list of daily specials, which best shows off the kitchen staff's abilities. Don't worry if you find yourself craving Italian later in the night; Areo's kitchen stays open past 11pm.

Belleville 😄

006

French ✗

330 5th St. (at Fifth Ave.)

Subway:	4 Av - 9 St	Open daily noon - 11pm
Phone:	718-832-9777	
Fax:	N/A	
Web:	www.bellevillebistro.com	
Prices:	🍴	

Belleville executes the informal French bistro concept perfectly, from décor to ambience to food. Decorated to appear old, Belleville appears comfortably worn, with tinned walls and ceilings, distressed mirrors and an antique bar. Tables nuzzle close to one another and sultry jazz plays in the background. In nice weather, windows open out on Brooklyn's busy Fifth Avenue and sidewalk seating.

Once you're settled at your table, expect pleasant service and a reasonably priced menu featuring well-prepared bistro classics from onion soup to duck confit to steak tartare with frites. This is a welcoming neighborhood place for a lingering lunch, a romantic dinner, weekend brunch, or simply an afternoon coffee.

Blue Ribbon Sushi

007

Japanese

278 Fifth Ave. (bet. 1st St. & Garfield Pl.)

Subway:	Union St	Sun – Thu 5pm - midnight
Phone:	718-840-0408	Fri – Sat 5pm - 2am
Fax:	N/A	
Web:	www.blueribbonrestaurants.com	
Prices:	$$	

Brooklyn sushi lovers need not venture to Manhattan anymore with a Blue Ribbon Sushi located right here in Park Slope. This neighborhood favorite is the sister of the original location in SoHo *(119 Sullivan St.)* and is right next door to the casually elegant Blue Ribbon Brooklyn, just as the two are neighbors in SoHo.

As you'd expect, this location provides equally delicate fare with original touches—but in larger surroundings and at a less frenetic pace (and a no-reservations policy). Delight in the freshest sushi (which changes daily based on market availability), or go beyond the status quo with the Blue Ribbon roll (half of a lobster topped with caviar). To help you narrow down your choices, sushi and sashimi are classified according to which ocean—the Atlantic or the Pacific—the fish comes from.

Brooklyn Fish Camp

008

Seafood

162 Fifth Ave. (bet. De Graw & Douglass Sts.)

Subway:	Union St	Mon – Sat noon - 3pm & 6pm - 11pm
Phone:	718-783-3264	Closed Sun
Fax:	718-783-3281	
Web:	www.brooklynfishcamp.com	
Prices:	$$	

Since many Brooklyn residents work in Manhattan, the borough tends to be pretty sleepy during the day, and it can be hard to find a good place for lunch (and nearly impossible to find a good piece of fish). Brooklyn Fish Camp has solved that problem, at least for fish lovers in Park Slope. At lunch it caters to families, with plenty of space for strollers.

An offshoot of the original Mary's Fish Camp in the West Village, this casual eatery (which doesn't take reservations) sails away with top-notch seafood and enthusiastic service. The menu changes daily, based on the market, but owner Mary Redding's famous lobster rolls, fried-fish sandwiches, freshly grilled fish and a selection of steamed or fried shellfish are always available. Be sure to order a side of spicy Old Bay French fries to share.

Brooklyn

Chestnut

Contemporary ✗

009

271 Smith St. (bet. De Graw & Sackett Sts.)

Subway:	Carroll St	Tue – Sat 5:30pm - 11pm
Phone:	718-243-0049	Sun 11am - 3pm & 5:30pm - 11pm
Fax:	718-243-2932	Closed Mon
Web:	www.chestnutonsmith.com	
Prices:	$$	

Some restaurants name their establishments with bad puns and some use their street address, but the owners of Chestnut christened their Carroll Gardens eatery with a moniker that perfectly sums up their philosophy. The name, like the restaurant, is comforting, seasonal and reminds diners that the best supermarket is nature itself. It's clear that time has been well spent here sourcing the best ingredients, whose natural flavors are allowed to shine.

Come on Tuesday or Wednesday night to take advantage of Chestnut's prix-fixe value menus, or order à la carte and feast on halibut with guanciale and wild mushrooms or stuffed pork chop with agrodolce figs.

Down-home style characterizes the dining room, and the young team provides personable and chatty service.

DuMont

American ✗

010

432 Union Ave. (bet. Devoe St. & Metropolitan Ave.)

Subway:	Lorimer St	Open daily 11am - 3pm & 6pm - 11pm
Phone:	718-486-7717	Closed Thanksgiving & December 25 - 26
Fax:	718-486-9084	
Web:	www.dumontrestaurant.com	
Prices:	$$	

DuMont may look like just one more Williamsburg restaurant, but don't pass this one by. Inside, an antique sheen is reflected in the tile floor, and the weathered tin walls and ceiling. Rock music plays in the background, bringing the atmosphere up to the present.

Chefs Cal Elliott and Polo Dobkin are DuMont's two hidden secrets. Formerly of Gramercy Tavern, they propose a list of seasonal specials along with a short menu of all-American fare such as barbecue ribs, and DuMac and cheese (made with radiatore pasta and cheddar, parmesan and gruyère cheeses, studded with bits of bacon). Even the specialty cocktail list is unique, with espresso martinis, Moscow mules and Grand Dad's lemonade.

For a weeknight burger and beer, try DuMont Burger at 314 Bedford Avenue.

Brooklyn

Eliá

011

8611 Third Ave. (bet. 86th & 87th Sts.)

Subway:	86 St	Tue – Thu 5pm - 10pm
Phone:	718-748-9891	Fri – Sat 5pm - 11pm
Fax:	718-748-9879	Sun 4pm - 9pm
Web:	N/A	Closed Mon
Prices:	$$	

You've spent the day on your scooter tooling around Santorini, the sun is starting to set, and now it's time for dinner… Okay, so you're in Brooklyn, and it's a cold Tuesday in February, but the sunny feel of this Bay Ridge taverna will nonetheless transport you to warmer climes. Whitewashed brick walls and marine blues in the modest dining room evoke sun-washed stucco buildings and the color of the Aegean Sea.

Along with the usual Greek favorites, the menu lists items (like the fish of the day) that come simply prepared and well flavored—as they do in the Greek islands—with bounteous amounts of fragrant olive oil and lemon. The best part? The upscale cuisine served here also comes with a palatable price tag.

Five Front

012

5 Front St. (bet. Dock & Old Fulton Sts.)

Subway:	High St	Mon & Wed – Thu 5:30pm - 11pm
Phone:	718-625-5559	Fri 5:30pm - midnight
Fax:	718-625-5523	Sat 11am - midnight
Web:	www.fivefrontrestaurant.com	Sun 11am - 11pm
Prices:	$$	Closed Tue

Tucked into the up-and-coming neighborhood dubbed DUMBO (for Down Under the Manhattan Bridge Overpass), Five Front takes its name from its address on busy Front Street. The restaurant is located just a block or so from the esplanade, with its fantastic views of Lower Manhattan. Weather permitting, the best seats at Five Front are in its spacious bamboo-filled garden, which nestles under the span of the Brooklyn Bridge.

Locals favor this pleasant space to savor sophisticated American fare, much of it interpreted with Italian accents. Inspired choices include Moroccan braised lamb and monkfish with manila clams and chorizo. At dinner, the three-course, fixed-price meal adds another option to the already reasonably priced menu.

Frankies 457 Spuntino 😊

013

457 Court St. (bet. 4th Pl. & Luquer St.)

Subway:	Carroll St	Open daily 11am - 11pm
Phone:	718-403-0033	
Fax:	718-403-9260	
Web:	www.frankiesspuntino.com	
Prices:	🥜	

One of a handful of full-service restaurants open for lunch on Court Street, this narrow brick storefront glows warmly day and night. The initial food preparation takes place in the basement kitchen, while the rustic meals are assembled in the casual dining room, behind a counter stacked with charcuterie and crusty breads. This practice fills the room with mouth-watering aromas, as meatball parmigiana sandwiches and warm bowls of house-made gnocchi are plated and brought to the table.

Frankies attracts diners from young area newcomers to old-school Brooklynites, who know red sauce as "gravy." Weather permitting, the best spot to dine is the inviting back garden, illuminated by strings of tiny lights.

Visit the new Manhattan location at 17 Clinton Street on the Lower East Side (neither location takes reservations).

Garden Café

014

620 Vanderbilt Ave. (at Prospect Pl.)

Subway:	7 Av	Tue – Thu 6pm - 9pm
Phone:	718-857-8863	Fri – Sat 6pm - 10pm
Fax:	N/A	Closed Sun & Mon
Web:	N/A	
Prices:	$$	

This little unassuming gem of a restaurant has operated for 20 years in Prospect Heights, a neighborhood which is now mostly gentrified. Owner John Policastro does the cooking, using premium ingredients; his charming wife, Camille, runs the front of the house, seeing to the needs of her guests.

It may not be trendy, but this family-run cafe draws an epicurean crowd with its excellent cuisine. At night there's but one set menu, and it's a real bargain considering the high quality of the food here. Don't expect fancy presentations or fussy ingredients, but do expect to be dazzled by simplicity.

Oddly, there's no garden here; the name comes from the ambience inside the restaurant, which is set about with lots of green plants, cane chairs, candlelight and soft music playing in the background.

Brooklyn

The Grocery

015

288 Smith St. (bet. Sackett & Union Sts.)

Subway:	Carroll St	Mon – Thu 5:30pm - 10pm
Phone:	718-596-3335	Fri – Sat 5:30pm - 11pm
Fax:	N/A	Closed Sun
Web:	N/A	
Prices:	$$	

Can you tell a restaurant by its façade? In this case, you can. The inviting Grocery, its name etched on the glass window in front, beckons diners to experience the warm hospitality and charming ambience inside the avocado-green dining room.

Co-owners Charlie Kiely and Sharon Pachter run this Carroll Gardens establishment with watchful eyes; she oversees the dining room, he presides over the kitchen. The chef lends his flair to flavorful American dishes, and the well-chosen wine list thoughtfully includes a few half-bottles. The concise contemporary menu showcases items such as semolina-crusted fluke and slow-rendered duck breast.

Since the tiny restaurant only seats 30 people, reservations are a must. In summer, though, the pleasant garden out back increases The Grocery's capacity.

Henry's End

016

44 Henry St. (bet. Cranberry & Middagh Sts.)

Subway:	High St	Mon – Thu 5:30pm - 10pm
Phone:	718-834-1776	Fri – Sat 5:30pm - 11pm
Fax:	718-855-9036	Sun 5pm - 10pm
Web:	www.henrysend.com	
Prices:	$$	

Nearly under the bridge in Brooklyn Heights, two blocks from the esplanade with its fine views of Lower Manhattan, Henry's End serves up American dishes in a casual atmosphere. Bistro tables are tightly packed in the small dining room, where the décor is fading and the walls are lined with black-and-white photographs of Brooklyn through the years.

Whether your tastes run to simple American classics (Southern fried chicken) or to more sophisticated preparations (wild Alaskan salmon), Henry's has something for you—and lots of it (portions are big here). Sample barbecued rattlesnake or antelope au poivre during the annual wild game festival (October through February). The ever-changing list of American wines by the glass is sure to provide a fitting accompaniment.

Brooklyn

Locanda Vini & Olii

017

129 Gates Ave. (at Cambridge Pl.)

Subway:	Clinton - Washington Avs
Phone:	718-622-9202
Fax:	718-622-9227
Web:	www.locandany.com
Prices:	$$

Tue – Thu 6pm - 10:30pm
Fri – Sat 6pm - 11:30pm
Sun 6pm - 10pm
Closed Mon, major holidays
& August 20 - September 10

Gracious host François Louy and his wife, Catherine, are not strangers to the restaurant business. Both from northern Italy, the couple comes with good credentials. François worked for the Cipriani restaurant group, and Catherine was a manager for Balthazar before the pair opened their own place in Clinton Hill. Located in a restored 100-year-old pharmacy, Locanda uses the old apothecary shelves and drawers to hold wine bottles, antique crockery and other supplies.

The menu changes daily, but the likes of house-made gnocchi in fresh tomato sauce, and branzino steamed en papillote in white wine and perfumed with fennel make a reliable prescription for a good meal. If you're dining with four or more, you may call ahead, if you like, and request a chef's tasting menu.

Noodle Pudding

018

38 Henry St. (bet. Cranberry & Middagh Sts.)

Subway:	High St
Phone:	718-625-3737
Fax:	N/A
Web:	N/A
Prices:	$$

Tue – Thu 5:30pm - 10:30pm
Fri – Sat 5:30pm - 11pm
Sun 5pm - 10pm
Closed Mon

Look for a warm greeting and friendly service once you find this restaurant, but don't look for a sign on the door—there isn't one. Brooklyn Heights cognoscenti know where to come for good conversation and generous portions of rustic Italian fare, including hearty pastas and grilled meats.

Diners have a great view of the Henry Street scene through the restaurant's large picture window, from well-spaced bistro tables. From risotto to osso buco, all the Italian favorites are on the menu here. You can savor the scene while you sip a cup of strong, aromatic espresso after your meal.

The restaurant (which doesn't accept reservations) takes its name from a baked potato dish that resembles Jewish kugel, a savory pudding baked with noodles and traditionally served on the Sabbath.

Brooklyn

Osaka

019

272 Court St. (bet. De Graw & Kane Sts.)

Subway:	Bergen St
Phone:	718-643-0044
Fax:	718-923-0173
Web:	www.osakany.com
Prices:	$$

Sun – Thu noon - 3pm & 5pm - 11pm
Fri – Sat noon - 3pm & 5pm - midnight

Osaka's plain brick façade blends in well with the village atmosphere of Cobble Hill. Inside the always crowded but small dining room, pistachio-colored walls, dark-blue linens and bamboo accents highlight the contemporary décor.

Named for Osaka-style sushi, with its larger pieces of fish over smaller beds of rice, the restaurant's menu offers an extensive selection of maki and chef's special rolls (there's even a "Viagra roll," with eel, avocado and sea urchin, the latter prized by many as an aphrodisiac) as well as raw seafood (sushi and sashimi are available as entrée plates or à la carte). Cooked entrées include tempura, teriyaki, broiled black cod and grilled duck breast. If you're looking for a good deal, try the special combination boxes, available for both lunch and dinner.

The Pearl Room

020

8201 Third Ave. (at 82nd St.)

Subway:	86 St
Phone:	718-833-6666
Fax:	718-680-4172
Web:	www.thepearlroom.com
Prices:	$$

Sun – Thu noon - 10:30pm
Fri – Sat noon - 11:30pm

The wave-shaped awning is your first clue to the type of cuisine you'll enjoy at this Bay Ridge fish emporium. Fresh from the sea comes an array of well-prepared dishes, from pan-seared sea bass to jumbo Panama shrimp. And speaking of jumbo, the portions here are nothing to sneeze at; rest assured you won't go away hungry. On weekends, the family-style brunch includes everything from homemade pastries and pancakes to steak and eggs.

Large windows add to the luminous feel of the room, with its shell-pink luster and fish-themed Cubist-style paintings on the walls. This is a place that is as inviting in winter, with its open fireplace, as it is in the summer, when diners appreciate the spacious garden terrace. Expect the service to be good-natured and attentive any time of year.

Brooklyn

Queen

021

84 Court St. (bet. Livingston & Schermerhorn Sts.)

Subway:	Borough Hall	Sun – Mon 11:30am - 10pm
Phone:	718-596-5955	Tue – Thu 11:30am - 10:30pm
Fax:	718-254-9247	Fri – Sat 11:30am - 11pm
Web:	N/A	
Prices:	$$	

What began in 1958 as a Brooklyn Heights pizza parlor has blossomed into a white-tablecloth restaurant offering fine regional Italian fare. The plain dining area, with its neat rows of tables marching down the room, may lack pizzazz, but the kitchen more than makes up for it with authentic dishes like homemade lasagna, chicken alla Cacciatora and veal saltimbocca Romana. Before you order, be sure to consider the long list of daily specials, which often overflow to a second page.

The friendly staff will make sure you feel like a king, or queen, serving up large portions of tasty specialties. Desserts range from simple biscotti and gelati to white-chocolate Amaretto semifreddo and sweet ricotta cheesecake.

If you're watching your pennies, go before 6pm for the bargain-priced prix-fixe menu.

Quercy

022

242 Court St. (bet. Baltic & Kane Sts.)

Subway:	Bergen St	Mon 5pm - 10:30pm
Phone:	718-243-2151	Tue – Thu & Sun 11am - 4pm
Fax:	718-243-2491	& 5pm - 10:30pm
Web:	N/A	Fri – Sat 11:30am - 11:30pm
Prices:	$$	

The bistro décor in this attractive Cobble Hill eatery hearkens back to the 1950s with its Formica bar, warm claret-colored walls and posters of mid-20th-century French actors hanging here and there.

The food is classic bistro, too—think beef Bourguignon, coq au vin, and, for dessert, tarte Tatin made with tart apples or luscious golden carmelized pears. Chef/owner Jean-François Fraysse named his establishment after his hometown in southwest France; the menu pays homage to his native region with dishes such as cassoulet and foie gras. In French fashion, the day's specials are written on a blackboard.

Hip Brooklyn residents frequent Quercy for that intangible *je ne sais quoi*, or perhaps it's just for the good French comfort food served in an inviting atmosphere.

Brooklyn

River Café

Contemporary 🍴🍴🍴

023

1 Water St. (bet. Furman & Old Fulton Sts.)

Subway: High St   Open daily 11:30am - 3pm & 5:30pm - 11pm
Phone: 718-522-5200
Fax: 718-875-0037
Web: www.rivercafe.com
Prices: $$$$

Location, location, location: these are the three best reasons to eat at the River Café. Housed in a barge on the East River with the Statue of Liberty and Brooklyn Bridge in its sights, this landmark has been around since 1977. Spectacular views stretching across the river to Manhattan's Financial District make this a favorite spot of romantics who book tables by the window for special dates or marriage proposals.

At lunch you can order à la carte, while at dinner you must choose between three- or six-course tasting menus that spotlight products like wild King salmon, Maine lobster and Hudson Valley foie gras. For dessert, take your cue from your surroundings and order the chocolate marquise Brooklyn Bridge; it's topped with a chocolate model of the span that looms nearby.

Savoia

Italian 🍴

024

277 Smith St. (bet. De Graw & Sackett Sts.)

Subway: Carroll St   Open daily 11:30am - midnight
Phone: 718-797-2727
Fax: 718-797-3114
Web: N/A
Prices: 🍴🍴

Multicolored hand-painted plates and cruets add color to the uncovered tables as this popular Carroll Gardens restaurant. Two compact rooms create an intimate feel to a space decorated with tile floors and black-and-white photographs of Italy. The big, family-size farmhouse table makes the perfect spot for large groups.

Pizzas are a hot item here; they come fresh out of the wood-burning oven in the little, open kitchen, which is visible to diners. Toppings stray from the standards, with hot sopressata, fried eggplant and boiled egg among the many choices. There are plenty of other entrées, too—most of them with a southern Italian focus—from lasagna to Sicilian-style beef cutlet. Personable and relaxed service adds to Savoia's casual vibe.

Sea

025

114 N. 6th St. (bet. Berry & Wythe Sts.)

Subway:	Bedford Av
Phone:	718-384-8850
Fax:	718-384-8155
Web:	www.searestaurant.com
Prices:	$$

Sun – Thu 11:30am - 12:30am
Fri – Sat 11:30am - 1:30am

You could call this cool Williamsburg Thai restaurant bubbly, since the bubble is Sea's logo. This shape appears on the menu and on the cutouts of the wooden partitions dividing the dining spaces, and it reflects from the disco ball that hangs from the ceiling. Check out the lifesize Buddha that overlooks a pool in the middle of the dining room, but be forewarned that all this Zen-like ambience dissolves at night into pulsing DJ music.

Whatever time you go to this restaurant-cum-nightclub, the menu cites a wide selection of spicy Thai fare, from crispy basil spring rolls to noodle dishes and an array of curries and stir-frys. The volcanic chicken topped with spicy lava sauce is a surefire hit.

There's another Sea in the East Village *(75 Second Ave., between 4th and 5th Sts)*.

Stone Park Cafe

026

324 Fifth Ave. (at 3rd St.)

Subway:	Union St
Phone:	718-369-0082
Fax:	718-369-6548
Web:	www.stoneparkcafe.com
Prices:	$$

Mon – Thu 5:30pm - 10pm
Fri 5:30pm - 11pm
Sat 11am - 3pm & 5:30pm - 11pm
Sun 11am - 3pm & 5:30pm - 9pm

A run-down Park Slope bodega was given a facelift in the fall of 2004 and opened as this delightful, warm-hearted place that marks another example of Fifth Avenue's culinary coming of age. Named for the Old Stone House historical museum set in a little park across the street, Stone Park Cafe is casually decked out in earth tones and lime green, with brown paper covering the tablecloths.

Service here reflects the pride that the waitstaff clearly feels about the place, while the menu offers a selection of dishes well balanced between simple fare and more ambitious preparations. Best of all, the kitchen uses market-fresh ingredients, and knows when to leave well enough alone. Go for weekend brunch and start your day off with a Bellini, followed by the likes of house-smoked salmon or short rib hash and eggs.

Brooklyn

Tuscany Grill

Italian ✗

027

8620 Third Ave. (bet. 86th & 87th Sts.)

Subway:	86 St	Open daily 4:30pm – 11pm
Phone:	718-921-5633	
Fax:	N/A	
Web:	N/A	
Prices:	$$	

Many restaurants lay claim to being romantic, but there's something about the combination of candlelight and a plate of pasta (remember that scene in Disney's *Lady and The Tramp*?) that just seems to naturally foster *amore*. For more than a decade, Tuscany Grill has been providing such an ambience for its customers, who come to this Brooklyn Little Italy not only from the surrounding Bay Ridge area but from Manhattan as well.

The room has a rustic appeal with its dried flowers, pine sideboards and yellow-hued walls, while the menu, as the restaurant's name suggests, celebrates the robust fare of Tuscany (grilled pizza, roasted fish). Expect a wait at this cozy spot—especially on weekends—if you don't have a reservation.

ONE WAY

FRONT ST

DO NOT
ENTER

ALL
TRAFFIC

Manhattan Bridge seen from DUMBO

Queens

Astoria Blvd.	BX	Shore Pkwy.	BZ	
Atlantic Ave.	BCYZ	Southern Pkwy.	CDZ	
Braddock Ave.	DY	Springfield Blvd.	DXZ	
Broadway	AXBY	Sunrise Hwy.	DZ	
Brooklyn-Queens Expwy.	AYBX	Sutphin Blvd.	CYZ	
Clearview Expwy.	CXDY	Union Turnpike	CYDX	
College Point Blvd.	1 BX	Utopia Pkwy.	CXY	
Conduit Ave.	BZ	Van Wyck Expwy.	BXCZ	
Cross Bay Blvd.	BZ	Vernon Blvd.	AX	
Cross Island Pkwy.	CXDY	Whitestone Expwy.	BCX	
Cypress Ave.	ABY	Willets Point Blvd.	CX	
Ditmars Blvd.	ABX	Woodhaven Blvd.	BY	
Farmers Blvd.	CDZ	14th Ave.	BCX	
Flushing Ave.	AY	21st St.	AX	
Francis Lewis Blvd.	CXDY	31st St.	AX	
Grand Ave.	AY	46th Ave.	CX	
Grand Central Pkwy.	BXY	63rd Dr.	BY	
Greenpoint Ave.	AY	69th St.	BY	
Hempstead Ave.	DY	94th St.	BX	
Hillside Ave.	CDY	147th Ave.	CDZ	
Hollis Court Blvd.	CX	164th St.	CXY	
Home Lawn St.	2 CY	212th St.	DY	
Jackie Robinson Pkwy.	CYBZ			
Jackson Ave.	AY			
Jamaica Ave.	BZDY			
Jericho Pkwy.	DY			
Junction Blvd.	BXY			
Laurelton Pkwy.	DZ			
Lefferts Blvd.	CYZ			
Liberty Ave.	BZCY			
Linden Blvd.	CDYZ			
Little Neck Pkwy.	DXY			
Long Island Expwy.	AYDX			
Main St.	CXY			
Merrick Blvd.	CYDZ			
Metropolitan Ave.	ACY			
Myrtle Ave.	ABY			
Nassau Expwy.	CZ			
Northern Blvd.	ADX			
Parsons Blvd.	CX			
Queens Blvd.	AXCY			
Rockaway Blvd.	BYDZ			
Roosevelt Ave.	ABX			

BRIDGES

Bronx-Whitestone Bridge	3 CX
Kosciuszko Bridge	4 AY
Pulaski Bridge	5 AY
Queensboro Bridge	6 AX
Queens-Midtown Tunnel	7 AX
Throgs Neck Bridge	8 CX
Triborough Bridge	AX

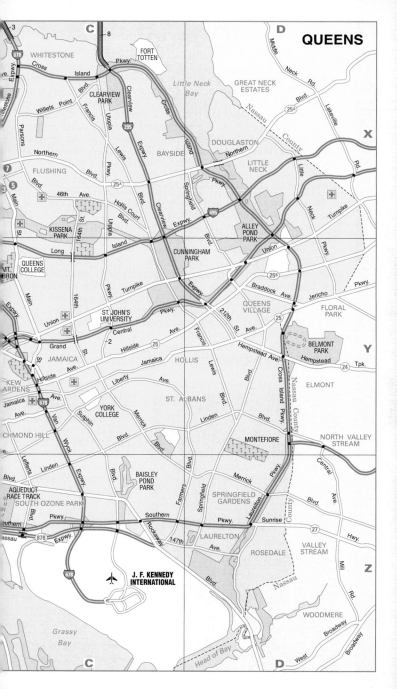

QUEENS

WHITESTONE

FORT TOTTEN

GREAT NECK ESTATES

CLEARVIEW PARK

Little Neck Bay

Nassau

DOUGLASTON

BAYSIDE

LITTLE NECK

FLUSHING

KISSENA PARK

CUNNINGHAM PARK

ALLEY POND PARK

QUEENS COLLEGE

MT. BRON

ST. JOHN'S UNIVERSITY

Braddock

QUEENS VILLAGE

FLORAL PARK

JAMAICA

HOLLIS

BELMONT PARK

KEW ARDENS

ST. ALBANS

ELMONT

YORK COLLEGE

MONTEFIORE

CHMOND HILL

NORTH VALLEY STREAM

AQUEDUCT RACE TRACK
SOUTH OZONE PARK

BAISLEY POND PARK

SPRINGFIELD GARDENS

LAURELTON

VALLEY STREAM

ROSEDALE

J. F. KENNEDY INTERNATIONAL

WOODMERE

Grassy Bay

Head of Bay

Queens

Almost as large as Manhattan, the Bronx, and Staten Island combined, the borough of Queens covers 120 square miles on the western tip of Long Island. Thousands of immigrants come here each year, drawn by the borough's relatively affordable housing and its tight-knit ethnic communities. Restaurants in these neighborhoods reflect Queens' ethnic diversity as well. Take a stroll through Astoria to find Greek grilled octopus and baklava. Try Jackson Heights for eclectic foods ranging from Indian tandoori dishes to Bolivian arepas. Flushing reigns as Queens' most vibrant Asian neighborhood.

A Bit of History – Queens' first permanent settlement was established by the Dutch at present-day Flushing in 1645. Clashes between Dutch and English settlers marked its early years. When the English took over the colony of Nieuw Amsterdam in 1664, they named this county Queens, after Catherine of Braganza, wife of King Charles II of England. Until the mid-19th century, Queens remained a sparsely populated area of small villages and farms. As New York City grew, urbanization of Queens accelerated, attracting successive waves of German and Irish immigrants. In 1898, Queens was incorporated as a borough of New York City, and new transportation facilities made it easier for residents to commute to Manhattan. By the 1970's, nearly 30 percent of Queens' residents were foreign born; that number has nearly doubled today.

Queens

© Martha Cooper

For years, there wasn't much to attract tourists to Queens. That is slowly changing as film studios and art museums make use of abandoned factories in Long Island City and Astoria. Sports thrive in **Flushing Meadows Corona Park** *(between 111th St. & Van Wyck Expwy.)*, which encompasses **Shea Stadium**, home of the New York Mets, as well as the **National Tennis Center**, where the U.S. Open is held each summer. Of course, visitors traveling to New York by air come to Queens whether they want to or not: both LaGuardia and Kennedy airports are located here.

Anna's Corner

001

Greek ✗

23-01 31st St. (at 23rd Ave.)

Subway: Astoria - Ditmars Blvd
Phone: 718-545-4000
Fax: N/A
Web: www.annas-corner.com
Prices: ✑

Mon – Thu 11am - midnight
Fri – Sun 11am - 1am

Greek restaurants are a dime a dozen in Astoria, but Anna's Corner stands out for its warm-weather-friendly décor and attentive service. This taverna occupies a prime corner of busy Astoria real estate and its location just a few blocks from the subway makes it an ideal choice for outer borough residents taking the quick ride for authentic Greek food.

The dining room is bright and airy with leafy plants and crisp white linens. From meze to main courses, a wide range of Greek fare comes in portions sized for sharing, and prices are easy on the wallet. From start to finish, Anna's staff is gracious, offering terrific assistance with the menu and thoughtfully presenting each guest with a taste of the house-made rice pudding at meal's end. Enjoy it with a potent cup of Greek coffee.

Bann Thai

002

Thai ✗

69-12 Austin St. (bet. 69th Rd. & Yellowstone Blvd.)

Subway: Forest Hills - 71 Av
Phone: 718-544-9999
Fax: 718-544-5928
Web: www.bannthairestaurant.com
Prices: ✑

Open daily 11:30am - 11pm

Located on a Forest Hills street surrounded by shops, this charming Thai place entices diners with what it bills as "authentic Thai cuisine." There's no hype to their claim; Thai-food connoisseurs will appreciate satay, spring rolls, noodle dishes, fried rice, vegetarian curries, and *tom yum goong* (Thai-style hot and sour soup made with shrimp, lemongrass, mushrooms, lime juice and hot chile). Chef's selections include *pad ma keur*, a luscious sauté of Japanese eggplant, shrimp, chicken, pork and basil leaves in ginger sauce.

Dining-room décor also rings true to Thailand with brightly painted walls, silk tapestries and Thai artifacts. And if you need more reasons to try Bann Thai, service is friendly and the prices are reasonable, especially at lunch.

Brick Cafe

003

Mediterranean ✗

30-95 33rd St. (at 31st Ave.)

Subway:	Broadway
Phone:	718-267-2735
Fax:	N/A
Web:	www.brickcafe.com
Prices:	$$

Sun – Thu 5pm - 11pm
Fri – Sat 11am - midnight

Resembling a European country inn, with its lace curtains, chunky wood tables, tin ceiling and knick-knacks set around the room, the Brick Cafe wraps diners in a rustic, romantic atmosphere. This storefront eatery, set on a residential street in Astoria, is a good place to take a date.

In the candlelit room, you can share plates that take their cues from the southern regions of France and Italy. Salads range from Caprese to Niçoise, while entrées include everything from penne alla vodka to striped bass oreganata. For dessert, tiramisu and crêpes Suzette represent the cafe's Franco-Italian tendencies.

Locals favor the weekend brunch, which includes everything from omelets and French toast to octopus carpaccio and tuna tartare.

Fiesta Mexicana

004

Mexican ✗

75-02 Roosevelt Ave. (at 75th St.)

Subway:	74 St - Broadway
Phone:	718-505-9090
Fax:	N/A
Web:	N/A
Prices:	⊜

Open daily 10am - 10pm

Just a few blocks from the Jackson Heights station, Fiesta Mexicana indulges sit-down diners as well as those on the run—the latter with its booming take-out business. A loyal clientele haunts this place for the delicious authentic Mexican food here. Although it's tempting, don't fill up on the chips and fantastic smoky salsa, so you'll have room for tasty *tacos de tinga* (soft corn tortillas stuffed with shredded roast pork and cooked in a chipotle tomato sauce). For dessert, the chocolate *tres leches* cake is always on the menu.

The restaurant has no liquor license, but a variety of seasonal *agua frescas*, blends of fresh fruit and water served over ice, are great thirst-quenchers. Be sure to bring cash, since Fiesta Mexicana doesn't accept credit cards.

Gum Fung 😊

Chinese ✗

136-28 39th Ave. (bet. Main & 138th Sts.)

Subway: Flushing - Main St   Open daily 9am - 11pm
Phone: 718-762-8821
Fax: N/A
Web: N/A
Prices: 😊

For any dim sum die-hard in the New York area, Gum Fung is Mecca. The huge, bright dining room sits in the heart of Flushing's Chinatown, easily accessible by either train or car. Diners here are greeted with open arms, and groups and families pack this place for the bite-size offerings served from carts that are maneuvered around the room by members of the waitstaff. Once you're seated, settle in and pay careful attention to the procession of steamed and fried concoctions passing by your table. Spring rolls, sticky-rice packets, and steamed buns number among the multitude of delectable dim sum selections.

Corral some friends and come sample a little bit of everything. Just remember, for the best quality and variety, you have to get here early.

Jackson Diner 😊

Indian ✗

37-47 74th St. (bet. Roosevelt & 37th Aves.)

Subway: Jackson Hts - Roosevelt Av   Sun – Thu 11:30am - 10pm
Phone: 718-672-1232   Fri – Sat 11:30am - 10:30pm
Fax: 718-396-4164
Web: www.jacksondiner.com
Prices: 😊

S

You could call the décor in this Jackson Heights diner whimsical, or you could say it was gaudy, depending on your point of view. Either way, it's colorful and modern, from the 3-D leaves on the ceiling to the multi-hued chairs that are more functional than comfortable (you can excuse all this because diners are supposed to be basic).

Don't come expecting burgers and milkshakes, though, since this diner is all about Indian cooking. If you like curries, masala dosa and tandoori dishes, Jackson Diner won't disappoint. The inexpensive lunch buffet offers a wide variety of southern Indian dishes, including dessert, for one low price.

After lunch, spend some time exploring the immediate neighborhood, which teems with jewelry stores, sari shops and groceries, all peddling Indian wares.

Queens

KumGangSan

007

138-28 Northern Blvd. (bet. Bowne & Union Sts.)

Subway: Flushing - Main St   Open daily 24 hours
Phone: 718-461-0909
Fax: 718-321-2575
Web: www.kumgangsan.net
Prices: $$

Having hunger pangs in the middle of the night? If you happen to be near Flushing, Queens, make a beeline for KumGangSan; it's open 24/7. Named for a range of mountains (translated as "Diamond Mountains" in English) in North Korea, the restaurant offers simple comforts, but that's of little matter to the lines of faithful customers who come here to dine on the large selection of authentic dishes (noodles, bowls of steaming broth, barbecued meats, casseroles) all made with seasonings imported from Korea. Meals begin here with a series of *panchan* (small dishes) before moving on to the appetizers and main courses.

In summer, snag a table on the terrace, with its burbling fountain. There's a second location in Midtown West *(49 W. 32nd St.)*, which is open all night, too.

Malagueta

008

25-35 36th Ave. (at 28th St.)

Subway: 36 Av   Tue – Sun noon - 10pm
Phone: 718-937-4821   Closed Mon
Fax: 718-937-4821
Web: N/A
Prices:

The neighborhood may be nondescript and the comfort may be basic here, but those aren't the reasons for coming to this tiny South American eatery. Authentic Brazilian food and reasonable prices are the reasons, and it would be a shame to visit Queens and miss this place. While most people associate Astoria with Greek food, you'll surely be rewarded for trying something different here.

At Malagueta, chef/owner Herbet Gomes, who grew up in a little town in northern Brazil, dishes up the likes of *acaraje* (black-pea fritters), *salpicao* (traditional Brazilian salad) and *moqueca de camarão* (shrimp stew with palm oil, onions, peppers and coconut milk); *feijoada*, the national dish of Brazil, is offered only on Saturday. Just be sure to save room for the creamy-sweet passion fruit mousse.

Queens

Piccola Venezia

Italian XX

009

42-01 28th Ave. (at 42nd St.)

Subway:	Steinway St	Open daily noon - 11pm
Phone:	718-721-8470	
Fax:	718-721-2110	
Web:	www.piccola-venezia.com	
Prices:	$$$	

Even if Astoria is not threaded by canals, Piccola Venezia will make you think of Venice—or at least its cuisine. Since 1973 this restaurant has been pleasing diners with its ample menu, which emphasizes northern Italian fare. Begin your meal with a grilled octopus or fried calamari appetizer before tucking into a plate of pasta. There's also a long list of daily specials to make your decision more challenging. And if you still can't find anything to suit your fancy, the kitchen honors special requests.

Piccola Venezia welcomes children and will happily tailor meals to picky eaters (i.e., half-portions or pasta without sauce). The amiable manager greets guests as if they were eating in his home. You may arrive a stranger, but you'll leave feeling like part of a big Italian family.

S'Agapo ☺

Greek X

010

34-21 34th Ave. (at 35th St.)

Subway:	Steinway St	Open daily noon - midnight
Phone:	718-626-0303	
Fax:	718-626-0303	
Web:	N/A	
Prices:	$$	

When in Astoria, go where the Greeks go, and in the case of S'Agapo ("I love you" in Greek), you'll quickly discover why this place is always crammed with Greeks, locals and Manhattanites sipping ouzo or a great bottle of wine from the well-assembled list.

Located on a quiet residential block bordering Astoria and Long Island City, S'Agapo is owned and managed by a charming couple from Crete. The taverna focuses on providing authentic food at palatable prices, with knowledgeable and personal service.

Rustic preparations of perfectly grilled fish, lamb, and an extensive assortment of cold and hot appetizers mean that no diner goes away hungry. A number of Cretan specialties (house-made lamb sausage, Cretan cheese dumplings), as well as the quiet outdoor terrace, set S'Agapo apart.

Sapori d'Ischia

011

Italian

55-15 37th Ave. (at 56th St.)

Subway:	Northern Blvd
Phone:	718-446-1500
Fax:	718-446-0134
Web:	N/A
Prices:	$$

Tue – Sat 11:30am - 3pm
& 5:30pm - 11pm
Sun 2pm - 11pm
Closed Mon

Remember the movie *Big Night*? Like the Baltimore Italian restaurant that starred in that film, Sapori d'Ischia doesn't serve sides of spaghetti. In fact, their "house rules," posted at the bar, spell out a number of other things the restaurant doesn't do (for instance, they don't serve butter, grate cheese atop seafood or put lemon peel in espresso).

Set on an industrial-looking block in Woodside, Sapori d'Ischia started out as a wholesale Italian foods business. Over the years, owner Frank Galano (who runs the place with his son Antonio), added a market and then a small trattoria to the premises. Today, delectable pastas, low prices and a convivial atmosphere complete with live piano entertainment keep customers coming back for more.

718 - Seven One Eight

012

French

35-01 Ditmars Blvd. (at 35th St.)

Subway:	Astoria - Ditmars Blvd
Phone:	718-204-5553
Fax:	718-204-2507
Web:	www.718restaurant.com
Prices:	$$

Sun – Thu noon - 10:30pm
Fri – Sat noon - 11pm

What's in a name? In this case, 718 refers to the Queens' area code, not the restaurant's street address. No matter. This cozy French bistro provides a welcome addition to the Greek and Italian places that pervade the Astoria dining scene.

With its solid French base, the cuisine displays Spanish and American influences, all realized with fresh, seasonal products: shrimp meets mango in a salad, rack of lamb pairs with piquillo peppers, and thin-crust *tartes flambées* pay homage to that traditional Alsatian dish. Banana and chocolate bread pudding, and warm apple tart round out the scrumptious dessert menu.

Come Friday night to watch the belly dancer (shows at 9:30pm and 10:30pm) and listen to music from the Casbah. If you're out partying late, 718 offers a tapas menu every day until 2am.

Queens

Spicy & Tasty

013

39-07 Prince St. (at 39th Ave.)

Subway:	Flushing - Main St	Open daily 11am - 11pm
Phone:	718-359-1601	
Fax:	N/A	
Web:	N/A	
Prices:	⚭	

Teeming with a dizzying array of restaurants, bakeries and shops all catering to Flushing's booming Asian population, this Chinatown block draws a mix of New Yorkers in search of authentic Chinese food.

A neighborhood newcomer, Spicy & Tasty fills that bill with fiery Szechuan cuisine that is remarkably consistent. Delicious dishes contain a symphonic blend of different degrees of heat, ranging from the mouth-numbing effect of Szechuan peppercorns to whole chiles marinated in sour vinegar that are merely warm by comparison. A few mild selections, which are no less tasty, will appeal to more prudent palates. Count on the kind staff for sound guidance regarding what to order.

The spacious dining room eschews Chinese lanterns and red walls in favor of light colors and wood sculptures.

Sripraphai ☺

014

64-13 39th Ave. (bet. 64th & 65th Sts.)

Subway:	Woodside - 61 St	Thu – Tue 11:30am - 10pm
Phone:	718-899-9599	Closed Wed
Fax:	N/A	
Web:	N/A	
Prices:	⚭	

The Thai crowd is your first hint that owner Sripraphai Tipmanee serves the real thing at her eponymous restaurant. Her food is spicy, and she doesn't cop out by catering to American tastes. Probably the most authentic Thai restaurant in New York City, Sripraphai is well worth the 20-minute subway ride out to Queens.

Crispy catfish salad, with puréed, fried catfish over shredded green papaya, fresh chiles and lettuce, is a particularly flavorful starter; curry and noodle dishes with varying heat levels are much-ordered entrées on the enormous menu. Hard-to-find Thai ingredients, sauces, and sweets are available for purchase at the attractive take-out counter.

Bring cash and be prepared to wait, since this restaurant doesn't accept credit cards or reservations.

Queens

Taverna Kyclades

015

Greek 🍴

33-07 Ditmars Blvd. (bet. 33rd & 35th Sts.)

Subway:	Astoria - Ditmars Blvd
Phone:	718-545-8666
Fax:	718-726-4766
Web:	www.tavernakyclades.com
Prices:	🥢

Mon – Thu noon - 11pm
Fri – Sat noon - 11:30pm
Sun noon - 10pm

Known for its large Greek population, Astoria doesn't lack for tavernas. This one, located on one of the commercial hubs of Greek Astoria, stands out for its seafood. A trophy swordfish decorates the exposed brick wall of the tiny dining room, where the waitstaff is clad appropriately in blue and white (the colors of the Greek flag).

Lunch is simple here, with a short menu of fish entrées supplemented by a few Greek grills and, of course, *spanikopita* (spinach pie layered with feta cheese and phyllo). Dinner presents a wider choice of main dishes emphasizing the fruits of the sea (from calamari to shrimp stuffed with crabmeat), though concessions are made to land lubbers with lamb chops, chicken kebabs, and T-bone steaks. Desserts are only offered in the evening, and reservations are not accepted.

Tournesol

016

French 🍴

50-12 Vernon Blvd. (bet. 50th & 51st Aves.)

Subway:	Vernon Blvd - Jackson Av
Phone:	718-472-4355
Fax:	N/A
Web:	N/A
Prices:	$$

Open daily 11:30am - 3pm
& 5pm - 11:30pm

A sunflower grows in Long Island City, in the form of this *petit morceau* of a bistro, whose name means "sunflower" in French. Not far outside the Queens-Midtown Tunnel, this charming place defies its unappealing concrete jungle location. With only 40 seats, Tournesol is a family affair, run by brother-and-sister team Pascal Escriout (formerly of Artisanal) and Patricia Escriout-Morvan.

In the simple, cheery dining room, you can feast on dishes from the South of France; the good news is that you only have to travel a single stop on the 7 train from Grand Central Station to get here. The changing menu lists the likes of sautéed snails with tarragon sauce, terrine of duck liver, braised beef cheeks and dark-chocolate marquise. If you're around on the weekend, try Tournesol's French-style brunch.

Trattoria l'Incontro

Italian ✗✗

017

21-76 31st St. (at Ditmars Blvd.)

Subway:	Astoria - Ditmars Blvd	Tue – Sun noon - 10pm
Phone:	718-721-3532	Closed Mon
Fax:	718-626-3375	
Web:	www.trattorialincontro.com	
Prices:	$$	

From the warm welcome you'll receive at Trattoria l'Incontro, you'll know immediately how important the customers are to Abruzzi native Tina Sacramone and her son, Rocco, who rule the kitchen. Indeed, at this Astoria Italian restaurant, the hospitality is as important as the food. The chef is frequently spotted in the dining area, greeting regulars and making sure everyone is happy with dishes such as Tina's homemade pastas. Risotto here is served in a crisp parmesan "bowl," a typical example of how the chef manages to improve on classic Italian cuisine.

In the main dining room, beams punctuate the ceiling, and paintings of the Italian countryside fill the walls. The brick pizza oven, which is visible to diners, turns out a host of savory pies—and even a sweet one stuffed with chocolate.

Water's Edge

American ✗✗✗

018

4-01 44th Dr. (at the East River)

Subway:	23 St - Ely Av	Mon – Fri noon - 3pm & 5:30pm - 11pm
Phone:	718-482-0033	Sat 5:30pm - 11pm
Fax:	718-937-8817	Closed Sun
Web:	www.watersedgenyc.com	
Prices:	$$$	

Waterside dining with magnificent Manhattan views draws patrons to the Water's Edge. The entire back wall of the restaurant is made of windows, affording superb views of the East River and the skyscrapers of Midtown. Elegant table settings and Louis XV-style chairs mark the dining room, decked out with original artwork and Oriental rugs, while live piano music sets the stage for romance.

Menus change seasonally here; but expect skillfully prepared contemporary dishes like grilled sturgeon with sorrel whipped potatoes, and duck with caramelized peaches and braised endive.

If you're coming from Manhattan, why not skip the cab ride and go in style? Make dinner reservations at Water's Edge, and you can take the complimentary boat shuttle to the restaurant from the 34th Street pier.

Queens

Staten Island

9/11 Memorial

Staten Island

New York City's "forgotten borough," Staten Island is primarily a bedroom community, culturally and economically related more to New Jersey than New York. The island, 14 miles long and 8 miles wide, boasts more wide-open green space than anywhere else is in the city.

To reach any of the restaurants here, you'll have to drive over the Verrazano-Narrows Bridge, or take the ferry. The borough's biggest attraction, the celebrated Staten Island Ferry carries over three-and-a-half-million tourists and commuters a year between Manhattan's South Ferry and St. George terminals, passing the Statue of Liberty each way. Stunning views of the Manhattan skyline and New York Harbor, especially at night, are priceless. So is the fare—the ride is free!

A Bit of History – Staten Island got its name in the early 1600s from Dutch merchants, who dubbed it Staaten Eyelandt (Dutch for "State's Island"). The first permanent settlement was established at Oude Dorp by Dutch and French Huguenot families in 1661. Over the next two centuries, the island thrived on farming and agriculture, ferrying goods to nearby Manhattan and New Jersey.

Staten Island's economy grew considerably in 1898, after its citizens voted to incorporate as one of the five boroughs of Greater New York City. This move attracted hardworking immigrants — many of Italian and Irish descent—to its farms and factories, and hard-playing society folks to its resort hotels. The boom went bust after World War I, when many residents left to make their fortunes on the mainland. The borough blossomed once again when the Verrazano-Narrows Bridge opened in 1964, linking the island with Brooklyn and bringing an influx of Manhattanites seeking refuge from the buzzing energy of New York.

Historic Richmond Town

© Martha Cooper

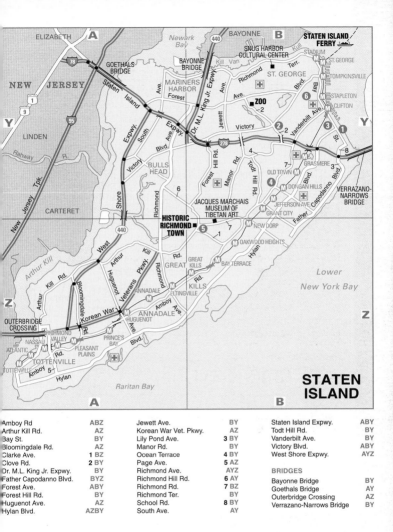

Amboy Rd	ABZ	Jewett Ave.	BY	Staten Island Expwy.	ABY
Arthur Kill Rd.	AZ	Korean War Vet. Pkwy.	AZ	Todt Hill Rd.	BY
Bay St.	BY	Lily Pond Ave.	**3** BY	Vanderbilt Ave.	BY
Bloomingdale Rd.	AZ	Manor Rd.	BY	Victory Blvd.	ABY
Clarke Ave.	**1** BZ	Ocean Terrace	**4** BY	West Shore Expwy.	AYZ
Clove Rd.	**2** BY	Page Ave.	**5** AZ		
Dr. M.L. King Jr. Expwy.	BY	Richmond Ave.	AYZ	**BRIDGES**	
Father Capodanno Blvd.	BYZ	Richmond Hill Rd.	**6** AY	Bayonne Bridge	BY
Forest Ave.	ABY	Richmond Rd.	**7** BZ	Goethals Bridge	AY
Forest Hill Rd.	BY	Richmond Ter.	BY	Outerbridge Crossing	AZ
Huguenot Ave.	AZ	School Rd.	**8** BY	Verrazano-Narrows Bridge	BY
Hylan Blvd.	AZBY	South Ave.	AY		

Today's Staten Island – Though isolated, Staten Island is not without its attractions. Its sandy, relatively uncrowded **beaches**, especially South Beach, make for a lovely outing. **Historic Richmond Town**, a 25-acre village *(441 Clarke St.)*, marks the site of one of the earliest settlements on the island. History comes alive here, thanks to costumed guides who demonstrate crafts (printmaking, tinsmithing, weaving) and regale visitors with tales about 19th-century life in the former county seat. An unexpected treasure, the **Jacques Marchais Museum of Tibetan Art** houses rare objects from Tibet, Nepal, China, Mongolia and India in an enchanted setting atop Lighthouse Hill.

Aesop's Tables

001

Contemporary ✗

1233 Bay St. (bet. Maryland & Scarboro Aves.)

Bus:	51 & 81	Tue – Sat 5:30pm - 10:30pm
Phone:	718-720-2005	Sun 11:30am - 3:30pm & 4pm - 8pm
Fax:	N/A	Closed Mon
Web:	N/A	
Prices:	$$	

Aesop's Tables occupies a renovated storefront on the island's east shore. Since it opened in 1991, this place has attracted a mixed crowd (from the island as well as the other boroughs) who have become fans of this charming place.

The menu changes regularly, following seasonal ingredients from Long Island and New Jersey farms, but American fare here can include anything from meatloaf to salmon roasted on a cedar plank. The simple, garlicky baked clams perfectly define this restaurant's appealing country cooking.

In the cozy dining room, where blue-and-white bistro chairs nuzzle up to little square tables, the specials are posted on a blackboard framed by silk flowers. Out back, the leafy garden, lit by candles at night, makes a great setting in which to eat on a balmy summer night.

American Grill

002

American ✗

1180 Victory Blvd. (at Clove Rd.)

Bus:	53, 61, 62	Sun – Mon 11:30am - 9pm
Phone:	718-442-4742	Tue – Thu 11:30am - 10pm
Fax:	718-448-7189	Fri – Sat 11:30am - 11pm
Web:	N/A	
Prices:	$$	

Red neon letters announce this West Brighton restaurant run by husband-and-wife team Charles and Melissa Santangelo, both graduates of the Culinary Institute of America. Charles mans the stoves, while Melissa manages the front of the house with an expert eye.

Inside, the dining room sports a simple décor, pleasantly embellished with wood wainscoting and color caricatures of its famous patrons.

The food is all-American, prepared with good products. Herb- and mustard-crusted salmon, pan-seared pork tenderloin, and hanger steak with hand-cut fries are among the menu's highlights. Don't pass up the sides, which include creamed spinach and macaroni gratin. American Grill also serves a well-priced lunch and brunch to its loyal followers.

Bayou Restaurant

003

1072 Bay St. (bet. Chestnut & St. Marys Aves.)

Bus:	51 & 81	Mon – Thu 11:30am - 11pm
Phone:	718-273-4383	Fri – Sat 11:30am - midnight
Fax:	N/A	Sun noon - 10pm
Web:	www.bayoustatenisland.com	
Prices:	$$	

Hop the ferry from Manhattan to Bayou, where the good times roll and the down-home Creole cooking will make you yearn for The Big Easy. Despite its location in a nondescript Staten Island neighborhood, if you close your eyes and step inside this faithfully recreated New Orleans bistro, you might think you've been transported to the French Quarter. Exposed brick walls make a gallery for trumpets, banjos, Mardi Gras beads, and portraits of favorite son, Louie Armstrong.

At Bayou, the party never ends, and the mood is infectious. The menu showcases what N'awlins does best, offering classics like chicken and andouille gumbo, catfish po' boys with roasted-pecan gravy, seafood jambalaya, and crawfish étouffée. There's even grilled alligator, and for dessert, don't forget the fried cheesecake.

Carol's Cafe

004

1571 Richmond Rd. (at Four Corners Rd. & Seaview Ave.)

Bus:	X15, 74, 76, 84, 86	Wed – Fri 6pm - 10pm
Phone:	718-979-5600	Sat 5pm - 11pm
Fax:	718-987-4509	Closed Sun – Tue
Web:	www.carolscafe.com	
Prices:	$$$	

Well-known on Staten Island for the cooking school she operates above her restaurant, owner and namesake Carol Frazzetta presides over the kitchen here. Frazzetta graduated from Le Cordon Bleu and studied at the Culinary Institute of America before opening Carol's Cuisine (the cooking school) in 1972. It was only natural that she would follow that act with her own cafe.

Decorated with a feminine touch, evident in the pink-linen napkins, fresh flowers on the tables and hanging plants that decorate the interior, Carol's Cafe only serves dinner. The seasonal menu travels through the U.S. and Europe for inspiration, fixing on the chef's favorite dishes. With entrées like oven-roasted beef brisket and pancetta- and mushroom-stuffed veal chop, homework never tasted quite so good.

Staten Island

The Parsonage

005

74 Arthur Kill Rd. (at Clarke Ave.)

Bus:	X15, 54, 74, 84	Tue – Thu 11:30am - 10pm
Phone:	718-351-7879	Fri – Sat 11:30am - 11pm
Fax:	718-351-4182	Sun 1pm - 9pm
Web:	N/A	Closed Mon
Prices:	$$	

For good food and fascinating history, head for The Parsonage. It's located in the heart of Historic Richmond Town, one of Staten Island's earliest settlements (established in the early 1700s), now a 25-acre living-history museum.

Built in 1855 to house the minister of the Dutch Reformed Church, the Gothic Revival-style parsonage boasts rooms restored with vintage wallpapers and Belle Époque chandeliers—an idyllic setting for a romantic meal. Choose from a prix-fixe seasonal menu at lunch, or an à la carte selection with Italian influences at dinner.

If you're visiting in summertime, note that since the restaurant is set within an extended museum, The Parsonage is popular with tourists.

Vida

006

381 Van Duzer St. (bet. Beach & Wright Sts.)

Bus:	78	Tue – Thu noon - 9:30pm
Phone:	718-720-1501	Fri – Sat noon - 10pm
Fax:	N/A	Closed Sun & Mon
Web:	N/A	
Prices:	$$	

Vida ("life" in Spanish) is an appropriate name for a restaurant at the center of a neighborhood's revitalization. Just five minutes from the waterfront in an area filled with faded, but soon-to-be-revamped Victorian homes, Vida opened over two years ago, breathing new life into this promising locale.

Terrific food at honest prices is the mantra for this endearing restaurant, where succulent, spicy-sweet pulled pork on crostini shares the menu with delicious salmon croquettes napped with saffron aïoli. Desserts, like the creamy pumpkin cheesecake, are baked in-house, and while the printed menu is full of delights, the best way to experience Vida is by ordering one of the daily specials.

Friendly service at this casual place cements its reputation as a true neighborhood restaurant.

Staten Island

Where to **stay**

Alphabetical list of Hotels

Where to stay

The Inn on 23rd

131 W. 23rd St. (bet. Sixth & Seventh Aves.)

Subway: 23 St (Seventh Ave.)
Phone: 212-463-0330
Fax: 212-463-0302
Web: www.innon23rd.com
Prices: rooms: $219 - $369

14
Rooms

The Inn on 23rd/Mark Viker

A warm and intimate atmosphere pervades this family-run bed-and-breakfast-style inn located in the heart of Chelsea. Situated in a renovated 19th-century town house, it offers guest rooms on five floors, each tastefully decorated in a different style and furnished with antiques, family heirlooms and artwork. All are spacious and comfortable with private, modern bathrooms; those on the top floor receive a nice dose of natural light. Care has been taken to minimize street noise with double-glazed windows and white-noise players. Business travelers will appreciate the satellite TV, two-line phones with voicemail and dataport, and complimentary high-speed Internet access.

A generous breakfast, served in the cozy second-floor library, includes goodies freshly baked by aspiring chefs from the New School Culinary Arts Program, which holds classes here. This is a rare find in Manhattan, reasonably priced for its comfort and setting, and appropriate for both business and leisure travelers.

Manhattan Chelsea

The Maritime

002

363 W. 16th St. (at Ninth Ave.)

Subway:	14 St - 8 Av
Phone:	212-242-4300
Fax:	212-242-1188
Web:	www.themaritimehotel.com
Prices:	rooms: $325 - $375 suites: $700 - $1,400 Restaurant: **$$**

121
Rooms
2
Suites
♿
♿

The Maritime Hotel

Ocean liner or hotel? The Maritime, designed for the National Maritime Union in 1966, was meticulously renovated in 2003 to blend the atmospheres of both. Striking five-foot porthole windows, warm teak walls and built-ins, and details in deep blues and greens enhance the air of nautical nostalgia. The lobby, in elegant yet simple retro style, exudes a relaxed and cool ambience.

Most of the cabinlike rooms, each with a marble bath, face the Hudson River and all offer CD/DVD players, flat-screen LCD TVs and wireless Internet access. Sybarites will love the feel of the custom-made 500-thread-count cotton sheets, while business travelers will appreciate the spacious work desk.

The hotel houses La Bottega, an Italian trattoria (where you can have breakfast), and chic Matsuri *(see restaurant listings)* for Japanese food. And to work off all that food, there's a 24-hour fitness room on-site.

Relax with a drink at Cabanas rooftop bar or visit trendy Hiro to experience the hip Chelsea scene. The Maritime is well situated for gallery hopping, as well as sampling Chelsea nightlife and upscale shopping.

Best Western Seaport Inn

001

33 Peck Slip (at Front St.)

Subway:	Fulton St
Phone:	212-766-6600
Fax:	212-766-6615
Web:	www.seaportinn.com
Prices:	rooms: $179 – $259

72
Rooms

Best Western Seaport Inn

Hard by the Brooklyn Bridge in Lower Manhattan, the Seaport Inn caters to both tourists and business travelers. The former enjoy its location in the popular South Street Seaport area, now known for its museums, shops and galleries. The latter find the hotel well situated for their business dealings in the Financial District. Both appreciate the inn's reasonable prices.

Inside this brick building you'll find clean, well-kept rooms sporting country-style furnishings, floral prints, and in-room safes and refrigerators. Some guestrooms even feature a terrace and a whirlpool tub. Complimentary high-speed Internet access is available throughout the hotel. In the morning, guests enjoy a continental breakfast, and in the afternoon, fresh-baked cookies are set out; both are included in the room rate.

Ask for a room on the 6th or 7th floor, where you'll have a private terrace overlooking the East River and the Financial District skyscrapers. And why not bring the family along? At the Seaport Inn, children 17 and under stay free in their parents' room.

The Ritz-Carlton, Battery Park

002

2 West St. (at Battery Pl.)

Subway:	Bowling Green
Phone:	212-344-0800
Fax:	212-344-3801
Web:	www.ritzcarlton.com
Prices:	rooms: $395 – $1,150 suites: $750 – $6,000 Restaurant: $$$

259
Rooms
39
Suites

The Ritz-Carlton Hotel

Rising 39 stories above Battery Park in its glass and brick tower, the Ritz commands a stunning view of the Statue of Liberty and New York Harbor. Rooms with harbor views are equipped with high-powered telescopes so you can better take in the dramatic waterscapes. If your room doesn't have a harbor view, don't despair; you can enjoy the same striking panorama—and a cocktail—from the Rise Bar on the 14th floor (the top floor of the hotel).

Guests here nestle in spacious rooms amid soothing pale colors, luxurious fabrics, Frette linens and marble bathrooms. Say the word and a butler will draw you a relaxing bath. Stay on the Club Level and you'll be treated to a complimentary breakfast and evening cocktails and hors d'oeuvres.

After a workout at the hotel's 2,500-square-foot health club, you can justify a caloric splurge at 2 West restaurant, which prides itself on its Prime Angus beef. While you're here, take some time to walk through the hotel's Art Deco-style public areas to see the impressive collection of modern art.

Wall Street is only a five-minute walk from the Ritz, and sightseers can catch ferries to the Statue of Liberty and Ellis Island right across the street.

Wall Street Inn

003

9 S. William St. (bet. Beaver & Broad Sts.)

Subway: Wall St (William St.)
Phone: 212-747-1500
Fax: 212-747-1900
Web: www.thewallstreetinn.com
Prices: rooms: $159 – $449

46
Rooms
&
🚲
🛎️

The Wall Street Inn

Tucked into one of the narrow streets laid out by the Dutch in the 17th century, this hotel fills two landmark buildings (1895 and 1920), previously occupied by Lehman Brothers. First-time guests soon become regulars here, drawn back time after time by the warm welcoming staff, well-appointed rooms, and moderate prices for the location.

Cheery rooms are tastefully done in period reproductions, and accented with fresh flowers and plants. All rooms have marble baths, but larger rooms on the 7th floor boast Jacuzzi tubs.

The location, right down the block from the New York Stock Exchange, and near South Street Seaport, is convenient for business travelers as well as families. Amenities such as in-room refrigerators, a small business center offering a full range of services, free high-speed Internet access, and a fitness facility equipped with a sauna and steam room, make the Wall Street Inn a good value for the price. And don't forget the complimentary continental breakfast.

The Carlton

001

88 Madison Ave. (at 29th St.)

Subway: 28 St (Park Ave. South)
Phone: 212-532-4100
Fax: 212-889-8683
Web: www.carltonhotelny.com
Prices: rooms: $249 – $389 suites: $750 – $2,000

296
Rooms
20
Suites

The Carlton

A traditional Beaux-Arts hotel dating back to 1904, The Carlton now sports a chic new look crafted by renowned interior designer David Rockwell. The 316-room hotel has an intimate European ambience, beginning with the polished woods and stylish mushroom and cream tones of the lobby, which boasts a two-story waterfall. Guestrooms and suites are awash in a palette of greens, browns and grays, and luxuriously equipped with Frette linens, mahogany furnishings and marble bathrooms. Pets are invited to tag along to this supremely comfortable hotel, where all rooms have iPod docking stations and complimentary wireless Internet access.

The Carlton's location just north of Madison Square Park, in the Flatiron/Gramercy neighborhood, affords views of the Empire State Building and busy Madison Avenue. Although The Carlton doesn't have an on-site gym, it does provide guests with complimentary access to Boom Fitness Center *(4 Park Ave.)*.

In addition to high style, The Carlton invites its guests to indulge in fine dining at Country *(see restaurant listings)*. This restaurant wins rave reviews from hotel guests and New Yorkers alike, and routinely draws an A-list clientele.

Inn at Irving Place

002

56 Irving Pl. (bet 17th & 18th Sts.)

Subway:	14 St - Union Sq
Phone:	212-533-4600
Fax:	212-533-4611
Web:	www.innatirving.com
Prices:	rooms: $415 - $565

12 Rooms

The Inn at Irving Place/Roy Wright

Once you step inside the doors of this small, unmarked luxury hotel, you'll be immersed in a bygone day. Built in 1834, two single-family brownstones (which contained everything from a speakeasy to a day spa over the years) now house the Inn at Irving Place. The cozy, charming lobby welcomes guests to a world filled with 19th-century antiques and a quiet grace.

Twelve individually decorated rooms are named for famous turn-of-the-century New Yorkers, many of whom once lived in the neighborhood (actress Sarah Bernhardt, author Washington Irving; interior designer Elsie de Wolfe). Don't think, however, that you'll lack for 21st-century comforts; Frette linens, Penhaligon's bathroom amenities, Sony CD players, VCRs, and wireless Internet connection come with each room.

In the morning, savor a continental breakfast in your room or in the parlor. Be sure to save time for afternoon tea (reservations required) in Lady Mendl's Victorian tea salon. Downstairs, clubby Cibar lounge offers a menu of martinis and light appetizers.

Manhattan Gramercy, Flatiron & Union Square

W - Union Square

003

201 Park Ave. South (at 17th St.)

Subway:	14 St - Union Sq
Phone:	212-253-9119
Fax:	212-253-9229
Web:	www.whotels.com
Prices:	rooms: $349 - $569 suites: $599 - $699

250
Rooms
20
Suites

Starwood Hotels & Resorts

The granite and limestone Guardian Life Building (1911) has been reborn as a posh W hotel overlooking Union Square. Designed by David Rockwell, the interior sports a contemporary look, from the polished two-story lobby with its sweeping staircase to soundproofed rooms with sleek leather headboards.

Comfort abounds in contemporary guest rooms, where you'll find goose-down comforters and pillows, cushy velvet armchairs, bath products from Bliss Spa, and terrycloth-lined robes. As for service, how can you argue with a hotel whose philosophy is "whatever you want, whenever you want it?" Just press the button on your room phone for everything from netting hard-to-get Knicks tickets to scheduling an in-room massage.

There's even a Pet Package, where your four-legged friend will be walked, groomed and pampered with special meals. Add Olives' tasty Mediterranean cuisine *(see restaurants listings)* and the intimate Underbar, and it's no wonder that W-Union Square attracts a brigade of beautiful people.

Gansevoort

001

18 Ninth Ave. (at 13th St.)

Subway:	14 St - 8 Av
Phone:	212-206-6700
Fax:	212-255-5858
Web:	www.hotelgansevoort.com
Prices:	rooms: $395 – $795 suites: $625 – $1,500

158
Rooms
20
Suites

Spa

heated

Hotel Gansevoort/David Joseph

Slick, sleek, swank: the first new upscale hotel in the Meatpacking District, the Gansevoort rises 14 stories above the burgeoning hip-dom of this once gritty area. Only the name, which belonged to the grandfather of Herman Melville, is historic. The lobby of this oh-so-cool property is outfitted in cherry-wood paneling and Matisse-inspired carpet. Eelskin-covered columns and mohair panels add texture, and special attention has been paid to lighting effects throughout. Elegant rooms wear a dusky palette with touches of color, and huge windows overlook, from the high floors, the Hudson River and surrounding city. Bathrooms are large and luxurious.

Ono *(see restaurant listings)* offers a hip scene and contemporary Japanese restaurant, but the coup de grace is the hotel's rooftop, complete with its popular bar and 45-foot-long heated pool with underwater music.

Gansevoort's newest additions are the Hiro Salon and the GSpa and Lounge, both located in the basement. By day, you can pamper yourself with a multitude of treatments at the sultry spa; by night, the spa equipment is removed and the space morphs into a lounge. It's quite the neighborhood hot spot.

Washington Square

002

103 Waverly Pl. (at MacDougal St.)

Subway: W 4 St - Wash Sq
Phone: 212-777-9515
Fax: 212-979-8373
Web: www.washingtonsquarehotel.com
Prices: rooms: $155 - $265 Restaurant: $$

160 Rooms

Washington Square Hotel

At the heart of the heart of New York City for over a century, the Washington Square Hotel overlooks its namesake park, a Greenwich Village landmark since 1826 and crossroads for the city's bohemian world of jazz, literature, poetry and politics. Family ownership since 1973 accounts for the hotel's friendly and welcoming atmosphere.

Its Art Deco décor, original artwork, and custom-designed furniture create a jazzy mood, especially in the Deco Room lobby bar. Recent renovations freshened rooms with 1930s-style appointments, pillow-top mattresses, and terrycloth robes. Jewel-tone walls establish a restful aura, while Deco details, such as faux ostrich-feather headboards, add a touch of playfulness. Rooms are equipped with complimentary high-speed Internet, with wireless access available in the bar and lobby areas.

Continental breakfast comes compliments of the house, but for lunch or dinner, North Square restaurant dishes up contemporary bistro fare. Take time for afternoon tea, served from Monday to Saturday (3pm to 5pm).

The Hotel on Rivington

001

107 Rivington St. (bet. Essex & Ludlow Sts.)

Subway: Delancey St
Phone: 212-475-2600
Fax: 212-475-5959
Web: www.hotelonrivington.com
Prices: rooms: $350 – $600 suites: $700 – $5,000 Restaurant: **$$$**

90
Rooms
20
Suites

Hotel on Rivington/Nicholas Koenig

The Hotel on Rivington has taken utmost advantage of its status as the first tall building in this swiftly gentrifying neighborhood. With floor-to-ceiling glass walls on at least two sides, rooms in its 21 stories offer stunning, unobstructed views of the surrounding cityscape.

The remarkable result of a collaboration of cutting-edge architects, designers, decorators and artists from around the world, this hotel combines sleek minimalist décor with ultramodern amenities, and, yes, comfort. If you notice anything but the view, you'll appreciate the Tempur-pedic mattresses, Frette linens, and wake-up calls synchronized with motorized curtains. The deluxe Italian-tile bathrooms are equipped with heated floors, steam showers and Japanese-style soaking tubs.

When you get hungry, check out chef Kurt Gutenbrunner's restaurant, Thor. In this airy space, topped by a soaring glass ceiling, you can savor market-fresh seasonal fare for breakfast, lunch, dinner, and weekend brunch.

You enter the lobby—accessible only to you and your invited guests—through the Eggtrance, designed as a deconstructed egg.

The Alex

001

205 E. 45th St. (bet. Second & Third Aves.)

Subway:	Grand Central – 42 St
Phone:	212-867-5100
Fax:	212-867-7878
Web:	www.thealexhotel.com
Prices:	rooms: $525 – $575 suites: $700 – $2,500

70
Rooms
133
Suites

The Alex Hotel

Opened in 2003, the Alex belongs to a new generation of sleekly understated hotels offering a Zen-inspired aesthetic, Scandinavian simplicity and space-age efficiency. A soothing, neutral palette dominates, punctuated with precious woods, bamboo, deluxe fabrics, Frette linens, and flat-panel liquid-crystal TVs in each room. Little luxuries like Frédéric Fekkai bath products and Dean & DeLuca snack trays round out the in-room amenities. Remarkable custom-designed furniture serves multiple purposes; Nightstands convert to writing tables and credenzas transform into flip-out desks, complete with T-1 high-speed Internet connections.

Need a printer? Request an "office on wheels" that also includes a fax and scanner along with office supplies. In the suites, only fully-equipped Poggenpohl kitchens will do.

Just off the lobby, restaurant Riingo *(see restaurant listings)* offers contemporary Japanese cuisine in addition to a full room-service menu. The hotel is conveniently located along Third Avenue between the United Nations and Grand Central Terminal.

Elysée

002

60 E. 54th St. (bet. Madison & Park Aves.)

Subway: 5 Av - 53 St
Phone: 212-753-1066
Fax: 212-980-9278
Web: www.elyseehotel.com
Prices: rooms: $295 suites: $525 - $650

89
Rooms
12
Suites
♿

Elysée Hotel

Since the 1920s, the Elysée has earned a reputation as a discreetly private haven for writers, actors and musicians. Vladimir Horowitz once lived in the suite where his piano still stands; Tennessee Williams lived and died here (in the Sunset Suite); and Marlon Brando made this his New York home.

The period atmosphere lingers on in the Neoclassical-style furnishings, careful service and recently redecorated rooms—some with terraces, kitchenettes or solariums. Lovely bathrooms are decorated in three tones of marble. Classic, yes, but modern conveniences like hotel-wide wireless Internet access and two-line phones are available here, too.

Complimentary breakfast, afternoon tea and cookies, and evening wine and cheese are served in the Club Room. The Elysée may be best known—and loved—for its engaging Monkey Bar, where murals of frolicking monkeys, olive-shaped barstools and piano music draw an attractive clientele. Drop in for a hefty Porterhouse at the adjoining steakhouse at the Monkey Bar *(see restaurant listings)*.

Manhattan Midtown East & Murray Hill

Four Seasons New York

003

57 E. 57th St. (bet. Madison & Park Aves.)

Subway: 59 St
Phone: 212-758-5700
Fax: 212-758-5711
Web: www.fourseasons.com
Prices: rooms: $675 – $1,095 suites: $1,750 – $3,450 Restaurant: **$$$**

304
Rooms
61
Suites

Four Seasons New York

Noted architect I.M. Pei designed the monumentally elegant Four Seasons New York in 1993. Indeed, nothing is small about this property. The tallest hotel building in the city, the limestone-clad tower soars 52 stories in a Postmodern style that draws heavily on the 1920s. Inside the 57th Street entrance, you'll walk into a grand foyer decorated with temple-like pillars, marble floors and a 33-foot backlit onyx ceiling.

The hotel also boasts the city's largest rooms, which, at 600 square feet, are doubtless among the most luxurious as well. A recent refurbishment installed plasma-screen TVs in the opulent bathrooms, which also feature marble soaking tubs that fill in just 60 seconds. Top-drawer service includes a 24-hour concierge, perks for pets and children, and a fabulous newly redesigned spa offering a full spectrum of massages, facials and body treatments. You'll find state-of-the-art exercise equipment, along with a whirlpool, steam room and sauna in the hotel's fitness facility.

In summer 2006, the Four Seasons welcomed its eagerly anticipated new restaurant, L'Atelier de Joël Robuchon, featuring wonderful contemporary French cuisine by the renowned French chef.

Library

004

299 Madison Ave. (at 41st St.)

Subway:	Grand Central - 42 St
Phone:	212-983-4500
Fax:	212-499-9099
Web:	www.libraryhotel.com
Prices:	rooms: $345 - $525

60
Rooms

Library Hotel

Nothing warms a room like books, and the Library Hotel proves the point. Steps from the New York Public and the Pierpont Morgan libraries, this boutique inn makes great use of its collection of 6,000 volumes. Each floor is numbered after a category in the Dewey Decimal system, and rooms contain books on a particular subject. History buff? Request the Biography room on the 9th floor. Literature your thing? Head to the 8th floor.

Furnishings are simple, and, though small, rooms are comfortable and quiet. Well equipped for business travelers, the hotel provides in-room high-speed Internet access, and computer stations in its business center. Enjoy a continental breakfast daily, snacks throughout the day and a wine reception on weekday evenings. Bottled spring water and Belgian chocolates come with each room, as does a VCR. Guests can choose their favorite movies from the hotel's video library of the American Film Institute's Top 100.

The hotel's pleasant public spaces, including the Writer's Den with its fireplace and comfy chairs, and the terrace Poetry Garden, are perfect for—what else?—reading.

New York Palace

455 Madison Ave. (bet. 50th & 51st Sts.)

Subway: 51 St
Phone: 212-888-7000
Fax: 212-303-6000
Web: www.newyorkpalace.com
Prices: rooms: $595 - $895 suites: $950 - $2,600

805
Rooms
88
Suites

New York Palace

The opulent Palace joins the historic 1882 Villard town houses with a contemporary 55-story tower built in 1980. The hotel's public spaces occupy the lavishly restored town homes built in the Italian Renaissance style, which you can enter through the lovely carriage courtyard on Madison Avenue. Fifth Avenue shopping, Rockefeller Center and Midtown cultural attractions all lie within easy walking distance.

Modern hotel rooms in the tower (floors 41 through 54), including 88 suites, are done in either traditional or modern style and provide all the amenities. The Palace houses a 7,000-square-foot spa and fitness club along with 22,000 square feet of excellent conference facilities. West-facing rooms have a stunning view of St. Patrick's Cathedral, just across Madison Avenue.

Gilt *(see restaurant listings)*, the Palace's new restaurant, premiered in December 2005 with cutting-edge cuisine and classic service in the space formerly occupied by Le Cirque 2000. Stop by the adjacent Gilt Bar and Lounge for a sophisticated cocktail in a striking contemporary setting.

Roger Smith

006

501 Lexington Ave. (at 47th St.)

Subway: 51 St
Phone: 212-755-1400
Fax: 212-758-4061
Web: www.rogersmithhotel.com
Prices: rooms: $265 – $425 suites: $399 – $529

96
Rooms
39
Suites

Roger Smith Hotel

Full of playful character—and art—the Roger Smith offers a casual, warm ambience cultivated by an attentive and welcoming young staff. In the public spaces, you'll find rotating exhibits of original artwork, and the hotel even owns and operates its own contemporary art gallery at the corner of 47th Street.

Spacious rooms in the bed-and-breakfast vein are individually decorated in crisp American country style, some with wrought-iron bed frames, and some with antique four-poster beds. Bathrooms remain in good condition, despite the fact that the building dates to 1929. Sunny junior suites claim coveted corner locations and come equipped with pull-out sofas for extra guests.

By special agreement, Roger Smith guests may use the New York Sports Club next door, and the hotel provides an iMac in the lobby for accessing your e-mail. Pets and children are welcome; kids 16 and under stay for free in their parents' room. All in all, the Roger Smith offers a good rate for its comfort, convenience and atmosphere.

Manhattan Midtown East & Murray Hill

Roger Williams

131 Madison Ave. (at 31st St.)

Subway: 33 St
Phone: 212-448-7000
Fax: 212-448-7007
Web: www.hotelrogerwilliams.com
Prices: rooms: $280 - $420

190
Rooms
♿
🦽

Hotel Roger Williams

Clean lines and pure color best describe the freshly renovated Roger Williams. In a departure from fashionable dark woods and minimalist palettes of gray and beige, colorful highlights accent the furnishings here. Light fills the lobby through 20-foot-high windows, and comfortable seating areas provide a classy meeting place.

Simple interior design and furniture give "the Roger" a distinctly Scandinavian air. The rooms, 15 with terraces (nice for romantic alfresco dining), feature flat-screen TVs, wireless high-speed Internet access, and modern bathrooms, though some only have showers (no tubs). Thoughtful touches include Egyptian cotton linens, Aveda toiletries, mini-bars and umbrellas. Most rooms have spectacular views of the nearby Empire State Building.

A "help-yourself" European-style breakfast (stocking everything from fresh-baked pastries to meats and cheeses) is available in the Breakfast Pantry each morning, and jazz plays by candlelight several evenings a week in the lounge. Located at 31st Street, the Roger is convenient to Madison Square Garden, Macy's and the trendy shops and restaurants of Midtown.

Manhattan Midtown East & Murray Hill

70 Park Avenue

008

70 Park Ave. (at 38th St.)

Subway: Grand Central - 42 St
Phone: 212-973-2400
Fax: 212-973-2401
Web: www.70parkavenuehotel.com
Prices: rooms: $275 - $500 suites: $375 - $600

201
Rooms
4
Suites
&

Kimpton New York/David Phelps

In elegance and style, this Kimpton hotel lives up to the fashionable residential neighborhood it occupies. A few blocks from Grand Central Station, and convenient to Madison and Fifth avenues, 70 Park takes its design cue from its historic façade. The interior color scheme, from lobby to guest rooms, ranges from limestone gray to shimmery bronze and light cocoa brown; a sandstone and limestone fireplace makes a notable centerpiece in the lobby.

Très chic, yes, but all set in a friendly and relaxing atmosphere. The rooms, comfortably contemporary, brim with electronic amenities, including CD/DVD players, and 42-inch flat-screen TVs with a yoga channel for hotel guests (yoga mats are available upon request). There's Wi-Fi Internet access throughout the property as well.

Tea and coffee are set out in the bar each morning, and after a hard day at work or play, you can mix and mingle at the evening wine receptions. Located off the lobby, Silverleaf Tavern serves a short menu of pub grub, as well as a full bar and a good selection of wines by the glass. As is the case at most Kimpton properties, pets are welcome here.

The St. Regis

The St. Regis Hotel

2 E. 55th St. (at Fifth Ave.)

Subway:	5 Av - 53 St
Phone:	212-753-4500
Fax:	212-787-3447
Web:	www.stregis.com/newyork
Prices:	rooms: $895 – $1,095 suites: $1,500 – $7,000 Restaurant: **$$$**

171
Rooms
66
Suites

Manhattan **Midtown East & Murray Hill**

Stylish and elegant, and with service close to perfection, the St. Regis reigns among the city's finest hotels. Commissioned by John Jacob Astor in 1904, this Beaux-Arts confection at the corner of Fifth Avenue is located just blocks from Central Park, MOMA and other Midtown attractions. Its public spaces and lobby, from the painted ceilings to the marble staircase, are steeped in Gilded Age opulence.

A recent redesign updated the elegant guestrooms with silk wall coverings and custom-made furniture. Guests in the spacious suites (the smallest is 600 square feet; they range up to 3,400 square feet) are cosseted with extra luxuries, such as a bouquet of fresh roses delivered daily. Unparalleled service includes a butler you can call on 24 hours a day, an on-site florist, complimentary garment pressing when you arrive, and the on-site Remède spa. Their signature massage calms jangled nerves with a mix of Shiatsu, Swedish, deep-tissue and reflexology.

Be sure to stop in the King Cole Bar to peek at Maxfield Parrish's famous mural, and to sip a Bloody Mary, which was introduced here in the 1920s.

The Vincci Avalon

010

16 E. 32nd St. (bet. Fifth & Madison Aves.)

Subway:	33 St
Phone:	212-299-7000
Fax:	212-299-7001
Web:	www.theavalonny.com
Prices:	rooms: $259 – $450 suites: $375 – $700 Restaurant: **$$**

70
Rooms
30
Suites

The Vincci Avalon

A classic European-style boutique property, the Avalon appeals especially to business travelers whose work takes them to the nearby Gramercy Park, lower Madison, Flatiron and Murray Hill areas. The lobby is elegant, if busy with pillars, patterns and paneling. Withdraw to the library/club room, complete with fireplace, for a bit more tranquility.

In addition to its superior rooms, the hotel has 30 large suites boasting traditional comforts designed in a conventional European style. They are particularly well outfitted for professionals, with two-line telephones equipped with dataports and speaker capability, and T1 lines for Internet access. Many rooms enjoy a view of the Empire State Building. Each guestroom has two 27-inch television sets, as well. Jacuzzi tubs, bidets and double sinks furnish the Italian-marble baths in the larger suites. Guests enjoy complimentary access to Bally's Sports Club and health spa.

A full American breakfast is available in the Avalon Bar and Grill, which also serves lunch and dinner.

Manhattan Midtown East & Murray Hill

The Waldorf=Astoria

011

301 Park Ave. (bet. 49th & 50th Sts.)

Subway:	51 St
Phone:	212-355-3000
Fax:	212-872-7272
Web:	www.waldorfastoria.com
Prices:	rooms: $420 - $638 suites: $706 - $1,479 Restaurant: **$$$**

1235
Rooms
250
Suites

♿

🛁

(Spa)

💆

The Waldorf=Astoria

Nothing says New York high society like the Waldorf=Astoria. Built in 1931, the hotel blends exquisite Art Deco ornamentation and lavish Second Empire furnishings. The original Waldorf, built in 1893, was demolished along with its companion, the Astoria, to make room for the Empire State Building. The huge "new" hotel (including its boutique counterpart with a private entrance, the Waldorf Towers) occupies the entire block between Park and Lexington avenues at 49th Street. Its lobby features a striking inlaid-tile mosaic and Deco chandelier. A $400-million renovation refreshed the grand dame, and deluxe fabrics and classic furniture dress the richly appointed and beautifully maintained rooms and suites, all outfitted with sumptuous marble baths.

With 1,500 employees, a full-service spa, four bars, and four restaurants—including Inagiku *(see restaurant listings)* for Japanese specialties, the Bull and Bear *(see restaurant listings)* for steak, and elegant Peacock Alley, which recently received a redesign—you'll want for little here. Take an afternoon break for tea on the Cocktail Terrace, overlooking the Park Avenue lobby.

W - The Tuscany

012

120 E. 39th St. (bet. Lexington & Park Aves.)

Subway: Grand Central - 42 St
Phone: 212-686-1600
Fax: 212-779-7822
Web: www.whotels.com
Prices: rooms: $300 - $480 suites: $450 - $500

111
Rooms
11
Suites
&

Starwood Hotels & Resorts

Tucked away on tree-lined 39th Street, not far from Grand Central Station, The Tuscany (not to be confused with its sister spot, W New York - The Court, located on the same block and designed for business travelers) cultivates a sensual, relaxed atmosphere. It begins in the cozy lobby (or "living room" in W speak) done up in luxuriant purples, greens and browns. Velvets and satins, rich woods and supple leather add to the lush feeling of the space, which beckons as a comfortable spot for a drink or a private conversation.

Spacious rooms, highlighted by bold, deep colors and textures, feature original contemporary furnishings. Pillow-top mattresses, goose-down duvets, and spa robes make for a comfy stay. Bathrooms, however, are on the small side. In-room electronics include access to a CD/DVD library (high-speed Internet access is available for a fee). W's signature "Whatever, Whenever" service is available 24/7 by pressing "0" on your cordless, dual-line phone.

Athletic types will want to visit Sweat, the on-site fitness center. Before or after your workout, you can grab a quick bite at W Cafe.

Algonquin

59 W. 44th St. (bet. Fifth & Sixth Aves.)

Subway:	42 St - Bryant Pk
Phone:	212-840-6800
Fax:	212-944-1419
Web:	www.algonquinhotel.com
Prices:	rooms: $249 - $509 suites: $399 - $699 Restaurant: **$$$**

150
Rooms
24
Suites

Algonquin Hotel

New York's oldest operating hotel was fully renovated in 2004 but remains true to its classically elegant roots and timeless aura. Best known for the circle of literati, including Dorothy Parker and Robert Benchley, who lunched in the Round Table Room in the years after World War I, the Algonquin preserves the feel and look of a fine Edwardian club.

Rooms have been smartly upgraded to include all modern amenities (tastefully hidden); top-quality fabrics and fittings lend rich jewel tones to the accommodations. You may not want to arise from your pillow-top mattress, 350-thread-count linen sheets, and the famous "Algonquin Bed." (Order one for home, if you like.) Each of the suites adds a fully stocked refrigerator.

For a taste of 1930s cafe society, step into the Oak Room, the legendary cabaret where famous audiences and performers (the likes of Harry Connick Jr. and Diana Krall got their starts here) made merry. The mood lingers, and shows still go on, with such talent as Andrea Marcovicci and Jack Jones.

Casablanca

147 W. 43rd St. (bet. Broadway & Sixth Ave.)

Subway: 42 St - Bryant Pk
Phone: 212-869-1212
Fax: 212-391-7585
Web: www.casablancahotel.com
Prices: rooms: $239 - $329 suites: $339 - $429

43
Rooms
5
Suites

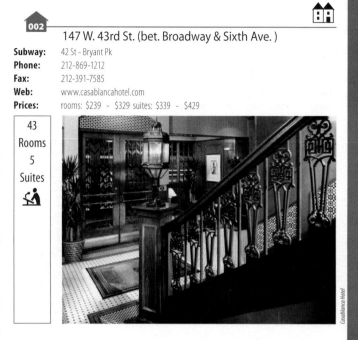

Casablanca Hotel

Manhattan Midtown West

No surprises here—except perhaps that the concept of designing a hotel after the famous Bogart movie works without being kitschy or overdone. The illusion begins as you enter through the ornate doors into the small tiled lobby, and while there is no nightclub on the premises, up a flight of stairs you'll find a tamer version of the famous Rick's. Complimentary continental breakfast is served here, or you can relax by the fireplace later for tea or champagne. A pianist—not necessarily named Sam—entertains on Fridays. You'll find a computer here to surf or check your e-mail, and high-speed Internet access comes complimentary in each room.

The Casablanca ambience extends into the fair-sized rooms as well, which are furnished with Moroccan-inspired fabrics and carved headboards. Bathrooms are done up nicely in dark and light tile, just exotic enough to evoke a more remote setting than Midtown. Despite the hotel's Times Square location, most rooms are surprisingly quiet.

From Monday through Saturday beginning at 5pm (until 8pm), guests are treated to a cheese and champagne reception in the common area.

Chambers

15 W. 56th St. (bet. Fifth & Sixth Aves.)

Subway:	57 St
Phone:	212-974-5656
Fax:	212-974-5657
Web:	www.chambershotel.com
Prices:	rooms: $395 - $450 suites: $850 - $2,000

72
Rooms
5
Suites
♿

Manhattan Midtown West

Chambers Hotel

Behind its latticework door, the soaring lobby of this sophisticate sets the mood. It's all about art here: the hotel displays over 500 original pieces by young artists. Lobby furnishings and design details in various textures—warm wood floors, leather rugs, velvet sofas—complete the look of a swank town home. On the mezzanine, roving waiters provide refreshments all day, while books, art, and stylish seating create a comfortable atmosphere.

Explore the hotel's 14 floors, as each hallway houses a site-specific work of art. Guest rooms resemble urbane loft spaces with wide-plank hardwood floors and an eclectic but handsome blend of warm and cool materials—gray-washed oak furniture and details in blackened steel, chenille, leather, glass and artist's canvas. Ask and you'll receive; services include babysitters, a car and driver, in-room massage, and even a personal trainer on call.

For sophisticated contemporary fare, make dinner reservations at Town *(see restaurant listings)*; this restaurant also provides the hotel's room service.

City Club

004

55 W. 44th St. (bet. Fifth & Sixth Aves.)

Subway: 42 St - Bryant Pk
Phone: 212-921-5500
Fax: 212-944-5544
Web: www.cityclubhotel.com
Prices: rooms: $325 suites: $995

62
Rooms
3
Suites

City Club Hotel

What started life in 1904 as a gentleman's club is now an urbane and sophisticated hotel. The City Club prides itself on its small, private lobby, more like the entryway to an exclusive residence than to a hotel.

Rooms are small but set about with pillows and other accessories that make them feel like guest rooms in a swank private home. Handsome black-marble bathrooms include spacious tubs or showers with bidets, a telephone and TV speakers. All guests enjoy complimentary high-speed Internet access as well as in-room DVD players and electronic safe-deposit boxes. Truly spectacular are the hotel's three duplex suites, decked out with private terraces and circular stairways that lead up to the sleeping room from a well-appointed sitting room below.

For kicked-up brasserie fare, try Daniel Boulud's DB Bistro Moderne *(see restaurant listings)*, which connects to the lobby via a paneled wine bar.

Essex House

005

160 Central Park South (bet. Sixth & Seventh Aves.)

Subway:	57 St - 7 Av
Phone:	212-247-0300
Fax:	212-315-1839
Web:	www.jumeirahessexhouse.com
Prices:	rooms: $300 – $500 suites: $600 – $4,000 Restaurant: **$$$**

515
Rooms
25
Suites

Essex House

This well-known Art Deco landmark opened in 1931 in its commanding site at the very foot of Central Park. Within easy walking distance of Carnegie Hall and the shops and restaurants of Fifth Avenue and the Time Warner Center, the Essex House welcomes guests in its impressive marble lobby.

A recent change in ownership passed this former Westin hostelry into the hands of the Dubai-based Jumeirah hospitality group. Big changes lie ahead for the Essex House. Look for a major makeover to bestow a new style on the 515-room hotel, including high-tech amenities like an "electronic butler," a touch-screen system that will allow guests to customize their stay here.

In the meantime, you can still sip a cocktail at Journeys, the hotel's clubby, masculine lounge, or delight in luxuries such as complimentary Mercedes car service within a several-mile radius. And you can still work out or relax with a massage at the fitness center and spa. As for the future, expect everything to change for the better, as the new owners give this stately grand dame a 21st-century facelift.

Iroquois

006

49 W. 44th St. (bet. Fifth & Sixth Aves.)

Subway:	42 St - Bryant Pk
Phone:	212-840-3080
Fax:	212-719-0006
Web:	www.iroquoisny.com
Prices:	rooms: $385 - $485 suites: $610 - $1,090 Restaurant: $$$

105
Rooms
9
Suites
&

The Iroquois

Well-known, well-kept and comfortable, the historic Iroquois evokes the mood of a private mansion. Modern European furnishings added during a recent renovation suit its 1923 vintage. A cozy library offers a computer with high-speed Internet access as well as a selection of classic books.

Newly remodeled guestrooms are swathed in chocolate-brown, and offer luxuries like Frette linens, Simmons Beautyrest mattresses and goose-down pillows. Italian marble bathrooms sparkle in peach and cream. All rooms have both tub and shower, while the nine suites are equipped with Jacuzzis. If you're sleeping in, press the button on your doorknob for privacy. Given the hotel's queenly grace, it's ironic to remember that bad boy James Dean lived in suite 803 from 1951 to 1953.

Amenities include a 24-hour health club featuring a Finnish sauna for the ultimate in relaxation. To savor the contemporary American cuisine at Triomphe restaurant, be sure to make a reservation; the intimate room is tiny and popular with theatergoers.

Le Parker Meridien

007

118 W. 57th St. (bet. Sixth & Seventh Aves.)

Subway: 57 St
Phone: 212-245-5000
Fax: 212-719-0006
Web: www.parkermeridien.com
Prices: rooms: $295 - $495 suites: $750 - $5,000 Restaurant: **$$**

691
Rooms
40
Suites

Le Parker Meridien/Andrew Bordwin

The Parker Meridien underwent a complete refurbishment in 2002. Its grand Neoclassical lobby has been updated with modern touches in lighting, seating and carpeting. While the large lobby suits the hotel's size, the service is surprisingly personal.

Ergonomic, well-planned accommodations bear the touch of a hotel-savvy designer. They are reasonable in size and uncluttered—streamlined, in fact—with Aeron desk chairs and Scandinavian-style cherry and cedar wood furniture. Showers are big enough for two, and desks allow ample room to work, if you must. In the suites, televisions are cleverly mounted to swivel for viewing from any angle.

Get your workout in at Gravity, the resident fitness club, offering spa services, and group fitness classes. You can do your laps at the penthouse pool. Fuel up first at Norma's, known for serving tasty breakfast dishes until mid-afternoon. For dinner try Seppi's, a French-style bistro, or, for a great burger, check out the rough-and-ready Burger Joint.

Metro

008

45 W. 35th St. (bet. Fifth & Sixth Aves.)

Subway:	34 St - Herald Sq
Phone:	212-947-2500
Fax:	212-279-1310
Web:	www.hotelmetronyc.com
Prices:	rooms: $175 - $360 suites: $275 - $495 Restaurant: **$$**

179
Rooms
3
Suites

Hotel Metro/Linda Davis

Though not hip or stylish, the Hotel Metro is nonetheless a good stay for the money. Located in the heart of the Garment District (light sleepers take note that the hotel's location is not a quiet one), New York's fashion center, the building was constructed in 1901. An Art-Deco inspired lobby leads into a spacious breakfast room/lounge where complimentary breakfasts are served each morning, and tea and coffee are available during the day.

Guest rooms have been recently refurbished (the Metro opened its doors in 1995) and are equipped with mini-bars, and upgraded "plush-top" mattresses. Many of the marble bathrooms benefit from natural light, and the overall standard of housekeeping is good. The hotel now offers high-speed wireless Internet access, as well as a fully equipped business center.

From the large rooftop bar (open from May through September), you'll have stunning views of the Empire State Building and the surrounding neighborhood, which includes Macy's, for all you hard-core shoppers.

Manhattan Midtown West

The Peninsula

700 Fifth Ave. (at 55th St.)

Subway:	5 Av - 53 St
Phone:	212-956-2888
Fax:	212-903-3949
Web:	www.peninsula.com
Prices:	rooms: $725 - $995 suites: $1,200 - $5,900 Restaurant: **$$$**

185
Rooms
54
Suites

The Peninsula, New York

Still sparkling from its $45-million restoration in 1998, this magnificent 1905 hotel serves beautifully as Peninsula's flagship U.S. property. When built as The Gotham, it was the city's tallest skyscraper, towering 23 stories.

Plush rooms exude a timeless elegance, and Art Nouveau accents complement their rich colors and appointments. Ample in size and well conceived for business travelers, each guest room provides a silent fax machine, wireless Internet access, and a bottled-water bar (with your choice of still or sparkling water). Service is a particularly strong suit at the Peninsula, and the smartly liveried staff effortlessly execute your every request.

You could spend hours in the 35,000-square-foot, three-story Peninsula Spa and Health Club, complete with its Jacuzzi, sauna, steam rooms, and luxurious indoor pool, but don't be late for afternoon tea or cocktails at the intimate Gotham Lounge. Ascend to the Pen-Top Bar and Terrace before retiring to intimate Fives restaurant (on the second floor) for a romantic meal.

Manhattan Midtown West

Hotel QT

125 W. 45th St. (bet. Sixth & Seventh Aves.)

Subway:	Times Sq - 42 St
Phone:	212-354-2323
Fax:	212-302-8585
Web:	www.hotelqt.com
Prices:	rooms: $175 - $425

140 Rooms
♿
🛏
🏊

Nikolas Koenig

The good life doesn't have to come at a high price at the Hotel QT. This unique, contemporary hotel brings cheap chic to the heart of Times Square, and offers an uncommonly good value in a city well known for its outrageously priced guest quarters.

Owned by Andre Balazs, who runs such hip hotels as The Mercer in New York and Chateau Marmont in Los Angeles, Hotel QT is a fantastic choice for those with champagne tastes and beer budgets. Guestrooms are simply decorated in a modern monastic style and boast flat-screen TVs, high-speed Internet access and platform and bunk beds topped with Egyptian cotton sheets. Complimentary buffet breakfast is included with each stay.

A youthful vibe penetrates the QT, where a sleek steel kiosk stocked with sundries serves as the reception desk. On the lobby level, the pool with its swim-up bar boasts a great scene of young urban professionals on business and holiday; meanwhile, the mezzanine lounge pulses with nightly DJ performances. A small fitness center with steam room and sauna is available to guests 24 hours a day, and in lieu of a restaurant or room service, the hotel stocks a library of take-out menus from area restaurants.

The Ritz-Carlton, Central Park

011

50 Central Park South (at Sixth Ave.)

Subway:	5 Av - 59 St
Phone:	212-308-9100
Fax:	212-207-8831
Web:	www.ritzcarlton.com
Prices:	rooms: $695 – $1,350 suites: $1,695 – $3,950 Restaurant: **$$$**

213
Rooms
48
Suites

Spa

The Ritz-Carlton Hotel

Renovated as the city's newest Ritz-Carlton in 2002, this classic Central Park hotel was built in 1929 as the St. Moritz. The reception lobby remains intimate to invoke a small luxury property, but the lobby lounge opens into a grand two-story space.

The facelift cut the number of guest rooms in half to create sumptuous accommodations of generous size. Steeped in Old World elegance, they offer the best in electronic amenities rivaled only by old-fashioned touches such as a bath butler, a telescope to explore Central Park, and, in the top-end suites, a choice of fine bed linens. For that extra personalized service, reserve a room on the Club Level, where guests have access to the exclusive Club Lounge that offers complimentary food and beverages daily.

Jet lag got you down? A visit to La Prairie provides the ultimate in spa treatments and pampering. Stop by the hotel's plush Star Lounge for proper afternoon tea or a well-shaken pre- or post-dinner martini.

Sofitel

012

45 W. 44th St. (bet. Fifth & Sixth Aves.)

Subway:	47-50 Sts - Rockefeller Ctr
Phone:	212-354-8844
Fax:	212-354-2480
Web:	www.sofitel.com
Prices:	rooms: $329 suites: $599 Restaurant: **$$$**

346
Rooms
52
Suites

Sofitel

Combining the best of French and American sensibilities, the Sofitel doesn't feel like a modern, 30-story tower hotel. Rich marble and leather greet guests in the spacious lobby filled with sofas and armchairs. Nicely sized guest rooms are attractively decorated with large windows (ask for a room on a higher floor for better views) and artwork that relates to both New York and Paris. Exceptional marble bathrooms include separate shower and tub. Wi-Fi Internet access and an on-site fitness center complete the picture. Pets are welcome here, too.

For cocktails, try Gaby Bar, a stylish lounge in the Art Deco tradition, with plenty of tables and comfortable chairs. Its companion restaurant, Gaby, serves French cuisine with Asian accents. The Sofitel's ideal location, between Rockefeller Center and the Empire State Building, and just east of Times Square and the theater district, is equally convenient for business and leisure travelers.

The Warwick

65 W. 54th St. (at Sixth Ave.)

Subway:	57 St
Phone:	212-247-2700
Fax:	212-247-2725
Web:	www.warwickhotelny.com
Prices:	rooms: $265 – $725 suites: $385 – $5,000 Restaurant: $$$

359
Rooms
67
Suites

The Warwick Hotel

Newspaper magnate William Randolph Hearst built the Warwick in 1927 so that his lady friend, Marion Davies, could host their band of Hollywood and theatrical friends in style. The 33-story hotel underwent a major facelift in 2001, and the smart guest rooms haven't lost their traditional feeling. Larger than many city hotel quarters, rooms here incorporate slick modern touches such as temperature controls that sense your presence. Go for broke and book the Suite of the Stars, where Cary Grant lived for 12 years; it boasts 1,200 square feet of space and its own wrap-around terrace.

For business travelers, high-speed Internet access is available throughout the hotel, and the business center in the lobby offers 24-hour fax and copying services. There's also an on-site fitness facility.

After working, or working out, treat yourself to a meal at Murals on 54, in full view of Dean Cornwall's wonderful murals depicting the history of Sir Walter Raleigh. Commissioned by Hearst in 1937 for the hotel's former Raleigh Room, these paintings have now been restored to their original luster.

The Mercer

147 Mercer St. (at Prince St.)

Subway: Prince St
Phone: 212-966-6060
Fax: 212-965-3838
Web: www.mercerhotel.com
Prices: rooms: $440 - $680 suites: $1,250 - $2,450

67
Rooms
8
Suites
&

The Mercer / Thomas Loof

Manhattan SoHo & NoLita

Even if your name isn't Leonardo DiCaprio, Cher or Calvin Klein, you'll be equally welcome at The Mercer. Housed in a striking Romanesque Revival-style building erected in 1890, the hotel caters to the glitterati with discreet, personalized service and intimate elegance. The modern lobby feels like your stylish friend's living room, complete with coffee-table books and an Apple computer for guests' Internet use.

A Zen vibe pervades the guest rooms, fashioned by Parisian interior designer Christian Liaigre with high, loft-like ceilings, large windows that open, and soothing neutral palettes. Spacious baths with oversize marble soaking tubs, 400-thread-count Egyptian cotton sheets, flat-screen TVs, and complimentary access to nearby fitness facilities (Crunch and New York Sports Club) number among the amenities.

Sure, the hotel offers 24-hour room service, but in this case the food comes from Jean-Georges Vongerichten's Mercer Kitchen *(see restaurant listings)*, located in the basement. Don't fret if you get a room facing the street; soundproofing filters out the noise.

Sixty Thompson

60 Thompson St. (bet. Broome & Spring Sts.)

Subway: Spring St (Sixth Ave.)
Phone: 212-431-0400
Fax: 212-431-0200
Web: www.60thompson.com
Prices: rooms: $299 – $490 suites: $650 – $1,000

85
Rooms
13
Suites
♿

Sixty Thompson

With its spare 1940s look inspired by French designer Jean-Michel Frank, Sixty Thompson absolutely oozes SoHo style. The lobby, decorated in gray, brown, and moss-green tones, is accented by bouquets of fresh flowers, and natural light floods in from floor-to-ceiling windows.

Room sizes vary, but all sport a minimalist look, with crisp, white Frette linens standing out against a wall of dark, paneled leather. Amenities include flat-screen TVs in all the rooms, and high-speed wireless Internet access. (Business travelers take note that Sixty Thompson has replaced the requisite in-room desk with a sitting area in its standard rooms.) Bathrooms are tiled with chocolate-colored marble and stocked with spa products by Fresh. For those who don't appreciate the smell of cigarette smoke in their room, the hotel devotes two entire floors to non-smoking chambers.

Be sure to check out the rooftop bar on the 12th floor, where you can sip a cocktail while you drink in great city views. In good weather, the rooftop scene is a hot one, whereas the lobby bar bustles year-round with a cool crowd. Downstairs, Kittichai restaurant *(see restaurant listings)* specializes in Thai cuisine.

Manhattan SoHo & NoLIta

Soho Grand

310 West Broadway (bet. Canal & Grand Sts.)

Subway:	Canal St (Sixth Ave.)
Phone:	212-965-3000
Fax:	212-965-3200
Web:	www.sohogrand.com
Prices:	rooms: $639 - $749 suites: $5,000

363
Rooms
2
Suites

Soho Grand Hotel

The architecture of this hip hotel (opened in 1996) recalls SoHo's industrial past, from the exposed-brick walls to the superb suspended steel staircase that connects the ground floor to the main lobby.

Two metal dog statues stand near the elevator, reminding guests of the Soho Grand's pet-friendly policy—what else would you expect from the same folks who own Hartz Mountain Industries? There's even a fish bowl in every room; if you grow attached to your new fishy friend, you're welcome to take him home with you.

And speaking of rooms, they're done in tones of gray and gold, with large picture windows overlooking the neighborhood. You'll relax in state-of-the-art style with Bose Wave CD/radios, in-room fax machines and broadband Internet connections. Feel like splurging? Reserve one of the airy, two-bedroom penthouse loft suites. They boast their own wrap-around terraces for enjoying the awesome cityscape.

If you can't get a reservation at the Soho Grand, the hotel's nearby sister, the Tribeca Grand Hotel, may be able to accommodate you.

Cosmopolitan

001

95 West Broadway (at Chambers St.)

Subway:	Chambers St (West Broadway)
Phone:	212-566-1900
Fax:	212-566-6909
Web:	www.cosmohotel.com
Prices:	rooms: $149 - $199

120
Rooms

Cosmopolitan

Located in the heart of TriBeCa, the Cosmopolitan ranks as the longest continually operated hotel in New York City, dating back to 1853. This hotel pulls in a big business-travel and European clientele; fans of the Cosmopolitan tend to come back year after year.

Newly renovated rooms may be small, simple and practical, but they are perfectly maintained. All guest chambers have private bathrooms and color TVs; ask for a room on the back side of the hotel, if you're worried about the street noise. Although the Cosmopolitan doesn't have a restaurant, the Soda Shop, located in the same building, serves breakfast, lunch and dinner in a charming soda-fountain setting. Of course, TriBeCa's myriad restaurants are nearby.

The hotel lies just a five-minute walk from Wall Street, SoHo and Chinatown, and the Chambers Street subway station is practically right outside the door. Don't expect fawning service or a multitude of amenities—although guests do receive free passes to the New York Sports Club—and you won't be disappointed. The cleanliness, location and modest price are reasons enough to stay here.

Bentley

001

500 E. 62nd St. (at York Ave.)

Subway: Lexington Av - 59 St
Phone: 212-644-6000
Fax: 212-207-4800
Web: www.nychotels.com
Prices: rooms: $175 - $250 suites: $225 - $350 Restaurant: **$$**

161
Rooms
36
Suites

Bentley Hotel

Manhattan Upper East Side

Trendy it's not, but the Bentley nevertheless offers oversize rooms for a good price in an area that's within walking distance of the subway, the shops and restaurants of Midtown, and the attractions of Central Park. The Art Deco lobby makes a sleek first impression, with its beige and brown furnishings, boxy lamps and geometric-print area rugs.

Belgian linens, down comforters, and streamlined furnishings highlight the comfortable, contemporary-style rooms. In many of them, large windows—especially on the south side—take in views of the East River and the nearby Queensboro Bridge. For families, the Bentley's suites are a particularly good value; these spacious rooms include pull-out sofas or futons. All guests receive free passes to a nearby health club.

If you're not up for going out for dinner, the hotel's rooftop restaurant offers a limited menu and affords a glittering nighttime panorama of the City That Never Sleeps. The Bentley doesn't serve breakfast, but guests do have complimentary access to the cappuccino bar (located off the lobby) 24 hours a day.

The Carlyle

35 E. 76th St. (at Madison Ave.)

Subway: 77 St
Phone: 212-744-1600
Fax: 212-717-4682
Web: www.thecarlyle.com
Prices: rooms: $650 - $950 suites: $950 - $6,000

123
Rooms
58
Suites

The Carlyle

Since it opened across from Central Park in 1930, The Carlyle has hosted every American president since Truman, along with a roster of foreign dignitaries from Prime Minister Nehru to Princess Diana—how's that for an A-list?

Named for British historian Thomas Carlyle, the hotel epitomizes luxury with its fine artwork, Baccarat crystal light fixtures, and nothing-is-too-much-to-ask service. Though small, individually decorated classic (Carlyle-speak for "standard") rooms are dressed in Louis XVI style with original Audubon prints, 440-thread-count Italian linens, plush carpets and lavish marble baths. Nearly half of the Carlyle's roomy suites feature a Steinway or a Baldwin baby-grand piano.

For entertainment, there's Café Carlyle, where Woody Allen regularly jams with the Eddie Davis New Orleans jazz band. Bemelmans Bar, renowned for its whimsical mural of characters from artist Ludwig Bemelmans' famous *Madeline* series of children's books, is a popular place for a cocktail. Bring the kids by for Madeline Tea, served from noon until 4pm.

Manhattan **Upper East Side**

The Lowell

003

28 E. 63rd St. (bet. Madison & Park Aves.)

Subway: Lexington Av - 63 St
Phone: 212-838-1400
Fax: 212-319-4230
Web: www.lowellhotel.com
Prices: rooms: $500 - $850 suites: $1,150 - $7,000 Restaurant: $$$

40
Rooms
30
Suites

The Lowell Hotel

A block from Central Park and close to Madison Avenue boutiques, The Lowell occupies a landmark 1928 building on a tree-lined Upper East Side street. The hotel's intimate size, discreet staff and sumptuous ambience are the reasons most fans give for coming back time after time.

From the moment you step inside the silk-paneled lobby, you'll sense the European elegance that defines The Lowell. Guests here are cosseted in lavish suites, most of which have working fireplaces and private terraces (the Garden Suite has two terraces) and iPod docking stations. A recent renovation added new marble-clad baths—complete with mini TVs and Bulgari toiletries—king size, half-canopy beds, new designer fabrics and upgraded kitchens to all accommodations.

The well-equipped fitness room adds thoughtful touches like magazines, cool towels, and fruit. If it's aerobics classes or an indoor pool you want, guests have complimentary access to the posh Equinox Fitness Club nearby.

Savor a hearty steak in the hotel's clubby Post House restaurant, or drop by the aristocratic Pembroke Room, all swagged in English chintz, for breakfast, afternoon tea or weekend brunch.

The Pierre

004

2 E. 61st St. (at Fifth Ave.)

Subway:	5 Av – 59 St
Phone:	212-838-8000
Fax:	212-758-7675
Web:	www.tajhotels.com/pierre
Prices:	rooms: $610 - $1,065 suites: $775 - $1,400 Restaurant: **$$$**

149
Rooms
52
Suites

The Pierre

Opened in 1930 by Charles Pierre Casalasco, The Pierre (now a Taj hotel) has pampered the crème de la crème of New York society for decades. The location of the Neoclassical-style building is unparalleled: overlooking lovely Central Park, The Pierre stands near the prestigious shops of Fifth Avenue—a big plus for hard-core shoppers.

Inside, handmade carpets, silk draperies, and ebullient bouquets of fresh flowers are just a sampling of the luxury that awaits you. Murals abound, from The Rotunda tea room and lounge to the 1,600-square-foot fitness center (which even has a room for massage therapy). Outfitted with wingback chairs, mahogany furnishings, and black and white marble baths, rooms have an old-fashioned elegance. Several of the 52 suites feature terraces with awesome city or Central Park views.

Elevator operators wearing white gloves epitomize the quality of service at a hotel where the business center and the concierge are available 24 hours a day. Oenophiles dining at the Cafe Pierre will be happy to know that the hotel boasts a 10,000-bottle wine cellar.

The Regency

005

540 Park Ave. (at 61st St.)

Subway: Lexington Av - 63 St
Phone: 212-759-4100
Fax: 212-826-5674
Web: www.loewshotels.com
Prices: rooms: $489 - $899 suites: $929 - $4,500 Restaurant: **$$$**

266
Rooms
85
Suites

The Regency, A Loews Hotel

A multimillion-dollar renovation spiffed up this flagship of Loew's hotel properties, just two blocks east of Central Park. Lush fabrics, Frette linens, CD players, TVs in the bathrooms, and double-paned windows are a few of the amenities you'll find in the contemporary-style rooms—the smallest of which is 225 square feet. Even Fido gets the royal treatment here with his own room-service menu and a dog-walking service.

Boasting a staff-to-guest ratio of 1 to 1, the hotel delights in serving its guests. Forget your reading glasses? Need a humidifier in your room? The Regency's staff is only too happy to oblige. Business travelers will appreciate rooms equipped with large writing desks, fax/printers, and high-speed Internet access. And if you need a haircut before that big meeting, there's even a beauty salon and barbershop on-site.

For that power breakfast, you need not go any farther than the hotel's 540 Park restaurant. For night owls, Feinstein's at The Regency (named for its owner, pop vocalist and songwriter Michael Feinstein) offers big-name cabaret acts six nights a week.

Hotel Wales

006

1295 Madison Ave. (bet. 92nd & 93rd Sts.)

Subway: 96 St (Lexington Ave.)
Phone: 212-876-6000
Fax: 212-860-7000
Web: www.waleshotel.com
Prices: rooms: $219 - $399 suites: $319 - $750 Restaurant: **$$**

46
Rooms
41
Suites

Hotel Wales

Built in 1902, the Hotel Wales sits atop Carnegie Hill, on the same block with the mansion of steel magnate Andrew Carnegie. Close to Upper East Side museums (including the Metropolitan Museum of Art), the hotel exudes a countryside feel in its soothing lobby, complete with a fireplace, marble staircase, coffered ceiling and mosaic floor.

All rooms profited from a 2000 renovation, which preserved the turn-of-the-century spirit with period furnishings, Belgian linens, down comforters, fresh flowers, and sepia-tone photographs of the neighborhood. Bathrooms are on the small side.

Spend some time on the rooftop terrace taking in the city views, or squeeze in a workout at the hotel's fitness studio. Continental breakfast is served each morning in the Pied Piper Room, decorated as a Victorian-era parlor. The Wales also includes Sarabeth's restaurant, loved by locals for its homemade breads, pastries and fruit preserves (available for sale), as well as its weekend brunch.

Excelsior

001

45 W. 81st St. (bet. Central Park West & Columbus Ave.)

Subway: 81 St - Museum of Natural History
Phone: 212-362-9200
Fax: 212-580-3972
Web: www.excelsiorhotelny.com
Prices: rooms: $169 - $279 suites: $189 - $459

120
Rooms
80
Suites

Excelsior

Located within a dinosaur bone's throw from the American Museum of Natural History, the 16-story Excelsior sits in the center of the action of the Upper West Side touring scene. Parents can charge their hearts' delight at the shops on nearby Columbus Avenue, then let the kids lead the charge through Central Park.

A country-French motif characterizes the décor of the reasonably priced standard rooms and one- and two-bedroom suites, while newly renovated bathrooms, sporting sparkling white tiles, remind you of why you love to stay in hotels. Bear in mind that while the street-view bedrooms are brighter, the rooms on the back side of the hotel offer peace and quiet. Wi-Fi Internet access is available throughout the property, and if you forgot your laptop, an Internet station is available for guests in the Excelsior's lobby.

The concierge will gladly arrange for theater tickets and restaurant reservations. But after a day of museum-hopping, why not retire to the Entertainment Room, where you can work out in the fitness center, peruse the books in the well-stocked library, or simply relax in front of the TV?

Mandarin Oriental

ᴀ◠ᴀ◠ᴀ

80 Columbus Circle (at 60th St.)

Subway: 59 St - Columbus Circle
Phone: 212-805-8800
Fax: 212-805-8888
Web: www.mandarinoriental.com
Prices: rooms: $725 - $1,095 suites: $1,800 - $8,400

202
Rooms
46
Suites

Mandarin Oriental Hotel/George Apostolidis

Occupying floors 35 to 54 in the north tower of the Time Warner Center, the Mandarin Oriental affords sweeping views of Central Park and the city, while bathing its guests in über-luxury. If the views from the floor-to-ceiling windows in your room don't do it for you, walk across the marble-floored lobby to the Lobby Lounge and take in the dramatic panorama while you sip—what else?—a Manhattan.

All of the 251 soundproofed guest rooms reflect subtle elegance with their Asian color schemes and 1940s-style furniture; most bathrooms are equipped with soaking tubs set near picture windows. Flat-panel LCD televisions can be found in both the bedroom and bath. And don't forget about the fitness center with its indoor lap pool, or the 14,500-square-foot, full-service spa. The latter is equipped with amethyst-crystal steam rooms, and a private VIP spa suite complete with its own sauna and fireplace.

Granted, the Time Warner Center contains some must-try restaurants, but why leave the hotel floors when you can enjoy contemporary Asian cuisine as well as stellar views on the 35th floor at Asiate *(see restaurant listings)*?

On the Ave

003

2178 Broadway (at 77th St.)

Subway: 79 St
Phone: 212-362-1100
Fax: 212-787-9521
Web: www.ontheave.com
Prices: rooms: $275 – $395 suites: $475 – $995

260
Rooms
7
Suites
&

On the Ave Hotel

Only a short walk away from Lincoln Center and Central Park, this early 20th-century structure was recently renovated and updated with early 21st-century accommodations. Flat-screen plasma TVs, T1 Internet connections, and Italian black-marble bathrooms will appeal to the cool in you, while Frette robes, down duvets, and the complimentary Belgian chocolates left on your pillow at turndown will leave you feeling appropriately pampered. Suite amenities include homemade cookies delivered to your room, and private balconies (in some suites).

Nightly piano music in the lobby makes a nice prelude to a refreshing sleep in feather beds adorned with 310-thread-count Italian cotton linens. Rooms on the top three floors boast balconies and afford views of the Hudson River or the trees of Central Park. If your room doesn't have a view, take the elevator to the landscaped balcony on the 16th floor; this pleasant space is equipped with Adirondack chairs for relaxing. All this, plus the pet-friendly hotel has a 24-hour business center, too.

Manhattan Upper West Side

Trump International Hotel & Tower

004

1 Central Park West (at Columbus Circle)

Subway: 59 St - Columbus Circle
Phone: 212-299-1000
Fax: 212-299-1150
Web: www.trumpintl.com
Prices: rooms: $705 – $725 suites: $995 – $2,400

38 Rooms
129 Suites

Trump International Hotel & Tower

Don't let the diminutive lobby fool you; the accommodations here are oh-so-The Donald. Inhabiting the 3rd through the 17th floors of this 52-story tower, the hotel offers luxurious guest rooms and suites that promise spectacular views of Manhattan through their floor-to-ceiling windows.

Appropriate for business or pleasure, lodgings at Trump International are that perfect mix of posh yet approachable. Shades of cinnamon, paprika or sage define the décor, while marble bathrooms, complete with Jacuzzi tubs, invite you for a relaxing soak above the hustle and bustle of the Big Apple. Or, for an even more "at home in the city" feel, choose a suite with a sleek European-style kitchen.

Over-the-top amenities include 42-inch plasma TVs, CD and DVD players, personalized business cards, a 6,000-square-foot fitness center equipped with a pool, a spa, and personal trainers. Not to mention in-room catering from the hotel's stellar restaurant Jean-Georges *(see restaurant listings)*. Last, but not least, the hotel's signature Attaché Service provides each guest with their own concierge—would you expect anything less from The Donald?

Coming Soon

New York City has a dynamic, ever-changing restaurant landscape, and each week presents word of an exciting opening. As of today, we have heard rumors that the future holds many new high-profile establishments, expanding the city's gastronomic boundaries. If indeed these spots successfully open their doors, it is worth mentioning a few.

There is certainly movement going on in New York's top hotel dining rooms. Not only is the Rhiga Royale hotel being transformed to the stylish London NYC, but Gordon Ramsay is moving in with his volatile kitchen antics. Also, the Dubai-based Jumeirah group will begin their ambitious transformation of the Essex House later this year and Alain Ducasse is bidding them adieu. He is expected to close the end of 2006 and open in the posh St. Regis space that was once Lespinasse. The much anticipated L'Atelier de Joël Robuchon opened August 8th, 2006 in the Four Seasons Hotel replacing 5757, and the reservations line is already overheating. The Ritz-Carlton Central Park is shuttering Atelier, a talented kitchen that never caught on, and allowing Laurent Tourondel to continue the expansion of his BLT empire with a BLT Market. Ian Schrager opened his Gramercy Park Hotel with keys to the gated park an alluring amenity. This fall, Alan Yau, the force behind some of London's hottest spots, will open Park Chinois, bringing a taste of his hip Asian style to Gramercy Park. Finally, Gilt has seen Paul Liebrandt come and go. The New York Palace's plan is to import Christopher Lee from Striped Bass in Philadelphia and set sail in a different direction.

After a long and ugly struggle with their union, Harry Cipriani is set to re-open around Labor Day in their home at the Sherry-Netherland Hotel. Socialites are brushing off their Manolos and bartenders readying the Bellinis. Similarly, the uptown set will have a new number for their speed dial as Le Caprice is importing a second location from across the pond.

The Time Warner Center continues to develop their restaurant collection. Landmarc will open a second address where Charlie Trotter never materialized, and Michael Lomonaco will feature Porter House New York where V Steakhouse failed to thrive. Top chefs are following the trend from traditional restaurant to lounge-style dining. Gray Kunz has assembled an A-team to support his project converting a former Rockefeller town house in Midtown West to Grayz, a lounge with ingredient-oriented beverages and finger food to match.

On the less grandiose side, a midtown outpost of Steven Hanson's popular Dos Caminos is slated to open in September, sure to keep the after-work crowd satiated with prickly pear margaritas. Jeffrey Chodorow will open Kobe Club in the space formerly occupied by Mix, and a gastropub where neither Rocco's nor Caviar & Banana remain. Rumors of the humorous name have been circulating.

Of course, this is not a comprehensive list, only a sampling of what is expected to arrive in the Big Apple. But plans change and deals fall through, so our inspectors will be sure to visit before possibly adding them to our selection. We look forward to next year's edition as we continue our quest to discover new restaurants for the Michelin Guide New York City 2008.

August 31st, 2006

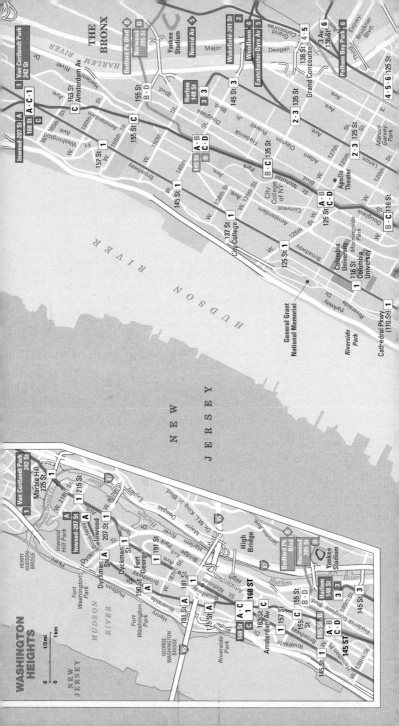